Optimizing Contemporary Application and Processes in Open Source Software

Mehdi Khosrow-Pour
Information Resources Management Association, USA

A volume in the Advances in Systems Analysis,
Software Engineering, and High Performance
Computing (ASASEHPC) Book Series

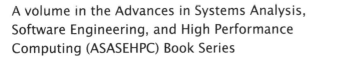

Published in the United States of America by
IGI Global
Engineering Science Reference (an imprint of IGI Global)
701 E. Chocolate Avenue
Hershey PA, USA 17033
Tel: 717-533-8845
Fax: 717-533-8661
E-mail: cust@igi-global.com
Web site: http://www.igi-global.com

Library of Congress Cataloging-in-Publication Data

Names: Khosrow-Pour, Mehdi, 1951- editor.
Title: Optimizing contemporary application and processes in open source
  software / Mehdi Khosrow-Pour, editor.
Description: Hershey, PA : Engineering Science Reference, [2018] | Includes
  bibliographical references.
Identifiers: LCCN 2017039684| ISBN 9781522553144 (hardcover) | ISBN
  9781522553151 (ebook)
Subjects: LCSH: Open source software.
Classification: LCC QA76.76.O62 O68 2018 | DDC 005.3--dc23 LC record available at https://lccn.loc.gov/2017039684

This book is published in the IGI Global book series Advances in Systems Analysis, Software Engineering, and High Performance Computing (ASASEHPC) (ISSN: 2327-3453; eISSN: 2327-3461)

British Cataloguing in Publication Data
A Cataloguing in Publication record for this book is available from the British Library.

All work contributed to this book is new, previously-unpublished material. The views expressed in this book are those of the authors, but not necessarily of the publisher.

For electronic access to this publication, please contact: eresources@igi-global.com.

Advances in Systems Analysis, Software Engineering, and High Performance Computing (ASASEHPC) Book Series

Vijayan Sugumaran
Oakland University, USA

ISSN:2327-3453
EISSN:2327-3461

MISSION

The theory and practice of computing applications and distributed systems has emerged as one of the key areas of research driving innovations in business, engineering, and science. The fields of software engineering, systems analysis, and high performance computing offer a wide range of applications and solutions in solving computational problems for any modern organization.

The **Advances in Systems Analysis, Software Engineering, and High Performance Computing (ASASEHPC) Book Series** brings together research in the areas of distributed computing, systems and software engineering, high performance computing, and service science. This collection of publications is useful for academics, researchers, and practitioners seeking the latest practices and knowledge in this field.

COVERAGE

- Network Management
- Enterprise information systems
- Parallel Architectures
- Performance Modelling
- Distributed Cloud Computing
- Virtual Data Systems
- Computer Networking
- Software engineering
- Metadata and Semantic Web
- Engineering Environments

IGI Global is currently accepting manuscripts for publication within this series. To submit a proposal for a volume in this series, please contact our Acquisition Editors at Acquisitions@igi-global.com or visit: http://www.igi-global.com/publish/.

Titles in this Series

For a list of additional titles in this series, please visit: www.igi-global.com/book-series

Aligning Perceptual and Conceptual Information for Cognitive Contextual System Development Emerging Research and Opportunities
Gary Kuvich (IBM, USA)
Engineering Science Reference • copyright 2018 • 172pp • H/C (ISBN: 9781522524311) • US $165.00 (our price)

Applied Computational Intelligence and Soft Computing in Engineering
Saifullah Khalid (CCSI Airport, India)
Engineering Science Reference • copyright 2018 • 340pp • H/C (ISBN: 9781522531296) • US $225.00 (our price)

Enhancing Software Fault Prediction With Machine Learning Emerging Research and Opportunities
Ekbal Rashid (Aurora's Technological and Research Institute, India)
Engineering Science Reference • copyright 2018 • 129pp • H/C (ISBN: 9781522531852) • US $165.00 (our price)

Solutions for Cyber-Physical Systems Ubiquity
Norbert Druml (Independent Researcher, Austria) Andreas Genser (Independent Researcher, Austria) Armin Krieg (Independent Researcher, Austria) Manuel Menghin (Independent Researcher, Austria) and Andrea Hoeller (Independent Researcher, Austria)
Engineering Science Reference • copyright 2018 • 482pp • H/C (ISBN: 9781522528456) • US $225.00 (our price)

Large-Scale Fuzzy Interconnected Control Systems Design and Analysis
Zhixiong Zhong (Xiamen University of Technology, China) and Chih-Min Lin (Yuan Ze University, Taiwan)
Information Science Reference • copyright 2017 • 223pp • H/C (ISBN: 9781522523857) • US $175.00 (our price)

Microcontroller System Design Using PIC18F Processors
Nicolas K. Haddad (University of Balamand, Lebanon)
Information Science Reference • copyright 2017 • 428pp • H/C (ISBN: 9781683180005) • US $195.00 (our price)

Probabilistic Nodes Combination (PNC) for Object Modeling and Contour Reconstruction
Dariusz Jacek Jakóbczak (Technical University of Koszalin, Poland)
Information Science Reference • copyright 2017 • 312pp • H/C (ISBN: 9781522525318) • US $175.00 (our price)

Model-Based Design for Effective Control System Development
Wei Wu (Independent Researcher, USA)
Information Science Reference • copyright 2017 • 299pp • H/C (ISBN: 9781522523031) • US $185.00 (our price)

701 East Chocolate Avenue, Hershey, PA 17033, USA
Tel: 717-533-8845 x100 • Fax: 717-533-8661
E-Mail: cust@igi-global.com • www.igi-global.com

Table of Contents

Detailed Table of Contents

Munish Saini, Guru Nanak Dev University, India
Kuljit Kaur Chahal, Guru Nanak Dev University, India

Many studies have been conducted to understand the evolution process of Open Source Software (OSS). The researchers have used various techniques for understanding the OSS evolution process from different perspectives. This chapter reports a meta-data analysis of the systematic literature review on the topic in order to understand its current state and to identify opportunities for the future. This research identified 190 studies, selected against a set of questions, for discussion. It categorizes the research studies into nine categories. Based on the results obtained from the systematic review, there is evidence of a shift in the metrics and methods for OSS evolution analysis over the period of time. The results suggest that there is a lack of a uniform approach to analyzing and interpreting the results. There is need of more empirical work using a standard set of techniques and attributes to verify the phenomenon governing the OSS projects. This will help to advance the field and establish a theory of software evolution.

Kaniz Fatema, American International University, Bangladesh
M. M. Mahbubul Syeed, American International University, Bangladesh
Imed Hammouda, South Mediterranean University, Tunisia

Open source software (OSS) is currently a widely adopted approach to developing and distributing software. Many commercial companies are using OSS components as part of their product development. For instance, more than 58% of web servers are using an OSS web server, Apache. For effective adoption of OSS, fundamental knowledge of project development is needed. This often calls for reliable prediction models to simulate project evolution and to envision project future. These models provide help in supporting preventive maintenance and building quality software. This chapter reports on a systematic literature survey aimed at the identification and structuring of research that offers prediction models and techniques in analysing OSS projects. The study outcome provides insight into what constitutes the main contributions of the field, identifies gaps and opportunities, and distils several important future research directions. This chapter extends the authors' earlier journal article and offers the following improvements: broader study period, enhanced discussion, and synthesis of reported results.

Chapter 3

Sangeeta Lal, Jaypee Institute of Information Technology, India
Neetu Sardana, Jaypee Institute of Information Technology, India
Ashish Sureka, Ashoka University, India

Log statements present in source code provide important information to the software developers because they are useful in various software development activities such as debugging, anomaly detection, and remote issue resolution. Most of the previous studies on logging analysis and prediction provide insights and results after analyzing only a few code constructs. In this chapter, the authors perform an in-depth, focused, and large-scale analysis of logging code constructs at two levels: the file level and catch-blocks level. They answer several research questions related to statistical and content analysis. Statistical and content analysis reveals the presence of differentiating properties among logged and nonlogged code constructs. Based on these findings, the authors propose a machine-learning-based model for catch-blocks logging prediction. The machine-learning-based model is found to be effective in catch-blocks logging prediction.

Chapter 4

Mohamed Guendouz, Dr. Moulay Tahar University of Saïda, Algeria
Abdelmalek Amine, Dr. Moulay Tahar University of Saïda, Algeria
Reda Mohamed Hamou, Dr. Moulay Tahar University of Saïda, Algeria

This chapter discusses the design and the implementation of a recommender system for open source projects on GitHub using the collaborative-filtering approach. Having such a system can be helpful for many developers, especially those who search for a particular project based on their interests. It can also reduce searching time and make search results more relevant. The system presented in this chapter was evaluated on a real-world dataset and using various evaluation metrics. Results obtained from these experiments are very promising. The authors found that their recommender system can reach better precision and recall accuracy.

Chapter 5

Utku Köse, Suleyman Demirel University, Turkey

Using open software in e-learning application is one of the most popular ways of improving effectiveness of e-learning-based processes without thinking about additional costs and even focusing on modifying the software according to needs. Because of that, it is important to have an idea about what is needed while using an e-learning-oriented open software system and how to deal with its source codes. At this point, it is a good option to add some additional features and functions to make the open source software more intelligent and practical to make both teaching-learning experiences during e-learning processes. In this context, the objective of this chapter is to discuss some possible applications of artificial intelligence to include optimization processes within open source software systems used in e-learning activities. In detail, the chapter focuses more on using swarm intelligence and machine learning techniques for this aim and expresses some theoretical views for improving the effectiveness of such software for a better e-learning experience.

Drawing praxis from Bowen University, Nigeria and other libraries worldwide, the chapter unveils the limitless capabilities of Koha ILS to successfully manage core library house-keeping functions—cataloging, acquisitions, circulation control, patrons' management, OPAC, serials, and report generation—in one seamless whole. Web-based features like its flexibility, adaptability, interoperability, MARC, Z39.50, patrons' ability for online logging in, registration, renewal, and many more were revealed. Also, reasons for its global adoptability, benefits, likely challenges, and solutions from practitioners were also highlighted. The chapter concludes that despite the puny but eventually surmounted challenges, Koha holds unlimited potential for libraries of any shape/size by just garnering from the experiences of subsisting users of the software globally.

Chapter 7

Open source software (OSS) is well established in sectors as diverse as aviation, health, telecommunications, finance, publishing, education, and government. As nations increasingly rely on knowledge assets to grow, the adoption of OSS will have profound economic consequences. This chapter identifies the mechanisms inherent to OSS production that help fuel innovation in knowledge-based economies. As a collaborative and open production model, OSS is conceptualized as a prototype of open innovation. OSS-related software development jobs are widely diffused throughout the economy, help build a skilled labour force, and offer wages significantly above the national average. OSS is thus believed to be a strong contributor to growth in high-value employment in the US. The authors also posit that, as industries are exposed to the benefits of OSS as a result of the broad diffusion of OSS-related jobs, open innovation processes outside software development may be adopted through a process of learning and imitation.

Chapter 8

To chapter concerns emerging cybernetics, which is the school of "meaning to lead" and is particularly associated with the idea of dominations and controls. This chapter initially anatomizes the sociology of software cybernetics into two broad movements—free/libre and open source software (FLOSS) and proprietary close source software (PCSS)—to argue a good software governance approach. This chapter discusses (a) in what matters and (b) for what reasons software governance of Turkey has locked into the ecosystems of PCSS and, in particular, considers causes, effects, and potential outcomes of not utilizing FLOSS in the state of Turkey. The government has continuously stated that there are no compulsory national or international conventions(s) and settlement(s) with the ecosystems of PCSS and that there is no vendor lock-in concern. Nevertheless, the chapter principally argues that Turkey has taken a pragmatic decision-making process of software in the emerging cybernetics that leads and contributes to techno-social externality of PCSS hegemonic stability.

Chapter 9

A literature survey study was conducted to explore the state-of-the-art of open source software and the opportunities and challenges faced by this segment of the software industry in seven Arab countries: Tunisia, Egypt, Jordan, Saudi Arabia, Qatar, Oman, and UAE. A framework and road map for OSS is derived and presented from interviews conducted in the UAE with at least four experts from each of the following categories: governments and ministries, IT companies, universities, and IT enthusiasts. This is the first study of its kind in this part of the world and is expected to make a significant contribution to the direction for open source software in the region and beyond.

Preface

The development and use of open source software (OSS) is constantly changing, thus creating a need for knowledge resources that will empower professionals, academic educators, researchers, students, programmers, and industry consultants all over the world. *Optimizing Contemporary Application and Processes in Open Source Software* is a vital reference source that will meet these needs by exploring the latest coverage on all aspects of open source software and processes from different fields, covering topics such as fault prediction, recommender systems, collaborative filtering, and e-learning software.

This reference source is organized into nine chapters contributed by global experts, drawing on their experiences, observations, and research surrounding open source, source code analysis, and empirical software engineering and measurement. The book starts with a general overview, and progresses toward coverage that is more industry and region-specific, focusing on current economic and governance issues surrounding open source software in the United States and also in the Arab World. A brief description of each of the chapters can be found in the following paragraphs.

In Chapter 1, "A Systematic Review of Attributes and Techniques for Open Source Software Evolution Analysis," the authors have used various techniques for understanding the open source software evolution process from different perspectives. This paper reports a meta-data analysis of the systematic literature review on the topic in order to understand its current state and to identify opportunities for the future. This research identified 190 studies, selected against a set of questions, for discussion. It categorizes the research studies into nine categories. Based on the results obtained from the systematic review, there is evidence of shift in the metrics and methods for open source software evolution analysis over a period of time.

In Chapter 2, "Demography of Open Source Software Prediction Models and Techniques," the authors explore how for effective adoption of open source software, fundamental knowledge of project development is needed. This often calls for reliable prediction models to simulate project evolution and to envision project future. These models provide help in supporting preventive maintenance and building quality software. The chapter reports on a systematic literature survey aimed at the identification and structuring of research that offer prediction models and techniques in analyzing open source software projects. The study outcome provides insight in what constitutes the main contributions of the field, identifies gaps and opportunities, and distils several important future research directions.

In Chapter 3, "Logging Analysis and Prediction in Open Source Java Project," the authors explore how log statements presented in source code provide important information to software developers because they are useful in various software development activities such as debugging, anomaly detection, and remote issue resolution. Most of the previous studies on logging analysis and prediction provide insights and results after analyzing only a few code constructs. The authors performed an in-depth, focused, and large-scale analysis of logging code constructs at two levels: the file level and catch-blocks level. They answer several research questions related to statistical and content analysis. Statistical and content analysis reveal presence of differentiating properties among logged and non-logged code constructs. Based on these findings the authors proposed a machine learning based model for catch-blocks logging prediction.

In Chapter 4, "Open Source Projects Recommendation on GitHub," the authors discuss the design and implementation of a recommender system for open source projects on the GitHub website using the collaborative-filtering approach. Having such a system can be helpful for many developers, especially those who search for a particular project based on their interests. The system presented in this chapter was evaluated on a real-world dataset and using various evaluation metrics. Results obtained from these experiments are very promising, and the authors found that their recommender system can reach better precision and recall accuracy.

In Chapter 5, "Optimization Scenarios for Open Source Software Used in E-Learning Activities," the author discusses how using open software in e-learning applications today is one of the most popular ways of improving the effectiveness of e-learning based processes without thinking about additional costs and even focusing on modifying the software according to needs. Because of that, it is important to have an idea about what is needed while using an e-learning oriented open software system and how to deal with its source codes. The author explores some possible applications of artificial intelligence to include optimization processes within open source software systems used in e-learning activities. In detail, the chapter focuses more on using swarm intelligence and machine learning techniques for this aim and express some theoretical views for improving effectiveness of such software for a better e-learning experience.

In Chapter 6, "Unlocking the Unlimited Potentials of Koha OSS/ILS for Library House-Keeping Functions: A Global View," the authors unveil the limitless capabilities of Koha ILS to successfully manage core library house-keeping functions-cataloging, acquisitions, circulation control, patrons' management, OPAC, serials, report generation in one seamless whole. The chapter concludes that despite the puny but eventually surmounted challenges, Koha holds unlimited potential for libraries of any shape/size.

In Chapter 7, "Open Growth: The Economic Impact of Open Source Software in the USA," the authors explain how open source software (OSS) is well established in sectors as diverse as aviation, health, telecommunications, finance, publishing, education, and government. As nations increasingly rely on knowledge assets to grow, the adoption of open source software will have profound economic consequences. The authors identify the mechanisms inherent to open source software production that help fuel innovation in knowledge-based economies. As a collaborative and open production model, open source software is conceptualized as a prototype of open innovation. The authors also posit that, as industries are exposed to the benefits of open source software as a result of the broad diffusion of open source software-related jobs, open innovation processes outside software development may be adopted through a process of learning and imitation.

In Chapter 8, "Strategy of Good Software Governance: FLOSS in the State of Turkey," the authors discuss how software governance in Turkey has locked into the ecosystems of proprietary closed source software, and in particular takes into consideration the causes, effects, and potential outcomes of not utilizing free (libre) and open source software in the state of Turkey. The government has continuously stated that there are no compulsory national or international conventions(s) and settlement(s) with the ecosystems of proprietary closed source software and that there is no vendor lock-in concern. The authors principally argue that Turkey has taken a pragmatic decision-making approach to software in the emerging cybernetics, which leads and contributes to techno-social externality of proprietary closed source software hegemonic stability.

In Chapter 9, "Towards Sustainable Development Through Open Source Software in the Arab World," the author explores the state-of-the-art of open source software and the opportunities and challenges faced by this segment of the software industry in seven Arab countries — Tunisia, Egypt, Jordan, KSA, Qatar, Oman and UAE. A framework and roadmap for open source software is presented and is derived from interviews conducted in the UAE with at least four experts from each of the following categories: governments and ministries, IT companies, universities and IT enthusiasts. This is the first study of its kind in this part of the world and is expected to make a significant contribution to the direction for open source software in the region and beyond.

The comprehensive coverage this publication offers is sure to contribute to an enhanced understanding of all topics, research, and discoveries pertaining to open source software. Furthermore, the contributions included in this publication will be instrumental in the expansion of knowledge offerings in the software industry and relevant research fields, inspiring readers to further contribute to current discoveries, while creating possibilities for further research and development.

Chapter 1
A Systematic Review of Attributes and Techniques for Open Source Software Evolution Analysis

Munish Saini
Guru Nanak Dev University, India

Kuljit Kaur Chahal
Guru Nanak Dev University, India

ABSTRACT

Many studies have been conducted to understand the evolution process of Open Source Software (OSS). The researchers have used various techniques for understanding the OSS evolution process from different perspectives. This chapter reports a meta-data analysis of the systematic literature review on the topic in order to understand its current state and to identify opportunities for the future. This research identified 190 studies, selected against a set of questions, for discussion. It categorizes the research studies into nine categories. Based on the results obtained from the systematic review, there is evidence of a shift in the metrics and methods for OSS evolution analysis over the period of time. The results suggest that there is a lack of a uniform approach to analyzing and interpreting the results. There is need of more empirical work using a standard set of techniques and attributes to verify the phenomenon governing the OSS projects. This will help to advance the field and establish a theory of software evolution.

1. INTRODUCTION

Due to the rising dominance of Open Source Software (OSS) in the software industry; not only are practitioners, but researchers as well as academicians also keen to understand the OSS development and evolution process. OSS development involves various stakeholders ranging from contributing volunteers to commercial software vendors. There is need to understand the OSS development model in general

DOI: 10.4018/978-1-5225-5314-4.ch001

and OSS evolution in particular so that the evolution process can be improved, if need be, for the future systems.

OSS evolution has attracted a lot of attention in the last decade. Easy and free availability of data on open source projects has resulted in a splurge of studies in this domain. As a result, the number of empirical studies related to OSS is much more in number in comparison to other topics in the field (Stol and Babar, 2009). Various methods have been employed in the past for analysis and prediction of OSS evolution. It is necessary to systematically summarise the empirical evidence obtained on these methods from the existing literature so that it is easy to comprehend the research work in this area, and reveal gaps in the existing work. As per the existing work in this direction, a few studies focusing on the survey of literature in the domain have been published. Fernandez- Ramil et al. (2008) discuss, in an informal way, a small sample (seven in numbers) of OSS evolution studies. Breivold et al. (2010) carry out a systematic literature review of OSS evolution studies (41 in numbers) focusing only on the evolvability characteristic of OSS systems. Syeed et al. (2013) follows a systematic literature review protocol to analyze studies on OSS Evolution. They present review of 101 research papers but their focus is on a limited set of categories of studies. Stol and Babar (2009) reviewed empirical studies reported in four International OSS conferences to assess quality of the papers from the perspective of the way they report the empirical research in OSS. Unlike the present study, their target is not review of studies on OSS evolution but assessment of quality of empirical research papers involving OSS systems. This chapter presents a systematic literature review of an extensive list of research papers published on the subject between the period of 1997 and 2016.

A number of research publications on OSS evolution have explored the phenomenon from different dimensions using different approaches. Broadly two dimensions are taken: Evolution in OSS structure, and Evolution in OSS community. Software structure exploration includes source code analysis, version history analysis, and repository information analysis. Community structure exploration includes social network analysis. Both the dimensions cannot be isolated from each other. They are useful when put together, and complement each other in answering questions regarding the OSS development and evolution process. Analyzing the links between the software structure and the developer community helps in improving software evaluation and quality.

In this chapter, we report a meta-data analysis on comprehensive review on OSS evolution published in the time period of 1997 to 2016 along with discussion on the project attributes and techniques used for analyzing software evolution (Chahal and Saini, 2016a; 2016b).

The rest of the paper is organized as follows: Section 2 presents the research questions that are addressed in this systematic review and the research criteria followed in this study for selection of primary studies. Section 3 presents the answers to the research questions identified in this work. Section 4 gives conclusions and future directions obtained from this systematic review.

2. RESEARCH METHODOLOGY

The review process follows a systematic review protocol (Kitchenham, 2007) so as to reduce the research bias. The review process included the following steps: 1) Defining the research questions, 2) Choosing a search strategy and study selection criteria, and 3) Data Extraction and Synthesis.

To begin with, research questions set the motivation for collection of relevant research studies. An objective quality assessment criterion helps in deciding the selection of studies as per their focus on research questions and quality of presentation as well. OSS evolution studies are categorized under various heads to put the related work at one place for easy understanding. The chapter summarizes the techniques and the empirical evidence available in the reviewed papers. A set of 9 different categories (see Table 1), with further subcategories, are identified for understanding the variety of techniques and methods for OSS evolution.

For detailed review methodology refer to our previous publications (Chahal and Saini, 2016a; 2016b).

3. RESULTS AND DISCUSSION

This section presents the details of the studies focusing on evolution of OSS systems. After a thorough analysis, 190 studies are selected for discussion here. All these studies address different aspects of the OSS evolution. First, we describe the meta-analysis of the research studies discussing their publication sources, and publication year. Then the results for each research question are discussed in the subsequent sections.

3.1. The Meta-Data Analysis

This section presents the meta-data analysis of the research studies identified for discussion in this chapter.

3.1.1. Publication Sources

Table 2 summarizes the details of the publications in top journals, conferences, workshops, and symposium along with the number indicating the count for studies (the table shows only the publications with count more than 3). Majority of the publications are in the International Conference on Software Maintenance (ICSM),IEEE Transactions on Software Engineering, International Conference on Software Engineering, International Workshop on Principles of Software Evolution, and Journal of Software Maintenance and Evolution: Research and Practice. A significant portion of the studies is published as conference papers with the ICSM attracting most of the work in this domain. Interestingly, International

Table 1. Research questions

Sr. No.	Research Question
1.	Which attributes and techniques have been used for OSS evolution analysis?
2.	Which attributes and techniques have been used for OSS evolution prediction?
3.	Is there any evidence of difference in the evolution of OSS v/s CSS?
4.	How do artifacts, other than source code, evolve in OSS systems?
5.	How has the choice of programming languages changed over the period of time in OSS evolution?
6.	What is the state of software development paradigms such as software reuse in the OSS evolution?
7.	How has the community contribution evolved?
8.	What part of the software evolution process has been automated?
9.	What is the state of the theory of OSS evolution?

Table 2. A summary of top publications

Publication Name	Type	Number
International Conference on Software Maintenance	Conference	18
IEEE Transactions on Software Engineering	Journal	8
International Conference on Software Engineering	Conference	7
International Workshop on Principles of Software Evolution	Workshop	7
Journal of Software Maintenance and Evolution: Research And Practice	Journal	6
Journal of Systems and Software	Journal	4
Journal of Empirical Software Engineering	Journal	4
Working Conference on Reverse Engineering	Conference	4
International Conference on Open Source Systems	Conference	4
International Workshop on Mining Software Repositories	Conference	4
Journal of Software: Evolution and Process	Journal	4
Journal of Information and Software Technology	Journal	3
Conference on Software Maintenance and Reengineering	Conference	3
International Workshop on Emerging Trends in Software Metrics	Workshop	3
International Software Metrics Symposium	Symposium	3
IEEE Software	Journal	3

Conference on Open Source Systems lags way behind ICSM for giving space to studies on OSS evolution, despite its focus on the core domain. It has been observed that researchers prefer to publish their work in conferences as compared to journals (Hermenegildo, 2012). Perhaps the reason is that journal papers are long and take more time to get the work published, whereas conferences let a researcher present, and publish work quickly. Conferences also provide opportunities for social/professional networking with other researchers in the field. Unfortunately, in some countries publishing work in conference proceedings is not encouraged. The University Grants Commission, India in its latest guidelines for promotion of university/college teachers does not assign any API (Application Performance Indicators) score for research publications in conferences. Only the paper presenter can claim the score, not the co-authors.

Figure 1 indicates that the journals have the second highest count in the total number of publication sources. Moreover, the research in this domain is not limited to journals or conferences; there are symposiums, workshops, book chapters, technical reports, and other forms of publication as well.

We further explored and found that majority of the publications (Journals/proceedings) are in IEEE (see Figure 2). Next is the ACM for sponsoring conferences alone or with IEEE (ACM/IEEE). In others category, there are publishers like Academia, IGI global, SECC, SERSC, Pearson, Science Direct etc., where publications related to software evolution can be found.

3.1.2. Year Wise Distribution

Figure 3 indicates that in almost all the years (from 1997-2016), there is a study on the software evolution. Therefore, it has been consistently a topic of active interest for the research community. Figure 3 shows that number of research studies increased continuously until 2009. After that the number dropped.

Figure 1. Type of Publication

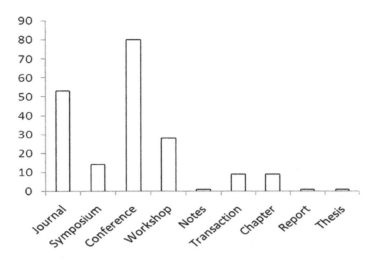

Figure 2. Top Publishers for OSS evolution Studies

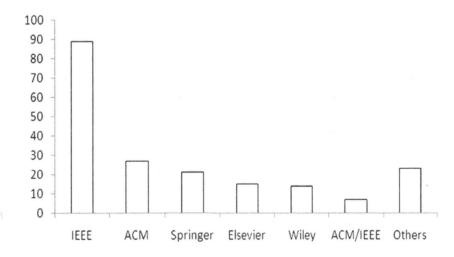

It may be attributed to the shift in focus from evolution of single systems (reviewed in this chapter) to evolution of OSS eco systems (out of scope of this study (see section 2 Table 1). The significant drop in the year 2016 may be due to the fact that data for the complete year is not recorded in the study (as it may not be available online at the time of data collection).

3.1.3. Perspectives of OSS Evolution

In this study, our main focus is on measuring and analyzing the evolution of OSS projects. In addition to it, various tools, methods, and techniques that were used to measure the evolution of OSS projects. As indicated in Table 1, in this study 9 different categories, with further subcategories, are identified for understanding the variety of techniques and methods for OSS evolution.

Figure 3. Year wise distribution of studies

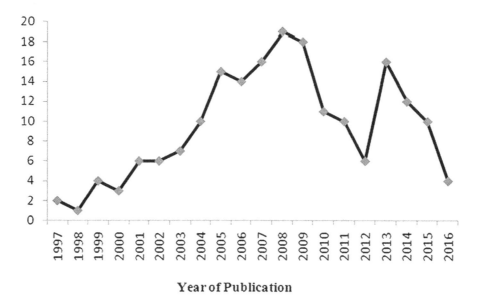

Year of Publication

Figure 4 shows that software evolution category has the highest peak in the graph. It is obvious due to the focus of this study on the topic. Other main areas on which this study have explored and given the details about evolution techniques and tools are of: software development, software maintenance, code analysis, visualization, and change analysis. This study also pointed that software evolution can be analyzed from the point of view of programming languages, co-evolution, software growth, prediction, software quality, and software communities etc.

3.2. OSS Evolution Analysis: Techniques and Empirical Results

Taking research questions as the points of reference, this section presents the various studies selected in this SLR to analyze their contribution in advancing the state of the art. It summarizes the techniques and the empirical evidence available in the reviewed papers. For a detailed discussion, please refer to these papers (Chahal and Saini, 2016a; 2016b).

3.2.1. RQ 1: Which Attributes and Techniques Have Been Used for OSS Evolution Analysis?

Based on the studies, we identified the following categories to understand the attributes and techniques the researchers used to analyze OSS evolution.

Broadly, the data is extracted from the following sources, and researchers employ various techniques for analyzing the data:

- **Source Code Analysis:** Measuring different aspects of code has been of interest of researchers as well as practitioners in the software engineering field since long time back, when software measurement was looked up to as a tool to make software development a scientific process. The idea

Figure 4. Various perspectives of OSS evolution

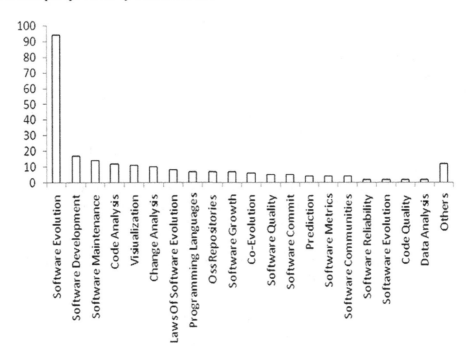

was to make progress in the software development measurable, so that it can be monitored and controlled. Moreover, code quality was thought of as a basis to ensure quality of a software product. Therefore, source code measurement attracted a lot of attention. Among the traditional set of source code metrics, we can include size, complexity, coupling and cohesion metrics. As the paradigms change, more metrics are added to measure the new features such as inheritance in Object Oriented Systems. After extracting the source code, it is analyzed from various perspectives. We noticed the following techniques for analyzing the software evolution in the review papers:

- Using Metrics
  - Growth Analysis (Godfrey and Tu, 2000; Lehman et al., 2001; Robles et al., 2005; Koch, 2007)
  - Complexity Analysis (Tahvildari et al., 1999; Stewart et al., 2006; Darcy et al., 2010; Girba et al.,2005b)
  - Modularity Analysis (Milev et al., 2009; Capiluppi, 2009; Alenezi and Zarour, 2015; Olszak et al., 2015)
  - Architectural Analysis (Capiluppi, 2004a; LaMantia et al., 2008; Wermilinger et al., 2011; Le et al., 2015; Alenezi and Khellah, 2015)
- Topic Models Based Approach (Hassan et al., 2005a; Thomas et al., 2014, Hu et al., 2015)
- Complex Systems Theory (Wu et al., 2007; Herraiz et al., 2008; Gorshenev and Pismak, 2003)
- Graph/Network Analysis Based Approach (Jenkins and Kirk,2007; Murgia et al., 2009; Wang et al., 2009; Ferreira et al., 2011; Pan et al., 2011; Chaikalis et al., 2015; Kpodjedo et al., 2013)

   - ○   Information Theory Based Approach (Abd-El-Hafiz, 2004; Arbuckle, 2009; Arbuckle, 2011)
   - ○   Qualitative Reasoning Based Approach (Smith et al., 2005)
- **Source Code Management System or Repository:** OSS development is a complex activity involving volunteers. There is need to analyze an OSS system from a wider perspective, i.e. beyond its source code files, to understand and improve the software development process (Robles et al., 2006a). An OSS project management team uses several types of repositories to track the activities of a software project as it progresses (Hassan et al., 2005b). Examples of such repositories are – Code repositories, historical repositories, and run-time repositories. Several techniques and attributes have been explored in the research literature to analyze the change management information available in a code repository.
   - ○   Change analysis (Gefen and Schneberger, 1996; Kemerer and Slaughter, 1997; Schach et al.,2003; Barry et al., 2003; Gupta et al., 2008; Ali and Maqbool, 2009; Hindle et al., 2009a; Meqdadi et al., 2013; Saini and Kaur, 2014a; Ahmed et al., 2015)
   - ○   Change request analysis (Herraiz et al., 2007a; Goulão et al., 2012)
   - ○   Commit analysis (Hattori and Lanza, 2008; Hindle et al., 2009a; Alali et al., 2008; Agrawal et al., 2015; Santos et al., 2016)

3.2.2. RQ2: Which Attributes and Techniques Have Been Used for OSS Evolution Prediction?

Prediction or forecast states the way things are going to occur in future. Time series analysis is the most commonly used tool (Yuen, 1985; 1987; 1988) to predict future attributes, e.g. size, defects of software systems. The software evolution metrics (based on project/process attributes) undertaken for prediction include

- Monthly number of changes (Herraiz, 2007a; Kemerer and S. Slaughter, 1999),
- Change requests (Goulão et al.,2012; Kenmei et al.,2008),
- Size & complexity (Caprio et al., 2001; Fuentetaja et al. 2002),
- Defects (Kläs et al., 2010; Raja et al., 2009),
- Clones (Antoniol et al., 2001), and
- Maintenance effort (Yu, 2006).

   Various techniques used for software evolution prediction include. The review studies explore the following models for OSS evolution prediction:

- ARIMA (Caprio et al., 2001; Kenmei et al., 2008)),
- ARMA models (Zhongmin et al., 2010),
- Hybrid models such as ARIMA and SVN (Kemerer and Slaughter,1999; Goulão et al., 2012),
- Data mining techniques (Ratzinger et al., 2007; Siy et al., 2007),
- Signal processing techniques (Dalle et al., 2006),
- Linear regression models (Zimmermann et al.,2007),
- Simulation tools (Smith et al., 2006; Lin, 2013).

A perusal of the existing research in this area shows ARIMA modelling as the most frequently used prediction procedure. However, OSS development is a wobbly process. Unlike the traditional development in which the environment is controlled, OSS development is based on contributions from volunteers who could not be forced to work even if something is of high priority for the project (Godfrey et al., 2000). Along with this unplanned activity, there is a lack of planned documentation related to requirements, and detailed design (Herraiz et al., 2007c). Classical time series techniques are inappropriate for analysis and forecasting of the data which involve random variables (Herraiz et al., 2007b; Kemerer et al., 1999). Fuzzy time series can work for domains which involve uncertainty. Saini and Kaur (2014b) propose to use a computation method of forecasting based on fuzzy time series (Singh, 2008) to predict the number of commits in OSS projects. Fuzzy time series can work for domains which involve uncertainty. Open source projects, sans any tight organizational support, face many uncertainties. Uncertainty lies in uncontrolled development environment such as availability of contributors at any point of time. Due to uncertainty, there is a large fluctuation in consecutive values. Analysis of monthly commits of three OSS projects, Eclipse, PostgreSQL, and Wildfly, indicates that the computation method outperforms the naive random walk model. When the study was expanded to seven OSS projects, the computation method did even better than the ARIMA models (Saini and kaur, 2016).

3.2.3. RQ 3: Is There Any Evidence of Difference in the Evolution of OSS v/s CSS?

Proprietary systems or Closed Source Systems (CSS) are developed following a strict organizational control. With OSS systems getting popular, a comparison of the CSS development process model with the new bazaar style development approach is but natural.

Based on the review, some studies have focused on the comparison of characteristics of OSS with CSS from their evolutionary behavior point of view. They pointed that the evolution of OSS and CSS may or may not vary in terms of

- Growth rate (Paulson et al., 2004); Robles et al., 2003; Capiluppi et al., 2004b; Xie et al., 2009; Neamtiu et al., 2013; Ferreira et al., 2011).
- System features (Mockus et al., 2002)
- Quality of code (Stamelos et al., 2002)
- Creativity (Paulson et al., 2004)
- Changing rate (Paulson et al., 2004)
- Modularity (Paulson et al., 2004)
- Effort estimation models (Fernandez- Ramil et al., 2008)
- Bug-fixing process and release frequency (Rossi et al., 2009)

Unlike CSS systems, OSS systems do not have a constrained growth due to increasing complexity as they evolve. However, software evolution is a discontinuous phenomenon in both the cases.

3.2.4. RQ 4: How Do Artifacts, Other Than Source Code, Evolve in OSS Systems?

Several software artifacts co-evolve with source code. The researchers have studied the evolution of source code with various artifacts, such as

- Build systems (Robles et al., 2006b; Adams et al., 2008; McIntosh et al., 2012)
- Comments (Fluri et al., 2009)
- Test-code (Marsavina et al., 2014)
- Changes related to database schema (Qiu et al., 2013)
- Database related activities (Goeminne et al., 2014)

There are a few studies in which artifacts other than source code are studied together

- Test-code and production code (Zaidman et al., 2011)
- Infrastructure as Code (IaC) files along with three other types of files – source code, test, and build files (Jiang and Adams, 2015)

3.2.5. RQ 5: How Has the Choice of Programming Languages Changed Over the Period of Time in the OSS Evolution?

The development of OSS has initiated a revolution in the development process of software, as most of the software systems nowadays are developed with the support for multiple programming languages (Delorey et al., 2007). However, the choice of programming languages has changed over the period of time.

- Trend in the popularity of different set of programming languages (Karus and Gall, 2011; Bhattacharya et al., 2011)
  - ○ Scripting and Interpreter based (platform independent) languages are more popular (Robles et al., 2006b)
- Choice of language viz-a-viz developer productivity, and defect density (Phipps, 1999; Myrtveit et al., 2008)
- Choice of language and gender of the developers (Dattero and Galup, 2004)

3.2.6. RQ 6: What Is the State of Software Development Paradigms Such as Software Reuse in the OSS Evolution?

Software reuse is a means for overcoming software crisis (Pressman, 2010). McIlroy (1968) pointed towards the reuse of code to build large reliable software systems in a controlled and cost effective way. It has been observed that OSS projects make extensive use of (third party) reusable software components (Zaimi et al., 2015). A few other papers that studied software reuse aspects in OSS projects are as follows:

- Developers' choice of evolutionary reuse for cost efficiency (Capra, 2006).
- Differences in the nature of evolution of libraries v/s applications (Vaucher and Sahraoui, 2007).
- The effect of reuse based development style on the evolution of software systems (Gupta et al., 2008).
- The evolutionary aspects of reusable software components (Kaur, 2013).

3.2.7. RQ 7: How Has the Community Contribution Evolved?

The development of OSS is not a well-planned activity (Goulão et al., 2012). A few people start an OSS project, users of the OSS system contribute to make changes to satisfy their own requirements, and the system starts evolving. Users and developers of an OSS project are called the OSS community. Community drives the evolution of OSS (Girba et al., 2005a). Research studies discussed the OSS community from different points of view:

- To identify reasonable community size to sustain an OSS project (Mockus et al., 2002; Capiluppi, 2003).
- The community dynamics (Nakakoji et al., 2002).
- Stability of the Community support (Robles et al., 2005).
- Developer productivity (Capiluppi et al., 2004b).
- Inequality in work distribution in OSS projects (Koch et al., 2007; Mockus et al., 2002)
- Team profile and structure in large vs small OSS projects (Xu et al., 2005)
- The deadline effect (Lin et al., 2013).
- Predicting next release date on the basis of community activity (Weicheng et al., 2013).

3.2.8. RQ 8: What Part of the Software Evolution Process Has Been Automated?

Automated support for a software engineering task is always appreciated as it can not only help to handle large volumes of data but also makes the task easily repeatable. Several tools have been created to handle comparison of successive versions of OSS systems, and to answer software evolution related questions. Some of these tools are

- Beagle (Tu and Godfrey, 2002)
- Kenyon (Bevan et al., 2005)
- Ferret (Rainer et al., 2008).
- Churrasco (D'Ambros and Lanza, 2010)
- CodeVizard (Zazworka and Ackermann, 2010).
- Replay (Hattori et al., 2013)

3.2.9. RQ 9: What Is the State of Theory of OSS Evolution?

In software evolution, Lehman's laws (1974, 1978, 1996) can be the best (and the only) example of a theory, though many empirical studies have refuted these laws in the context of OSS evolution. Several studies checked the applicability of Lehman's laws:

- Anomaly in the applicability of the laws (Godfrey and Tu, 2000, Robles et al., 2005).
- Confirmed the two laws related to continuous change (1st law), and continuous growth (6th law) (Godfrey and Tu, 2000, 2001; Bauer and Pizka, 2003; Wu and Holt, 2004; Robles et al., 2005; Herraiz et al., 2006; Koch, 2005, 2007; Mens et al., 2008; Israeli and Feitelson, 2010; Vasa, 2010; and Neamtiu et al., 2013).

- The fourth law confirmed only in (Israeli and Feitelson, 2010).
- The fifth law confirmed only in (Vasa, 2010).
- Only Bauer and Pizka (2003) confirm all the eight laws.
- Lehman's laws for small v/s large systems (Roy and Cordy, 2006; Koch, 2007).

All these studies lack a uniform approach to analyze and interpret the results. There are multiple interpretations of the statements defining the laws. The metrics for measuring the constructs to validate the laws are defined differently in different studies.

With the availability of tools and data resources in the public domain, researchers can now repeat experiments and build empirical evidence to confirm/refute the laws. However, collecting empirical evidence is only the first stage for theory building. It has to be followed by hypothesis formulation, testing, and then optimization (Godfrey and German, 2008). In the new context, laws should be reformulated to suit the changing software development paradigms as they have not been since 1996.

4. CONCLUSION AND FUTURE GUIDELINES

Open Source Software has been able to get a lot of attention of the research community as it is easy not only to prove a new concept, but also to repeat the experiments on OSS data sets available in the public domain. The meta-data analysis depicts valuable facts such as:

- Most of the contributors prefer to publish their work in conferences as compared to journals.
- The evolution of OSS is measured by using different methods, tools and techniques.
- IEEE and ACM are among the publishers who published research related to OSS evolution.

Some of the other major revelations of the review results are as follows:

- Software size has been the most common attribute to analyze evolution of OSS projects. Several types of metrics have been employed to measure software size. These metrics range from coarse grained level metrics such as number of files, modules, and functions, to fine grained level metrics such as number of LOC, methods, and classes. Several approaches, other than source code analysis using metrics, to analyze OSS evolution have also been employed in the research literature.
- Lately, metrics related to change activity have also been included to understand OSS evolution. These metrics measure changes in source code such as number of program elements (functions/classes/methods) changed in consecutive versions. Change activity as recorded in SCM systems is also used in a few cases. Most of the work deals with finding change size, change effort distributions. A few studies do change profile analysis as OSS systems evolve. But that is restricted to a few of the change categories e.g. adaptive v/s non-adaptive changes, or corrective v/s non-corrective changes. A fine-grained view of the changes can help to answer amount of progressive/ regressive work performed in a software system as it evolves. It can also be used to validate Lehman's 2nd law as Gonzalez-Barahona (2014) points to the lack of information available in this regard in their study of the glibc system.

- Herraiz et al. (2007c) observed that there are no long term correlations in the time series representing OSS activity. There is need to explore other alternative methods for time series analysis (rather than ARIMA) to deal with the uncertain evolutionary behavior of OSS systems.
- A shift in the programming languages, from procedural to object oriented, has been noticed as OSS systems, as subject systems in the corresponding studies, evolved over the period of time.
- Techniques and tools have been devised to tackle large amounts of data generated in software evolution analysis and prediction. Software evolution automation offers to collect volumes of data in a consistent manner. Software evolution visualization helps in understanding the transitions in complex and large systems in an easy way. Big data analytics can also help to analyze large sets of data generated during software evolution. Data analytics can be used to manage and understand the complex web of software evolution as it happens in source code and other related repositories.

REFERENCES

Abd-El-Hafiz, S. (2004). *An Information Theory Approach to Studying Software Evolution. Alexandria Engineering Journal, 43*(2), 275–284.

Adams, B., De Schutter, K., Tromp, H., & De Meuter, W. (2008). The evolution of the Linux build system. *Electronic Communications of the EASST, 8.*

Agrawal, K., Amreen, S., & Mockus, A. (2015). Commit quality in five high performance computing projects. In *International Workshop on Software Engineering for High Performance Computing in Science* (pp. 24-29). IEEE Press. doi:10.1109/SE4HPCS.2015.11

Ahmed, I., Mannan, U., Gopinath, R., & Jensen, C. (2015). An Empirical Study of Design Degradation: How Software Projects Get Worse over Time. *Proceedings of the 2015 ACM/IEEE International Symposium on Empirical Software Engineering and Measurement*, 1 – 10. doi:10.1109/ESEM.2015.7321186

Alali, A., Kagdi, H., & Maletic, J. (2008). What's a Typical Commit? A Characterization of Open Source Software Repositories. In *Proceedings of the 16th International Conference on Program Comprehension* (pp. 182-191). IEEE. doi:10.1109/ICPC.2008.24

Alenezi, M., & Khellah, F. (2015). Architectural Stability Evolution in Open-Source Systems. In *Proceedings of the International Conference on Engineering & MIS 2015 (ICEMIS '15)*. ACM. doi:10.1145/2832987.2833014

Alenezi, M., & Zarour, M. (2015). Modularity Measurement and Evolution in Object-Oriented Open-Source Projects. In *Proceedings of the International Conference on Engineering & MIS (ICEMIS '15)*. doi:10.1145/2832987.2833013

Ali, S., & Maqbool, O. (2009). Monitoring Software Evolution Using Multiple Types of Changes. In *Proceedings of the 2009 International Conference on Emerging Technologies* (pp. 410-415). IEEE. doi:10.1109/ICET.2009.5353135

Antoniol, G., Casazza, G., Penta, M., & Merlo, E. (2001). Modeling Clones Evolution through Time Series. In *Proceedings of the IEEE International Conference on Software Maintenance* (pp. 273-280). IEEE.

Arbuckle, T. (2009). Measure Software and its Evolution-using Information Content. In *Proceedings of the joint international and annual ERCIM workshops on Principles of Software Evolution (IWPSE) and Software Evolution (Evol) Workshops* (pp. 129-134). ACM. doi:10.1145/1595808.1595831

Arbuckle, T. (2011). Studying Software Evolution using Artifacts Shared Information Content. *Science of Computer Programming*, *76*(12), 1078–1097. doi:10.1016/j.scico.2010.11.005

Barry, E., Kemerer, C., & Slaughter, S. (2003). On the Uniformity of Software Evolution Patterns. *Proceedings of the 25th International Conference on Software Engineering*, 106-113. doi:10.1109/ICSE.2003.1201192

Bauer, A., & Pizka, M. (2003). The Contribution of Free Software to Software Evolution. In *Proceedings of the Sixth International Workshop on Principles of Software Evolution* (pp. 170-179). IEEE. doi:10.1109/IWPSE.2003.1231224

Bevan, J., Whitehead, E. Jr, Kim, S., & Godfrey, M. (2005). Facilitating Software Evolution Research with Kenyon. *Software Engineering Notes*, *30*(5), 177–186. doi:10.1145/1095430.1081736

Bhattacharya, P., & Neamtiu, I. (2011). Assessing Programming Language Impact on Development and Maintenance: A Study on C and C++. In *Proceedings of the 33rd International Conference on Software Engineering (ICSE)* (pp. 171-180). IEEE. doi:10.1145/1985793.1985817

Breivold, H., Chauhan, M., & Babar, M. (2010) A Systematic Review of Studies of Open Source Software Evolution. *Proceedings of the 17th Asia Pacific Software Engineering Conference (APSEC)*, 356-365. doi:10.1109/APSEC.2010.48

Capiluppi, A. (2003). Models for the Evolution of OS Projects. In *Proceedings of International Conference on Software Maintenance (ICSM)*. IEEE. doi:10.1109/ICSM.2003.1235407

Capiluppi, A. (2009). Domain Drivers in the Modularization of FLOSS Systems. Open Source EcoSystems: Diverse Communities Interacting. In C. Boldyreff, K. Crownston, B. Lundell et al. (Eds.), *Proceedings of the 5th IFIP WG 2.13 International Conference on Open Source Systems OSS '09*. Skovde, Sweden: Springer. doi:10.1007/978-3-642-02032-2_3

Capiluppi, A., Morisio, M., & Ramil, J. (2004a). The Evolution of Source folder structure in actively evolved Open Source Systems. In *Proceedings of the 10th International Symposium on Software metrics (METRICS '04)* (pp. 2-13). IEEE Computer Society, doi:10.1109/METRIC.2004.1357886

Capiluppi, A., Morisio, M., & Ramil, J. (2004b). Structural Evolution of an Open Source System: A case study. *Proceedings of the International Workshop on Program Comprehension*. doi:10.1109/WPC.2004.1311059

Capra, E. (2006). Mining Open Source web repositories to measure the cost of Evolutionary reuse. In *Proceedings of the 1st International Conference on Digital Information Management* (pp. 496-503). IEEE.

Caprio, F., Casazza, G., Penta, M., & Villano, U. (2001). Measuring and predicting the Linux kernel Evolution. *Proceedings of the Seventh Workshop on Empirical Studies of Software Maintenance*, 77.

Chahal, K. K., & Saini, M. (2016a). Open Source Software Evolution: A Systematic Literature Review (Part 1). *International Journal of Open Source Software and Processes*, *7*(1), 1–27. doi:10.4018/IJOSSP.2016010101

Chahal, K. K., & Saini, M. (2016b). Open Source Software Evolution: A Systematic Literature Review (Part 2). *International Journal of Open Source Software and Processes*, *7*(1), 28–48. doi:10.4018/IJOSSP.2016010102

Chaikalis, T., & Chatzigeorgiou, A. (2015). Forecasting Java Software Evolution Trends Employing Network Models. *IEEE Transactions on Software Engineering*, *41*(6), 582–602. doi:10.1109/TSE.2014.2381249

D'Ambros, M., & Lanza, M. (2010). Distributed and Collaborative Software Evolution Analysis with Churrasco. *Science of Computer Programming*, 75.

Dalle, J. M., Daudet, L., & den Besten, M. (2006). Mining CVS signals. *Proceedings of the Workshop on Public Data about Software Development*, 12-21.

Darcy, P., Daniel, L., & Stewart, K. (2010). Exploring Complexity in Open Source Software: Evolutionary Patterns, Antecedents, and Outcomes. In *Proceedings of the 2010 43rd Hawaii International Conference on System Sciences (HICSS)*. IEEE Press. doi:10.1109/HICSS.2010.198

Dattero, R., & Galup, S. (2004). Programming languages and Gender. *Communications of the ACM*, *47*(1), 99–102. doi:10.1145/962081.962087

Delorey, D., Knutson, C., & Giraud-Carrier, C. (2007). Programming language trends in Open Source development: An evaluation using data from all production phase Sourceforge Projects. *Proceedings of the Second International Workshop on Public Data about Software Development (WoPDaSD'07)*.

Fernandez-Ramil, J., Lozano, A., Wermilinger, M., & Capiluppi, A. (2008). Empirical Studies of Open Source Evolution. In T. Mens & S. Demeyer (Eds.), *Software Evolution* (pp. 263–288). Berlin: Springer. doi:10.1007/978-3-540-76440-3_11

Ferreira, K., Bigonha, A., Bigonha, S., & Gomes, M. (2011). Software Evolution Characterization-a Complex Network Approach. *Proceedings of the X Brazilian Symposium on Software Quality-SBQS*, 41-55.

Fluri, B., Würsch, M., Giger, E., & Gall, H. (2009). Analyzing the Co-Evolution of Comments and Source code. *Software Quality Journal*, *17*(4), 367–394. doi:10.1007/s11219-009-9075-x

Fuentetaja, E., & Bagert, D. (2002). Software Evolution from a Time-series Perspective. In *Proceedings International Conference on Software Maintenance* (pp. 226-229). IEEE. doi:10.1109/ICSM.2002.1167769

Gefen, D., & Schneberger, S. (1996). The Non-homogeneous Maintenance Periods: a Case Study of Software Modifications. In *Proceedings International Conference on Software Maintenance* (pp. 134-141). IEEE. doi:10.1109/ICSM.1996.564998

Girba, T., Kuhn, A., Seeberger, M., & Ducasse, S. (2005a). How Developers Drive Software Evolution. In *Proceedings of the Eighth International Workshop on Principles of Software Evolution* (pp. 113-122). IEEE. doi:10.1109/IWPSE.2005.21

Girba, T., Lanza, M., & Ducasse, S. (2005b). Characterizing the Evolution of Class Hierarchies. In *Proceedings of the Ninth European Conference on Software Maintenance and Reengineering (CSMR)* (pp. 2-11). IEEE. doi:10.1109/CSMR.2005.15

Godfrey, M., & German, D. (2008). Frontiers of software maintenance track. In *International Conference on Software Engineering* (pp. 129-138). IEEE.

Godfrey, M., & Tu, Q. (2000). Evolution in Open Source Software: A case study. In *Proceedings of the International Conference on Software Maintenance* (pp. 131–142). IEEE. doi:10.1109/ICSM.2000.883030

Godfrey, M., & Tu, Q. (2001). Growth, Evolution, and Structural Change in Open Source Software. In *Proc. of the 2001 Intl. Workshop on Principles of Software Evolution (IWPSE-01)* (pp. 103-106). IEEE.

Goeminne, M., Decan, A., & Mens, T. (2014). Co-evolving Code-related and Database-related Changes in a Data-intensive Software System. *Proceedings of the IEEE Conference on Software Maintenance, Reengineering and Reverse Engineering (CSMR-WCRE)*, 353–357. doi:10.1109/CSMR-WCRE.2014.6747193

Gonzalez-Barahona, J. M., Robles, G., Herraiz, I., & Ortega, F. (2014). Studying the laws of software evolution in a long-lived FLOSS project. *Journal of Software: Evolution and Process*, *26*(7), 589–612. PMID:25893093

Gorshenev, A., & Pismak, M. (2003). Punctuated Equilibrium in Software Evolution. *Physical Review E: Statistical, Nonlinear, and Soft Matter Physics*, *70*(6). PMID:15697556

Goulão, M., Fonte, N., Wermelinger, M., & Abreu, F. (2012). Software Evolution Prediction Using Seasonal Time Analysis: A Comparative Study. *Proceedings of 16th European Conference Software Maintenance and Reengineering (CSMR)*, 213-222. doi:10.1109/CSMR.2012.30

Gupta, A., Cruzes, D., Shull, F., Conradi, R., Rønneberg, H., & Landre, E. (2008). An examination of Change Profiles in reusable and non-reusable Software Systems. *Journal of Software Maintenance and Evolution: Research and Practice*, *22*(5), 359–380.

Hassan, A., Mockus, A., Holt, R., & Johnson, P. (2005b). Special issue on Mining Software Repositories. *IEEE Transactions on Software Engineering*, *31*(6), 426–428. doi:10.1109/TSE.2005.70

Hassan, A., Wu, J., & Holt, R. (2005a). Visualizing Historical Data Using Spectrographs. In *Proceedings of the 11th IEEE International Software Metrics Symposium (METRICS '05)*. IEEE Computer Society. doi:10.1109/METRICS.2005.54

Hattori, L., D'Ambros, M., Lanza, M., & Lungu, M. (2013). Answering Software Evolution Questions: An Empirical Evaluation. *Information and Software Technology*, *55*(4), 755–775. doi:10.1016/j.infsof.2012.09.001

Hattori, L., & Lanza, M. (2008). On the Nature of Commits. In *Proceedings of the 23rd IEEE/ACM International Conference on Automated Software Engineering-Workshops* (pp. 63-71). IEEE.

Hermenegildo, M. V. (2012). *Conferences vs. journals in CS, what to do? Evolutionary ways forward and the ICLP/TPLP model*. Leibniz-ZentrumfürInformatik.

Herraiz, I., Gonzalez-Barahona, J., & Robles, G. (2007a). Forecasting the Number of Changes in Eclipse using Time Series Analysis. In *Proceedings of the 2007 Fourth International Workshop on Mining Software Repositories MSR'07* (pp. 32-32). IEEE. doi:10.1109/MSR.2007.10

Herraiz, I., Gonzalez-Barahona, J., & Robles, G. (2007b). Towards a Theoretical Model for Software Growth. In *Proceedings of the Fourth International Workshop on Mining Software Repositories* (p. 21). IEEE Computer Society. doi:10.1109/MSR.2007.31

Herraiz, I., Gonzalez-Barahona, J., Robles, G., & German, D. (2007c).On the prediction of the Evolution of libre Software Projects. In *Proceedings of the 2007 IEEE International Conference on Software Maintenance (ICSM '07)* (pp. 405-414). IEEE. doi:10.1109/ICSM.2007.4362653

Herraiz, I., Gonzlez-Barahona, J., & Robles, G. (2008). Determinism and Evolution. In A. Hassan, M. Lanza, & M. Godfrey (Eds.), *Mining Software Repositories*. ACM. doi:10.1145/1370750.1370752

Herraiz, I., Robles, G., González-Barahona, J., Capiluppi, A., & Ramil, J. (2006). Comparison between SLOCs and Number of files as Size Metrics for Software Evolution analysis. In *Proceedings of the 10th European Conference on Software Maintenance and Reengineering (CSMR '06)* (p. 8). IEEE. doi:10.1109/CSMR.2006.17

Hindle, A., German, D., Godfrey, M., & Holt, R. (2009a). Automatic Classification of Large Changes into Maintenance Categories. In *Proceedings of the 17th International Conference on Program Comprehension ICPC'09* (pp. 30-39). IEEE.

Hu, J., Sun, X., Lo, D., & Bin, L. (2015). Modeling the Evolution of Development Topics using Dynamic Topic Models. *Proceedings of the 2015 IEEE 22nd International Conference on Software Analysis, Evolution and Reengineering*, 3-12. doi:10.1109/SANER.2015.7081810

Israeli, A., & Feitelson, D. (2010). The Linux Kernel as a Case Study in Software Evolution. *Journal of Systems and Software*, *83*(3), 485–501. doi:10.1016/j.jss.2009.09.042

Izurieta, C., & Bieman, J. (2006). The Evolution of FreeBSD and Linux. In *Proceedings of the 2006 ACM/IEEE international symposium on Empirical Software engineering* (pp. 204-211). ACM. doi:10.1145/1159733.1159765

Jenkins, S., & Kirk, S. (2007). Software Architecture Graphs as Complex Networks: A Novel Partitioning Scheme to Measure Stability and Evolution. *Information Sciences*, *177*(12), 2587–2601. doi:10.1016/j.ins.2007.01.021

Jiang, Y., & Adams, B. (2015). Co-Evolution of Infrastructure and Source Code: An Empirical Study. In *Proceedings of the 12th Working Conference on Mining Software Repositories (MSR '15)* (pp. 45-55). Piscataway, NJ: IEEE Press. doi:10.1109/MSR.2015.12

Karus, S., & Gall, H. (2011). A Study of Language Usage Evolution in Open Source Software. In *Proceedings of the 8th Working Conference on Mining Software Repositories* (pp. 13-22). ACM. doi:10.1145/1985441.1985447

Kaur, K. (2013). Analyzing Growth Trends of Reusable Software Components. In H. Singh & K. Kaur (Eds.), *Designing, Engineering, and Analyzing Reliable and Efficient Software*. Hershey, PA: IGI Global; doi:10.4018/978-1-4666-2958-5.ch003

Kemerer, C., & Slaughter, S. (1997). A Longitudinal Analysis of Software Maintenance Patterns. In *Proceedings of the eighteenth international conference on Information Systems* (pp. 476-477). Association for Information Systems.

Kemerer, C., & Slaughter, S. (1999). An Empirical Approach to Studying Software Evolution. *IEEE Transactions on Software Engineering*, 25(4), 493–509. doi:10.1109/32.799945

Kenmei, B., Antoniol, G., & Penta, M. (2008). Trend Analysis and Issue Prediction in Large-scale Open Source Systems. In *Proceedings of the 12th European Conference on Software Maintenance and Reengineering (CSMR'08)* (pp. 73-82). IEEE. doi:10.1109/CSMR.2008.4493302

Kitchenham, B. (2007). *Guidelines for Performing Systematic Literature Review in Software Engineering*. Technical report EBSE-2007-001.

Kläs, M., Elberzhager, F., Münch, J., Hartjes, K., & Von Graevemeyer, O. (2010). Transparent Combination of Expert and Measurement Data for Defect Prediction: an Industrial Case Study. In *Proceedings of the 32nd ACM/IEEE International Conference on Software Engineering* (Vol. 2, pp. 119-128). ACM. doi:10.1145/1810295.1810313

Koch, S. (2005). Evolution of Open Source System Software Systems - a Large Scale Investigation. *Proceedings of the First International Conference on Open Source Systems*.

Koch, S. (2007). Software Evolution in Open Source Projects—a Large-scale Investigation. *Journal of Software Maintenance and Evolution: Research and Practice*, 19(6), 361–382. doi:10.1002/smr.348

Kpodjedo, S., Ricca, F., Galinier, P., & Antoniol, G. (2013). Studying Software Evolution of Large Object Oriented Software Systems using an etgm Algorithm. *Journal of Software: Evolution and Process*, 25(2), 139–163.

LaMantia, M., Cai, Y., MacCormack, A., & Rusnak, J. (2008). Analyzing the Evolution of large-scale Software Systems using Design Structure Matrices and Design Rule Theory: Two Exploratory Cases. In *Proceedings of theSeventh Working IEEE/IFIP Conference on Software Architecture (WICSA '08)* (pp. 83-92). IEEE. doi:10.1109/WICSA.2008.49

Le, D., Behnamghader, P., Garcia, J., Link, D., Shahbazian, A., & Medvidovic, N. (2015). An Empirical Study of Architectural Change in Open-Source Software Systems. In *Proceedings of the 12th Working Conference on Mining Software Repositories (MSR '15)* (pp. 235-245). IEEE. doi:10.1109/MSR.2015.29

Lehman, M. (1996). Laws of Software Evolution Revisited. In *Proceedings of the European Workshop on Software Process Technology* (pp. 108-124). Springer-Verlag. doi:10.1007/BFb0017737

Lehman, M., Ramil, J., & Sandler, U. (2001). An Approach to Modeling Long-term Growth Trends in Software Systems. In *Proceedings of the International Conference on Software Maintenance* (pp. 219–228). IEEE.

Lin, S., Ma, Y., & Chen, J. (2013). Empirical Evidence on Developer's Commit Activity for Open-Source Software Projects. *Proceedings of the 25th International Conference on Software Engineering and Knowledge Engineering*, 455-460.

Marsavina, C., Romano, D., & Zaidman, A. (2014). Studying Fine-Grained Co-Evolution Patterns of Production and Test Code. *Proceedings of the 2014 IEEE 14th International Working Conference on Source Code Analysis and Manipulation (SCAM)*, 195-204. doi:10.1109/SCAM.2014.28

McIntosh, S., Adams, B., & Hassan, A. (2012). The Evolution of Java build Systems. *Empirical Software Engineering, 17*(4), 578–608. doi:10.1007/s10664-011-9169-5

McIlroy, M. (1968). *Mass Produced Software Components*. Keynote address in NATO Software Engineering Conference.

Mens, T., Fernández-Ramil, J., & Degrandsart, S. (2008). The Evolution of Eclipse. In *Proceedings of the 2008 IEEE International Conference on Software Maintenance (ICSM)* (pp. 386-395). IEEE. doi:10.1109/ICSM.2008.4658087

Meqdadi, O., Alhindawi, N., Collard, M., & Maletic, J. (2013). Towards Understanding Large-scale Adaptive Changes from Version Histories. In *Proceedings of the 2013 IEEE International Conference on Software Maintenance* (pp. 416-419). IEEE. doi:10.1109/ICSM.2013.61

Milev, R., Muegge, S., & Weiss, M. (2009). Design Evolution of an Open Source Project using an Improved Modularity Metric. In *Proceedings of the 5th IFIP WG 2.13 International Conference on Open Source Systems OSS '09*. Skovde, Sweden: Springer. doi:10.1007/978-3-642-02032-2_4

Mockus, A., Fielding, R., & Herbsleb, J. (2002). Two case studies of Open Source Software development: Apache and Mozilla. *ACM Transactions on Software Engineering and Methodology, 11*(3), 309–346. doi:10.1145/567793.567795

Murgia, A., Concas, G., Marchesi, M., Tonelli, R., & Turnu, I. (2009). Empirical study of Software Quality Evolution in Open Source Projects using Agile Practices. *Proceedings of the International symposium on Emerging Trends in Software Metrics (ETSM)*.

Myrtveit, I., & Stensrud, E. (2008). *An Empirical Study of Software development Productivity in C and C++*. Presented at NIK-2008 conference. Retrieved from www.nik.no

Nakakoji, K., Yamamoto, Y., Nishinaka, Y., Kishida, K., & Ye, Y. (2002). Evolution Patterns of Open-Source Software Systems and Communities. In *Proceedings of the international workshop on Principles of Software Evolution* (pp. 76-85). ACM. doi:10.1145/512035.512055

Neamtiu, I., Xie, G., & Chen, J. (2013). Towards a Better Understanding of Software Evolution: An Empirical Study on Open-Source Software. *Journal of Software: Evolution and Process, 25*(3), 193–218.

Olszak, A., Lazarova-Molnar, S., & Jørgensen, B. (2015). Evolution of Feature-Oriented Software: How to Stay on Course and Avoid the Cliffs of Modularity Drift. In *Proceedings of the 9th International Joint Conference Software Technologies, CCIS* (Vol. 555, pp. 183-201). Springer.

Pan, W., Li, B., Ma, Y., & Liu, J. (2011). Multi-Granularity Evolution Analysis of Software. *Journal of Systems Science and Complexity*, *24*(6), 1068–1082. doi:10.1007/s11424-011-0319-z

Paulson, J., Succi, G., & Eberlein, A. (2004). An Empirical Study of Open-Source and Closed-Source Software products. *IEEE Transactions on Software Engineering*, *30*(4), 246–256. doi:10.1109/TSE.2004.1274044

Phipps, G. (1999). Comparing Observed Bug and Productivity Rates for Java and C++. *Software, Practice & Experience*, *29*(4), 345–358. doi:10.1002/(SICI)1097-024X(19990410)29:4<345::AID-SPE238>3.0.CO;2-C

Pressman, R. (2010). *Software Engineering – A Practitioner's Approach* (7th ed.). McGraw Hill Education.

Qiu, D., Li, B., & Su, Z. (2013). An Empirical Analysis of the Co-Evolution of Schema and Code in Database Applications. In Meeting on Foundations of Software Engineering, ser. ESEC/FSE 2013 (pp. 125–135). ACM. doi:10.1145/2491411.2491431

Rainer, A., Lane, P., Malcolm, J., & Scholz, S. (2008). Using N-grams to Rapidly Characterise the Evolution of Software code. In *Proceedings of the 23rd IEEE/ACM International Conference on Automated Software Engineering Workshops* (pp. 43-52). IEEE. doi:10.1109/ASEW.2008.4686320

Raja, U., Hale, D., & Hale, J. (2009). Modeling Software Evolution Defects: A Time Series Approach. *Journal of Software Maintenance and Evolution: Research and Practice*, *21*(1), 49–71. doi:10.1002/smr.398

Ratzinger, J., Gall, H., & Pinzger, M. (2007). Quality Assessment Based on Attribute Series of Software Evolution. In *Proceedings of the 14th Working Conference on Reverse Engineering WCRE '07* (pp. 80-89). IEEE. doi:10.1109/WCRE.2007.39

Robles, G., Amor, J., Gonzalez-Barahona, J., & Herraiz, I. (2005). Evolution and Growth in Large Libre Software Projects. In *Proceedings of the International Workshop on Principles in Software Evolution* (pp. 165-174). IEEE. doi:10.1109/IWPSE.2005.17

Robles, G., Gonzalez-Barahona, J., & Merelo, J. (2006a). Beyond Source Code: The Importance of other Artifacts in Software Development. *Journal of Systems and Software*, *79*(9), 1233–1248. doi:10.1016/j.jss.2006.02.048

Robles, G., Gonzalez-Barahona, J., Michlmayr, M., & Amor, J. (2006b). Mining Large Software Compilations over Time: Another Perspective of Software Evolution. In *Proceedings of the 2006 international workshop on Mining Software repositories (MSR'06)* (pp. 3-9). ACM doi:10.1145/1137983.1137986

Robles-Martinez, G., Gonzlez-Barahona, J., Centeno-Gonzalez, J., Matellan-Olivera, V., & Rodero-Merino, L. (2003). Studying the Evolution of Libre Software Projects using Publicly Available Data. *Proceedings of the 3rd Workshop on Open Source Software Engineering*.

Rossi, B., Russo, B., & Succi, G. (2009) Analysis of Open Source Software Development Iterations by Means of Burst Detection Techniques, In Open Source EcoSystems: Diverse Communities Interacting. In *Proceedings 5th IFIP WG 2.13 International Conference on Open Source Systems* (pp. 83-93). Springer.

Roy, C., & Cordy, J. (2006). *Evaluating the Evolution of Small Scale Open Source Software Systems.* Academic Press.

Saini, M., & Kaur, K. (2014a). Analyzing the Change Profiles of Software Systems using their Change Logs. International Journal of Software Engineering, 7(2), 39-66.

Saini, M., & Kaur, K. (2014b). Software Evolution Prediction using Fuzzy Analysis. In *Proceedings of International Conference on Emerging Applications of Information Technology, organized by Computer Society of India at Indian Institute of Science.* Kolkata, India: IEEE Computer Society Press.

Saini, M., & Kaur, K. (2016). Fuzzy analysis and prediction of commit activity in open source software projects. *IET Software*, *10*(5), 136–146. doi:10.1049/iet-sen.2015.0087

Santos, E. A., & Hindle, A. (2016). Judging a commit by its cover; or can a commit message predict build failure?. *PeerJ PrePrints, 4*, e1771v1.

Schach, S., Jin, B., Yu, L., Heller, G., & Offutt, J. (2003). Determining the Distribution of Maintenance Categories: Survey versus Measurement. *Empirical Software Engineering*, *8*(4), 351–365. doi:10.1023/A:1025368318006

Singh, S. (2008). A Computational Method of Forecasting Based on Fuzzy Time Series. *Journal of Mathematics and Computers in Simulation*, *79*(3), 539–554. doi:10.1016/j.matcom.2008.02.026

Siy, H., Chundi, P., Rosenkrant, D., & Subramaniam, M. (2007). Discovering Dynamic Developer Relationships from Software Version Histories by Time Series Segmentation. In *Proceedings of the 2007 IEEE International Conference on Software Maintenance* (pp. 415-424). IEEE. doi:10.1109/ICSM.2007.4362654

Smith, N., Capiluppi, A., & Fernandez-Ramil, J. (2006). Agent-based Simulation of Open Source Software Evolution. *Software Process Improvement and Practice*, *11*(4), 423–434. doi:10.1002/spip.280

Smith, N., Capiluppi, A., & Ramil, J. (2005). A Study of Open Source Software Evolution Data using Qualitative Simulation. *Software Process Improvement and Practice*, *10*(3), 287–300. doi:10.1002/spip.230

Stamelos, I., Angelis, L., Oikonomou, A., & Bleris, G. L. (2002). Code quality analysis in open source software development. *Information Systems Journal*, *12*(1), 43–60. doi:10.1046/j.1365-2575.2002.00117.x

Stewart, K., Darcy, D., & Daniel, S. (2006). Opportunities and Challenges Applying Functional Data Analysis to the Study of Open Source Software Evolution. *Statistical Science*, *21*(2), 167–178. doi:10.1214/088342306000000141

Stol, K., & Babar, M. (2009). Reporting Empirical Research in Open Source Software: the State of Practice. In *Proceedings 5th IFIP WG 2.13 International Conference on Open Source Systems OSS '09.* Skovde, Sweden: Springer. doi:10.1007/978-3-642-02032-2_15

Syeed, M., Hammouda, I., & Systa, T. (2013). Evolution of Open Source Software Projects: A Systematic Literature Review. *Journal of Software, 8*(11).

Tahvildari, L., Gregory, R., & Kontogiannis, K. (1999). An Approach for Measuring Software Evolution using Source Code Features. In *Proceedings of the Sixth Asia Pacific Software Engineering Conference (APSEC '99)* (pp. 10-17). IEEE. doi:10.1109/APSEC.1999.809579

Thomas, S., Adams, B., Hassan, A., & Blostein, D. (2014). Studying Software Evolution using Topic Models. *Science of Computer Programming, 80,* 457–479. doi:10.1016/j.scico.2012.08.003

Tu, Q., & Godfrey, M. (2002). An Integrated Approach for Studying Architectural Evolution. In *Proceedings of the 10th International Workshop on Program Comprehension* (pp. 127-136). IEEE.

Turski, W. (1996). Reference Model for Smooth Growth of Software Systems. *IEEE Transactions on Software Engineering, 22*(8), 599–600.

Vasa, R. (2010). *Growth and Change Dynamics in Open Source Software Systems* (Ph.D. thesis). Swinburne University of Technology, Melbourne, Australia.

Vaucher, S., & Sahraoui, H. (2007). Do Software Libraries Evolve Differently than Applications?: An Empirical Investigation. In *Proceedings of the 2007 Symposium on Library-Centric Software Design* (pp. 88-96). ACM. doi:10.1145/1512762.1512771

Wang, L., Wang, Z., Yang, C., Zhang, L., & Ye, Q. (2009). Linux Kernels as Complex Networks: A Novel Method to Study Evolution. In *Proceedings of the 25th International Conference on Software Maintenance* (pp. 41-51). IEEE. doi:10.1109/ICSM.2009.5306348

Weicheng, Y., Beijun, S., & Ben, X. (2013). Mining GitHub: Why Commit Stops -- Exploring the Relationship between Developer's Commit Pattern and File Version Evolution. *Proceedings of the 20th Asia-Pacific Software Engineering Conference, 2,* 165–169. doi:10.1109/APSEC.2013.133

Wermilinger, M., & Ferreira, H. (2011). Quality Evolution track at QUATIC 2010. *Software Engineering Notes, 36*(1), 28–29. doi:10.1145/1921532.1960273

Wu, J., & Holt, R. (2004). Linker Based Program Extraction and its use in Software Evolution. *Proceedings of the International Workshop on Unanticipated Software Evolution,* 1-15.

Wu, J., Holt, R., & Hassan, A. (2007). Empirical Evidence for SOC Dynamics in Software Evolution. In *Proceedings of the International Conference on Software Maintenance* (pp. 244-254). IEEE. doi:10.1109/ICSM.2007.4362637

Xie, G., Chen, J., & Neamtiu, I. (2009). Towards a Better Understanding of Software Evolution: An Empirical Study on Open Source Software. In *Proceedings of the International Conference on Software Maintenance* (pp. 51-60). IEEE. doi:10.1109/ICSM.2009.5306356

Xu, J., Gao, Y., Christley, S., & Madey, G. (2005). A Topological Analysis of the Open Source Software Development Community. In *Proceedings of the 38th Annual Hawaii International Conference on System Sciences (HICSS'05).* IEEE.

Yu, L. (2006). Indirectly Predicting the Maintenance Effort of Open-Source Software. *Journal of Software Maintenance and Evolution: Research and Practice, 18*(5), 311–332. doi:10.1002/smr.335

Yuen, C. (1985). An empirical approach to the study of errors in large software under maintenance. *Proc. IEEE Int. Conf. on Software Maintenance*, 96–105.

Yuen, C. (1987). A statistical rationale for evolution dynamics concepts. *Proc IEEE Int. Conf. on Software Maintenance*, 156–164.

Yuen, C. (1988). On analyzing maintenance process data at the global and detailed levels. *Proc. IEEE Int. Conf. on Software Maintenance*, 248–255.

Zaidman, A., Rompaey, B., Deursen, A., & Demeyer, S. (2011). Studying the Co-Evolution of Production and Test Code in Open Source and Industrial Developer Test Processes through Repository Mining. *Empirical Software Engineering, 16*(3), 325–364. doi:10.1007/s10664-010-9143-7

Zaimi, A., Ampatzoglou, A., Triantafyllidou, N., Chatzigeorgiou, A., Mavridis, A., & Chaikalis, T. (2015). An Empirical Study on the Reuse of Third-Party Libraries in Open-Source Software Development. In *Proceedings of the 7th Balkan Conference on Informatics Conference* (pp. 4). ACM. doi:10.1145/2801081.2801087

Zazworka, N., & Ackermann, C. (2010). CodeVizard: a Tool to Aid the Analysis of Software Evolution. In *Proceedings of the 2010 ACM-IEEE International Symposium on Empirical Software Engineering and Measurement (ESEM '10)*. ACM doi:10.1145/1852786.1852865

Zhongmin, C., & Yeqing, W. (2010,). The application of theory and method of time series in the modeling of software reliability. In *Proceedings of the 2010 Second International Conference on Information Technology and Computer Science (ITCS)* (pp. 340-343). IEEE. doi:10.1109/ITCS.2010.89

Zimmermann, T., Premraj, R., & Zeller, A. (2007). Predicting Defects for Eclipse. *Proceedings of the Third International Workshop on Predictor Models in Software Engineering (Promise '07)*. doi:10.1109/PROMISE.2007.10

Chapter 2
Demography of Open Source Software Prediction Models and Techniques

Kaniz Fatema
American International University, Bangladesh

M. M. Mahbubul Syeed
American International University, Bangladesh

Imed Hammouda
South Mediterranean University, Tunisia

ABSTRACT

Open source software (OSS) is currently a widely adopted approach to developing and distributing software. Many commercial companies are using OSS components as part of their product development. For instance, more than 58% of web servers are using an OSS web server, Apache. For effective adoption of OSS, fundamental knowledge of project development is needed. This often calls for reliable prediction models to simulate project evolution and to envision project future. These models provide help in supporting preventive maintenance and building quality software. This chapter reports on a systematic literature survey aimed at the identification and structuring of research that offers prediction models and techniques in analysing OSS projects. The study outcome provides insight into what constitutes the main contributions of the field, identifies gaps and opportunities, and distils several important future research directions. This chapter extends the authors' earlier journal article and offers the following improvements: broader study period, enhanced discussion, and synthesis of reported results.

INTRODUCTION

The use of Open Source Software (OSS) is increasingly becoming part of the development strategy and business portfolio of more and more IT organizations. This is, for example, demonstrated by the growing numbers of downloads of OSS code by companies (Samoladas;Angelis;& Stamelos, 2010). The primary

DOI: 10.4018/978-1-5225-5314-4.ch002

motivation is that OSS can offer huge benefits to an organization, with minimal development costs while taking advantage of free access to code and high quality driven by the power of distributed peer review (Capiluppi & Adams, Reassessing brooks law for the free software community, 2009). Successful OSS projects, such as Eclipse have reached thousands of downloads per day (Eclipse, 2013). However, such projects are typically complex, both from the point of view of the code base, and the community. They may consist of a wide range of components, and come with a large number of versions reflecting their development and evolution history.

In order to adopt an OSS component effectively, an organization often needs fundamental knowledge of the project development, composition, and the possible risks associated with its use. This is because OSS code is primarily developed outside the company by an ultra-wide distributed community (Thy;Ferenc;& Siket, 2005) (Samoladas;Angelis;& Stamelos, 2010). In particular, organizations might need to understand how an OSS project may evolve, as this may impact the future of the organization itself. Additionally, the concern of the quality and reliability of OSS components should be addressed adequately. From a proactive perspective, foreseeing the evolution of an OSS component may provide the organization with useful information including the kind of maintenance practices, resources, and strategic decisions need to be allocated and adopted in supporting their development strategies.

Accordingly, a wide range of prediction models have been proposed by the research community for the purpose of simulating the evolution and approximating the future of OSS projects, with regard to various aspects. For instance, a number of methods supporting error prediction have been developed to provide valuable information for preventive maintenance, and for building quality software. An example prediction scenario has been to foresee potential error prone segments of the code base for tracing down the modules that would most likely require future maintenance tasks (Thy;Ferenc;& Siket, 2005) (Yuming & Baowen, 2008). Despite the variety and volume of OSS prediction studies, it has been argued that the efforts for analysing the evolutionary behaviour of OSS systems still lag behind the high adoption levels of OSS. Furthermore, the focus of OSS prediction studies in general has been restricted to a small number of projects, which limits the generalizability of the methods and results. Such claims thus need empirical evidence (Russo;Mulazzani;Russo;& Steff, 2011).

This chapter is an enhanced version of the literature review that is aimed to provide an in-depth analysis of the prediction research work targeted to analysing OSS projects (Syeed, Hammouda, & Systa, 2014). To carry out this review a review protocol was developed following the guidelines presented in (Kitchenham, Procedures for performing systematic reviews, 2004), a detail discussion of which is resented in the following sections.

The outcome of this review would benefit the readers in following capacities: first, it offers a single point reference to the state-of-the-art studies on the topic; second, it offers a detail break down of what constitute the prediction study concerning OSS projects (e.g., which facets of prediction studies are mostly explored, what data sources are used, what methods and metrics are used along with others), and third, it distils the gaps and opportunities to formulate future research directions. This chapter reflects the following enhancement: (1) a broader study period with enhanced list of articles (65 peer reviewed articles), (2) enhanced discussion on the research question highlighting the results taken from current publications, (3) synthesis on the reported results, and (3) a more elaborated discussion.

This chapter is structured as follows. In REVIEW METHODOLOGY the research questions and the review protocol are discussed. Answers to the research questions, and a synthesis on the reported results are presented in sections REVIEW RESULT and SYNTHESIS respectively. A discussion on open areas in the field of OSS and prediction are presented in section AVENUE TO FUTURE WORK.

Section THREATS TO VALIDITY throws light on the validity issues related to the review protocol. Finally, concluding remarks are presented in the CONCLUSION section. Additionally, a complete list of reviewed articles can be found in section REFERENCES section and the data collection table can be downloaded from the following link (OSS prediction studies: Data collection Table, 2017).

REVIEW METHODOLOGY

Evidence-based Software Engineering (EBSE) relies on aggregating the best available evidence to address engineering questions posed by researchers. A recommended methodology for such studies is Systematic Literature Review (SLR) (Kitchenham, ym., 2010). Performing an SLR involves several discrete tasks, which are defined and described by Kitchenham (Kitchenham, Procedures for performing systematic reviews, 2004). As a starting point, SLR recommends to pre-define a review protocol to reduce the possibility of researcher bias (Kitchenham, Procedures for performing systematic reviews, 2004). Along those guidelines and following the review process described in (Cornelissen;Zaidman; Deursen;Moonen;& Koschke, 2009), Figure 1 shows the tasks involved in this review protocol. These tasks are discussed in the subsequent subsections.

It has to be noted that the following procedure is replicated to select and analyse the latest 13 articles which published between 2012 and March 2017. Therefore, this chapter reviewed a total of 65 articles (of which 52 articles are taken from the journal).

Research Questions

The research questions defined for this study fall within the context of OSS projects and prediction strategies. In total, we have formulated 9 questions, as presented in Table 1. These questions are proposed to portray the holistic view of OSS prediction studies, covering aspects, for instance, the focus of the study, methodological detail, case study projects, prediction methods, metric suites, OSS data sets and validation process. A subset of these questions is typical for SLR conducted for prediction studies (Catal & Diri, A systematic review of software fault prediction studies, 2009).

Article Selection

This section describes the article selection process (phase (b) in Figure 1) that includes defining the inclusion criteria for article selection, an automated keyword search process to search digital libraries, a manual selection from the initial set of articles, and the reference checking of the listed articles.

- **Inclusion/Exclusion Criteria:** Along the research questions shown in Table 1, we have defined a set of selection criteria in advance that should be satisfied by the reviewed articles. Articles that fail to pass either of these criteria are excluded from the review. The criteria set for the article selection are as follows:
- Subject area of the articles must unveil strong focus on prediction. Authors must explicitly state the type of prediction performed (e.g., fault, quality, security, effort, survivability, success prediction) and provide detailed evidence of metrics, methods, and data sets exploited.

Figure 1. Systematic literature review process (adopted from (Cornelissen;Zaidman;Deursen;Moon en;& Koschke, 2009))

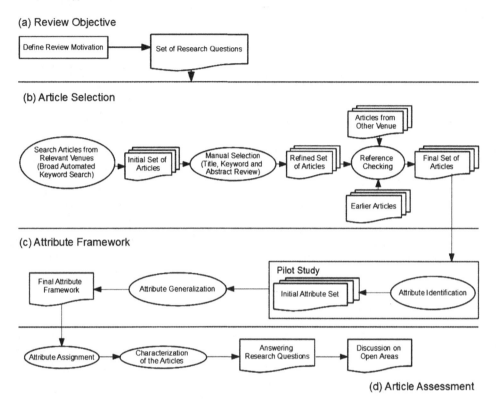

- Articles must exhibit a profound relation to OSS projects and take into consideration those aspects that are particularly attributed to the OSS community and projects. Articles using OSS as a case study are taken into account if they satisfy the above criterion.
- Articles published in referred journals and conferences are included for the review. Books are not considered in this study.

The suitability of the articles was determined against the above mentioned selection criteria through a manual analysis (discussed later in this section) of title, keywords, abstract. In case of doubt conclusions are checked (Brereton; Kitchenham; Budgen; Turner; & Khalil, 2007).

Automated Keyword Search

Automatic keyword search is a widely used strategy in literature surveys (e.g., (Beecham; Baddoo; Hall; Robinson; & Sharp, 2008) (Dyba & Dingsyr, 2008)). Thus, we performed a broad automated keyword search to get the initial set of articles. First two authors of this article were responsible for the search process. Six digital libraries were searched, a list of which is given bellow:

- IEEE Computer Society Digital Library
- ACM

Table 1. Research Questions

Category	Sl. No.	Research Question	Main Motivation
Target	RQ1	Which facets of prediction approaches were explored, and how many articles were published under each facet?	To identify the focus area of the prediction work (e.g., fault or defect prediction) and to decompose the articles according to their study focus.
	RQ2	Does the interest on "OSS prediction study" follow an increasing trend?	To identify the beginning and growth of research interest in the field OSS project prediction.
Target Group	RQ3	What is the portfolio of projects analyzed for prediction studies and what are the domains of the projects?	To determine the mode of prediction studies (e.g., horizontal or vertical) by statistically measuring the studied OSS projects and their domains.
Approach and Results	RQ4	What are the research approaches followed in the studies?	To identify the general trend of research methodology used in research.
	RQ5	What datasets or data sources of OSS projects are mostly exploited?	To identify the data sources of OSS projects those are used for prediction.
	RQ6	What metric suites are evaluated and what tools are used for metric data collection?	To explore the metric suites used for the prediction study and frequently used tools for data extraction.
	RQ7	What are the methods used in prediction models?	To explore the prediction methods used in OSS.
	RQ8	How are the research methodology and results validated?	To identify the approaches employed to evaluate the research approaches in mitigating associated validity threats.
	RQ9	How are the prediction models validated?	To identify the approaches utilized in validating the performance of the prediction models.

- ScienceDirect
- SpringerLink
- Google Scholar
- FLOSShub

To the knowledge of the authors, the above libraries provide the most popular sources for open source related research articles. All searches were based on the title, keywords and abstract. The time period for this search was from January, 2000 to March, 2013.

Knowing the fact that construction of search strings varies among libraries, we first defined search terms according to our inclusion criteria. Then to form the search strings, we combined these search terms following the guidelines of each digital library. The list of search terms that were used is as follows.

Terms representing OSS: "Open source" or OSS or "Open Source Software" or "Open Source Software projects" or FLOSS or "Libre Software" or "F/OSS".

Terms representing prediction: "Prediction" or "Prediction model" or "Fault prediction" or "Defect prediction" or "Test effort prediction" or "Correction cost prediction" or "Reusability prediction" or "Security prediction" or "Effort prediction" or "Quality prediction".

The automated keyword search resulted in 1047 articles. From this list of articles, we excluded those that were obviously false positives. False positives include results, e.g., from other fields than software engineering and computer science. The first two authors reviewed the results of each search independently looking at the title, and the venue of the articles. The output of this step was the common selection of 84 articles consisting of 24 journal articles and 60 conference articles.

Manual Selection

Recent studies (Brereton;Kitchenham;Budgen;Turner;& Khalil, 2007) (Cornelissen;Zaidman;Deurse n;Moonen;& Koschke, 2009) pointed out that (a) current digital libraries on software engineering do not provide good support for automated keyword search due to lack of consistent set of keywords, and (b) the abstracts of software engineering articles are relatively poor in comparison to other disciplines. Thus, it is possible that the 84 articles identified in the earlier step might contain irrelevant ones and some relevant might be missing. Due to this, the first two authors performed a manual selection of these articles by reviewing the title, keywords and abstract (and in case of doubt, checking the conclusion (Brereton;Kitchenham;Budgen;Turner;& Khalil, 2007)). To reduce the researcher bias in this selection process, the domain expert (third author) examined the selected articles against the selection criterion. Any disagreement was resolved through discussion. This process ended up with 50 articles consisting of 16 journal articles and 34 conference articles.

- **Reference Checking:** To ensure the inclusion of other relevant but missing articles (as mentioned above), the first two authors independently performed a non-recursive search through the references of the 50 selected articles. This process identified 2 additional conference articles.
- **Final Set of Articles:** The article selection process finally ended up with 52 articles (16 journal and 36 conference articles). A complete list of these articles is presented in section LIST OF REVIEWED ARTICLES.

Attribute Framework

The next step in the review protocol was the construction of an attribute framework (phase (c) in Figure 1). This framework was used to characterize the selected articles and to answer the research questions. Following is a brief description of this process.

- **Attribute Identification:** The attribute set was derived based on two criteria: (a) The domain of the review (i.e., prediction of OSS projects) and (b) the research questions. A pilot study was run for this step, as shown in phase (c) of Figure 1. This phase consists of a number of activities:

First, we performed an exploratory study on the structure of 5 randomly selected articles (from the pool of 52 articles). This study led to a set of seven general attributes that can be used to describe the articles and to answer the research questions. This attribute list is shown in the Attribute column of Table 2.

Second, this list of attributes was refined further into a number of specific sub-attributes to get a precise description of each of the general attributes and fine tune the findings on the research questions. To do this, we made a thorough study of the same set of articles and wrote down words of interest that could be relevant for a particular attribute (e.g., "fault prediction", or "effort prediction" for the Study Target attribute). The result after reading all articles was a (large) set of initial sub attributes. This data extraction task was performed by the first two authors of this survey.

- **Attribute Generalization and Final Attribute Framework:** We further generalized the attributes and sub-attributes to increase their reusability (Cornelissen;Zaidman;Deursen;Moonen;& Koschke, 2009). For example, sub-attributes "mailing list archive" or "chat history" are intuitively generalized to Communication.

To reduce the change of researcher bias in this stage, two step validations were done. First, the attributes and associated sub-attributes were identified and then generalized independently by the first two authors. Then they were merged to a single set of attributes through discussion. Second, the final attribute list selected by the first two authors was examined and validated by the domain expert (third author), who did not have any connection with the attribute identification process. Table 2 shows the final set of attributes and their connection to the research questions in answering them.

Table 2. Attribute Framework

Attribute	Sub Attribute	Brief Description	RQ Addressed
General		Publication Type, Year of Publication.	RQ2
Study Type		Empirical, comparative, case study, tool implementation.	RQ4
Study Target		Study facets (e.g., fault prediction).	RQ1
Case Study	OSS projects studied	List of OSS Projects studied.	RQ3
	Programming language	Target programming languages of OSS projects.	
	Project Domain	Application domain of the OSS projects covered.	
Data Source	Source code	Code base, CVS/SVN.	RQ5
	Contribution	Change log, bug tracking systems.	
	Communication	Mailing list archive, chat history.	
	External sources	Sourceforge, github, ohloh.	
Methodology	Method	Implication or application of prediction methods.	RQ6 and RQ7
	Metric	Implication or application of metrics / features / attributes for prediction.	
	Tool implementation	Implementation of a tool to automate prediction.	
	Tool used	Existing tools, algorithms used for study.	
Validation	Validation of the study	Validation process of the research methodology.	RQ8 and RQ9
	Validation of the prediction model	Validation process of the accuracy and applicability of a prediction model.	

Article Assessment

The article assessment step consists of four distinct activities as shown in phase (d) of Figure 1. In this section, we focus on the first two steps.

- **Attribute Assignment:** Using the attribute framework from the previous section, we processed all articles and assigned the appropriate attribute sets to each of the articles. These attributes effectively capture the essence of the articles in terms of the research questions and allow for a clear distinction between (and comparison of) the articles under study.

The assignment process was performed independently by the first two authors of this survey. During this process, authors claim of contribution is assessed against the results presented in the articles. For example, to validate the claim on the target of the study (e.g., fault/defect prediction), we assessed what relevant data sources are explored, what metrics and methods are used, and the duration and process of the data collection. Also, we did not draw any conclusions from what was presented in an article if it was not explicitly mentioned. For example, we left the attribute field study type empty if it was not mentioned in the article.

- **Characterization of the Reviewed Articles:** Since the attribute assignment process is subject to different interpretations, different reviewers may predict different attribute subsets for the same article (Cornelissen; Zaidman; Deursen; Moonen; & Koschke, 2009). Thus to ensure the quality of the assignment and to reduce the reviewer bias (Cornelissen; Zaidman; Deursen; Moonen; & Koschke, 2009) following measures were taken: (a) attributes assigned to an article by the two authors were cross-checked, and any conflicts and disagreements were resolved through discussion, and (b) the domain expert assessed the final attribute assignment table against the reviewed articles. This table can be downloaded here (OSS prediction studies: Data collection Table, 2017).

Next, the results of this review have been presented by answering the research questions and discussing future research agenda.

REVIEW RESULT

Given the article selection and attribute assignment, the next step is to present and interpret the study findings. We start with discussing answers to the research questions based on the study outcome.

RQ1: Which facets of the prediction approaches were explored, and how many articles were published under each facet?

An in-depth study of the selected articles led us to decompose the OSS prediction articles into a number of facets. Figure 2 presents the complete listing of these facets along with article count under each facet. According to this figure, articles are highly skewed towards fault prediction and reliability prediction facets. Traditionally, software fault prediction approaches use software metrics and fault data from previous releases to predict fault-prone modules for the next release. Research under reliability

Figure 2. Focus area of the prediction studies

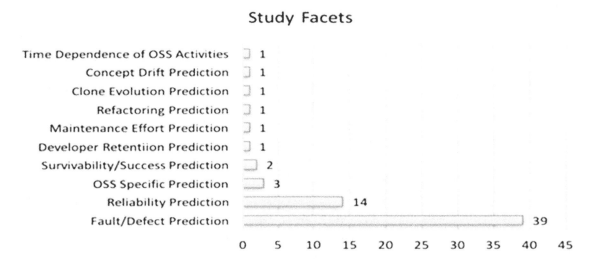

Study Facets

Time Dependence of OSS Activities — 1
Concept Drift Prediction — 1
Clone Evolution Prediction — 1
Refactoring Prediction — 1
Maintenance Effort Prediction — 1
Developer Retentiion Prediction — 1
Survivability/Success Prediction — 2
OSS Specific Prediction — 3
Reliability Prediction — 14
Fault/Defect Prediction — 39

0   5   10   15   20   25   30   35   40   45

prediction studies the stability, volatility, vulnerability and residual defects within OSS projects, among others. Alongside a recent trend is devoted to explore the OSS specific properties in prediction. This includes for instance, predicting the popularity of repositories, predicting future forks of a project based of past trend, and trustworthiness.

Among the Facets, Software Fault/Defect Prediction Is Studied Extensively

RQ2: Does the interest on "oss prediction study" follow an increasing trend?

Although our study period started from the beginning of the year 2000, we got the first article published in year 2005 (according to the article selection criteria). Figure 3 is a line curve which plots publication year on the x-axis and the number of articles published in that year on the y-axis for the articles under review. Exposition of the curve reveals that research on this domain is recent (the first article in year 2005), and follows a growing trend in terms of number of publications till the year 2012. However, a sharp decline since then has been noted.

Research in the Domain of OSS Project Prediction Is One of the Key Interest for the Researchers

RQ3: What is the portfolio of projects analysed for prediction studies and what are the domains of the projects?

The realm of open source consists of thousands of projects. These projects have diverse characteristics including different application domain, community size, evolution pattern, and success history. Our review identified that prediction studies mostly used data from the flagship OSS projects that are large in size with a large user and developer community, and that belong to popular application domains. Findings suggest that Development Platform, Application Software and Application Suite are the most

Figure 3. Year-wise distribution of the prediction studies

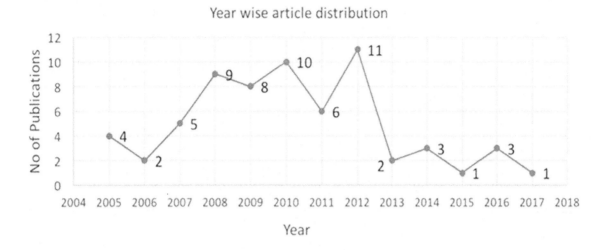

popular application domains (Figure 4). Projects within those domains, such as Eclipse, NetBeans, Mozilla, Apache, Office suites got the highest attention in the reviewed studies. Most of these projects enjoy more than 5 years of development and evolution history. Figure 5 presents the list of OSS projects that were studied at least in two articles.

This finding supports the fact that research to date is mostly vertical (Capiluppi, Models for the evolution of os projects, 2003) taking only the flagship projects into account. However, vast majority of projects do not belong to the domain of large and successful one (Boldyreff;Beecher;& Capiluppi, 2009). Therefore, reported results cannot be extended to broader population of OSS projects.

Figure 4. Application Domain of the OSS projects

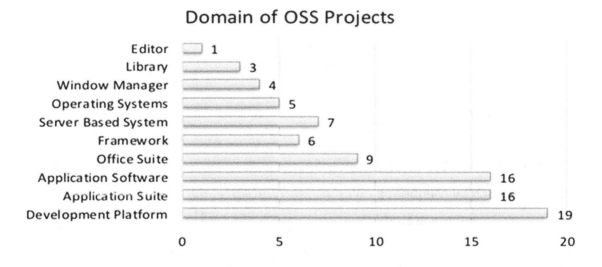

Figure 5. List of OSS projects studied

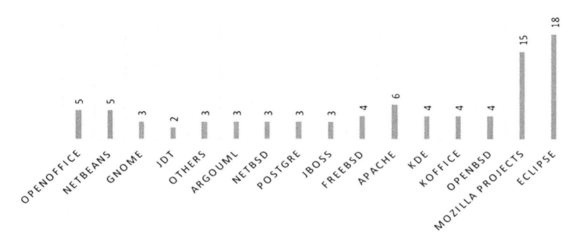

STUDY FREQUENCY OF OSS PROJECTS

Large and Successful OSS Projects are Often Selected as Case Study Projects

RQ4: What are the research approaches followed in the studies?

The research methodologies followed in the articles can be categorized into five distinct approaches: empirical study, case study, comparative study, survey, and tool implementation. Figure 6 shows the count of published articles according to this classification. As can be seen from the figure, 72% of the studies (47 articles out of 65) followed an empirical research approach.

Empirical Research Is the Most Frequent Research Methodology Used in the Articles

RQ5: What datasets or data sources of oss projects are mostly exploited?

Figure 6. Main focus of the prediction studies

Research Approach

Approach	Count
Comparative Study	1
Survey	2
Case Study on OSS Projects	5
Not Exactly Mentioned	28
Empirical Study	47

0   10   20   30   40   50

One of the most important aspects of prediction studies is the usage of project datasets. These datasets of OSS projects are termed as repositories which contain a plethora of information on the underlying software and its development processes (Cook;Votta;& Wolf, 1998) (Atkins;Ball;Graves;& Mockus, 1999). These data sources offer several benefits: the approach is cost effective, requires no additional instrumentation, and does not depend on or influence the software process under consideration (Cook;Votta;& Wolf, 1998). Sources for such data can be divided into two broad categories, e.g., project sources and external sources, as shown in Figure 7. Project sources are managed and maintained by the respective project with the aid of data management tools, e.g., source code version control systems (e.g., CVS, SVN, GIT), bug tracking systems (e.g., Bugzilla), mailing list archives and others. However, many third-party hosting sites offer facilities in hosting and maintaining project data, e.g., Sourceforge, and Ohloh. In this study, these sources are categorized as external sources. Utilization count of the sources under these two categories is summarized in Figure 7.

As shown in this figure, repositories maintained by the respective projects have a clear popularity over the external sources. Among the project sources, bug tracking systems and the source code version management systems were mostly explored. This is reasonable as majority of the reviewed articles are skewed towards fault/defect prediction of the software (as discussed in RQ1), and the sources listed above are the primary candidate for that. Among the external sources, SourceForge (Schilling;Laumer;& Weitzel, 2012) is one of the most popular repository hosting thousands of OSS projects and having over four million downloads per day (Schilling;Laumer;& Weitzel, 2012).

Repositories Maintaining Source Code (e.g., SVN/CVS) and Bug Reports (e.g., Bugzilla, Jira, Email Archives) Are Mostly Explored in the Prediction Studies

RQ6: What metric suites are evaluated and what tools are used for metric data collection?

Distributions of metric suites in the articles are shown in Figure 8. A good sample of the reviewed articles (16 out of 65) used class-level metrics, followed by method and source-code level (11 articles)

Figure 7. Data Sources for OSS Prediction Studies

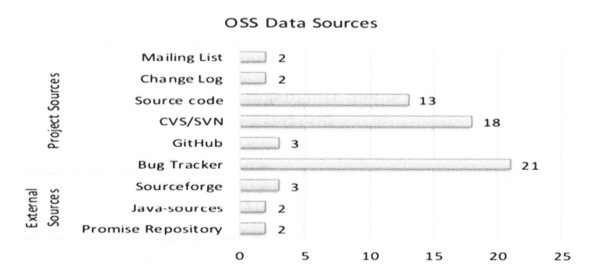

Figure 8. List of Metric Suites

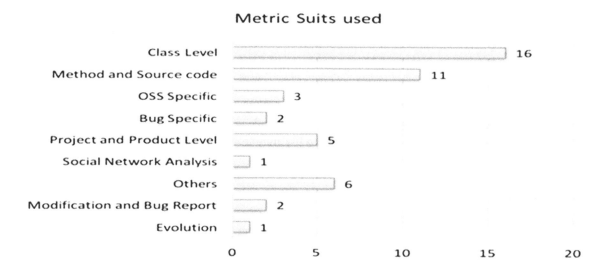

metrics. When class-level metrics are used instead of method-level/ source-code level metrics, predicted fault-prone modules are the classes instead of methods. Yet, more specific parts of source code that are fault-prone can be identified with method/source code level metrics. Both categories of metrics fit well within OSS projects as the majority of projects studied in the reported articles are implemented using object oriented languages (Figure 9). As a side not, the use of such languages is limited to only three languages, namely, JAVA, C++ and C. Even though these languages are the most popular ones, yet the studies left a side many other contemporary languages. This affects the completeness of fault prediction studies, a discussion on which is made in the AVENUE TO FUTURE WORK section.

Among the class-level metrics, the CK (Chidamber & Kemerer metrics) suite, proposed in 1994, is the most popular one. It is being used by several software tool vendors and researchers working on fault prediction (Catal & Diri, A systematic review of software fault prediction studies, 2009). Apart from this, other popular metric suites are MOOD (metrics for object-oriented design), QMOOD (quality metrics for object-oriented design), and L&K (Lorenz and Kidd's metrics). These metrics are used for programs that are developed using object oriented programming.

Figure 9. Programming language distribution among the studied OSS projects

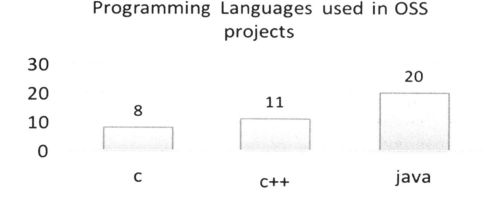

Within method/source code level metrics, Halstead (proposed in 1977) and McCabe (proposed in 1976) metrics have been the most popular ones. Method-level metrics can be collected for programs developed with structured programming or object-oriented programming paradigms. Because source code developed with these paradigms include methods.

A summary of the analysis of the metrics reported in the reviewed articles from the point of view of performance can be found in Table 3. In this table, statistical significance of the metrics (based on prediction accuracy) is classified into three categories, e.g., significant (or best), satisfactory (or good), and bad predictors, keeping alignment to the classification used in the reviewed articles. Additionally, metrics are classified in the category contradictory if they are identified as significant/satisfactory predictors, as well as, bad predictors in the reviewed articles.

Amongst the metric suites, class level metrics, e.g., CK metrics show strong predictive capability (P.M. & Duraiswamy, 2011) in general, although few of the metrics performance are inconclusive. For instance, DIT (Depth of Inheritance Tree) is noted as a satisfactory predictor in (Wahyudin;Schatten; Winkler;Tjoa;& Biffl, 2008) (Subramanyan & Krishnan, Empirical analysis of ck metrics for object-oriented design complexity- Implications for software defects, 2003), but classified as a bad predictor in (Thy;Ferenc;& Siket, 2005) (Shatnawi & Li, 2008). Similar results exist for LOC (Lines Of Code) metric. Within individual studies, the LOC is reported as a significant predictor for fault prediction (Catala;Sevima;& Diri, 2011) (Li;Herbsleb;& Shaw, 2005) (Thy;Ferenc;& Siket, 2005). According to these studies, the LOC metric alone performs better (or similar) compared to the CK metrics. Within other individual studies, LOC is reported to have poor predictive power (Knab;Pinzger;& Bernstein, 2006). Results analogous to this also exist in literature beyond the context of OSS (Fenton & Ohlsson, 2000) (Bell;Ostrand;& Weyuker, 2006).

Apart from fault prediction metrics, the use of SNA (Social Network Analysis) metrics shows a considerable decrease in false positives rates without compromising the detection rates (Gerger;Basar;& aglayan, 2011). Recently, a different trend of prediction work has been carried out in (Schilling;Laumer;& Weitzel, 2012), where prediction of developer retention in OSS projects has been studied. For doing this, actual Person-Job and Person-Team Fit parameters were used as metrics. Reported results have identified that the level of developer retention is positively related to facts like participant's level of relevant development experience and familiarity with the coordination practices within the team. Further, the level of retention has been found to be negatively associated with the level of academic qualification and underrating the contributions of a developer. In other words, developers who are undervalued, or having high academic degrees are inclined to leave projects.

Recent studies also explore OSS project specific metrics to predict several aspects of the projects. For instance, predicting future forking trend of a project based on the fork history, or determining the trustworthiness of a project.

Data collection for metrics is traditionally supported by a wide range of data collection and analysis tools. We, thereby, bring together the tools used in each reviewed article, the list of which is presented in Figure 10, along with their usage count. As can be seen from the figure, Weka is the most popular among the used tools. The reason might be that Weka provides a comprehensive collection of machine learning algorithms both for data mining and for generating prediction models that distinguish between the class of files "No bug" and the class "One or more bug". Most of the other tools used are third party software. Thus, the quality of the data is limited to the accuracy of such tools.

Figure 10. Tools used for metric data collection and modelling

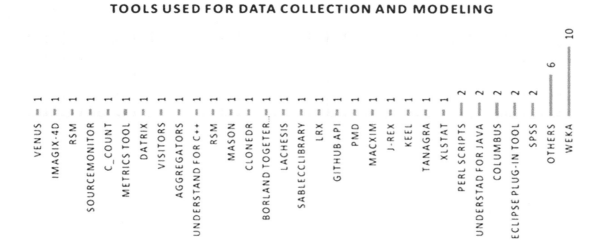

TOOLS USED FOR DATA COLLECTION AND MODELING

RQ7: What are the methods used in prediction models?

Methods and algorithms that are used to build fault/defect prediction models, primarily fall into two categories: statistical methods and machine learning algorithms. As can be seen from Figure 11, 46% (30 out of 65) of the articles exploited statistical methods whereas 29% (19 out of 65) used machine learning algorithms. We summarize in Table 4, the key performance evaluation of these models extracted from the reviewed articles.

Researchers apply statistical methods, such as univariate or multivariate linear regression, logistic regression, or cox regression to predict faults. However, statistical models are considered black box solutions because the relationship between input and response cannot be seen easily (Almeida & Matwin, 1999). Also, a model that has been validated with a specific project's data is not convenient to be used in another project. The reason is that these models are highly dependent on data (Almeida & Matwin, 1999) and that data varies significantly from one project to another. According to our findings statistical models (e.g., linear regression), despite their significantly accurate results (see Table 4), are subject to a specific project release. Therefore, a model trained with the dataset of one release cannot be applied readily to subsequent releases. Additionally, the performance evaluation of a logistic algorithm resulted low classification accuracy compared to that of machine learning methods, for example decision tree algorithms (Table 4).

Machine learning algorithms, on the other hand, provide several powerful algorithms to address these problems. Examples include Naive Bayes and decision tree algorithms (e.g., J48, C4.5). As reported in Table 4, the models built with machine learning algorithms showed (a) high classification accuracy (according to quality assessment parameters), (b) had low false classification rate, and (c) had better performance compared to logistic regression. However, performance evaluation of these algorithms across projects (either, within the same domain or different) and among subsequent releases of a project are yet to be conducted for the OSS domain.

Table 3. Metric performance evaluation

Metric Category and Example	Statistical Significance
Class level metrics (E.g. CK, MOOD, QMOOD, L&K)	- Pareto's law holds which implies that the majority of faults is rooted in a small proportion of classes. - Significant metrics are CBO, RFC, LOC, WMC, RFC, LCOM, LCOMN, CTA, CTM, OCMEC, LCOM3, and OSAVG. - Satisfactory metrics include NOC, DIT, NOOM, NOAM, NOA, NOO, LCOM, CSA, CSO, NPAVGC, SDIT, SNOC, POF, and PDIT. - Bad predictors are NOC and DIT. - Metrics that resulted in contradictory performance include NOC and DIT. - Compared to other metrics, CK metrics showed consistent fault prediction capability for OSS object oriented software. - Also, an Eclipse plug-in based tool implementing the Naive Bayes algorithm with class level metrics resulted in the same performance as with WEKA tools Naive Bayes implementation. **Reference:** (English;Exton;Rigon;& Cleary, 2009), (Yuming & Baowen, 2008), (Thy;Ferenc;& Siket, 2005), (P.M. & Duraiswamy, 2011), (Shatnawi & Li, 2008), (Korua & Liu, 2007), (Catala;Sevima;& Diri, 2011), (Johari & Kaur, 2012), (Singh & Verma, 2012), (Okutan & Yildiz, 2012), (Zimmermann;Premraj;& Zeller, Predicting Defects for Eclipse, 2006)
Method and Source code level metrics (E.g., Halstead, McCabe, Cyclomatic complexity)	- Significant source code metrics are size, if statements, Nested routine declarations, Include files, switch and case usage, Data type declarations, and Accumulated McCabe complexity. - Significant method level metrics are Number of method calls and Number of methods. - Metrics (or Predictors) obtained from one project can be applied to (a) different projects with a reasonable accuracy and (b) projects within the same domain with higher accuracy. **Reference:** (Zimmermann;Premraj;& Zeller, Predicting Defects for Eclipse, 2006), (Phadke & Allen, 2005), (Ferzund;Ahsan;& Wotawa, 2008), (Zimmermann;Nagappan;Gal;Giger;& Murphy, 2009)
Evolution metrics (E.g. linesChangePer-Change, linesActivityRate, coChangedFiles, linesChange.)	- High quality prediction models can be built using evolution metrics. These models can identify refactoring prone/non refactoring prone classes very accurately. Additionally, an increase in refactoring has a significant positive impact on the quality of the software. - Prediction accuracy of the metrics varies among projects. - Significant metrics in this category include coChangedNew, linesActivityRate, coChangedFiles, linesChangePerChange, linesActivityRate, coChangedFiles, changeFrequencyBefore, and coChangedNew. **Reference:** (Ratzinger;Sigmund;Vorburger;& Gall, 2007), (J. Ratzinger, 2008), (Lee;Lee;& Baik, 2011), (Kenmei;Antoniol;& Penta, 2008)
SNA metrics (E.g., Betweenness Centrality, Closeness Centrality, Barycenter Centrality.)	- Considerably decreases high false alarm rates without compromising the defect detection rates. - Considerably increases low prediction rates without compromising low false alarm rates compared to churn metrics. - Information flow within the developer communication network has significant effect on code quality. **Reference:** (Biçer;Basar;& Çaglayan, 2011)
Project and Product metrics (E.g., RDD, RCD, Software Documentation Completeness.)	- Significant metrics are Resolved Defects/Reported Defects (RDD), Closed Defects/Reported Defects (RCD), Changes by peripheral developers/total changes (CBD), Class Data Abstraction Coupling (CDA), and TechMailing. - Models proposed based on this metric class resulted high prediction accuracy for the studied projects. **Reference:** (Wahyudin;Schatten;Winkler;Tjoa;& Biffl, 2008), (Lee;Lee;& Baik, 2011), (English;Exton;Rigon;& Cleary, 2009)
Modification and Bug report metrics (E.g., sharedMRs, nrPRs, reporter(bug).)	- Bug report metrics having significant performance are assignee, reporter, and monthOpened (in which month the bug is reported). - Modification and Bug report metrics with satisfactory performance includes nrMRs (checkins of a *.cpp file), sharedMRs (the number of times a file was checked in together with other files), and nrPRs (the number of reported problems). - Between 60% and 70% of incoming bug reports can be correctly classified into fast and slowly fixed. **Reference:** (Giger;Pinzger;& Gall, 2010), (Knab;Pinzger;& Bernstein, 2006)
Other metrics	- Heuristic metrics: Significant predictors are MFM (Most Frequently Modified) and MFF (Most Frequently Fixed). Bad predictors are MRM (Most Recently Modified) and MRF (Most Recently Fixed). - Historical metrics: Significant predictors are files age, DA (number of distinct authors), and FC (frequency of change). Additionally, old unstable or old fluctuating files are the most fault-prone ones. The number of defects found in the previous release of a file does not correlate with its current defect count. **Reference:** (Hassan & Holt, The Top Ten List: Dynamic Fault Prediction, 2005), (Illes-Seifert & Paech, 2010)

Figure 11. Methods for Prediction

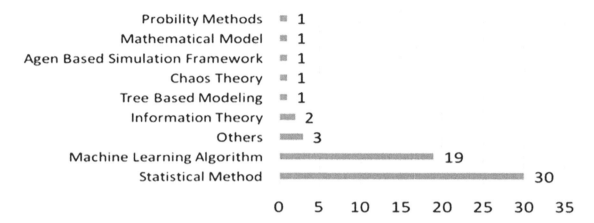

Prediction methods used

Statistical Method — 30
Machine Learning Algorithm — 19
Others — 3
Information Theory — 2
Tree Based Modeling — 1
Chaos Theory — 1
Agen Based Simulation Framework — 1
Mathematical Model — 1
Probility Methods — 1

Statistical Methods Are Mostly Used to Build Fault/Defect Prediction Models

RQ8: How are the research methodology and results validated?

Threats to validity in experimental studies can be classified into three broader categories. They are, external, internal, and construct validities (Subramanyan & Krishnan, Empirical analysis of ck metrics for object-oriented design complexity: Implications for software defects, 2003). External validity refers to the extent to which reported results can be generalized to the whole population (or outside the study settings). Internal validity means that changes in the dependent variables can be safely attributed to changes in the independent variables. Construct validity means that the independent and dependent variables accurately model the abstract hypotheses.

Our review results concerning these validity issues reveal that 52% (27 out of 52) of the articles reported one or more of the validity threats concerning the underlying research methodology and research results. These articles either reported quantifiable measure to minimize one or more of the validity threats or admitted the threat as a delinquent to the study. Figure 12 presents the number of articles that discuss the validity threats concerting the study. As can be seen from the figure, 20 articles out of 65 addresses internal validity threat, whereas, only 13 studies cited external validity. This implies that a large part of the studies (52 out of 65) needs to be extended to a broader domain of OSS projects for generalizability of the reported results. Many of these studies also recommend further replication of the approach across other OSS projects to gain confidence on reported results (English;Exton;Rigon;& Cleary, 2009) (Shatnawi & Li, 2008). Relating to this, in (Turhan;Menzies;Bener;& Stefano, 2009) it is reported that for defect prediction models there exists very little evidence on their cross-project applicability.

Table 4. Performance evaluation of Prediction models

Prediction Model and Example	Model Performance
Statistical Method (Linear Regression)	- Linear regression can be used to build accurate prediction models using evolution metrics. - Univariate linear regression analysis showed that many class level metrics are strongly related to maintainability. Whereas, multivariate linear regression demonstrates reasonable prediction accuracy. - According to ROC measure, MMLR model showed better performance in predicting severity levels of faulty classes, than the multivariate logistic regression (MLR) model. Additionally, these models identify more severe errors slightly better than they can do to less severe errors. However, a prediction model used in one release cannot be used in subsequent releases without training it with that release data. - Linear regression model using evolution metrics resulted in good performance according to mean absolute error (MAE), and root mean square error (RMSE) measure. - Linear regression model using both source code metrics and product and project metric resulted in good classification accuracy. - Linear regression models that include subset of Martin metrics achieved competitive accuracy, and that the models outperformed the ones that do not include Martin metrics in predicting the number of pre-release faults in packages. - Quality assessment of the models are done with Precision, Recall, Accuracy, mean absolute error (MAE), root mean square error (RMSE), magnitude of relative error (MRE), and receivable operating characteristics (ROC) curve. **Reference:** (Shatnawi & Li, 2008), (Ratzinger;Gall;& Pinzger, Quality assessment based on attribute series of software evolution, 2007), (Yuming & Baowen, 2008), (Ekanayake;Tappolet;Gall;& Bernstein, 2009), (Wahyudin;Schatten;Winkler;Tjoa;& Biffl, 2008), (Hassan, Predicting Faults Using the Complexity of Code Changes, 2009), (Elish;Al-Yafei;& Al-Mulhem, 2011)
Statistical Method (Regression Analysis, Correlation)	- Logistic regression model resulted in low recall (only few of the defect-prone files were correctly identified as defect-prone) in predicting post-release defects for files/packages have post-release. However, precision value shows that classified files have very low false positives. - Logistic regression model resulted a bit lower rate in false negative (TYPE II) classification as compared to decision tree models using source code metrics. - Cox proportional hazards modeling with recurrent events identified significant relationship between the logarithmic transformation of class size and defect-proneness. - Quality assessment of the models is done with Precision, Recall, and Accuracy. **Reference:** (Koru;Zhang;& Liu), (Zimmermann;Premraj;& Zeller, Predicting Defects for Eclipse, 2006), (Phadke & Allen, 2005)
Machine Learning Algorithms (Decision Tree, e.g., J48, C4.5, LMT, Random Forest)	- Decision tree models with initial and post-submission bug report data showed adequate performance when compared to random classification. Between 60% and 70% of incoming bug reports can be correctly classified into fast and slowly fixed. The best performing prediction models were obtained with 14-days or 30-days of post-submission data. However, implementation of a fully automated system based on these models is questionable. - A Decision tree learner (J48) can predict defect densities at source code/class level with acceptable accuracies. J48 along with other prediction models identifies refactoring prone classes with high accuracy and recall. - Decision tree model (C4.5) performs better than logistic regression model with significantly low false negative (TYPE II) classification. - Random Forest algorithm classifies fault prone classes with high accuracy, recall, F-measure, and AUC. - The classification accuracy (using Weka tool) varies between 68% and 92% for different releases of the projects. - Quality assessment of the models is done with Precision, Recall, F-measure, Accuracy, and AUC. **Reference:** (Gerger;Basar;& aglayan, 2011), (Knab;Pinzger;& Bernstein, 2006), (Phadke & Allen, 2005), (Zimmermann;Nagappan;Gal;Giger;& Murphy, 2009), (Ferzund;Ahsan;& Wotawa, 2008)
Machine Learning Algorithms (Naive Bayes)	- Naive Bayes has performed better than J48 according to ROC, Precision, Recall, F-measure, Accuracy and Mean absolute error measures. - Model built with Naive Bayes algorithm and using SNA metrics either (a) considerably decreases high false alarm rates without compromising the detection rates, or (b) considerably increases low prediction rates without compromising low false alarm rates. - Quality assessment of the models are done with Precision, Recall, F-measure, Accuracy, ROC curve, Mean absolute error, Probability of detection(pd), and Probability of false alarms(pf). **Reference:** (P. Singh, 2012), (Catala;Sevima;& Diri, 2011), (Biçer;Basar;& Çaglayan, 2011)
Machine Learning Algorithms (Neural network, KStar, Adtree)	- Univariate models built with Neural Network, KStar, and Adtree do not offer improved fault-proneness discrimination ability compared to using the complexity metrics directly. - The neural network model resulted in the weakest model (according to precision and completeness) compared to logistic regression and decision tree models. **Reference:** (Y. Zhoua, 2010), (Thy;Ferenc;& Siket, 2005)

Figure 12. Validation of the research methodology

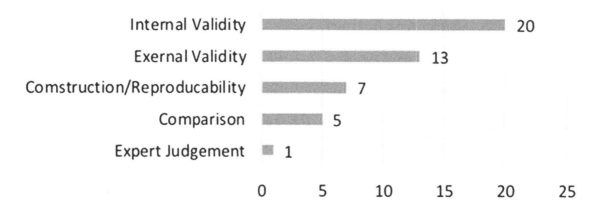

Threat to validity

Majority of the Studies Suffer From External Validity Threats and Thus Fall Short in Generalizing the Results to the Population of OSS Projects

RQ9: How are the prediction models validated?

There are many ways in which the performance of a prediction model can be measured. Indeed, many different categorical and continuous performance measures are used in the articles. A list of such measures is presented in Figure 13. There is no one best way to measure the performance of a model. This depends on factors like class distribution of the training data, how the model has been built, and how the model will be used. In assessing the performance of a classification model, the evaluation measures applied most are (a) precision/ correctness (the ratio of the number of classes correctly predicted as fault prone to the number of classes predicted as fault-prone), (b) recall/ sensitivity (the ratio of the number of classes correctly predicted as fault prone to the total number of classes that are actually fault prone), and (c) accuracy (the ratio of number of classes correctly predicted to the total number of classes) (Kaur & Malhotra, 2008).

It should be noted that cross comparison of studies is sometimes difficult if uniform performance measures are not reported. Current literature (Kitchenham, ym., 2010) in this regard reports that the ROC (Receivable Operating Characteristics) curves, AUC (Area Under the Concentration-time curve), and ARE (Average Relative Error) are effective when comparing the ability of modelling techniques. They are particularly useful to cope with different datasets and for continuous studies.

SYNTHESIS

This chapter is dedicated in pursuing a systematic literature review on the topic- prediction methods and techniques for OSS projects. Under the hood, 65 research articles published in peer reviewed journals and conferences are reviewed systematically to answer 9 key queries related to the topic.

Figure 13. Validation of the prediction model

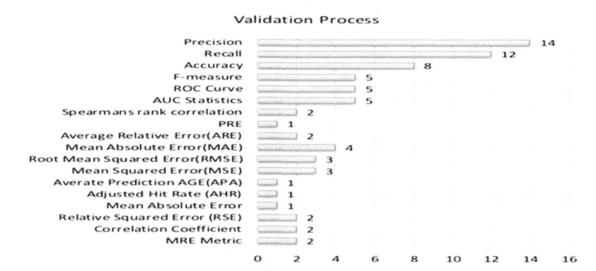

According to the recorded response of the review, it is noted that OSS prediction studies have largely focused on Fault/Defect prediction and Reliability prediction. Many methods, models, metrics and data sources are presented, explored and analysed for predicting defects of OSS projects. Such interest in research is reasonable since dealing with software faults is a vital and foremost important task in software development (Santosh & Kumar, 2016). Presence of faults is always detrimental to the quality and reliability of the software, and has a negative impact on the development and maintenance cost of the software (Menzies, et al., 2010). Therefore, locating fault prone segments within a software should help improving its quality and reliability.

As cited in (Gupta & Saxena, 2017), prediction of software defect can only be possible either based on historical data accumulated during implementation of similar or same software projects or it can be developed using design metrics collected during design phase of software development. In this regard, this review reported extensive use of source code version control (e.g., CVS, SVN, GIT) and bug reporting systems (e.g., Bugzilla, Jira) for extracting historical data on both development and error tracking and resolution.

Contemporary software development utilizes Object-oriented (OO) approach as a de-facto standard for implementing software (Gupta & Saxena, 2017). In line to this observation, this review reported that majority of the projects studied for prediction are implemented using OO languages (e.g., JAVA and C++). Consequently, use of OO metrics (e.g, class level and method level metrics) are predominantly used in prediction studies.

In identifying defects, two main categories of prediction methods are predominantly used by the studies. They are, statistical methods and machine learning methods. According to the review outcome, statistical methods have popularity over machine learning methods. However, due to better performance in prediction machine learning algorithms are being used more and more in the studies.

OSS projects are often multifaceted endeavour. It comprises of number of components that are often absent in their commercial counterpart. For instance, the development practices, the community of developers and users, their communications, collaborations, contributions and management concerning a project. All these factors should have a deep impact on the overall quality of the software that OSS project produces. Therefore, data concerning these factors (e.g., mailing archives, communication channels regarding bug resolving, discussion forums) should be exploited in prediction studies alongside the traditional approaches.

AVENUE TO FUTURE WORK

The final step of the survey (see Figure 1) consists of formalizing the tacit knowledge acquired through the study of the review articles to distil further research directions and recommendations. This is mainly conducted through the analysis of the research questions and the results reported in the articles.

On Data Sources and Data Quality

The quality of the data used for metrics in prediction (especially in fault prediction) has significant potential to undermine the efficacy of a model. Data quality is complex and many aspects of the data are important to ensure reliable predictions (Hall;Beecham;Bowes;Gray;& Counsell, 2012). Yet, collecting good quality data in OSS projects is very hard due to their use of different data management systems (Figure 7), tools, and techniques for managing historical data. This makes it difficult to ensure availability and quality of the data required for metric suites, which may hinder the comparability of the results (Askari & Holt, 2006). Also collected data is usually noisy and often needs to be cleaned (Caglayan;Bener;& Koch, 2009) for reliable fault prediction (Jiang;Lin;Cukic;& Menzies, 2009). None-the-less the size of training and test dataset has an impact on the accuracy of the prediction (Jiang;Lin;Cukic;& Menzies, 2009). Yet, without good quality and clearly reported data, it is difficult to gain confidence in the predictive results. Taking these issues in consideration, future studies may focus on the followings.

- Proposing standard approaches to assess the quality and quantity of the data required to build reliable prediction models.
- Proposing and adopting standard approaches for data collection, considering different available data sources. Data cleaning mechanisms should be explicitly addressed. This will make the reported results more cohesive and comparable.
- Addressing the issue of confidence on the tool performance to gain overall confidence on the data quality and results.

On the Methods

Prediction research in OSS projects is skewed towards fault/defect prediction, as shown in Figure 3. Consequently, fault prediction models are mostly used, which can be broadly classified into statistical methods and machine learning algorithms (Figure 11). Our review identified the dominance of statistical methods over machine learning algorithms in the articles (as shown in Figure 11). However, statistical methods have their limiting factors, and thus the following recommendations could be considered.

- Exploring the potential of machine learning methods for prediction. We argue that machine learning algorithms have better features than statistical methods (Catal & Diri, A systematic review of software fault prediction studies, 2009).

- Using simpler models as they have relatively better prediction performance. For instance, Naive Bayes and Logistic regression, in particular, seem to be the techniques used in models that are performing relatively well (Hall;Beecham;Bowes;Gray;& Counsell, 2012).

On Predictive Performance of the Methods

Performance comparison across studies is only possible if studies report a set of uniform measures (Hall;Beecham;Bowes;Gray;& Counsell, 2012). Additionally, any uniform set of measures should give a full picture of correct and incorrect classification. Prediction studies utilize a number of measuring techniques (as listed in Figure 13 in the Appendix), namely precision, recall, accuracy, ROC curve, and AUC. According to our findings, 63% of the reviewed articles (33 out of 52 articles) did not report performance measure of the model. Thus, future works may focus on the followings areas to increase confidence on the prediction models and their comparability.

- Using uniform measures such as ROC curves, AUC, and Average Relative Error (ARE) to improve the comparing ability of modelling techniques. These are particularly useful to cope with different datasets and for continuous studies.
- Exploring the potential of cost and/or effort aware measurement for prediction models. This takes into account the cost/effort of falsely identifying modules and has been increasingly reported as useful (Lessmann;Baesens;Mues;& Pietsch, 2008) (Zimmermann;Herzig;Nagappan;Zeller;& Murphy, 2010).
- Developing heuristics and recommendations for reliable measure selection. Inappropriate measures can present a misleading picture of predictive performance and can undermine the reliability of predictions (Catala;Sevima;& Diri, 2011).

On the Metrics

Class level metrics and source code metrics are used predominantly in the studied literature (as reported in Figure 8). Overall these metrics have good prediction accuracy. Yet, conflicting results among studies exist concerning the performance of some metrics, as discussed in RQ6. Thus the following need to be considered in future works.

- Identifying factors that can influence performance inconsistency. This may include, among other factors, the diverse nature of OSS data sources, unavailability of required data, and hindering the metric accuracy while applying to certain prediction models.
- Developing heuristics and best practices to minimize the factors that lead to inconsistency of the metric performance and to provide reliable results.

Traditionally defect prediction models rely on metrics that represent the state of the software system at a specific moment in time. These metrics are used to capture a particular snapshot or release of a project to predict the next one. But metrics capturing changes over time in projects also play a significant role in prediction. For example, metrics presenting software evolution were used to predict the need of refactoring (Y. Zhoua, 2010) and quality of OSS projects (Lee;Lee;& Baik, 2011) with significant accuracy. Though such results are encouraging, these metrics are not mature enough to gain prediction confidence. Thus, future study can consider the following recommendations.

- Deriving an empirically validated set of evolution metrics for fault prediction.
- Performing exploratory studies to verify whether it can complement the existing metric suites to experience better prediction results.

Additionally, metrics modelling the community dynamics of OSS projects can play a pivotal role in predicting the future of the project, including fault prediction. Current research (as discussed in RQ6) gives affirmative indication towards this direction.

On OSS Community and Prediction

What sets open source development apart from the traditional proprietary setting is the developer community driving the project. Hence it seemed natural to include the community aspect as one of the questions. However, although the structure, social connections and internal communication of OSS communities have gained significant interest, research effort devoted to studying the community in relation to prediction appears quite the opposite (as shown in Figure 2). For instance, such topic has been studied in (Bettenburg & Hassan, 2010) where the authors investigated the impact of social structures between developers and end-users on software quality. Their results give support to thinking that social structures in the community do hold prediction power in addition to the source code centric approaches. It is also suggested that combining metrics focusing on code and social aspects work as a better prediction model than either alone. On a similar note, development communities and their communication have been studied from the prediction point of view (Wolf;Schroter;Damian;& Nguyen, 2009) outside the scope of OSS giving prediction power to communication structure measures in build failures. A similar result is reported in (Bird;Nagappan;Gall;Murphy;& Devanbu, 2009) in which developer information is used as an element within a socio-technical network of variables, which offered better predictive performance. This suggest the following questions could be studied in future works.

- How can community structures be used as a predictive instrument?
- Can metric suites and models be community-oriented? Would this complement traditional approaches to achieve improved prediction accuracy?

On the Generalizability Issue

Decisions made under the selected research methodology lead to the generalizability concern of the reported results. One major concern is that the population of case study OSS projects is skewed towards the flagship ones (Figure 4 and Figure 5), having a long history of project evolution with large user and developer community. Thus, the reported results fall short in representing the wider population of OSS projects [many projects are small and not successful].

Moreover, prediction models applied in one project may not be applicable to others. The reason is that these models are highly dependent on data (Almeida & Matwin, 1999) and that data varies significantly from one project to another. Also, statistical models are strongly tied to a specific release of a project, and therefore, a model trained with one snapshot of a project cannot be applied to subsequent releases.

Additionally, data collection process for metrics should have traceability to increase confidence on the metric performance. All these issues contributed to the validity of the reported results, especially the generalizability dimension (Figure 12). The following points could be taken care in future studies to address external validity.

- Approaches and techniques for data selection, collection and processing should be made explicit to increase the confidence on metric performance.
- Metric and method selection should be justified with uniform measurement techniques.
- Case study projects should be selected in order to increase the generalizability of the reported results.

On the Programming Languages

For fault prediction studies, it is important to include programming language as one of the criterion for predicting numbers of faults. According to the study results in (Ostrand;Weyuker;& Bell, 2003), it has been noted that Makefiles, SQL, shell, HTML, and "other" files had significantly higher fault rates than java files when holding all else constant, while c files had significantly lower rates. There might be several factors contributed to this fact, e.g., different languages may be designed for different tasks and functionalities, and given the same functionality, different language may require diverse amount of codes lines to achieve the functionality (Ostrand;Weyuker;& Bell, 2003). However, the exact impact of programming languages on fault prediction are yet inconclusive (Ostrand;Weyuker;& Bell, 2003). This observation, however, raises a validity threat towards the fault prediction results reported to date for OSS, as only 3 of the most popular programming languages (Ranking, 2014) (Figure 9) are considered in the studies. Keeping this in mind, future studies should carefully pick divertive languages and incorporate them within the prediction model.

THREATS TO VALIDITY

Carrying out a literature review is mostly a manual task. Thus, most threats to validity relate to the possibility of researcher bias (Cornelissen;Zaidman;Deursen;Moonen;& Koschke, 2009). To minimize this, we adopted guidelines on conducting SLR suggested by Kitchenham (Kitchenham, Procedures for performing systematic reviews, 2004). In particular, we documented and reviewed all steps we made in advance, including selection criteria and attribute definitions.

In what follows, description related to validity threats pertaining to article selection, attribute framework, and article characterization.

Article Selection

Following the advice of Kitchenham (Kitchenham, Procedures for performing systematic reviews, 2004), the inclusion criteria is defined based on the research questions and during the definition of the review protocol, which may reduce the likelihood of bias. Only articles satisfying this selection criterion have been considered in this study. For collecting relevant articles, we first performed automated keyword search and then performed manual selection. The first step condenses the selection bias whereas the later ensures the relevance of the selected articles. Finally, a non-recursive search through the references of the selected articles is performed. This increases the representativeness and completeness of our selection. To minimize the selection bias and reviewer bias further, a domain expert (third author) verified the relevance of the selected articles against the selection criterion.

Attribute Framework

The construction of the attribute framework may be the most subjective step (Cornelissen; Zaidman; Deursen; Moonen; & Koschke, 2009). Thus we took a two-step validation measure to minimize bias. First, the attribute set is derived based on the research questions and domain of study. A pilot study was run by the first two authors in which five articles were randomly selected to derive these attributes. The resultant attribute sets from both the authors were then merged through discussion to get the final set of attributes. Second, the representativeness of this attribute framework is then examined by the domain expert (third author).

Article Assessment

Similar to the construction of the attribute framework, the process of assigning the attributes to the research articles is subjective and may be difficult to reproduce (Cornelissen; Zaidman; Deursen; Moonen; & Koschke, 2009). We address this validation threat through a two-step evaluation process as discussed in section REVIEW METHODOLOGY.

CONCLUSION

In this chapter, we have reported a systematic literature review (SLR) on the prediction studies of open source software projects. To carry out this review we adopted a review protocol following the guidelines presented in (Kitchenham, Procedures for performing systematic reviews, 2004) and (Cornelissen; Zaidman; Deursen; Moonen; & Koschke, 2009). A set of 65 articles were reviewed in the study, which is the result of a systematic article selection process defined in the protocol. Through a detailed reading of a subset of the selected articles, we derived an attribute framework that was consequently used to characterize the articles in a structured fashion. We also posed a set of research questions in advance that are investigated and answered throughout the study. The attribute framework was sufficiently specific to characterize the articles in answering the research questions. None-the-less, an elaborated discussion on the validity of the review process is also presented.

The characterization of the reviewed articles will help researchers to investigate previous prediction studies from the perspective of metrics, methods, datasets, tool sets, and performance evaluation and validation techniques in an effective and efficient manner. We also put an elaborated discussion on the most significant research results. In summary, this article provides a single point reference on the state-of-the-art of OSS prediction studies which could benefit the research community to establish future research in the field.

To the best of our knowledge this is the first study that provides a systematic review on prediction studies of OSS projects. However, systematic literature review in the field of software fault prediction was first conducted in (Catal & Diri, A systematic review of software fault prediction studies, 2009). Focus area of this review was the articles on software fault prediction with a specific focus on metrics, methods and datasets. Later on, this work was extended in (Catal, Software fault prediction: A literature review and current trends, 2011) incorporating more articles and presenting current trends on the field of fault prediction. But these reviews concerned fault prediction studies only and were not targeting open source projects.

Yet in comparing our results concerning fault prediction with these studies, we noted contradictions. For instance, the dominance of statistical methods in OSS fault prediction contradicts with the findings reported in (Catal & Diri, A systematic review of software fault prediction studies, 2009). This study pointed out that machine learning algorithms are gaining more interest (they increased from 18% to 66%) over statistical methods (they decreased from 59% to 14%) for prediction. This difference in findings might be for two reasons, (a) the survey in (Catal & Diri, A systematic review of software fault prediction studies, 2009) focused only on fault prediction studies of in-house software, whereas our survey covers the entire domain of prediction studies on OSS projects, and (b) prediction studies are relatively new (as discussed in RQ2) in OSS. However, it will be promising to see that researchers explore the potential of machine learning methods in OSS prediction studies which is also suggested in (Catal & Diri, A systematic review of software fault prediction studies, 2009).

ACKNOWLEDGMENT

We would like express our sincere gratitude to Late Prof. Tarja Systä, Department of Pervasive Computing, Tampere University of Technology, Finland, for her invaluable contributions to the journal version of this chapter.

REFERENCES

Almeida, M. D., & Matwin, S. (1999). Machine learning method for software quality model building. *International symposium on methodologies for intelligent systems*, 565-573.

Askari, M., & Holt, R. (2006). Information theoretic evaluation of change prediction models for large-scale software. *International workshop on Mining software repositories*, 126–132. doi:10.1145/1137983.1138013

Atkins, D., Ball, T., Graves, T., & Mockus, A. (1999). Using version control data to evaluate the impact of software tools. *International Conference on Software Engineering*, 324-333. doi:10.1145/302405.302649

Beecham, S., Baddoo, N., Hall, T., Robinson, H., & Sharp, H. (2008). Motivation in software engineering: A systematic literature review. *Information and Software Technology*, *50*(9-10), 860–878. doi:10.1016/j.infsof.2007.09.004

Bell, R., Ostrand, T., & Weyuker, E. (2006). Looking for bugs in all the right places. Intl Symp. Software Testing and Analysis, 61-72.

Bettenburg, N., & Hassan, A. (2010). Studying the impact of social structures on software quality. *International Conference on Program Comprehension*, 124–133. doi:10.1109/ICPC.2010.46

Biçer, S., Basar, A., & Çaglayan, B. (2011). Defect prediction using social network analysis on issue repositories. *International Conference on Software and Systems Process*, 63-71.

Bird, C., Nagappan, N., Gall, H., Murphy, B., & Devanbu, P. (2009). *Putting it all together: Using socio-technical networks to predict failures*. Intl Symp. Software Reliability Eng.

Boldyreff, C., Beecher, K., & Capiluppi, A. (2009). Identifying exogenous drivers and evolutionary stages in Floss projects. *Journal of Systems and Software, 82*(5), 739–750.

Brereton, P., Kitchenham, B. A., Budgen, D., Turner, M., & Khalil, M. (2007). Lessons from applying the systematic literature review process within the software engineering domain. *Journal of Systems and Software, 80*(4), 571–583. doi:10.1016/j.jss.2006.07.009

Caglayan, B., Bener, A., & Koch, S. (2009). Merits of using repository metrics in defect prediction for open source projects. *CSE Workshop Emerging Trends in Free/Libre/Open Source Software Research and Development*, 31–36. doi:10.1109/FLOSS.2009.5071357

Capiluppi, A. (2003). *Models for the evolution of os projects*. ICSM. doi:10.1109/ICSM.2003.1235407

Capiluppi, A., & Adams, P. J. (2009). Reassessing brooks law for the free software community. *IFIP Advances in Information and Communication Technology, 299*, 274–283. doi:10.1007/978-3-642-02032-2_24

Catal, C. (2011). Software fault prediction: A literature review and current trends. *Expert Systems with Applications, 38*(4), 4626–4636. doi:10.1016/j.eswa.2010.10.024

Catal, C., & Diri, B. (2009). A systematic review of software fault prediction studies. *Expert Systems with Applications, 36*(4), 7346–7354. doi:10.1016/j.eswa.2008.10.027

Catala, C., Sevima, U., & Diri, B. (2011). Practical development of an Eclipse-based software fault prediction tool using Naive Bayes algorithm. *Expert Systems with Applications, 38*(3), 2347–2353. doi:10.1016/j.eswa.2010.08.022

Cook, J., Votta, L., & Wolf, A. (1998). Cost-effective analysis of in-place software processes. *IEEE Transactions on Software Engineering, 24*(8), 650–663. doi:10.1109/32.707700

Cornelissen, B., Zaidman, A., Deursen, A., Moonen, L., & Koschke, R. (2009). A systematic survey of program comprehension through dynamic analysis. *IEEE Transactions on Software Engineering, 35*(5), 684–702. doi:10.1109/TSE.2009.28

Dyba, T., & Dingsyr, T. (2008). Empirical studies of agile software development: A systematic review. *Information and Software Technology, 50*(9-10), 833–859. doi:10.1016/j.infsof.2008.01.006

Eclipse. (2013). Retrieved from Eclipse: http://www.eclipse.org/proposals/packaging/

Ekanayake, J., Tappolet, J., Gall, H., & Bernstein, A. (2009). *Tracking Concept Drift of Software Projects Using Defect Prediction Quality*. MSR. doi:10.1109/MSR.2009.5069480

Elish, M., Al-Yafei, A., & Al-Mulhem, M. (2011). Empirical comparison of three metrics suites for fault prediction in packages of object-oriented systems: A case study of Eclipse. *Advances in Engineering Software, 42*(10), 852-859.

English, M., Exton, C., Rigon, I., & Cleary, B. (2009). *Fault detection and prediction in an open-source software project*. PROMISE. doi:10.1145/1540438.1540462

Fenton, N. E., & Ohlsson, N. (2000). Quantitative analysis of faults and failures in a complex software system. *IEEE Transactions on Software Engineering, 26*(8), 797–814. doi:10.1109/32.879815

Ferzund, J., Ahsan, S., & Wotawa, F. (2008). Analysing Bug Prediction Capabilities of Static Code Metrics in Open Source Software. *International Conferences IWSM*, 331-343.

Gerger, S. B., Basar, A., & Aglayan, B. (2011). Defect prediction using social network analysis on issue repositories. *ICSSP*, 63–71.

Giger, E., Pinzger, M., & Gall, H. (2010). *Predicting the fix time of bugs*. RSSE.

Hall, T., Beecham, S., Bowes, D., Gray, D., & Counsell, S. (2012). A systematic literature review on fault prediction performance in software engineering. *IEEE Transactions on Software Engineering, 38*(6), 1276–1304. doi:10.1109/TSE.2011.103

Hassan, A. (2009). *Predicting Faults Using the Complexity of Code Changes*. ICSE. doi:10.1109/ICSE.2009.5070510

Hassan, A., & Holt, R. (2005). *The Top Ten List: Dynamic Fault Prediction*. ICSM.

Illes-Seifert, T., & Paech, B. (2010). Exploring the relationship of a files history and its fault-proneness: An empirical method and its application to open source programs. *Information and Software Technology, 52*(5), 539–558. doi:10.1016/j.infsof.2009.11.010

Jiang, Y., Lin, J., Cukic, B., & Menzies, T. (2009). *Variance analysis in software fault prediction models*. Intl Symp. Software Reliability Eng. doi:10.1109/ISSRE.2009.13

Johari, K., & Kaur, A. (2012). Validation of object oriented metrics using open source software system: An empirical study. *Software Engineering Notes, 37*(1), 1–4. doi:10.1145/2088883.2088893

Kaur, A., & Malhotra, R. (2008). Application of random forest in predicting fault-prone classes. *International Conference on Advanced Computer Theory and Engineering*, 37 – 43. doi:10.1109/ICACTE.2008.204

Kenmei, B., Antoniol, G., & Penta, M. D. (2008). *Trend Analysis and Issue Prediction in Large-Scale Open Source Systems*. CSMR. doi:10.1109/CSMR.2008.4493302

Kitchenham, B. (2004). *Procedures for performing systematic reviews*. Technical Report TR/SE-0401, Keele University, and Technical Report 0400011T.1, National ICT Australia.

Kitchenham, B., Pretorius, R., Budgen, D., Brereton, O. P., Turner, M., Niazi, M., & Linkman, S. (2010). Systematic literature reviews in software engineering- a tertiary study. *Information and Software Technology, 52*(8), 792–805. doi:10.1016/j.infsof.2010.03.006

Knab, P., Pinzger, M., & Bernstein, A. (2006). *Predicting defect densities in source code? les with decision tree learners.* MSR.

Koru, A. G., Zhang, D., & Liu, H. (2007). Modeling the effect of size on defect proneness for open-source software. *Third International Workshop on Predictor Models in Software Engineering.*

Korua, A., & Liu, H. (2007). Identifying and Characterizing change-prone classes in two large-scale open-source products. *Journal of Systems and Software, 80*(1), 63–73. doi:10.1016/j.jss.2006.05.017

Lee, W., Lee, J., & Baik, J. (2011). *Software reliability prediction for open source software adoption systems based on early lifecycle measurements.* COMPSAC. doi:10.1109/COMPSAC.2011.55

Lessmann, S., Baesens, B., Mues, C., & Pietsch, S. (2008). enchmarking classi?cation models for software defect prediction: A proposed framework and novel findings. *IEEE Transactions on Software Engineering, 34*(4), 485–496. doi:10.1109/TSE.2008.35

Li, P. L., Herbsleb, J., & Shaw, M. (2005). Finding predictors of? eld defects for open source software systems in commonly available data sources: a case study of openbsd. *International Software Metrics Symposium (METRICS).* doi:10.1109/METRICS.2005.26

Okutan, A., & Yildiz, O. (2012). *Software defect prediction using Bayesian networks.* Journal Empirical Software Engineering.

OSS prediction studies: Data collection Table. (2013). Retrieved from OSS prediction studies: Data collection Table: http://literature-review.weebly.com/

Ostrand, T., Weyuker, E., & Bell, R. (2003). Predicting the Location and Number of Faults in Large Software Systems. *IEEE Transactions on Software Engineering.*

Perry, D., Porter, A., & Votta, L. (2000). Empirical studies of software engineering: A roadmap. *The Future of Software Engineering.*

Phadke, A., & Allen, E. (2005). *Predicting Risky Modules in Open-Source Software for High-Performance Computing.* SE-HPCS. doi:10.1145/1145319.1145337

P.M., S., & Duraiswamy, K. (2011). An Empirical Validation of Software Quality Metric Suites on Open Source Software for Fault-Proneness Prediction in Object Oriented Systems. *European Journal of Scientific Research, 52*(2).

Ranking, S. (2014). *Top 10 Programming Languages.* Retrieved from Top 10 Programming Languages: http://spectrum.ieee.org/computing/software/top-10-programming-languages

Ratzinger, J. T. S. (2008). On the Relation of Refactoring and Software Defects. MSR, 35-38.

Ratzinger, J., Gall, H., & Pinzger, M. (2007). Quality assessment based on attribute series of software evolution. *Working Conference on Reverse Engineering,* 80–89. doi:10.1109/WCRE.2007.39

Ratzinger, J., Sigmund, T., Vorburger, P., & Gall, H. (2007). Mining software evolution to predict refactoring. *International Symposium on Empirical Software Engineering and Measurement,* 354–363. doi:10.1109/ESEM.2007.9

Russo, B., Mulazzani, F., Russo, B., & Steff, M. (2011). Building knowledge in open source software research in six years of conferences. *IFIP Advances in Information and Communication Technology, 365*, 123–141. doi:10.1007/978-3-642-24418-6_9

Samoladas, I., Angelis, L., & Stamelos, I. (2010). Survival analysis on the duration of open source projects. *Information and Software Technology, 52*(9), 902–922. doi:10.1016/j.infsof.2010.05.001

Schilling, A., Laumer, S., & Weitzel, T. (2012). Who Will Remain? An Evaluation of Actual Person-Job and Person-Team Fit to Predict Developer Retention in FLOSS Projects. *Hawaii International Conference on System Sciences*, 3446–3455.

Shatnawi, R., & Li, W. (2008). The effectiveness of software metrics in identifying error-prone classes in post-release software evolution process. *Journal of Systems and Software, 81*(11), 1868–1882. doi:10.1016/j.jss.2007.12.794

Singh, P. S. V. (2012). Empirical Investigation of Fault prediction capability of object oriented metrics of open source software. JCSSE, 323 – 327.

Singh, P., & Verma, S. (2012). *Empirical Investigation of Fault prediction capability of object oriented metrics of open source software*. JCSSE.

Subramanyan, R., & Krishnan, M. (2003). Empirical analysis of ck metrics for object-oriented design complexity- Implications for software defects. *IEEE Transactions on Software Engineering, 29*(4), 297–310. doi:10.1109/TSE.2003.1191795

Syeed, M., Kilamo, T., Hammouda, I., & Systä, T. (2012). Open Source Prediction Methods: a systematic literature review. In *IFIP International Conference of Open Source Systems* (pp. 280-285). Springer. doi:10.1007/978-3-642-33442-9_22

Thy, T., Ferenc, R., & Siket, I. (2005). Empirical validation of object-oriented metrics on open source software for fault prediction. *IEEE Transactions on Software Engineering, 31*(10), 897–910. doi:10.1109/TSE.2005.112

Turhan, B., Menzies, T., Bener, A. B., & Stefano, J. D. (2009). On the relative value of cross-company and within-company data for defect prediction. *International Symposium on Empirical Software Engineering and Measurement2009, 14*(5), 540–578. doi:10.1007/s10664-008-9103-7

Wahyudin, D., Schatten, A., Winkler, D., Tjoa, A. M., & Biffl, S. (2008). *Defect prediction using combined product and project metrics a case study from the open source apache. myfaces project family*. Euromicro Conference Software Engineering and Advanced Applications. doi:10.1109/SEAA.2008.36

Wolf, T., Schroter, A., Damian, D., & Nguyen, T. (2009). Predicting build failures using social network analysis on developer communication. *International Conference on Software Engineering*, 1-11. doi:10.1109/ICSE.2009.5070503

Yuming, Z., & Baowen, X. (2008). *Predicting the maintainability of open source software using design metrics*. Academic Press.

Zhoua, Y. (2010). On the ability of complexity metrics to predict fault-prone classes in object-oriented systems. *Journal of Systems and Software, 83*(4), 660–674. doi:10.1016/j.jss.2009.11.704

Zimmermann, T., Herzig, K., Nagappan, N., Zeller, A., & Murphy, B. (2010). *Change bursts as defect predictors*. Intl Symp. Software Reliability Eng.

Zimmermann, T., Nagappan, N., Gal, H., Giger, E., & Murphy, B. (2009). *Cross-project Defect Prediction- A Large Scale Experiment on Data vs. Domain vs. Process*. ESEC/FSE.

Zimmermann, T., Premraj, R., & Zeller, A. (2006). Predicting Defects for Eclipse. *Third International Workshop on Predictor Models in Software Engineering*.

ADDITIONAL READING

Badri, M., Badri, L., Flageol, W., & Toure, F. (2016). Source code size prediction using use case metrics: An empirical comparison with use case points. *Innovations in Systems and Software Engineering*, 1–17.

Borges, H., Hora, A., & Valente, M. T. 2016. Predicting the Popularity of GitHub Repositories, *International Conference on Predictive Models and Data Analytics in Software Engineering, Article no.* 9.

Bouktif, S., Sahraoui, H., & Ahmed, F. (2014). Predicting Stability of Open-Source Software Systems Using Combination of Bayesian Classifiers [. *ACM Transactions on Management Information Systems*, *5*(1), 3. doi:10.1145/2555596

Braunschweig, B., Dhage, N., Viera, M. J., Seaman, C., Sampath, S., & Koru, A. G. 2012. Studying Volatility Predictors in Open Source Software, *International Symposium on Empirical Software Engineering and Measurement (ESEM)*, Pages 181-190. doi:10.1145/2372251.2372286

Bucholz, R., & Laplante, P. A. (2009). A dynamic capture model for software defect prediction. *Innovations in Systems and Software Engineering*, *5*(4), 265–270. doi:10.1007/s11334-009-0099-y

Catala, C., Sevima, U., & Diri, B. (2011). Practical development of an Eclipse-based software fault prediction tool using Naive Bayes algorithm. *Expert Systems with Applications*, *38*(3), 2347–2353. doi:10.1016/j.eswa.2010.08.022

Chen, F., Li, L., Jiang, J., & Zhang, L. 2014. Predicting the Number of Forks for Open Source Software Project, *International Workshop on Evidential Assessment of Software Technologies*, Pages 40-47. doi:10.1145/2627508.2627515

Ekanayake, J., Tappolet, J., Gall, H. C., & Bernstein, A. (2012). Time variance and defect prediction in software projects. *Empirical Software Engineering*, *17*(4), 348–389. doi:10.1007/s10664-011-9180-x

Ekanayake, J., Tappolet, J., Gall, H. C., & Bernstein, A. (2012). Time variance and defect prediction in software projects. *Journal Empirical Software Engineering*, *17*(4-5), 348–389. doi:10.1007/s10664-011-9180-x

English, M., Exton, C., Rigon, I., & Cleary, B. 2009. Fault Detection and Prediction in an Open-Source Software Project. *Proceedings of the 5th International Conference on Predictor Models in Software Engineering (PROMISE)*. doi:10.1145/1540438.1540462

Ferzund, J., Ahsan, S. N., & Wotawa, F. (2008). Analysing Bug Prediction Capabilities of Static Code Metrics in Open Source Software, Software Process and Product Measurement. *Lecture Notes in Computer Science, 5338*, 331–343. doi:10.1007/978-3-540-89403-2_27

Garcia, H. V., & Shihab, E. 2014. Characterizing and Predicting Blocking Bugs in Open Source Projects, *11th Working Conference on Mining Software Repositories (MSR)*, Pages 76-81.

Giger, E., Pinzger, M., & Gall, H. 2010. Predicting the Fix Time of Bugs, *Proceedings of the 2nd International Workshop on Recommendation Systems for Software Engineering*. doi:10.1145/1808920.1808933

Gitzel, R., Krug, S., & Brhel, M. (2010). *Towards A Software Failure Cost Impact Model for the Customer: An Analysis of an Open Source Product*. PROMISE. doi:10.1145/1868328.1868354

Gyimothy, T., Ferenc, R., & Siket, I. (2005). Empirical Validation of Object-Oriented Metrics on Open Source Software for Fault Prediction. *IEEE Transactions on Software Engineering, 31*(10), 897–910. doi:10.1109/TSE.2005.112

Illes-Seifert, T., & Paech, B. (2010). Exploring the relationship of a files history and its fault-proneness: An empirical method and its application to open source programs. *Information and Software Technology, 52*(5), 539–558. doi:10.1016/j.infsof.2009.11.010

Koru, A. G., Zhang, D., & Liu, H. (2007). Modeling the Effect of Size on Defect Proneness for Open-Source Software. *ICSE, 2007*, 115–124.

Korua, A. G., & Liu, H. (2007). Identifying and Characterizing change-prone classes in two large-scale open-source products. *Journal of Systems and Software, 80*(1), 63–73. doi:10.1016/j.jss.2006.05.017

Lavazza, L., Morasca, S., Taibi, D., & Tosi, D. 2010. Predicting OSS Trustworthiness on the Basis of Elementary Code Assessment, *ACM-IEEE International Symposium on Empirical Software Engineering and Measurement, Article no*. 36. doi:10.1145/1852786.1852834

Luo Li, P., Shaw, M., & Herbsleb, J. (2005). Finding Predictors of Field Defects for Open Source Software Systems in Commonly Available Data Sources: A Case Study of OpenBSD. *METRICS, 05*, 32.

Malhotra, R., & Khanna, M. (2016). An exploratory study for software change prediction in object-oriented systems using hybridized techniques. *Automated Software Engineering, 24*(87), 1–45.

Okutan, A., & Yildiz, O. T. (2012). *Software defect prediction using Bayesian networks*. Journal Empirical Software Engineering.

Phadke, A. A., & Allen, E. B. (2005). Predicting Risky Modules in Open-Source Software for High-Performance Computing. *Proceedings of SE-HPCS, 05*, 60–64. doi:10.1145/1145319.1145337

Samoladas, I., Angelis, L., & Stamelos, I. (2010). Survival analysis on the duration of open source projects. *Information and Software Technology, 52*(9), 902–922. doi:10.1016/j.infsof.2010.05.001

Shanthi, P. M., & Duraiswamy, K. (2011). An Empirical Validation of Software Quality Metric Suites on Open Source Software for Fault-Proneness Prediction in Object Oriented Systems. *European Journal of Scientific Research, 51*(2).

Shatnawia, R., & Li, W. (2008). The effectiveness of software metrics in identifying error-prone classes in post-release software evolution process. *Journal of Systems and Software, 81*(11), 1868–1882. doi:10.1016/j.jss.2007.12.794

Shihab, E., Ihara, A., Kamei, Y., Ibrahim, W. M., Ohira, M., Adams, B., & Matsumoto, K. et al. (2013). Studying re-opened bugs in open source software. *Empirical Software Engineering, 18*(5), 1005–1042. doi:10.1007/s10664-012-9228-6

Ullah, N. (2015). A method for predicting open source software residual defects. *Journal of Software Quality, 23*(1), 55–76. doi:10.1007/s11219-014-9229-3

Yu, L. (2006). Indirectly predicting the maintenance effort of open-source software. *Journal of Software Maintenance and Evolution: Research and Practice., 18*(5), 311–332. doi:10.1002/smr.335

Zanetti, M. S., Scholtes, I., Tessone, C. J., & Schweitzer, F. 2013. Categorizing Bugs with Social Networks: A Case Study on Four Open Source Software Communities, *International Conference on Software Engineering*, Pages 1032-1041. doi:10.1109/ICSE.2013.6606653

Zhou, Y., & Xu, B. (2008). Predicting the Maintainability of Open Source Software Using Design Metrics. *Wuhan University Journal of Natural Sciences, 13*(1), 14–20. doi:10.1007/s11859-008-0104-6

Zhoua, Y., Xua, B., & Leung, H. (2010). On the ability of complexity metrics to predict fault-prone classes in object-oriented systems. *Journal of Systems and Software, 83*(4), 660–674. doi:10.1016/j.jss.2009.11.704

Zimmermann, T., Premraj, R., & Zeller, A. 2006. Predicting Defects for Eclipse. *Proceedings of the Third International Workshop on Predictor Models in Software Engineering.*

Chapter 3
Logging Analysis and Prediction in Open Source Java Project

Sangeeta Lal
Jaypee Institute of Information Technology, India

Neetu Sardana
Jaypee Institute of Information Technology, India

Ashish Sureka
Ashoka University, India

ABSTRACT

Log statements present in source code provide important information to the software developers because they are useful in various software development activities such as debugging, anomaly detection, and remote issue resolution. Most of the previous studies on logging analysis and prediction provide insights and results after analyzing only a few code constructs. In this chapter, the authors perform an in-depth, focused, and large-scale analysis of logging code constructs at two levels: the file level and catch-blocks level. They answer several research questions related to statistical and content analysis. Statistical and content analysis reveals the presence of differentiating properties among logged and nonlogged code constructs. Based on these findings, the authors propose a machine-learning-based model for catch-blocks logging prediction. The machine-learning-based model is found to be effective in catch-blocks logging prediction.

INTRODUCTION

Logging is an important software development practice that is used to record important program execution points in the source code. The recorded log generated from program execution provides important information to the software developers at the time of debugging. Fu et al. (2014) conducted a survey of Microsoft developers, asking them their opinion on source code logging. Results of the survey showed that 96 percent of the developers consider logging statements the primary source of information for problem diagnosis. In many scenarios, logging is the only information available to the software developers

DOI: 10.4018/978-1-5225-5314-4.ch003

for debugging because the same execution environment is unavailable (which makes bug regeneration difficult) or the same user input is unavailable (because of security and privacy concerns) (Yuan et al., 2012). Yuan et al. (2012) showed in their characterization study that the bug reports consisting of logging statements get fixed 2.2 times faster compared to the bug reports not consisting of any logging statements. Logging statements are not only useful in debugging, but they are also useful in many other applications, such as anomaly detection (Fu et al., 2009), performance problem diagnosis (Nagaraj et al., 2012), and workload modeling (Sharma et al., 2011).

Logging statements are important, but they have an inherent cost and benefit tradeoff (Fu et al., 2014). A large number of logging statements can affect system performance because logging is an I/O-intensive activity. An experiment by Ding et al. (2015) and Sigelman et al. (2010) reveal that in the case of search engines, logging can increase average execution time of requests by of 16.3%. Similar to excess logging, less logging is also problematic. An insufficient number of logging statements can miss important debugging information and can lessen the benefits of logging. Hence, developers need to avoid both excessive and insufficient logging. However, previous research and studies show that developers often face difficulty in optimal logging, that is, identifying which code construct to log in the source code (Fu et al., 2014; Zhu et al., 2015). It happens because of lack of training and the domain experience required for optimal logging. For example, Shang et al. (2015) reported an incident of a user from a Hadoop project complaining about less logging of catch-blocks. Recently the software engineering research community has conducted studies to understand the logging practices of software developers in order to build tools and techniques to help with automated logging. The current studies provide limited characterization study or conduct analysis on fewer code constructs. There are gaps in previous studies, as they do not analyze all the code constructs in detail, which this study aims to fill.

The work presented in this chapter is the first large-scale, in-depth, and focused study of logged and nonlogged code constructs at multiple levels. High-level (source code files) and low-level (catch-blocks) analysis were conducted to identify relationships between code constructs and logging characteristics. Based on the finding of this multilevel analysis authors proposed a machine leanirng based model for log statement prediction for catch-blocks. . A case study was performed on three large, open-source Java projects: Apache Tomcat (Apache Tomcat, n.d.), CloudStack (Apache CloudStack, n.d.), and Hadoop (Page, n.d.). Empirical analysis reveals several interesting insights about logged and nonlogged code constructs at both the levels. The machine learning based model give encouraging results for catch-blocks logging prediction on Java projects.

RELATED WORK

This section presents the closely related work and the novel research contributions of the study presented in this chapter in context to existing work. The authors categorize the related work in three dimensions: 1) improving source code logging, 2) uses of logging statements in other applications, and 3) applications of LDA in topic identification.

Improving Source Code Logging

Yuan et al. (2012) analyze source code and propose *ErrorLog* tool that logs all the generic exception patterns. However, logging all the generic exception can cause excess of log statements in the source code. Fu et al. (2014) empirically analyzed logging practices of software developers on two industrial systems. They addressed three research questions in their study: first, finding code snippets that were logged frequently; second, identifying the distinguishing characteristics of logged and nonlogged code constructs; and third, building a tool for logging prediction. They analyzed 100 randomly chosen logging statements and identified the most frequently logged code construct types. They performed detailed analysis of return value check and exception snippets. They computed the logging ratio of each unique exception type and reported that the majority of the exception types falls in the range of a medium logging ratio (i.e., 10 percent to 90 percent). They analyzed 70 nonlogged catch-blocks and identified the main reasons for not inserting a logging statement in the catch-block. They reported the correlations among the presence of some specific keywords that affect the logging decision such as "delete," "remove," "get," etc. The machine learning–based tool proposed by Fu et al., which used contextual information from the code, gave an F-score of 80 percent to 90 percent. This shows that contextual information can be an important factor when making logging decisions. This study extends the characterization study performed by Fu et al. on many dimensions. First, the study performed by Fu et al. presents results on the basis of manual analysis of only a few code constructs, whereas in this work the authors present their analysis using much larger code constructs. Second, the authors extended their study by answering many more research questions at two levels. Third, the authors analyzed open-source Java project, whereas they analyzed closed-source C# projects. Hence, the results in this chapter can be reproduced by the software engineering research community. Zhu et al. (2015) extended the study performed by Fu et al. by using more features for building the logging prediction. However, their study also lack comprehensive analysis of the features used for building the logging prediction model.

Yuan et al.'s (2012b) work involved empirically analyzing modifications to log messages. They reported many interesting findings from their empirical analysis performed on four large open-source projects. Yuan et al. (2012b) reported that 18 percent of all the committed revisions modify logging code, and 26 percent of the time developers modify the verbosity level of the logging code as an afterthought. Forty-five percent and 27 percent of the time developers modify the text and variable of the log messages, respectively, to incorporate changes in the execution information. Based on these findings, they proposed a simple code clone-based technique to find inconsistent verbosity levels in the source code. In another study, Yuan et al. (2012c) propose model for enhancing the content of log statements. Chen et al. (2016) replicated the study performed by Yuan et al. (2012b) for Java projects and reported several differences in results as compared to the results reported by Yuan et al. (2012b). Kabinna et al.'s (2016) work on predicting the stability of logging statements using features from three different domains: context, developer, and content. In another study, Kabinna et al.'s (2016b) work on empirically analyzing migration of log libraraies in Java projects. Li et al. (2016) worked on predicting verbosity level of log statement. In another study, Li et al. (2016b) worked on predicting just in time log changes. In contrast to these studies, our work focuses on finding distinguishing features of logged and non-logged code constructs and to predict logged code constructs. This book chapter is based on our previous published work (Lal et al., 2015, Lal & Sureka, 2016; Lal et al., 2016b). This work is found to be useful and has been extended for if-blocks logging prediction (Lal et al., 2016) and cross-project catch-blocks and if-blocks logging prediction (Lal et al., 2017a; Lal et al., 2017b).

Uses of Logging Statements in Other Applications

Logging statements have been found useful in various software development tasks (Mariani & Pastore, 2008; Nagaraj et al., 2012; Shang et al., 2015; Xu et al., 2009; Yuan et al., 2010). Shang et al. (2015) used logging statements present in a file to predict defects. Shang et al. (2015) proposed various product and process metrics using logging statements to predict post-release defects in software. Nagaraj et al. (2012) used good and bad logs of the system to detect performance issues. Nagaraj et al. (2012) also developed a tool, DISTALYZER, that helps developers find components responsible for poor system performance. Xu et al.'s (2009) work involved mining console logs from distributed systems at Google. They used logging information to find anomalies in the system. The authors verified anomalies were detected at the time when the system raised performance-related issues. They reported that performance issues are raised at the same time when anomalies are detected in system. Yuan et al. (2010) proposed a technique for finding the root cause of the failures by using logging information. They developed a tool, SherLog, that can use logs to find information about failed runs. SherLog can find important information about failures without requiring any re-execution of the code. All these studies focused on using log information in other applications such as finding root causes and performance issue detection. In contrast to these studies, the work described in this chapter focuses on the comparison between logged and nonlogged code constructs at two levels.

LDA Applications in Topic Identification

LDA is a popular topic modeling technique (Blei et al., 2003). It has been utilized widely in various software engineering applications to discover meaningful topics (Barua et al., 2012; Pagano & Maalej, 2013; Thomas et al., 2014; Tian et al., 2009). Tian et al. (2009) used LDA for software categorization. They proposed a system that can learn topic models from the identifier and comments present in the source code and can categorize software into one of the 43 programming languages such as C, C++, Java, PHP, Perl, etc. Thomas et al. (2014) used LDA topic models for software evolution analysis. Results reported by them show that topic models are effective in discovering actual code changes. Pagano et al. (2013) used LDA to study blogging behavior of committers and noncommitters. Results showed that committers' blogs consist of topics related to features and domain concepts, and 15 percent of the time blogs consist of topics related to source code. In contrast, blogs of noncommitters consist of topics related to conferences, events, configuration and deployment. Barua et al. (2012) used LDA on a StackOverflow questions and answers dataset in order to discover the most popular topics among the developer community. Results showed that a wide variety of topics are present in the developer discussions. They also showed that topics related to Web and mobile application development are gaining popularity compared to other topics. All these previous studies show the effectiveness of LDA topic models in the software engineering applications, and hence the authors of this chapter choose LDA for topic analysis. However, in contrast to these studies, the authors used LDA for topic identification in logging and nonlogging code constructs. To the best of their knowledge, LDA has never been used for topic modeling in this context.

Table 1. Details of individual research questions addressed in each research dimension

Research Dimension	Research Questions
Statistical analysis of high-level code constructs (source code files)	1. Is distribution of the logged files skewed? 2. Do logged files have greater complexity compared to that of nonlogged files? 3. Is there a positive correlation between file complexity and log statement count?
Statistical analysis of low-level code constructs (catch-blocks)	4. Do try-blocks associated with logged catch-blocks have greater complexity compared to that of nonlogged catch-blocks? 5. What is the logging ratio of different exception types? 6. Is the exception type contribution the same in total catch-blocks as well as in total logged catch-blocks? 7. Are the top20 exception types and their respective logging ratios the same in all three projects? 8. Can logged and nonlogged catch-blocks co-exist?
Content-based analysis of low-level code constructs (catch-blocks)	9. Do try-blocks associated with logged and nonlogged catch-blocks have different topics?
Logging prediction model for low-level code constructs (catch-blocks)	10. Can we predict logged catch-blocks using machine learning based model?

RESEARCH DIMENSIONS AND RESEARCH QUESTIONS

Table 1 shows four main research dimensions (RDs) and respective research questions (RQs) considered in this work. Following is a brief description of each RD and respective RQs:

- **RD1 - Statistical Analysis of Source Code Files:** In RD1, the authors answer three main research questions related to the statistical properties of logged and nonlogged files. Statistical analysis is important because it provides insights about the logged and nonlogged code constructs without looking at the semantics of the code. The first and second RQs compute the percentage of logged files and their average SLOCs. The third RQ computes the correlation between file SLOC and respective logging count.

- **RD2 - Statistical Analysis of Catch-Blocks:** In RD2, the authors answer five research questions related to the statistical properties of logged and nonlogged catch-blocks. The fourth research question compares the complexities of the try-blocks associated with logged and nonlogged catch-blocks to investigate whether complexities of try-blocks have any effect on the corresponding catch-block logging decision or not. The fifth and seventh RQs compute the logging ratio of all the exception types and the top 20 exception types in all three projects. The sixth RQ computes the contribution of an exception type in total catch-blocks and total logged exception types. The eighth RQ investigates whether logged and nonlogged catch-blocks can co-exist.

- **RD3 - Content-Based Analysis of Catch-Blocks:** In RD3, the authors use an LDA-based topic modeling technique on the contextual information present in the try-blocks associated with logged and nonlogged catch-blocks. They hypothesize that the contextual information present in the try-blocks can reveal important information for the corresponding catch-block logging.

- **RD4 - Logging Prediction Model for Catch-Blocks:** In RD4, the authors use finding of this empirical study and propose machine learning based model for logged catch-blocks prediction.

Figure 1. Research method followed in this study

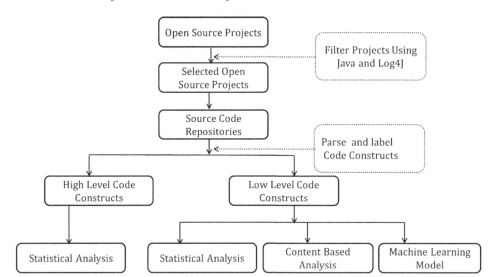

RESEARCH METHOD AND EXPERIMENTAL DATASET

This section presents the research methodology and experimental dataset details (refer to Figure 1). The research method consists of two phases: dataset selection and dataset preparation.

Dataset Selection Phase

In this phase, the authors selected open-source projects on which to conduct their experiments. Following are the list of properties and essential criteria which were taken into account while selecting the three open-source projects for the analysis:

1. **Type: Open Source:** The authors conducted their study on open-source software projects so that the work can be replicated and used for benchmarking and comparison.
2. **Programing Language: Java:** The authors selected a Java-based project for the study because Java is one of the most used programing languages (Kim, 2016;Krill, 2016).
3. **Logging Framework: Log4J:** The authors used Java projects utilizing the Log4J (Goers, n.d.) framework for logging. They targeted projects using the Log4J framework only because this is one of the widely used frameworks for Java logging.
4. **Number of Java Files: More Than 1,000:** The authors set this threshold so that they can draw statistically significant conclusions.
5. **Number of Catch-Blocks: More Than 1,000:** The authors set this threshold so that they can draw statistically significant conclusions.

Experimental Dataset Details

The authors selected three projects for their empirical study based on the criteria defined for the dataset selection phase: Apache Tomcat, CloudStack, and Hadoop. All three projects are long-lived Java projects with a development history of ≈7 to 17 years. Table 2 shows the SLOC of all three projects. SLOC are computed using the LocMetrics tool (LocMetrics, n.d.). Apache Tomcat, CloudStack and Hadoop have been previously used by the research community for logging and other studies (Kabinna et al., 2016; Lal & Sureka, 2016; Lal et al., 2016; Shang et al., 2015; Zimmermann et al.,2009). Following are the details of each project.

- **Apache Tomcat:** Apache Tomcat is open-source software developed under the umbrella of the Apache Software Foundation (Apache Tomcat, n.d). It is a Web server that implements many Java EE specifications like Java Servlet, Java EL, Java Sever Pages, and WebSocket. Logging is important in Apache Tomcat Web server; it has its own LogManager implementation; and it also supports private per-application logging configurations (Crossley, n.d.;Team, n.d.).
- **CloudStack:** CloudStack is open-source software developed by the Apache Software Foundation (Apache CloudStack, n.d). It provides public, private, and hybrid cloud solutions. It also provides a highly available and scalable Infrastructure as a Service (IaaS) cloud computing platform for deployment and management of networks of virtual machines. It provides support for many hypervisors such as VMware, KVM and Xen Cloud Platform (XCP). CloudStack provides large amounts of log entries, and for a CloudStack administrator investigating errors in the logs is an inevitable task (Kosinski, 2013).
- **Hadoop:** Hadoop is also developed by the Apache Software Foundation (Page, n.d). It is a framework that enables distributed processing of large datasets. It is scalable from a single server to multiple machines. The Apache Hadoop library is designed to detect and handle application-layer failures. Hadoop is one of the most widely used software platforms, and various tools have been developed to monitor the status of the Hadoop using generated logs (Shang et al., 2015; Rabkin & Katz, 2010).

Dataset Preparation Phase

In this step, the authors extract logging statements and target code constructs from the source code. Following are the details of the data preparation.

- **Files:** The authors extracted all the high-level (source code files) code constructs from the source code. They focused only on Java files in this work and removed other types of files such as CSS and XML. Table 2 shows statistics on the number of Java files extracted from each of the projects. For example, the Apache Tomcat project consists of 2,037 Java files, whereas the CloudStack project consists of 5,351 Java files. The authors extracted logging statements from each file (refer to Table 3). They marked a file as "logged" if it consisted of at least one logging statement; otherwise, it was marked as "non-logged."

- **Catch-Blocks:** Next the authors extract all the catch-blocks from the source code. They extracted all the catch-blocks from the Java files using the Eclipse Java source code parsing library (Beaton, n.d). However, a single try-block can have multiple catch-blocks. In such cases the authors considered all catch-blocks belonging to a single try-block as a separate instance. Figure 2 shows an illustrative example of separate instance creation. The authors marked a catch-block as "logged" if it consisted of at least one logging statement. Table 2 shows that the experimental dataset consists of 3,325, 12,591, and 7,947 catch-blocks in Apache Tomcat, CloudStack, and Hadoop, respectively. It also shows that 27 percent, 26.15 percent, and 22 percent of the catch-blocks are logged in Apache Tomcat, Hadoop, and CloudStack, respectively.
- **Logging Lines:** All three projects used in the empirical study are Java and Log4J based projects. However, the authors observed several inconsistencies in logging statement formats and hence created 26 regular expressions to extract all the logging statements. The authors observed two semantically different types of logging: first, in which the logging level is explicitly mentioned (for example, Type 1 and Type 2 logging statements in Listing 1) and second, in which the logging level is not mentioned explicitly (for example, Type 4 and Type 5 in Listing 1). The authors also observed several inconsistencies in the uses of the log levels. For example, Listing 1 shows three different ways in which the log level "warn"' is used in different datasets (refer to Type 1, Type 2, and Type 3 in Listing 1).

STATISTICAL ANALYSIS ON HIGH-LEVEL CODE CONSTRUCTS

The following subsections present the work on characterizing high-level code constructs (source code files). The authors answer research questions related to the distribution and complexity of logged files. They also analyze correlations between the logging count of a file and it's SLOC.

Figure 2. Catch-block instance creation from try-blocks

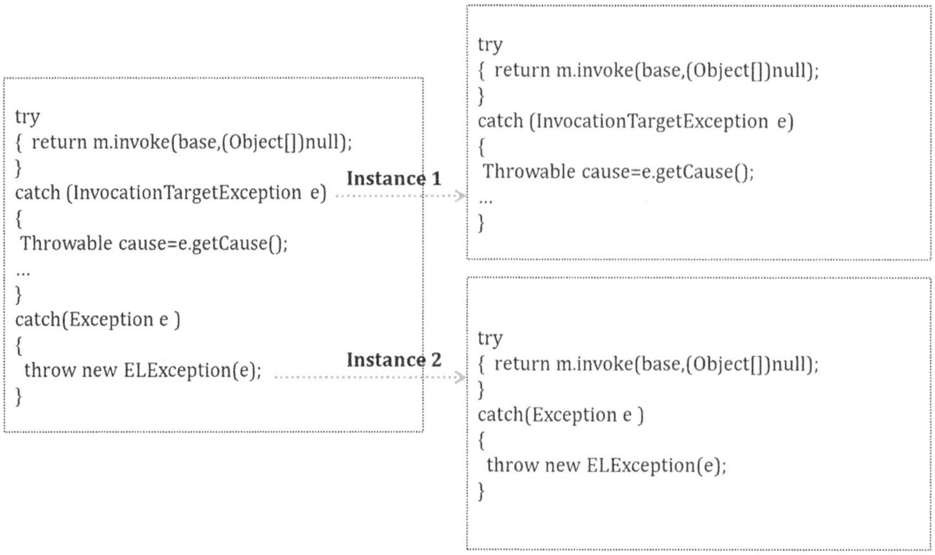

Listing 1. Example of logging statements taken from the dataset

```
/*-----------------Type 1: (Taken from Hadoop)----------------*/
LOG.warn(AuthenticationToken ignored: + ex.getMessage());
/*-----------------Type 2: (Taken from Hadoop)--------------*/
logWarningWhenAuxServiceThrowExceptions(service, AuxServicesEventType.APPLICATION_INIT, th);
/*-----------------Type 3: (Taken from Apache Tomcat)--------*/
Logger.getLogger(getLoggerName(getHost(),url)).log(Level.WARNING,""Unable to determine web application context.xml "" +
docBase,e);
/*-------------Type 4: (Taken from Apache Tomcat)---------*/
log("Error closing redirector: " + ioe.getMessage(),Project.MSG_ERR);
/*--------------Type 5: (Taken from Apache Tomcat)---------*/
project.log(wrong object reference + refId + - + pref.getClass());
```

Table 2. Experimental dataset details

Project	Apache Tomcat	CloudStack	Hadoop
Version	8.0.9	4.3.0	2.7.1
Logging Library	Log4J	Log4J	Log4J
Java File	2,037	5,351	6,332
SLOC	276,209	1,142,970	951,629
Log Line Count	2,703	10,428	10,108
Total Catch Blocks	3,325	12,591	7,947
Logged Catch Blocks	887 (27%)	2,790 (22.16%)	2,078 (26.15%)
Distinct Exception Types	120	163	265

RQ 1: Is the distribution of the logged files skewed?

The authors counted the number of files that consisted of at least one logging statement. Table 3 shows that only 17.9 percent, 14.9 percent, and 22.3 percent of files consisted of logging statements in Apache Tomcat, CloudStack, and Hadoop, respectively. This result shows that distribution of files containing logging statements is highly skewed, that is, less than 23 percent of files consist of logging statements. The authors believe that understanding the characteristics of source code for files that do not contain any logging statements can provide useful insights for logging prediction tools, as the tool does not need to predict logging in the files, given that there is no history of logging statements.

The distribution of files containing and not containing log statements is skewed as only ≈14 percent to 22.3 percent of files contain logging statements.

RQ 2: Do logged files have greater complexity compared to nonlogged files?

This subsection presents a comparison of the complexity of the logged and nonlogged files. The authors measured the complexity of a file using its SLOC. To compute SLOC, they removed all the blank lines, package statements, import statements, and comments from the file. They also removed lines containing only '{' or '}'. Table 3 shows the values of average SLOC of logged and nonlogged files for all three projects. The table also shows that for the Apache Tomcat project, the average SLOC value

Table 3. The count (%) of logged files in the total files. It also shows the average SLOC of logged and nonlogged files. LFC: Logged File Count; AS: Average SLOC; LF: Logged Files; NLF: Nonlogged Files

Project	Total Files	LFC (%)	AS	
			LF	NLF
Apache Tomcat	2,037	365 (17.9%)	**260.04**	69.37
CloudStack	5,351	798 (14.9%)	**290.81**	159.87
Hadoop	6,332	1414 (22.3%)	**254**	75.51

of logged and nonlogged files is 260.04 and 69.37. Results show a similar trend for other two projects, that is, the average SLOC of logged files is higher than that of nonlogged files. Average values provide useful statistics, but they lack significant details about the actual distribution. Hence the authors drew a box-and-whisker plot for the SLOC of logged and nonlogged files. The graph in Figure 3 shows that the median SLOC values of logged files is higher that of nonlogged files for all three projects. For example, the median SLOC value for logged files in the CloudStack project is 114.5, whereas the median SLOC value for nonlogged files in the CloudStack project is 46.0. Figure 3 also shows a higher interquartile range for logged files, which shows a higher spread of SLOC values in logged files compared to that of nonlogged files. The results presented in this subsection lead to many more questions regarding the analysis of more complex metrics (such as object-oriented metrics; Thwin & Quah 2005) of files to get a deeper understanding about the relation between file complexity and logging.

Logged files have greater complexity and spread (measured using SLOC of a file) as compared to that of nonlogged files.

RQ 3: Is there a positive correlation between file complexity and log statement count?

The box-and-whiskers plot of the previous subsection shows that files with higher SLOC (i.e., higher complexity) are more likely to contain logging statements. Hence the authors hypothesize that there exists a positive correlation between file SLOC and its log statement count, that is, the higher the SLOC, the higher the log statement count of the file. To test this hypothesis the authors created a scatter plot

Figure 3. SLOC comparison of logged and nonlogged files

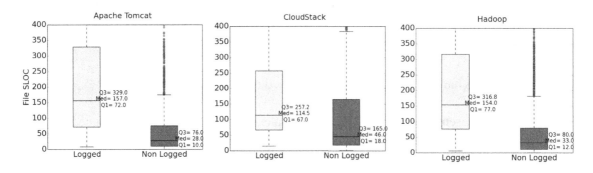

between file SLOC and the respective log statement count. Scatter plots are one of the simplest yet powerful methods to visualize correlations between two variables. The authors created two scatter plots: the first scatter plot was between the SLOC of all the files in the database and respective log statement count, and the second scatter plot was between the SLOC only of logged files and respective log statement counts. The authors also computed the Pearson correlation between file SLOC and log statement count (Welcome to Statistics, n.d.). They obtained correlation values of 0.58, 0.76, and 0.67 for Apache Tomcat, CloudStack, and Hadoop, respectively, which shows that a positive correlation exists between SLOC and log statement count of a file (refer to Figure 5). However, it is interesting to observe the correlation value between file SLOC and logging count decreases after the addition of nonlogged files (refer to Figure 4). The authors observed the presence of three (one in each project) very large, nonlogged files in all three projects. Figure 4 shows these three files, marked using a red circle. Manual analysis reveals that these three files are tool-generated files and hence do not consist of any log statements. Table 4 gives details about the files and the tool used to generate these files. The experimental results presented in this subsection show a positive correlation between file SLOC and log statement count. The authors believe that these findings can be utilized by logging prediction tools to predict logging in the files if they exceed some project-specific threshold of file SLOC.

A positive correlation exists between the SLOC of logged files and the logging count.

Figure 4. Scatter plot showing correlation between SLOC of the files and respective logging counts

Figure 5. Scatter plot showing correlation between SLOC of only logged files and respective logging counts

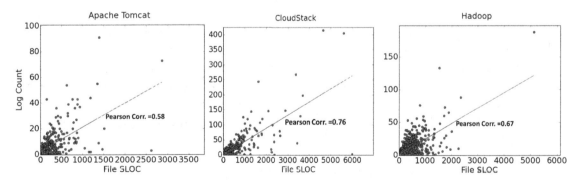

Table 4. Details of the three large nonlogged files

Project	File Name	File SLOC	Log Count	Analysis
Apache Tomcat	ELParser.java	2,272	0	Auto-generated using JJTree and JavaCC
CloudStack	AmazonEC2 Stub.java	250,323	0	Auto-generated using WSDL
Hadoop	Hamlet.java	19,431	0	Auto-generated using HamletGen

STATISTICAL ANALYSIS ON LOW-LEVEL CODE CONSTRUCTS

The following subsections work on characterizing low-level code constructs (catch-blocks). The authors answer research questions related to complexity, logging ratio distribution, and whether logged and nonlogged catch-blocks can exist together.

RQ4: Is the complexity of try-blocks associated with logged catch-blocks greater than that of nonlogged catch-blocks?

The authors compared the complexity of the try-blocks associated with logged and nonlogged catch-blocks. They wanted to analyze whether the complexity of a try-block acts a parameter when deciding to log corresponding catch-blocks or not. In this work, they considered three parameters to measure the complexity of a try-block: size of the try-block (SLOC count), operator count of the try-block and method call count.

Comparing SLOC of Try-Blocks Associated With Logged and Nonlogged Catch-Blocks

The authors computed SLOC of the corresponding try-blocks associated with logged and nonlogged catch-blocks. They computed SLOC using the same method described in a previous section. Listing 2 shows an example of a try-block from the Apache Tomcat project. The SLOC value of the try-block shown in Listing 2 is 2. Figure 6 shows box-and-whisker plots revealing the dispersion and skewness in SLOC for try-blocks associated with logged and nonlogged catch-block across three projects. The graph in Figure 6 reveals that the median and the third-quartile values for logged catch-blocks are more than the corresponding values for nonlogged catch-blocks in Apache Tomcat and Hadoop. For example, the third quartile and median for logged catch-blocks in the Apache Tomcat project is 7.0 and 2.0, respectively, whereas the third quartile and median for nonlogged catch-blocks in the Apache Tomcat project is 2.0 and 1.0, respectively. However, for the CloudStack project, the authors observed that the third quartile for logged catch-blocks is higher than the third quartile for the nonlogged catch-blocks but the median value is smaller. The box plots in Figure 6 also reveal that the interquartile range (width of the box: Q3 − Q1) for logged catch-blocks is higher than those of nonlogged try-blocks, indicating a higher spread.

Listing 2. Example of a try-block taken from the Apache Tomcat project

```
try{
lc=new LoginContext(getLoginConfigName());
lc.login();
}catch(LoginException e)
{
log.error(sm.getString(spnegoAuthenticator.serviceLoginFail),e);
response.sendError(HttpServletResponse.SC_INTERNAL_SERVER_ERROR);
return false;
}
Try-LOC: 2
Operator Count: 7 (()()() =)
Method Call Count: 2 (getLoginConfigName, login)
Catch Exception: LoginException
```

Figure 6. Comparison of SLOC of try-blocks associated with logged and nonlogged catch-blocks

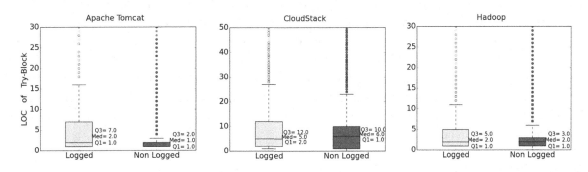

Figure 7. Comparison of operator count of try-blocks associated with logged and nonlogged catch-blocks

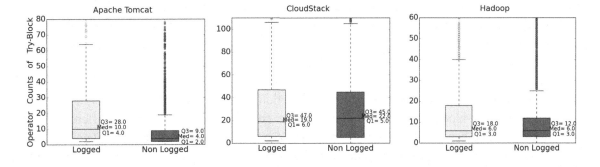

Comparing Operator Count of Try-Blocks Associated With Logged and Nonlogged Catch-Blocks

Counting the total number of operators in a program has been widely used as a metric to measure the complexity of given source code. The Halstead metric for computing program complexity is based on counting the total and distinct numbers of operators and operands in the source code (Virtual Machinery, n.d.). The authors created a list of 19 arithmetic operators (=, *, +, −, %, !, (,), [,], &, ?,:, >, <, |,

Figure 8. Comparison of method call count of try-blocks associated with logged and nonlogged catch-blocks

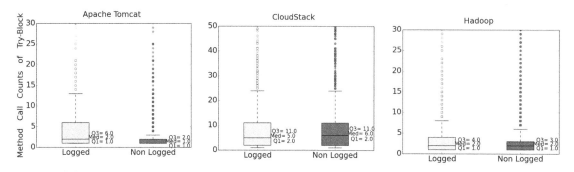

^, ~, /) that perform normal mathematical operations such as add, subtract, multiplication, division, and modulo. They counted the number of operators (from the list of 19) in the try-block linked to logged and nonlogged catch-blocks. The box plots in Figure 7 reveal that the third-quartile values for logged try-blocks (28, 47, and 18) are greater than the corresponding values (9, 45, and 12) for nonlogged try-blocks in Apache Tomcat, CloudStack, and Hadoop. The median values for Apache Tomcat indicate that logged try-blocks have greater complexity in terms of operator count. The authors observed that the median value for logged try-blocks and nonlogged try-blocks for the Hadoop project is the same. They believe that the lines-of-code metric is correlated to the number-of-operators metric, and hence they observe similar trends for both measures.

Comparing the Method Call Count of Try-Blocks Associated With Logged and Nonlogged Catch-Blocks

The Halstead complexity measure computes program complexity based on several factors, such as the number of distinct operators and operands, as well as the total number of operators and operands. Predefined library function and user-defined function calls are considered operators according to the Halstead complexity metric. A large number of methods (equivalent to operators) within a try-block increases both cognitive complexity and testing complexity. Listing 2 shows an example of a try-block with two executable statements, both of which are function calls (getLoginConfigName() and login()). There can be two try-blocks with the same number of executable statements but a different number of function calls, and hence the complexity measure based on method call count is different from the complexity measure based on lines of code, as well as the complexity measure based on total number of operators. The authors computed the number of function calls for every try-block in the source code dataset. Figure 8 shows the box plots for the number of methods for the three projects in the experimental dataset. It reveals that the third-quartile value for the logged try-block is higher than the corresponding values for the nonlogged try-block for the Apache Tomcat and Hadoop projects. For example, the median and third-quartile value for Apache Tomcat is 2.0 and 6.0, respectively, for the logged try-block, which is higher than the median and third-quartile value of 1.0 and 2.0, respectively, for the nonlogged try-block. The authors observed that for the CloudStack project, the third-quartile value is the same for both logged and nonlogged try-blocks. Results give an indication that complexity of try-blocks can be use as a parameters for catch-blocks logging prediction.

Try-blocks associated with logged catch-blocks have greater complexity than that of nonlogged catch-blocks for the Apache Tomcat and Hadoop projects.

RQ 5: What is the logging ratio trend of the various exception types?

This subsection statistically analyzes the logging ratio (LR_i) of distinct exception types in all three projects. The logging ratio of each exception type is computed using Equation 1 (refer to Table 5 for details about the acronyms used in this equation). The logging ratio metric is defined and used earlier by Fu et al. (2014) for analysis of exception types on C# projects. The logging ratio of an exception type shows the percentage of its logged catch-blocks ($TLCB_i$) to its total number of catch-blocks (TCB_i). For example, the "ChannelException" exception type in the Tomcat dataset has 25 catch-blocks, out of which 15 are logged. Hence, the logging ratio of ChannelException exception type i.e., $LR_{ChannelException}$, is 60 percent. Figure 9 shows the histogram of the logging ratio of distinct exception types for all three projects. In Figure 9, the x-axis shows the range of the logging ratio (with an interval of 10 percent) and the y-axis shows the percentage of the distinct exception types falling in that range. On top of each bar of the histogram, the distinct exception types falling in that logging ratio range are plotted and counted. For example, Figure 9a shows that 47 exception types in the Apache Tomcat project have a logging ratio between 0 percent and 10 percent. Fu et al. (2014) reported in their study that the majority of exception types belong to either a very high (>=90%) or low (<=10%) logging ratio range. Although they computed the results on C# projects and results of a Java project can differ, the authors observed results similar to Fu et al. (2014) with Java projects.

$$LR_i = \frac{\left|TLCB_i\right| * 100}{\left|TCB_i\right|} \tag{1}$$

The majority of the exception types in the Java project belong to either a very high (>=90%) or very low (<=10%) logging ratio.

RQ 6: Is the exception type contribution the same in total catch-blocks and in total logged catch-blocks?

Figure 9. Logging ratio of all three projects

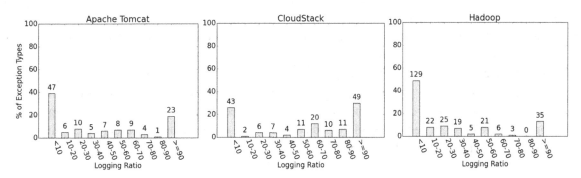

Table 5. Various acronyms used in Equation 1, Equation 2, and Equation 3

Variable Name	Acronym
Total Catch-Blocks in the Dataset	TCB_{DT}
Total Logged Catch-Blocks in the Dataset	$TLCB_{DT}$
Total Catch-Block of ith Exception Type	TCB_i
Total Logged Catch-Blocks of ith Exception Type	$TLCB_i$
Exception Type Ratio (Catch Count) of ith Exception Type	$ERCC_i$
Exception Type Ratio (Log Count) of ith Exception Type	$ERLC_i$
Logging Ratio of ith Exception Type	LR_i

This subsection measures the contribution of each exception type in total catch-blocks as well as in total logged catch-blocks. The authors define two metrics: Exception Type Ratio (Catch Count) [ERCC] and Exception Type Ratio (Log Count) [ERLC] for the same; refer to Equation 2 and Equation 3 for details (refer to Table 5 to get details on the acronyms used in these equations). ERCC defines the percentage of contribution of a particular exception type in total catch-blocks whereas ERLC defines it for logged catch blocks. ERCC computes the percentage of total catch-blocks of an exception type (TCB_i) to total catch-blocks in the dataset (TCB_{DT}), whereas the ERLC metric computes the percentage of total logged catch-blocks of an exception type ($TLCB_i$) to total logged catch-blocks in the dataset ($TLCB_{DT}$). For example, for the Apache Tomcat project we have TCB_{DT}= 3325 and $TLCB_{DT}$ =887. Now for 'ChannelException' exception type we have $TCB_{ChannelException}$=25 and $TLCB_{ChannelException}$=15. Hence, for ChannelException type we have value of ERCC=7.5 and ERLC=1.69. The motivation behind computing these two metrics is to find exception types that contribute a great deal to total catch-blocks and less to logged catch-blocks, or vice versa. For example, ChannelException type have comparatively less contribution in logged catch-blocks as compared to that in all catch-blocks because for it the value of ERCC metric is greater than ERLC metric. Early detection of such exception types can be beneficial to developers as well as logging prediction tools, because exception-specific rules can be created for such exception types. Figure 10 shows the histogram of ERCC metrics for all three projects. In Figure 10, the x-axis shows the ERCC range and the y-axis shows the sum of ERCC values of all the exception types falling in that ERCC range, that is, all the exception types falling in a particular group give an ERCC range and their ERCC value can be summed. On top of each bar is a count of unique exception types falling in that ERCC range. For example, Figure 10a shows that for the Apache Tomcat project 116 exception types have an ERCC metric value between 0 and 5 and sum of their ERCC values is 35, that is, 116 exception types together constitute 35 percent of total catch-blocks. Figure 10a also shows that two exception types in the Apache Tomcat project have ERCC values between 20 and 25 and together they constitute 42 percent of total catch-blocks. Figure 11 shows the histogram for ERLC metrics for all three projects. In Figure 11, the x-axis shows the ERCC range and the y-axis shows the sum of ERLC values of all the exception types falling in that ERCC range. The x-axis is the same in both graphs so the contribution of the same exception type in total catch-blocks (using the ERCC metric) and in total logged catch-blocks (using the ERLC metric) can be compared. Figure 11a shows that 116 exception types together constitute 38 percent of all logged catch-blocks, whereas these same 116 exception types constitute only 35 percent of total catch-blocks (refer to Figure 10a).

Figure 10b and Figure 11b show an interesting finding about four exception types (marked by arrows in the Figure) from the CloudStack project. These four exception types—ADBException, AxisFault, IllegalArgumentException, and XMLStreamException—have very large ERCC values (i.e., very large contribution in total catch-blocks), but very low ERLC values (i.e., much smaller contribution in the total logged catch-blocks). For example, the exception type "XMLStream" has 1,952 occurrences in the CloudStack project, but none of these occurrences are logged. Detection of such exception types can be beneficial for logging prediction tools, as the tool can learn the exception types that have such drastic differences in ERCC and ERLC values.

$$ERCC_i = \frac{|TCB_i| * 100}{|TCB_{DT}|} \tag{2}$$

$$ERLC_i = \frac{|TLCB_i| * 100}{|TLCB_{DT}|} \tag{3}$$

Some exception types in the CloudStack project have very high ERCC values (i.e., very large contribution in total catch-blocks) but very low ERLC values (i.e., much less contribution in the total logged catch-blocks).

RQ 7: Are the top 20 exception types and their respective logging ratios the same in all three projects?

This section presents an analysis of the logging ratio of the top 20 most frequent exception types in all three projects. The authors plotted a pie chart showing the contribution of the top 20 most frequent exception types in total catch-blocks. Figure 12 shows that the top 20 most frequent exception types contribute to ≈80 percent to 88 percent of the total catch-blocks for all three projects. Hence, analyzing the top 20 exception types can be crucial for the logging prediction tools, as ≈80 percent of the time the tool will be making a prediction for one of these top 20 exception types. In addition to this, if a similar trend exists regarding the logging ratio of the top 20 exception types across the projects, then it can be beneficial for cross-project logging prediction.

Figure 10. ERCC metric value for all three projects

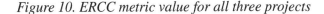
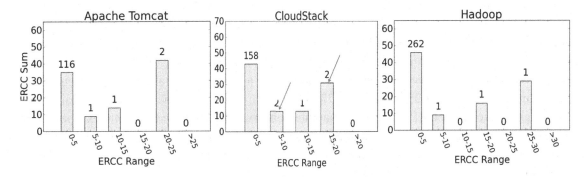

Figure 11. ERLC metric value for all three projects

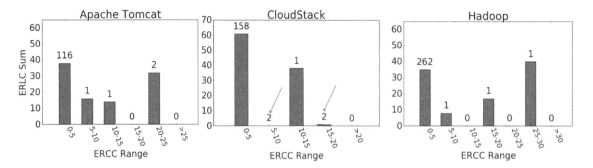

Table 6. Details of four exception types from the CloudStack project with very high ERCC but very low ERLC values. CCB: Count of Total Catch-Blocks; CLCB: Count of Total Logged Catch-Blocks; LR: Logging Ratio.

Exception Type	CCB	ERCC	CLCB	ERLC	LR
ADB Exception	960	0.0762	0	0	0
AxisFault	643	0.0511	0	0	0
IllegalArgumentException	1,971	0.1565	19	0.0068	0.0096
XMLStreamException	1,952	0.155	0	0	0

The authors wanted to answer two interesting research questions about the top 20 exception types: Are these top 20 exception types the same across all the projects, and do the top 20 exception types show common trends for logging ratios in all three projects? To answer these research questions, the authors computed the top 20 exception types, as well as their respective logging ratios (using Equation 1) for all three projects. The answer to the first question is "No." Results show that only 6 exception types are common among the three projects in the top 20 exception type list. Table 7 shows details of these six common exception types (Exception, IQException, Throwable, InterruptedException, IllegalStateException, and IllegalArgumentException) in all the three projects. The Throwable class is the superclass of all errors and exceptions in the Java language. The Exception class and its subclasses are a form of Throwable that indicates conditions that a reasonable application might want to catch. Throwable and Exception are higher-level classes (Exception extends Throwable, which extends the root of the class hierarchy Object), with several subclasses defining specific exception types; hence, they are common. the authors believe that classes like InterruptedException are common because Apache Tomcat, CloudStack, and Hadoop extensively use multithreading, and InterruptedException is thrown when a thread is waiting, sleeping, or otherwise occupied and the thread is interrupted. The authors compared logging ratios of six common exceptions in all three projects. Table 7 shows no specific trend for logging ratios across the three projects. For example, the exception type "Exception" has a low logging ratio for the Apache Tomcat and Hadoop projects (i.e., 37.25 percent and 27.72 percent), whereas for the CloudStack project, it has a high logging ratio (i.e., 66.81 percent). The authors observed similar trend for other exception types. Thus, the answer to the second research question is also "No." This indicates that the logging ratio of an exception type is project specific, and hence a cross-project defect-prediction technique might need more sophisticated features than logging ratio.

Figure 12. Pie chart of top 20 exception types, showing percentage in total contribution

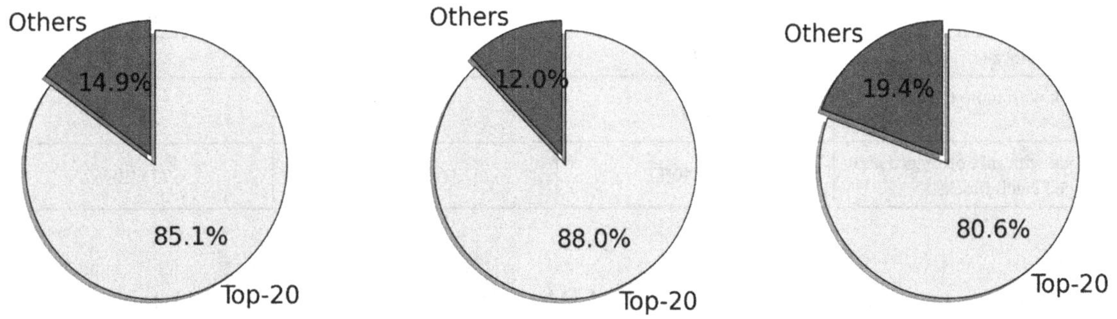

Table 7. Logging ratio details of 6 common exceptions in the top 20 exception type list of the three projects

Exception Type	Apache Tomcat	CloudStack	Hadoop
Exception	37.25%	66.81%	27.72%
IOException	27.41%	54.69%	36.69%
Throwable	45.66%	72.24%	53.05%
InterruptedException	6.12%	25.15%	23.28%
ClassNotFoundException	32.14%	4.48%	6.49%
IllegalArgumentException	23.19%	0.96%	16.67%

The most frequent exception types, as well as their respective logging ratios, are project specific.

RQ 8: Do logged and nonlogged catch-blocks coexist together?

The Java programing language allows associating multiple catch-blocks (each with a different exception type) to a single try-block. In this subsection, the authors' aim is to investigate whether a single try-block can have both logged and nonlogged catch-blocks or not. This research question is important to answer, as many times catch-block logging prediction tools use features from try-blocks. If the frequency of such try-blocks is very high, then it can affect the performance of such machine learning–based catch-block logging prediction tools. To answer this research question, the authors computed the count of try-blocks with both logged and nonlogged catch-blocks in all three projects. Table 8 shows that a very small percentage (i.e., ≈0.33 percent to 1.4 percent) of total try-blocks has both logged and nonlogged catch-blocks.

A very small percentage of try-blocks have both logged and nonlogged catch-blocks.

Content-Based Analysis of Low-Level Code Constructs

This section presents the experimental results of content-based analysis of low-level (catch-blocks) logged and nonlogged code constructs. The authors applied LDA for content analysis. LDA is a popular topic modeling technique and has been used widely in the past for topic identification in the source code and in many other research areas (Thomas et al., 2014; Maskeri et al., 2008; Pagano & Maalej, 2013). The

Table 8. Details of try-blocks with multiple catch-blocks

Project	Apache Tomcat	CloudStack	Hadoop
Unique try-blocks	2,914	9,899	7,171
Try-block with more than one catch-block	254	1,002	653
Try-block with mix of logged and nonlogged catch-blocks	41 (1.40%)	31 (0.31%)	77 (1.07%)

following subsections describe the steps of the LDA model creation, results of LDA topic modeling, and the authors' observations from the obtained results.

Preprocessing Steps for LDA Analysis

The preprocessing steps for LDA model creation are as follows:

1. To identify the topics present in the logged and nonlogged catch-blocks, the authors analyzed the contents of the try-blocks associated with logged and nonlogged catch-blocks. They created corpus consisting of the content of try-blocks associated with logged and nonlogged catch-blocks.
2. The authors performed prepossessing and removed all the English stop words, special characters, and operators. They removed English stop words such as "is," "the," and "of" from the analysis because they were mainly interested in identifying the core functionality of the code constructs that leads to logging. The authors then applied stemming on the obtained corpus. Stemming is useful in reducing inflected words to the same root words and hence helps in reducing the corpus size. The authors used the Python NLTK library for stop word removal and stemming (Natural Language Toolkit, n.d.).
3. The authors believe that words that occur in almost all the documents or that occur in very few documents may not be helpful in retrieving useful topics. Hence they removed all the words that occurred in 80 percent of the documents and in less than 2 percent of the documents.
4. The authors performed LDA for 10,000 runs because LDA gives better results when the number of iterations is increased. Previous studies in software engineering research have also used the same threshold value for LDA (Thomas et al., 2014).
5. The authors set the number of topics parameter for the LDA algorithm as 10.
6. The authors used a default value of other LDA parameters in the Python LDA library (Gensim, n.d.).

RQ 9: Do try-blocks associated with logged and nonlogged catch-blocks have different topics?

Table 9 shows the result obtained by LDA topic modeling on try-blocks associated with both logged and nonlogged catch-blocks. From this table, the authors observed that topics listed under try-blocks associated with logged and nonlogged catch-blocks are different. Hence they randomly picked some of the topics from the logged and nonlogged category and analyzed the differences in the associated code blocks. The authors drew the following interesting observations from this analysis:

1. They observed the "thread sleep" topic in the Apache Tomcat project. This topic is mentioned in the nonlogged catch-block category. The authors further analyzed occurrences of "thread sleep" in the Apache Tomcat project. They observed that in 84 occurrences of "thread sleep," it occurred 71 times in try-blocks associated with nonlogged catch-blocks.

2. The authors observed the presence of a topic related to "socket" in both try-blocks associated with logged and nonlogged catch-blocks. They analyzed all 43 try-blocks consisting of socket and wrapper words and found that in try-blocks associated with logged catch-blocks, the socket wrapper is mostly used for close or error functions, whereas for try-blocks associated with nonlogged catch-blocks, the socket function is used for timeout operations. LDA is able to detect this difference, as shown in the Apache Tomcat project regarding topics 4 (logged catch-blocks) and 3 (nonlogged catch-blocks).

3. The authors analyzed the "result stub (topic 1)" topic from the CloudStack project. They found 161 occurrences of try-blocks consisting of both words. They also noticed that catch-blocks associated with all 161 try-blocks are nonlogged. LDA is able to detect this because the "request stub" topic is not present in logged catch-blocks.

The contextual information present in the try-blocks provides important information for the associated catch-block logging.

Table 9. Topics discovered in try-blocks associated with logged and nonlogged catch-blocks

Project	Logged Catch-Block		Nonlogged Catch-Block	
Project	**Topic**	**Word**	**Topic**	**Word**
Apache Tomcat	1. channel file 2. method param 3. context log 4. **socket status**	1. channel, get, file, new, stream 2. method, get, param, valu, type 3. context, get, log, null, host 4. socket, statu, get, wrapper	1. **thread sleep** 2. channel read 3. **socket pool** 4. connect pool	1. results, thread, sleep, get 2. channel, close, read, buffer 3. socket, get, key, pool 4. get, connect, null, set, pool
CloudStack	1. byte key 2. response value 3. network 4. vm host	1. key, byte, new, pair, string 2. respons, valu, string, name, equal 3. network, ip, host, string, conn 4. vm, host, cmd, answer, state	1.**result stub** 2. pram om 3. java lang 4. stmt	1. result, stub, amazon, object, ec 2. om, factori, param, amazon, ec 3. class, java, lang, name, except 4. id, pstmt, string, set, long, rs
Hadoop	1. key id 2. assert 3. job conf 4. rm token	1. id, key, get, contain, info 2. request, fail, system, assert 3. job, get, name, map, conf, 4 token, rm, get, except, new	1. user token 2. key 3. get response 4. file path	1. token, user, arg, run, els 2. key, get, context, string 3. get, respons, job, request 4. file, path, fs, get, dir, statu

LOGGING PREDICTION MODEL FOR CATCH-BLOCKS

Using finding from our empirical analysis we propose a machine learning based catch-blocks logging prediction model, *LogOpt* (Lal & Sureka, 2016; Lal et al., 2016b). Based on this study we extract 46 distinguishing features for catch-blocks logging prediction (refer to Table 10 for details). These features have three properties: *Type, Domain*, and *Class*. *Type* of a feature specifies whether a feature is: t*extual, numeric or Boolean. Textual* features can take any textual value. *Numeric* features can take any positive numeric value. *Boolean* features can take value either 0 or 1. *Domain* of the feature specifies part of the source code from where the feature is extracted. We identified three domains: *try/catch, method_bt,* and *other*. If a feature extracted from try/catch-block it will have domain '*try/catch*'. If a feature extracted from the first line of the containing methods to the previous line of try-block associated with target catch-block, it will have domain '*method_bt*'. If a feature extracted from some other part of source code, it will have domain '*other*'. Features can belong to *positive class* feature of *negative class*. *Positive* class features are beneficial in predicting logged catch-blocks whereas *negative* class features are beneficial in predicting nonlogged catch-blocks. We use total 46 features for catch-blocks logging prediction model building (refer to Table 10)

LogOpt Model Building

Using the 46 features, the authors propose *LogOpt* model for catch-blocks logging prediction. *LogOpt* is a machine learning based model. For *LogOpt* model training, the authors, first extract all the catch-blocks from the dataset and label them as 'logged' or 'nonlogged'. A catch-block is marked as logged if it consists of at least one log statement; otherwise, it is marked as 'nonlogged'. Second, the authors extract all the 46 features (textual, numeric, and Boolean) from the all the instances. Uses of textual features directly for machine learning model building can increase in model complexity. Hence, in the third step authors applied feature preprocessing techniques to clean the textual features. Authors applied camel case conversion, lower case, stop word removal, stemming, and tf-idf (Han et al., 2011) conversion. Fourth, author combine tf-idf representation of textual features with Boolean and numeric features and create final feature vector. Authors, then train machine learning algorithms such as Radom Forest (RF), J48, Support Vector Machine (SVM), on the final feature vector to create the *LogOpt* model. This model is then used for logging prediction on new instances.

LogOpt Model Evaluation

Authors evaluate performance of *LogOpt* model on all the three project (Apache Tomcat, CloudStack, and Hadoop). For testing the performance of *LogOpt* model, authors divided the dataset into two parts in a ratio of 70:30 using stratified random sampling (Han et al., 2011). 70% of the dataset is used for training and 30% of the dataset is used for testing. Since, dataset sampling can lead to biases in the result the authors created 10 such random samples and reported average results. Authors evaluated performance of the model using several machine learning classifiers (RF, SVM, J48). SVM classifier performs the best and give the highest F1-score of 76.79% (Apache Tomcat), 84.32% (CloudStack), and 67.16% (Hadoop) (Lal & Sureka, 2016; Lal et al., 2016b).

Table 10. Features used for building catch-block logging prediction model. Class: Positive (P), Negative (N). Domain: Try/Catch (T), Method_bt (M), Other (O).

Type of Feature	Catch-Block Features (Class, Domain)	Explanation
Textual Features	1.Catch Exception Type (P,T) 2.Log Levels in Try Block (P,T) 3.Log Levels in Method_BT(P,M) 4.Operators in Try Block(P,T) 5.Operators in Method_BT(P,M) 6.Method Parameters (Type) (P,O) 7.Method Parameters (Name) (P,O) 8.Container Package Name (P,O) 9.Container Class Name (P, O) 10.Container Method Name (P,O) 11.Variable Declaration Name in Try Block(P,T) 12.Variable Declaration Name in Method_BT(P,M) 13.Method Call Name in Try Block(P,T) 14.Method Call Name in Method_BT(P,M)	1. Exception type of catch-block. 2. Verbosity level of the log statements present in the try-block. 3. Verbosity level of the log statements present in the method_bt section. 4. Arithmetic operators used in the try-block. 5. Arithmetic operators used in the method_bt section. 6. Type of parameters used in the containing method. 7. Name of the parameters used in the containing method. 8. Name of the containing package. 9. Name of containing class. 10. Name of the containing method. 11. Names of the variables declared in the try-block. 12. Name of the variables declared in the method_bt section. 13. Names of the methods called in try-block. 14. Names of the methods called in method_bt section.
Numerical Features	1.Size of Try Block [SLOC](P,T) 2.Size of Method_BT[SLOC](P,M) 3.Log Count Try Block(P,T) 4.Log Count in Method_BT(P,M) 5.Count of Operators in Try Block(P,T) 6.Count of Operators in Method_BT(P,M) 7.Variable Declaration Count in Try Block(P,T) 8.Variable Declaration Count in Method_BT(P,M) 9.Method Call Count in Try Block(P,T) 10.Method Call Count in Method_BT(P,M) 11.Method Parameter Count(P,O) 12.IF Count in Try Block(P,T) 13.IF Count in Method_BT(P,M)	1. SLOC of try-block. 2. SLOC of method_bt section. 3. Count of log statements in try-block. 4. Count of log statements in method_bt section. 5. Count of arithmetic operators in try-block. 6. Count of operators in method_bt section. 7. Count of variables declared in try-block. 8. Count of variables declared in method_bt section. 9. Count of methods called in try-block. 10. Count of methods called in method_bt section. 11. Count of parameters in containing method. 12. Count of if-statements in try-block. 13. Count of if-statements in method_bt section.
Boolean Features	1.Previous Catch Blocks(P,T) 2.Logged Previous Catch Blocks (P,T) 3.Method have Parameter (P, O) 4.Logged Try Block(P,T) 5.Logged Method_BT(P,M) 6.IF in Try(P,T) 7.IF in Method_BT(P,M) 8.Throw/Throws in Try Block(N,T) 9.Throw/Throws in Catch Block(N,T) 10.Throw/Throws in Method_BT(N,M) 11.Return in Try Block(N,T) 12.Return in Catch Block(N,T) 13.Return in Method_BT(N,M) 14.Assert in Try Block(N,T) 15.Assert in Catch Block(N,T) 16.Assert in Method_BT(N,M) 17.Thread.Sleep in Try Block(N,T) 18.Interrupted Exception Type(N,T) 19.Exception Object "Ignore" in Catch(N,T)	1. Previous catch-blocks are present. 2. Previous catch-blocks have any log statement. 3. Containing method has parameter. 4. Try-block has log statement. 5. Method_bt section has log statement. 6. Try-block has if-statement. 7. Method_bt section has if-statement. 8. Throw/throws statement present in the try-block. 9. Throw/Throws statement present in catch-block. 10. Throw/Throws statement present in the method_bt section. 11. 'Return' statement present in the try-block. 12. 'Return' statement present in the catch-block. 13. 'Return' statement present in the method_bt section. 14. 'Assert' statement present in try-block. 15. 'Assert' statement present in the catch-block. 16. 'Assert' statement present in the method_bt section. 17. 'thread.sleep' method called in try-block. 18. Catch-block exception types is 'InterruptedException'. 19. Exception class object name is 'ignore' in catch-block.
Total Features =	Textual (14) + Numeric (13)+ Boolean(19) =46 Feature	

CONCLUSION AND FUTURE WORK

Source code logging is an important software development practice, and tools and techniques that can help software developers make optimal and strategic logging decisions can be beneficial. Analysis of logged and nonlogged code constructs can provide useful insights to improve current logging prediction tools. In this chapter, the authors performed statistical and content-based analysis of source code files and catch-blocks from three large open-source Java projects. They answered several research questions in this chapter. Following are the main research findings of this work:

- Fewer files consist of logging statements.
- Source code files with logging statements have a much larger average SLOC compared to those without logging statements.
- There is a positive correlation between the SLOC of logged files and their respective log statement counts.
- Try-blocks associated with logged catch-blocks have greater complexity than that of nonlogged catch-blocks for the Apache Tomcat and Hadoop projects.
- Some exception types contribute greatly to total catch-blocks, whereas there is little or no contribution in total logged catch-blocks.
- The logging ratio of an exception type is project specific.
- The LDA-based topic modeling technique is effective in discovering topics of logged and nonlogged code constructs.

Authors proposed a machine leaning based model proposed for catch-blocks logging prediction. Machine learning based model is found to be effective in catch-blocks logging prediction and give the highest F1-score of 84.32% on CloudStack project .

The authors think that this work provides a future direction for three lines of work: *statistical analysis, content-based analysis, and machine leanring based logging prediction model.* Statistical analysis provides the ability to explore more deeply the features of logged code constructs. In this work, the authors analyzed a complexity metric (SLOC, operator count, etc.) with respect to logged and nonlogged code constructs. However, many other source code metrics, such as inheritance depth, and object-oriented metrics need to be evaluated for deeper analysis of logged and nonlogged files. Content-based research needs more exploration in terms of the topics present in the logged and nonlogged code constructs. In this work, the authors used LDA for topic modeling, and the initial results are encouraging. However, deeper analysis of code constructs with respect to multiple semantic techniques such as LDA and Latent Semantic Indexing (LSI) is required for in-depth analysis of the topics present in logged and nonlogged code constructs. In this work, authors propose a machine learning model based on static features from the source code for catch-blocks logging prediction. The proposed model can be extended for other type of code constructs such as if-blocks, while-loop, switch-case.

THREATS TO VALIDITY

- **Number and Type of Project:** The authors selected Apache Tomcat, CloudStack, and Hadoop projects for the study. All three projects are open-source, Java-based projects. Other types of projects, such as closed source, or projects written in other languages (e.g., C#, Python) need to be evaluated. Overall, the authors cannot draw any general conclusion that is applicable to all software logging. They believe that this study provides insight about logging practices of open-source, Java-based projects.

- **Quality of Ground Truth:** The authors assumed that logging statements inserted by software developers of Apache Tomcat, CloudStack, and Hadoop project are optimal. There is the possibility of errors or nonoptimal logging in the code by the developers, which can affect the results of the study. However, all three projects are long lived and are actively maintained; hence it is safe to assume that most of the code constructs have good (if not optimal) logging. The authors used 26 regular expressions to extract the logging statements from the source code. Manual analysis reveals that all the logging statements were extracted (to the best of the authors' knowledge). However, there is still a possibility that the regular expressions missed some types of logging statements in the source code.

- **Machine Learning Model Evaluation:** At the time of evaluating the performance of *LogOpt* model, authors removed the three tool generated files from the dataset. Authors believe that using data from tool generated files for training as well as for prediction can cause bias in the performance of model.

REFERENCES

Apache Cloudstack. (n.d.). Retrieved March 18, 2016, from https://cloudstack.apache.org/downloads.html

Apache Tomcat. (n.d.). Retrieved March 16, 2016, from https://tomcat.apache.org/download-80.cgi

Barua, A., Thomas, S. W., & Hassan, A. E. (2014). What are developers talking about? an analysis of topics and trends in stack overflow. *Empirical Software Engineering*, *19*(3), 619–654. doi:10.1007/s10664-012-9231-y

Beaton, W. (n.d.). *Eclipse Corner Article*. Retrieved March 12, 2016, from https://www.eclipse.org/articles/article.php?file=Article-JavaCodeManipulation

Blei, D. M., Ng, A. Y., & Jordan, M. I. (2003). Latent dirichlet allocation. *The Journal of Machine Learning Research, 3*, 993-1022.

Chen, B., & Jiang, Z. M. J. (2016). Characterizing logging practices in Java-based open source software projects–a replication study in Apache Software Foundation. *Empirical Software Engineering*, 1–45.

Crossley, A., & Shapira, Y. (n.d.). *Apache Tomcat 7*. Retrieved March 20, 2016, from https://tomcat. apache.org/tomcat-7.0-doc/logging.html

Ding, R., Zhou, H., Lou, J. G., Zhang, H., Lin, Q., Fu, Q., & Xie, T. et al. (2015, July). Log2: A Cost-Aware Logging Mechanism for Performance Diagnosis. *USENIX Annual Technical Conference*, 139-150.

Fu, Q., Lou, J. G., Wang, Y., & Li, J. (2009, December). Execution anomaly detection in distributed systems through unstructured log analysis. In *2009 ninth IEEE international conference on data mining* (pp. 149-158). IEEE. doi:10.1109/ICDM.2009.60

Fu, Q., Zhu, J., Hu, W., Lou, J. G., Ding, R., Lin, Q., . . . Xie, T. (2014, May). Where do developers log? an empirical study on logging practices in industry. In *Companion Proceedings of the 36th International Conference on Software Engineering* (pp. 24-33). ACM.

Gensim: Topic modelling for humans. (n.d.). Retrieved March 19, 2016, from https://radimrehurek.com/ gensim/models/ldamodel.html

Goers, R., Gregory, G., & Deboy, S. (n.d.). *Log4j – Log4j 2 Guide - Apache Log4j 2*. Retrieved October 23, 2015, from http://logging.apache.org/log4j/2.x/

Han, J., Pei, J., & Kamber, M. (2011). *Data mining: concepts and techniques*. Elsevier.

Kabinna, S., Bezemer, C. P., Hassan, A. E., & Shang, W. (2016, March). Examining the Stability of Logging Statements. *Proceedings of the 23rd IEEE International Conference on Software Analysis, Evolution, and Reengineering (SANER)*.

Kabinna, S., Bezemer, C. P., Shang, W., & Hassan, A. E. (2016b, May). Logging library migrations: a case study for the apache software foundation projects. In *Proceedings of the 13th International Conference on Mining Software Repositories* (pp. 154-164). ACM. doi:10.1145/2901739.2901769

Kim, L. (2015). *10 Most Popular Programming Languages Today*. Retrieved March 20, 2016, from http://www.inc.com/larry-kim/10-most-popular-programming-languages-today.htm

Kosinski, K. (2013, February). *Advanced CloudStack Troubleshooting using Log Analysis - a session at ApacheCon North America 2013*. Retrieved March 19, 2016, from http://lanyrd.com/2013/apachecon/ scbrfk/

Krill, P. (2015). *Java regains spot as most popular language in developer index*. Retrieved March 23, 2016, from http://www.infoworld.com/article/2909894/application-development/java-back-at-1-in-language-popularity-assessment.html

Lal, S., Sardana, N., & Sureka, A. (2015). Two Level Empirical Study of Logging Statements in Open Source Java Projects. *International Journal of Open Source Software and Processes*, 6(1), 49–73. doi:10.4018/IJOSSP.2015010104

Lal, S., & Sureka, A. (2016, February). LogOpt: Static Feature Extraction from Source Code for Automated Catch Block Logging Prediction. In *Proceedings of the 9th India Software Engineering Conference* (pp. 151-155). ACM. doi:10.1145/2856636.2856637

Lal, S., Sardana, N., & Sureka, A. (2016, June). LogOptPlus: Learning to Optimize Logging in Catch and If Programming Constructs. In *Proceedings of 40th Annual Computer Software and Applications Conference* (pp. 215-220). IEEE. doi:10.1109/COMPSAC.2016.149

Lal, S., Sardana, N., & Sureka, A. (2016b). Improving Logging Prediction on Imbalanced Datasets: A Case Study on Open Source Java Projects. *International Journal of Open Source Software and Processes*, *7*(2), 43–71. doi:10.4018/IJOSSP.2016040103

Lal, S., Sardana, N., & Sureka, A. (2017a). ECLogger: Cross-Project Catch-Block Logging Prediction Using Ensemble of Classifiers. *e-Informatica. Software Engineering Journal*, *11*(1), 9–40.

Lal, S., Sardana, N., & Sureka, A. (2017b). Three-level learning for improving cross-project logging prediction for if-blocks. *Journal of King Saud University-Computer and Information Sciences*. (in press)

Li, H., Shang, W., & Hassan, A. E. (2016). Which log level should developers choose for a new logging statement. *Empirical Software Engineering*, 1–33.

Li, H., Shang, W., Zou, Y., & Hassan, A. E. (2016b). Towards just-in-time suggestions for log changes. *Empirical Software Engineering*, 1–35.

LocMetrics. (n.d.). Retrieved March 19, 2016, from http://www.locmetrics.com/

Mariani, L., & Pastore, F. (2008, November). Automated identification of failure causes in system logs. In *Software Reliability Engineering, 2008. ISSRE 2008. 19th International Symposium on* (pp. 117-126). IEEE. doi:10.1109/ISSRE.2008.48

Maskeri, G., Sarkar, S., & Heafield, K. (2008, February). Mining business topics in source code using latent dirichlet allocation. In *Proceedings of the 1st India software engineering conference* (pp. 113-120). ACM. doi:10.1145/1342211.1342234

Nagaraj, K., Killian, C., & Neville, J. (2012). Structured comparative analysis of systems logs to diagnose performance problems. *9th USENIX Symposium on Networked Systems Design and Implementation (NSDI 12)*, 353-366.

Natural Language Toolkit. (n.d.). Retrieved March 19, 2016, from http://www.nltk.org/

Pagano, D., & Maalej, W. (2013). How do open source communities blog? *Empirical Software Engineering*, *18*(6), 1090–1124. doi:10.1007/s10664-012-9211-2

Page, B. W. (n.d.). *Welcome to Apache Hadoop!* Retrieved March 18, 2016, from http://hadoop.apache.org/#DownloadHadoop

Rabkin, A., & Katz, R. H. (2010, November). Chukwa: A System for Reliable Large-Scale Log Collection. LISA, 10, 1-15.

Sharma, B., Chudnovsky, V., Hellerstein, J. L., Rifaat, R., & Das, C. R. (2011, October). Modeling and synthesizing task placement constraints in Google compute clusters. In *Proceedings of the 2nd ACM Symposium on Cloud Computing* (p. 3). ACM. doi:10.1145/2038916.2038919

Shang, W., Nagappan, M., & Hassan, A. E. (2015). Studying the relationship between logging characteristics and the code quality of platform software. *Empirical Software Engineering, 20*(1), 1–27. doi:10.1007/s10664-013-9274-8

Sigelman, B. H., Barroso, L. A., Burrows, M., Stephenson, P., Plakal, M., Beaver, D., . . . Shanbhag, C. (2010). Dapper, a large-scale distributed systems tracing infrastructure. Technical report, Google, Inc.

Team, C. D. (n.d.). *Apache Commons Logging - Overview*. Retrieved March 18, 2016, from https://commons.apache.org/proper/commons-logging/

Thomas, S. W., Adams, B., Hassan, A. E., & Blostein, D. (2014). Studying software evolution using topic models. *Science of Computer Programming, 80*, 457–479. doi:10.1016/j.scico.2012.08.003

Thwin, M. M. T., & Quah, T. S. (2005). Application of neural networks for software quality prediction using object-oriented metrics. *Journal of Systems and Software, 76*(2), 147–156. doi:10.1016/j.jss.2004.05.001

Tian, K., Revelle, M., & Poshyvanyk, D. (2009, May). Using latent dirichlet allocation for automatic categorization of software. In *Mining Software Repositories, 2009. MSR'09. 6th IEEE International Working Conference on* (pp. 163-166). IEEE. doi:10.1109/MSR.2009.5069496

Virtual Machinery - Sidebar 2 - The Halstead Metrics. (n.d.). Retrieved March 19, 2016, from http://www.virtualmachinery.com/sidebar2.htm

Welcome to Statistics How To! (n.d.). Retrieved March 19, 2016, from http://www.statisticshowto.com/

Xu, W., Huang, L., Fox, A., Patterson, D., & Jordan, M. I. (2009, October). Detecting large-scale system problems by mining console logs. In *Proceedings of the ACM SIGOPS 22nd symposium on Operating systems principles* (pp. 117-132). ACM. doi:10.1145/1629575.1629587

Yuan, D., Mai, H., Xiong, W., Tan, L., Zhou, Y., & Pasupathy, S. (2010, March). SherLog: error diagnosis by connecting clues from run-time logs. In ACM SIGARCH computer architecture news (Vol. 38, No. 1, pp. 143-154). ACM. doi:10.1145/1736020.1736038

Yuan, D., Park, S., Huang, P., Liu, Y., Lee, M. M., Tang, X., & Savage, S. et al. (2012). Be conservative: enhancing failure diagnosis with proactive logging. *10th USENIX Symposium on Operating Systems Design and Implementation*, 293-306.

Yuan, D., Park, S., & Zhou, Y. (2012b, June). Characterizing logging practices in open-source software. In *Proceedings of the 34th International Conference on Software Engineering* (pp. 102-112). IEEE Press.

Yuan, D., Zheng, J., Park, S., Zhou, Y., & Savage, S. (2012c). Improving software diagnosability via log enhancement. *ACM Transactions on Computer Systems, 30*(1), 4. doi:10.1145/2110356.2110360

Zhu, J., He, P., Fu, Q., Zhang, H., Lyu, M. R., & Zhang, D. (2015, May). Learning to log: Helping developers make informed logging decisions. In *Software Engineering (ICSE), 2015 IEEE/ACM 37th IEEE International Conference on* (Vol. 1, pp. 415-425). IEEE.

Zimmermann, T., Nagappan, N., Gall, H., Giger, E., & Murphy, B. (2009, August). Cross-project defect prediction: a large scale experiment on data vs. domain vs. process. In *Proceedings of the the 7th joint meeting of the European software engineering conference and the ACM SIGSOFT symposium on The foundations of software engineering* (pp. 91-100). ACM. doi:10.1145/1595696.1595713

Chapter 4
Open Source Projects Recommendation on GitHub

Mohamed Guendouz
Dr. Moulay Tahar University of Saïda, Algeria

Abdelmalek Amine
Dr. Moulay Tahar University of Saïda, Algeria

Reda Mohamed Hamou
Dr. Moulay Tahar University of Saïda, Algeria

ABSTRACT

This chapter discusses the design and the implementation of a recommender system for open source projects on GitHub using the collaborative-filtering approach. Having such a system can be helpful for many developers, especially those who search for a particular project based on their interests. It can also reduce searching time and make search results more relevant. The system presented in this chapter was evaluated on a real-world dataset and using various evaluation metrics. Results obtained from these experiments are very promising. The authors found that their recommender system can reach better precision and recall accuracy.

INTRODUCTION

GitHub is a very popular crowdfunding software development platform, a social coding platform and a web based Git repository hosting service, allowing anyone to participate in open source project documentation, design, coding and testing in a social way. In order to participate in these activities, a developer must create an account, allowing him to share his own projects, forking other's projects and following other developers, Figure 1 shows a sample GitHub profile.

One of the most helpful implemented features on GitHub is the fork feature, which means making a full copy of the repository of the original project. Forking a repository allows the developer to freely experiment with the project without affecting the original copy, forking is considered as the first task

DOI: 10.4018/978-1-5225-5314-4.ch004

Figure 1. Example of a GitHub profile page

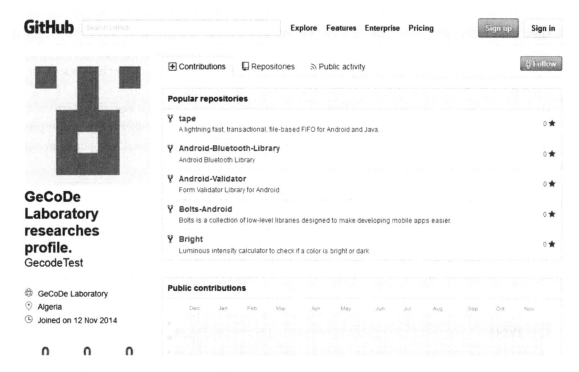

to do in order to make contributions to an existing project. Another implemented feature is the Star feature, when a developer gives a star to a repository it means that he is interested in this project. For example, a developer who is interested in mobile game development may give stars to some 2d mobile game libraries like: AndEngine, LibGDX, cocos1d-x and others.

Developers are always searching for good open source projects to make project prototypes or to enhance their own software projects with new features, GitHub provides them a search functionality to do this manually without any automatic recommendations provided, Figure 2 shows a sample search page. However, searching for suitable repositories can be a difficult task and may take a long time, it can also interpret the development process of a project, for that reason the existence of an automatic recommender system for GitHub repositories may be very helpful for developers to reduce search time and make search results more relevant and organized, these are the main benefits of such a system for all developers. However, developers may benefit differently from it according to their profile type and their professional skills, for instance: a professional developer is probably searching for new programming challenges or even for business opportunities, while a beginner is probably looking for good stuff to learn something new or to improve its skills, or he is simply searching for repositories to work on. The issue that arises in these cases is how we can find a relevant content on GitHub and recommend it to a user.

In this paper, the authors present a new system for recommending relevant GitHub repositories for developers; they use a collaborative-filtering approach and they model the user behaviors as a User-Item matrix so they can apply different recommendation methods like calculating similarities between users (developers) and items (repositories) and so on. Then, the authors evaluate their recommender system on a real data set using well-known evaluation metrics, the design and the implementation of this system will be discussed in detail in later sections.

The main contributions of the authors in this paper are as follows:

- They address a new problem which is the recommendation of code to developers, they study the problem of finding and recommending relevant repositories on GitHub website.
- They propose a new recommender system based on collaborative filtering techniques to recommend relevant repositories for developers on the GitHub website.
- They investigate the performance of their system by testing it on a real dataset; they perform technical experiments using well-known metrics to show the effectiveness of their proposed approach.
- They develop a small prototype to show system functionalities and how developers can benefit from it.

The outline of this paper is given as follows: Section 2 presents related work done in the field of collaborative-filtering and content –based techniques and shows some related work on GitHub. Section 3 defines the problem and illustrates a use case example. In section 4 the authors present their system approach and its architecture. Section 5 details the used data set. Section 6 illustrates the obtained results from our system evaluation. Finally, section 7 concludes this paper with conclusions and some future works.

Related Work

In this section the authors discuss some of the related research works in both collaborative-filtering approaches and GitHub recommender systems and data analysis.

Figure 2. Sample search results on GitHub

Collaborative-Filtering Recommender Systems

Collaborative-Filtering (CF) (Goldberg et al., 1992) approaches are a set of methods and algorithms used in recommender systems design and implementation, they are known for being simple to implement and also for their high accuracy of recommendation results.

CF techniques are grouped into three subcategories; Memory-Based, Model-Based and Hybrid techniques. Memory-based CF techniques use previous rating data for calculating similarities between users or items to make recommendations according to those calculated similarity values. In these techniques, most of the work is in calculating similarities, several similarity calculation algorithms were proposed in literature, among them, the Correlation-Based Similarity (Resnick et al., 1994) (Sarwar et al., 2001), Vector Cosine-Based Similarity (Sarwar et al., 2000), Conditional probability-based similarity (Deshpande & Karypis, 2004). However Memory-Based CF techniques present several limitations like data sparsity, to overcome these limitations, Model-Based CF techniques (Breese et al., 1998) have been proposed. Model-Based CF techniques use rating data to learn a model for predicting user rating, machine learning and data mining methods are used for learning these models, several techniques have been proposed, including, Bayesian Belief nets (BNs) CF models (Breese et al., 1998) (Su & Khoshgoftaar, 2006), Clustering CF models (Hofmann, 2004), and Latent Semantic CF models (Shani et al., 2002).

Content-Based Recommender Systems

Content-Based filtering recommendation approaches are based on a description of the item and a profile of user's preference, these algorithms analyze a set of documents and/or descriptions of items previously rated by a user, and build a model or profile of user interests based on the features of the objects rated by that user. Content-based recommender systems use keywords to represent both the item descriptions and user profiles, then, the attributes of the user profile are matched against the attributes of an item's description by measuring a similarity between them, The higher this similarity, the higher the chance that the item is recommended. Generally, methods from data mining and machine learning fields are used to represent items and build models, for example: the TF-IDF(Term frequency- inverse document frequency) is used to represent items from textual reviews, a user's review is analyzed by this method to extract pertinent keywords from it. For more details about these type of recommender systems, (Pazzani & Billsus, 2007) paper presents a good overview and literature review of content-based recommender systems.

GitHub Data Analysis and Its Recommender Systems

In this subsection the authors present some related research works that studied GitHub website, including the analysis of its data and some research papers interested in creating recommender systems for different GitHub functionalities.

In (Zhang et al., 2014), authors have studied different user behaviors on GitHub like forking, watching, commenting on issues, pull-requesting and membership to answer some research questions, the most important question for the authors of this paper was: "What types of user behavior data are suitable for recommending relevant projects?", after conducting several experiments on real data gathered from GitHub, they found that among all user behaviors, the Forking is suitable for recommending relevant projects. This result is very helpful to the authors; in fact they use this forking behavior as a developer rating for repositories in a form of 0/1 data.

Another problem in GitHub is the manual assignment of reviewers for pull-requests (PRs), this task may take time, this led authors in (Yu et al., 2014) to propose a reviewer recommender system for incoming pull-requests (PRs), in their approach they combined information retrieval and social networks analyses by taking advantages of the textual semantic of PRs, they implemented an online system for testing their approach to see how it can help other developers in the assignment of PRs reviewers, experiment results of their approach on a real dataset using Top-N recommendations showed good results.

On the other hand, several works were interested in the analysis of GitHub data, like analyzing the network structure of developer's distribution (Thung et al., 2013), visualization of GitHub data (Heller et al., 2011), in (Guzman et al., 2014) authors studied developer's comments on repositories commits.

PROBLEM DEFINITION AND USES CASES

This section defines formally the problem addressed in this paper and shows a use case of such a solution with an illustrative example.

Problem Definition

Let D a set of developers and R a set of repositories, the goal is to recommend repositories that would be interesting to developers. Formally, a recommendation algorithm takes sets D and R and learns a function f such that:

$$f : D \times R \to B$$

In other words, the function assigns a Boolean value to each developer-repository pair $\left(d, r\right)$, where this value indicates if developer d is interested in repository r.

In this paper we consider $M = \left\{m_{ij}\right\}$ the user-item matrix and $m_{ij} \in \left\{0,1\right\}$, where $m_{ij} = 1$ means that developer i is already interested in repository j while $m_{ij} = 0$ means that the developer is probably not interested in the repository or does not know about it. The task is to find repositories that would interest a developer and that are not watched by him/her.

Use Case

The authors give here an example to illustrate the issues involved in this paper. Consider a developer identified by "gueno" who is interested in mobile development, he is already interested in these repositories: (Libgdx, ask, bourbon, fastadapter, icepick), we consider also that there is six developers who are actually in the website. Table 1 shows a dataset which contains the developers and their preferred repositories including developer "gueno". The goal is to recommend repositories for "gueno" based on this dataset.

Table 1. Example dataset

Developer	Repositories
gueno	Libgdx, ask, bourbon, fastadapter, icepick
marc	Libgdx, fastadapter, icepick, ExoMedia, FileDownloader
steve	Libgdx, fastadapter, FileDownloader, joda-time-android
ninja	bourbon, fastadapter,
tim	ask, joda-time-android
hanna	icepick, FileDownloader, joda-time-android
gosling	icepick, bourbon, ExoMedia, FileDownloader

The authors propose a collaborative-filtering technique to deal with this problem. First, they create the user-item matrix M_{ij} from the information reported in Table 1, the matrix M_{ij} is shown in Table 2. Second, they calculate the similarity between developer "gueno" and every developer in the dataset using the matrix from Table 2, after calculation they sort the developers according to their similarities, the new set of developers is as follows:

marc(3), steve(2), gosling(2), ninja(2), hanna(1), tim(1).

From this list we can say that the most similar developer to "gueno" is "marc" with 3 common repositories, and then come developers: "steve", "gosling" and "ninja" with 2 common repositories. "hanna" and "tim" are not similar to "gueno" since they share only 1 from 8 repository with him. The authors conclude that "marc", "steve" and "gosling" are the most similar developers to "gueno", the next step consists of choosing repositories from common ones between them and recommend them to "gueno". The common repositories between "marc", "steve" and "gosling" are: "FileDownloader" and "ExoMedia", so these two repositories will be recommended to "gueno" with the following sorted list:

1.   FileDownloader
2.   ExoMedia

In this paper the authors propose to automate the above tasks by using collaborative-filtering techniques to calculate similarities between developers and to find the relevant repositories for a developer.

Table 2. User-Item matrix M

User/Item	Libgdx	ask	bourbon	fastadapter	icepick	ExoMedia	FileDownloader	joda-time-android
gueno	1	1	1	1	1	0	0	0
marc	1	0	0	1	1	1	1	0
steve	1	0	0	1	0	0	1	1
ninja	0	0	1	1	0	0	0	0
tim	0	1	0	0	0	0	0	1
hanna	0	0	0	0	1	0	1	1
gosling	0	0	1	0	1	1	1	0

PROPOSED APPROACH

This section describes in detail the design and the implementation of our recommender system; it also presents some of the background and methodologies used in recommender systems.

System Architecture

Our goal in this paper is to create a system capable of automatically recommending relevant GitHub repositories for developers, for that the authors propose a simple architecture suitable for this task, Figure 3. Illustrates it.

Firstly, data from GitHub is processed so the authors can generate the user-item matrix, this data is saved in a form of JSON (JavaScript Object Notation), the authors start by extracting forks for each repository in the database, the result of this operation is a list of key-value pairs, key is a user ID and value is the list of forked repositories IDs by this same user. Secondly, they generate the user-item matrix from these pairs of data; the authors will illustrate this task in detail in the following subsection.

The next step consists of making recommendations for developers using this generated user-item matrix. A recommender system is a system that can predict automatically user ratings for an item or more, or in the other case, can propose to him a ranked list of items. In this paper the authors are interested in this second particular case; the system finds a ranked list of relevant repositories for a developer.

Finally, the last step consists of evaluating our recommender system, the evaluation metrics will be discussed later.

User-Item Matrix Model

In collaborative-filtering techniques, a user-item matrix is often given where each entry is an unknown value or a rating assigned by a user to an item.

Figure 3. The architecture of our system

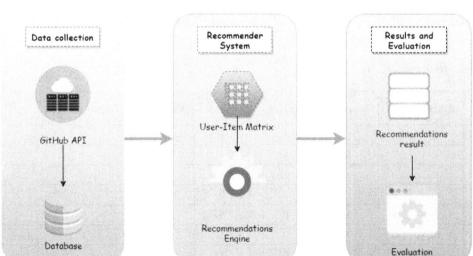

In this paper the authors choose to model user ratings in the user-item matrix as forking a repository, which means if a developer is already forking a repository, his rating value for it is 1, otherwise it is 0 (unknown rating), Table 3 is an example of a user-item matrix used by our system. Where $D_1 \dots D_4$ represent developers and $R_1 \dots R_3$ represent repositories.

Definition 1: Let $D = \left\{ d_1 \cdots d_n \right\}$ A set of all developers and $R = \left\{ r_1 \cdots r_m \right\}$ a set of all repositories, the user-item matrix or developer-repository matrix is:

$$M_{n \times m} \tag{1}$$

where

$$M_{i,j} = \begin{cases} 1, & \textit{if } d_i \textit{ forks } r_j; \\ 0, & \textit{otherwise.} \end{cases} \tag{2}$$

Recommendations Method

In this paper, a memory-based collaborative-filtering technique is used since our goal is to recommend a list of ranked repositories to a developer the authors use the Top-N recommendation method.

In Top-N recommendations, the task is to recommend a list of ranked items that will interest the user. That task does not exist in the actual GitHub website.

In order to compute these recommendations, the Top-N recommendation method analyzes the user-item matrix to find relations between users or items. There are two sub-methods, User-Based and Item-Based Top-N recommendation, in this paper the Item-Based technique (Breese et al., 1998) is used.

Item-Based Top-N Recommendation Algorithm

In this subsection the authors will describe how Item-Based Top-N recommendation algorithm works, in the contrary of user-based technique, which first finds similar users to a user *u* and then combines their ratings for an item *i* to predict the user *u* rating for that item, item-based technique performs collaborative filtering directly by finding the most similar items by calculating similarity between them, different steps of this algorithm are detailed as follows:

Table 3. Simple example of User-Item Matrix

User/Repository	R_1	R_2	R_3
D_1	1	1	0
D_2	0	1	0
D_3	1	0	0
D_4	0	0	1

Step 1: For each repository, the algorithm computes the *k* most similar repositories for it, this *k* number is also known as number of neighbors, the similarities are computed using a similarity calculation method; the authors will discuss some of them later.

Step 2: The algorithm removes the set *R* from the *k* most similar repositories; *R* is the set of already forked repositories, this means removing every similar repository that is already forked by the user. The result will be saved in the set *U*.

Step 3: Finally, the algorithm computes the similarity between each repository of the set *U* and the set *R*, this means calculating similarities between the user forked repositories and the *k* most similar ones for them, the result will be a list of repositories classed decreasingly according to their similarities.

Similarity Calculation

There are several mathematical formulas and algorithms to calculate similarities between two items. However they are not suitable for our case (binary ratings, 1 or 0), they are designed for five-star ratings where the rating vary between 0 and 5, in this paper the authors use a similarity method suitable for this type of rating, it is the Jaccard similarity coefficient (Lipkus, 1999) (Levandowsky & Winter, 1971).

The Jaccard similarity coefficient or the Jaccard index, is a measure for comparing similarity and diversity between sets (items or users), it is defined as the size of the intersection divided by the size of the union of the two sets, given two items *i* and *j*, the Jaccard similarity coefficient between them is denoted by *sim(i,j)*, given by:

$$\text{sim}(i, j) = J = \frac{R_{11}}{R_{01} + R_{10} + R_{11}} \tag{3}$$

where:

R_{11} represents the number of times the both items *i* and *j* have received a rating value of 1.

R_{01} represents the number of times the item *i* has received a rating value of 0 and the item *j* has received a rating value of 1.

R_{10} represents the number of times the item *i* has received a rating value of 1 and the item *j* has received a rating value of 0.

Since that our approach uses a 0/1 raring to represent user ratings for repositories, the Jaccard similarity coefficient is the most suitable similarity calculation method for our system, it is also simple and easy to implement.

DATA SET

The data set used in this paper is the Mining Software Repositories Challenge 2014 data set (MSR2014), this dataset was created especially for this challenge, it includes data from the top-10 starred software projects for the top programming languages on GitHub, which gives 90 projects and their forks. For each project, all data have been retrieved including issues, pull requests, organizations, followers, stars and labels.

In this paper, the authors use the version of MSR2014 from the GHTorrent project (Gousios, 2013; Gousios et al., 2014). Table 4 summarizes some statistical information about the data set, Figure 4. shows the distribution of programming languages over projects in the dataset.

EXPERIMENT RESULTS

In this section the authors present the experimental results taken from the evaluation of their system on a real data set presented earlier in this paper, they start by giving some evaluation metrics, then they describe the experimental setup, finally they discuss results obtained from these experiments.

Table 4. Statistical information about the data set

Type of Data	Count
Users	465,198
Repositories	1,204
Issues	126,308
Pull Requests	79,359
Commits	601,080

Figure 4. Language distributions over projects

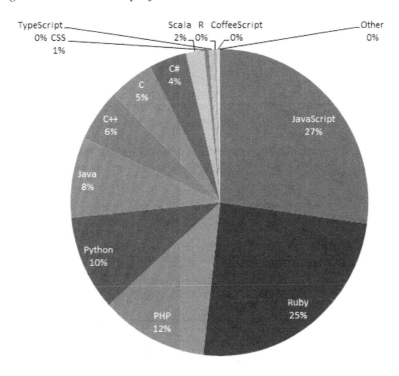

Evaluation Metrics

In this paper, the authors choose several evaluation metrics like MAE, Recall, Precision and F-Measure (Karypis, 2000).

Recall, Precision and F-Measure.

These three metrics are widely used in literature to evaluate recommender systems in term of relevancy. Based on the selection of items for recommendations and their relevancy, we can have four types of items outlined in Table 5. Given this table, we can define measures that use relevant information provided by users.

Precision is a measure; it defines the fraction of relevant items among recommended items:

$$P = \frac{N_{rs}}{N_s} \tag{4}$$

Recall provides the probability of selecting a relevant item for the recommendation:

$$R = \frac{N_{rs}}{N_r} \tag{5}$$

When we want to measure both of these two evaluations, we can combine both precision and recall by taking their harmonic mean in the F-measure:

$$F_1 = \frac{2 \times P \times R}{P + R} \tag{6}$$

Mean Absolute Error (MAE)

Mean Absolute Error (MAE) computes the average absolute difference between the true ratings and the predicted ratings, MAE calculation formula is given by:

Table 5. Partitioning of items with respect to their selection for recommendation and their relevancy

	Selected	Not Selected	Total
Relevant	N_{rs}	N_{rn}	N_r
Irrelevant	N_{is}	N_{in}	N_i
Total	N_s	N_n	N

$$MAE = \frac{\sum_{ij} \left| \hat{r}_{ij} - r_{ij} \right|}{n} \qquad (7)$$

where n is the number of predicted ratings, $\hat{r}_{ij}$ is the predicted rating, and r_{ij} is the true rating.

Experiment Setup

For the implementation of our system, the authors used Java on a Linux machine (Ubuntu 14.04), with the following performances: Intel Core I3 Processor, 8 GB DDR3 RAM.

For the evaluation, the authors used the k-fold cross validation method; in this paper k is chosen to be 10.

In K-fold cross validation the data set is divided randomly into K (almost) equal-sized non-overlapping parts, called the folds. Finally, the performance of the model is the average of the k performances.

Results and Discussions

In this subsection, results from evaluation of our system are discussed and summarized in different formats, tables and graphic images, to show obtained results.

In the first experiment, our goal is to see the effect of the number of neighbors on recommendation results, in this experiment the authors fixed the number n of Top-N recommendations to the number of total returned items, this means that all recommended repositories will be returned as recommendations result, and the number of neighbors k was varied. Figure 4. Shows obtained results.

Figure 4. Shows that the number of neighbors can affect slightly the mean absolute error when it is lower than 40, after that, when the number of neighbors is higher than 40, the mean absolute error

Figure 5. The effectiveness of the number of neighbors on mean absolute error

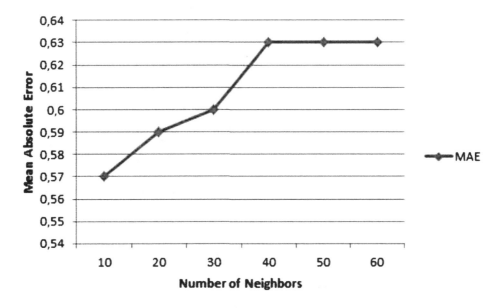

stabilizes at the value of 0.63. This means that our system can avoid many errors while recommending repositories for developers.

A second experiment was performed, this time to see the effect of the number of *N* recommendations on the values of precision and recall; the results of this experiment are illustrated by Figure 5.

Figure 5. Clearly exhibits the overall performance of the authors approach. They observe that the values of precision and recall are stable for all values of *N*, the precision reaches its highest value at *N* equal to 15, and this means that all returned items (recommended repositories) are approximately all relevant to the user. Always from this graph, the authors observe that the recall is stable at the value of 0.6 at almost values of *N*, this means that the probability of selecting relevant repositories for recommendations is higher.

From these results, the authors can calculate F-Measure, they found it stable at the value of 0.77 at all values of *N*, and this means that the recommendation results are very accurate.

From these evaluation results, the authors can say that their recommender system has good accuracy of recommendations; this makes it very helpful for GitHub developers to search for suitable repositories that correspond to their needs. However, no final conclusion will be given until deploying this recommender system concretely, so they can really see how it will respond to developer's needs.

The authors developed also a website prototype in which they have implemented their proposed solution, Figure 7 shows a screenshot of this proposed prototype taken from a developer profile. The list in the left side provides links to the various functionalities proposed by the system, as shown in the figure a developer may see his/her top repositories, explore others or recommend a repository to friend. The list in the right side show the top recommended repositories for the developer who are logged, it provides for each recommended repository the following information:

- The index: represents the order of the repository in the list.
- The name: the name of the repository.

Figure 6. The effectiveness of the number of recommendations

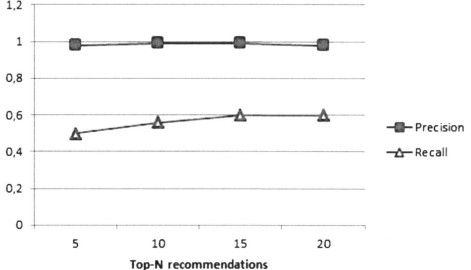

Figure 7. Screenshot of the proposed prototype

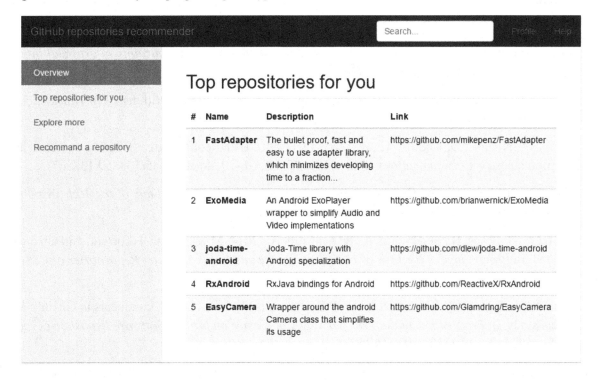

- The description: the description of the repository, basic information about it.
- The link: the URL link to the repository on GitHub.

CONCLUSION AND FUTURE WORKS

In this paper, the authors have presented a new recommender system for GitHub repositories based on the collaborative-filtering techniques. First, some related works on this domain have been discussed, then, the architecture of the system was given, and finally, a set of experiments have been done in order to evaluate the results of our recommender system.

Experimental results on a real data set collected from the GitHub website, using well known metrics and a 10-fold cross validation method, show that our system can help developers in searching for appropriate open source projects. The mean absolute error metric of our system has shown very encouraging results. Precision and recall values are also accurate.

As future works, the authors plan to test other features of GitHub in recommending repositories like: watch, star and comment; they plan to combine all these features in only one rating. The authors plan also to evaluate other collaborative-filtering techniques especially the model-based ones. Finally, the authors prepare to do a comparative study between different techniques of model representation and recommendation algorithms to see their effectiveness.

REFERENCES

Breese, J. S., Heckerman, D., & Kadie, C. (1998, July). Empirical analysis of predictive algorithms for collaborative filtering. In *Proceedings of the Fourteenth conference on Uncertainty in artificial intelligence* (pp. 43-52). Morgan Kaufmann Publishers Inc.

Deshpande, M., & Karypis, G. (2004). Item-based top-n recommendation algorithms. *ACM Transactions on Information Systems, 22*(1), 143–177. doi:10.1145/963770.963776

Goldberg, D., Nichols, D., Oki, B. M., & Terry, D. (1992). Using collaborative filtering to weave an information tapestry. *Communications of the ACM, 35*(12), 61–70. doi:10.1145/138859.138867

Gousios, G. (2013, May). The GHTorent dataset and tool suite. In *Proceedings of the 10th Working Conference on Mining Software Repositories* (pp. 233-236). IEEE Press.

Gousios, G., Vasilescu, B., Serebrenik, A., & Zaidman, A. (2014, May). Lean GHTorrent: GitHub data on demand. In *Proceedings of the 11th Working Conference on Mining Software Repositories* (pp. 384-387). ACM.

Guzman, E., Azócar, D., & Li, Y. (2014, May). Sentiment analysis of commit comments in GitHub: an empirical study. In *Proceedings of the 11th Working Conference on Mining Software Repositories* (pp. 352-355). ACM. doi:10.1145/2597073.2597118

Heller, B., Marschner, E., Rosenfeld, E., & Heer, J. (2011, May). Visualizing collaboration and influence in the open-source software community. In *Proceedings of the 8th Working Conference on Mining Software Repositories* (pp. 223-226). ACM. doi:10.1145/1985441.1985476

Hofmann, T. (2004). Latent semantic models for collaborative filtering. *ACM Transactions on Information Systems, 22*(1), 89–115. doi:10.1145/963770.963774

Karypis, G. (2001, October). Evaluation of item-based top-n recommendation algorithms. In *Proceedings of the tenth international conference on Information and knowledge management* (pp. 247-254). ACM.

Levandowsky, M., & Winter, D. (1971). Distance between sets. *Nature, 234*(5323), 34–35. doi:10.1038/234034a0

Lipkus, A. H. (1999). A proof of the triangle inequality for the Tanimoto distance. *Journal of Mathematical Chemistry, 26*(1-3), 263–265. doi:10.1023/A:1019154432472

Pazzani, M. J., & Billsus, D. (2007). Content-based recommendation systems. In *The adaptive web* (pp. 325–341). Springer Berlin Heidelberg. doi:10.1007/978-3-540-72079-9_10

Resnick, P., Iacovou, N., Suchak, M., Bergstrom, P., & Riedl, J. (1994, October). GroupLens: an open architecture for collaborative filtering of netnews. In *Proceedings of the 1994 ACM conference on Computer supported cooperative work* (pp. 175-186). ACM. doi:10.1145/192844.192905

Sarwar, B., Karypis, G., Konstan, J., & Riedl, J. (2000, October). Analysis of recommendation algorithms for e-commerce. In *Proceedings of the 2nd ACM conference on Electronic commerce* (pp. 158-167). ACM. doi:10.1145/352871.352887

Sarwar, B., Karypis, G., Konstan, J., & Riedl, J. (2001, April). Item-based collaborative filtering recommendation algorithms. In *Proceedings of the 10th international conference on World Wide Web* (pp. 285-295). ACM.

Shani, G., Brafman, R. I., & Heckerman, D. (2002, August). An MDP-based recommender system. In *Proceedings of the Eighteenth conference on Uncertainty in artificial intelligence* (pp. 453-460). Morgan Kaufmann Publishers Inc.

Su, X., & Khoshgoftaar, T. M. (2006, November). Collaborative filtering for multi-class data using belief nets algorithms. In *Tools with Artificial Intelligence, 2006. ICTAI'06. 18th IEEE International Conference on* (pp. 497-504). IEEE. doi:10.1109/ICTAI.2006.41

Thung, F., Bissyandé, T. F., Lo, D., & Jiang, L. (2013, March). Network structure of social coding in github. In *Software Maintenance and Reengineering (CSMR), 2013 17th European Conference on* (pp. 323-326). IEEE. doi:10.1109/CSMR.2013.41

Yu, Y., Wang, H., Yin, G., & Ling, C. X. (2014, September). Reviewer recommender of pull-requests in GitHub. In *Software Maintenance and Evolution (ICSME), 2014 IEEE International Conference on* (pp. 609-612). IEEE. doi:10.1109/ICSME.2014.107

Chapter 5
Optimization Scenarios for Open Source Software Used in E–Learning Activities

Utku Köse
Suleyman Demirel University, Turkey

ABSTRACT

Using open software in e-learning application is one of the most popular ways of improving effectiveness of e-learning-based processes without thinking about additional costs and even focusing on modifying the software according to needs. Because of that, it is important to have an idea about what is needed while using an e-learning-oriented open software system and how to deal with its source codes. At this point, it is a good option to add some additional features and functions to make the open source software more intelligent and practical to make both teaching-learning experiences during e-learning processes. In this context, the objective of this chapter is to discuss some possible applications of artificial intelligence to include optimization processes within open source software systems used in e-learning activities. In detail, the chapter focuses more on using swarm intelligence and machine learning techniques for this aim and expresses some theoretical views for improving the effectiveness of such software for a better e-learning experience.

INTRODUCTION

With the transformation of the society into information society, all fields of the life have started to change form according to needs of this new society form. Now, it is more important to reach to desired information rapidly and adapt it to the problems – tasks by using specific approaches of the digital world. Among all the improvements, the field of education has a unique place because it is both among objective fields to be changed and supportive fields to grow up individuals, who are appropriate members of the information society. At this point, the field of education has received many revolutionary changes in time and the educational experiences has become some type of special processes, which are done even we do not take place face-to-face in a real classroom environment. In this sense, the approach of

DOI: 10.4018/978-1-5225-5314-4.ch005

Distance Education and the E-Learning, which is a type of Distance Education as supported with computer, communication and multimedia technologies, have become very popular leading an unstoppable trend towards the future (Bates, 2005; Klašnja-Milićević et al., 2017a; Moore, 2013; Welsh et al., 2003).

E-Learning is today's effective form of education with its features and mechanisms to eliminate limitations regarding time and place. But as a result of rapid improvements in especially computer and communication technologies, it has become more common to run E-Learning processes just simply and considering other factors directly in order to improve effectiveness and efficiency of this process. As general, both teachers and students may need different supportive factors to make E-Learning better for them. Although it is more considerable to run E-Learning solutions instead of traditional educational approaches before, it is now more widely followed to find alternative ways of improving E-Learning experiences.

It is possible to see many different types of ways for improving effectiveness of E-Learning activities. In the associated literature, this issue is even widely discussed (Burgess, 2017; Dascalu et al., 2014; Hamburg et al., 2008; Johnson et al., 2008; Kalyuga & Sweller, 2005; Kechaou et al., 2011; Korres, 2017; Liaw, 2008; Macleod & Kefallonitis, 2017; Romero & Ventura, 2006; Shen et al., 2009; Song et al., 2004; Sun et al., 2008; Zhang et al., 2006). At this point, using open software in E-Learning application is today's one of the most popular ways of improving effectiveness of E-Learning based processes without thinking about additional costs and even focusing on modifying the software according to needs. Because of that, it is important to have idea about what is needed while using an E-Learning oriented open software system and how to deal with its source codes. Generally, it is a good option here to add some additional features and functions to make the open source software more intelligent and practical to make both teaching - learning experiences during E-Learning processes. That can be achieved better thanks to a strong scientific field: Artificial Intelligence. Approaches, methods, and techniques in Artificial Intelligence has a remarkable place in a multidisciplinary manner with all effective and efficient solution that have been provided so far, even for the most complex, and advanced types of problems. So, in the intersection of E-Learning and open source software systems, applications from Artificial Intelligence could be very effective to improve E-Learning. In the associated literature, we can see many different examples of Artificial Intelligence applications within E-Learning and Distance Education in a general manner (Aroyo & Dicheva, 2004; Brusilovsky & Peylo, 2003; Colchester et al., 2017; Herder et al., 2017; Klašnja-Milićević et al., 2017b; Kose & Koc, 2014; Schiaffino et al., 2008; Tang & McCalla, 2003; Van Eck, 2007; Villaverde et al., 2006; Wen-Shung Tai et al., 2008; Wenger, 2014; Woolf, 2010). But as an alternative, it will be a good way to think about some 'butterfly effects' by considering improve of open source based E-Learning software systems.

Considering the explanations so far, objective of this chapter is to discuss about some possible applications of Artificial Intelligence to include optimization processes within open source software systems used in E-Learning activities. Here, the main issue is achieving an actual mathematical optimization model or a solution process that can be accepted as 'optimizing something' in the active E-Learning habitat towards an improved E-Learning experience for both teachers and students. In detail, the chapter focuses more on using Swarm Intelligence and Machine Learning techniques for this aim and express some theoretical views for improving effectiveness of such software for a better E-Learning experience. It is believed that this research work will be a good opportunity to have ideas about possible optimization oriented applications within open source software systems of E-Learning and lead the interested readers to realize further investigations in this manner.

In the context of the chapter subject and scope, remaining content of the chapter is organized as follows: The next section is devoted to some brief introduction of today's known open source software solutions for E-Learning activities. With this section, it is aimed to give some essential information the readers for having idea about what types of open source E-Learning software systems are generally used. Following to that section, some examples of optimization scenarios are discussed – explained theoretically under the third section. In detail, there are some alternative scenarios supported by Swarm Intelligence and Machine Learning techniques to improve E-Learning processes over open source software systems. Here, more consideration has been tried to be given for achieving optimization by considering possible codes used within open source software systems. Next, some ideas derived for future research directions are expressed briefly under the fourth section and the chapter is ended by discussing about conclusions under the last section.

A BRIEF VIEW FROM OPEN SOURCE E-LEARNING SOFTWARE SYSTEMS

For a long time, there is a remarkable effort on developing open source E-Learning software. In this context, it is important that majority of such software systems are focused on ensuring learning management system (LMS) platforms to combine important features and functions useful for a typical E-Learning processes. On the other hand, there are also some software systems, which can be used as supportive actors to achieve a better organization of E-Learning. So, we can think about modular E-Learning approaches in which different open software systems are connected each other (In this chapter, such connection is associated with intelligent optimization scenarios as it can be understood). Because of that, we can provide some examples of open source E-Learning software by providing a categorization according to essential features provided by them.

The author has provided an example categorization before in order to list some free and open source software systems regarding E-Learning 2.0 (Kose, 2014). Because today's open source software systems are already based on principles regarding to Web 2.0, Web 3.0, and even Web 4.0, it is more important to use just the categorization approach here (For more information regarding the concepts of E-Learning 2.0, Web 2.0, Web 3.0, and Web 4.0, readers are referred to Aghaei et al., 2012; Downes, 2005; Ebner, 2007; Kose, 2010; Kose, 2014). Considering the categorization by Kose (2014), it is possible to examine the open source E-Learning software (as considering them also even services sometimes) under four categories as: (1) E-Learning Portals, (2) File Sharing Environments, (3) Social-Network Based Services, and (4) Specific – Special Applications and Services (Figure 1).

E-Learning Portals

Some well-known open source E-Learning software systems that can be examined as 'E-Learning Portal' can be explained briefly as follows:

Moodle

Moodle is one of the most popular E-Learning portals – learning managements systems with its stable, flexible and fast using style. The system is based on PHP programming language and uses MySQL or

Figure 1. Categories regarding open source E-Learning software (Kose, 2014)

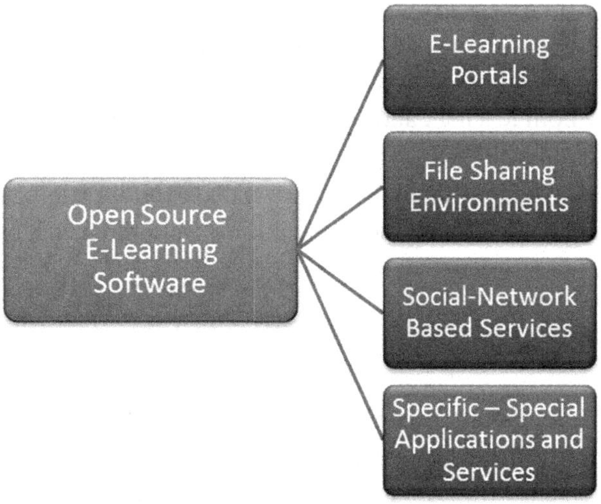

PostgreSQL for database management. It comes with many different features including dashboards, student tracking mechanisms, examinations – quizzes, organizing tools, course content sections, and many other ones as supported with multimedia elements. All over the world, there is a remarkable community of developers – supporters, so it is always possible to find alternative components – plug-ins, pre-made course contents, translations for the whole system, wide documentation on its use and development, and also instant help from different users – experts, who have mastered E-Learning experience with Moodle (Pappas, 2015; Web Resources Depot, 2009).

ATutor

ATutor is another alternative of open source E-Learning portal with its fast and user-friendly interface. ATutor employs a common interface in which teachers and students can perform their own tasks. As general, the system employs different features – functions including development and providing of courses – course content, arranging assessments, preparing polls, performing analyses over the data regarding performed E-Learning activities (Pappas, 2015).

Eduslide.Open Source

Eduslide.Open Source is a software system developed by The Virtual Training Company located in Virginia, USA. Over the system teachers can share their knowledge by creating custom courses by using Eduslide. Eduslide employs many different features for creating a whole online learning community. It comes with different tools such as wikis, forums, chats and quizzes. At this point, wikis, forums and chat tools can be employed for collaboration between teachers and students. Furthermore, it is also possible for teachers to use integrated project management tools for controlling students' learning process. On the other hand, it is also possible for teachers to create lesson objectives for task based learning activities over Eduslide. Another feature of the Eduslide is supporting the invitation based learning (Kose, 2014).

Claroline

Claroline is another portal based open source solution for E-Learning processes. In detail, the system has been designed by teachers and it provides all necessary needs for an effective and collaborative E-Learning experience for both teachers and students. As developed over PHP and use with MySQL database management, Claroline also has a wide support all over the world with translations into many languages. Some remarkable features of the system are related to online exercise preparing, learning path determination for students and also communication options over online chat or forums (Web Resources Depot, 2009).

eFront

As based on an Ajax structure, eFront is an E-Learning portal with many features and functions to organize flow of an E-Learning process. In detail, the system provides wide content authoring tools supported with multimedia elements, file managers and also digital libraries to store files, and some other tools like quiz, survey generators to achieve an effective E-Learning environment for both teachers and students (Web Resources Depot, 2009).

File Sharing Environments

File sharing environments are actually useful for not only E-Learning activities but also for all works associated with online file share over the Web. But here, it has been tried to give some idea about open source solutions for explaining the opportunities on providing own-service for file share among teachers and students within an E-Learning habitat.

YouTransfer

YouTransfer is a free and open source self-hosted file sharing solution that may be used along E-Learning activities. It seems that it has also some pricing options in some alternative using approaches but generally it can be used accordingly fast and easily as a file sharing module of a formed E-Learning structure. Except from its features and functions regarding file share, YouTransfer comes with also support regarding Firewalls in order to achieve a more secure and controllable self-hosted file share system on the back (Nesbitt, 2017).

FileDrop

FileDrop is another open source solution regarding file share but in order to run it, the software systems of Sandstorm.io or Sandstorm Oasis should be used, too. Generally, the FileDrop is a rapid and simple software to be used for sharing files directly to people over their e-mail addresses (Nesbitt, 2017).

LinShare

As another file sharing service as open source, LinShare provides more security features and functions to achieve a flexible and fast file sharing environment. With the use of well-known features like dragn-drop, it is possible to share files with varying sizes with people. So, it is another alternative form of open source file sharing that may be used through an E-Learning plan (Nesbitt, 2017).

ProjectSend

ProjectSend is an open source, self-hosted solution for file share and it comes with again security features – options to achieve a more secure, self-hosted file sharing environment. In detail, this system also enables users to share their files and even folders with people or groups, which can be adjusted before (Nesbitt, 2017).

Social-Network Based Services

Nowadays, there is no certain line between having social-network based features and just traditional using features within open source software systems. Because, today's trendy using features generally promote social interaction among users even it is the simplest system located over the Web, for particular tasks – activities. But in order to meet with the classification made before, some alternative open source solutions having more social features – functions have been combined here. Of course, these systems can be accepted as also E-Learning portals.

Elgg

Elgg is a generally a social-networking based open source solution as developed by Curverider Ltd. and open source community, for educational processes. Elgg employs some interactive tools like blogs, podcasting applications, file sharing applications, and even a RSS reader. In detail, it is possible for both teachers and students to search for other ones by using tags over the system and finally create some type of active learning communities – groups over the system environment. The tagging approach is a remarkable feature used widely over the system. As multimedia support, Elgg enables teachers and students to upload their photos, audio, and video files within blog posts easily, and even make comments and open discussions on objective topics (Kose, 2014).

OLAT

OLAT is an open source E-Learning software system, which provides a use oriented solution for getting more effectiveness in E-Learning experiences. In addition to the provided calendar tools, course pages, certificate system and approaches regarding file storage, the system also focuses on the use of social learning. The system also supports different types of devices so that teachers and students can experience the E-Learning activities over even their mobile devices (Pappas, 2015).

Opigno

Opigno is an E-Learning environment, which provides more interaction by using multimedia elements to some other tools that can used by system users. As general, it is possible over Opigno to use E-Learning authoring and course development tools, arrange course time tables and control – manage objective students' activities over the system. The system also comes with video galleries and thanks to some communication tools like chat and instant messaging, it promotes a collaborative teaching – learning experience (Pappas, 2015).

ILIAS

ILIAS is another open E-Learning platform, which comes with many features and functions to achieve a collaborative environment. In this context, the system employs a simple, fast, and flexible interface in order to organize a common E-Learning environment in which it is more effective to communicate each other and perform any other tasks (i.e. document share, reaching to other teachers – students, performing time based tests) regarding the planned E-Learning flow (Pappas, 2015; Web Resources Depot, 2009).

Dokeos

As based on PHP and MySQL to run database, Dokeos is more than just traditional E-Learning portal. Briefly, Dokeos employs a flash-based video conferencing system as integrated to enable teachers – students to experience online, interactive communication sessions. With also its coaching features – functions, the system employs assignment feedback, online chat, agenda, and forum tools to ensure a general E-Learning environment (Web Resources Depot, 2009).

Specific: Special Applications and Services

In addition to the mentioned open source software systems, there are many other E-Learning oriented tools that can be examined out of the categories considered before. Especially nowadays, there are many different types of specific E-Learning applications – services to support general E-Learning flow with their interactive features. Some remarkable ones are:

Fedena

Rather than just E-Learning oriented environment, Fedena allows users to manage the whole school with its wide analyzing tools. As developed by using Ruby on Rails, the system employs a flexible, fast interface to deal with all tasks regarding a school by including also tracking students, examinations, and many other statistical data associated with teachers and students (Morpus, 2016). It is remarkable here that use of general school management software systems can enable educational institutions to have more then they desired and achieve a more effective E-Learning experience by organizing the whole structure with some other software systems and as according to their needs. In addition to Fedena, some other remarkable open source school management software systems are: FeKara, SchoolTime, TS School, and Gibbon (Morpus, 2016).

Annotum

Annotum is an open source solution for writing and organizing scholarly articles over a Web platform supported with WordPress. In Annotum, it is possible to arrange articles by using many writing tools like document styles, citations, and even mathematical equations. From a general perspective, the system forms a general, blog based, article platform to support educational collaborations and information share (Pappas, 2011).

Open Meetings

As a specific and important need among E-Learning systems, OpenMeeting is a Web conferencing system, which tries to complete this need of online conferencing with an open source approach. In detail, the system supports also instant messaging, online whiteboard, document sharing and editing, audio based features, and even screen sharing in order to improve interactivity over active Web conferencing sessions (Pappas, 2016).

Big Blue Button

Big Blue Button is another open solution for Web conferencing through E-Learning activities. It is popular as like the Open Meetings and widely supported by the open source community as hosted over Google Code platform. As general, Big Blue Button provides all necessary Web conferencing tools like whiteboards, screen and document sharing, audio based features, and also some additional tools to perform zoom in, highlighting, and notes drawing over active white boards (Pappas, 2016).

In addition to open source Web conferencing solutions like Open Meetings and Big Blue Button, there are also many other open source software systems to achieve online, Web conferencing over an organized E-Learning process. Some of them are: MConf, VMukti, Jitsi, and WebHuddle (Pappas, 2016).

OPTIMIZATION SCENARIOS OVER OPEN SOURCE E-LEARNING SOFTWARE

Considering the open source software systems for E-Learning, it is possible to think about some optimization scenarios, which include use of Artificial Intelligence techniques. At this point, it is important here to adapt different open software systems in a modular manner to run an optimized way of E-Learning experience, which is beneficial for both teachers and students.

It is possible to derive many different optimization scenarios by using different features and functions of the related open source software systems. But some remarkable ones, which will direct the interested readers to think about more, can be explained briefly as follows:

Optimum Content: Data Providing

By making necessary code additions and adjusting database structure, it is possible for the E-Learning environments having course content to determine which course content can be provided to a specific student. At this point, it is possible to use a Machine Learning technique: Artificial Neural Network model to get some input data regarding student (i.e. exam results, content viewing information, course difficulty, student's academic success level) and receive output(s) indicating which content can be provided to the objective student. This can be done under a flexible Artificial Neural Network model in which number of artificial neurons, hidden layers, number of input / output neurons can be updated according to additional E-Learning tasks – activities done over the system. The author has already some example of optimizing research works introduced to the associated literature before (Kose, 2013; Kose & Arslan, 2017). At this point, this scenario of optimum content receiving can be done in even E-Learning plans using open source software systems in a modular manner. For example, outputs of specific E-Learning tools can be used as students' input data and an Artificial Neural Network among different types of E-Learning software systems can be used as a 'regulator' for determining the most optimum course content (even maybe quiz, file…etc.) to be provided for the objective student. Readers interested in having more information about Artificial Neural Networks are referred to (Kubat, 2015; Wang, 2003; Yegnanarayana, 2009; Zhu, 2017).

Optimizing Activities Students Can Perform

Whether it is included in an E-Learning portal or not, some specific activities can be enabled or disabled according to students' performance over the system. Of course, this scenario is not for limiting students' activities but an encouragement way to make them more active over the system environment. At this point, the same Artificial Neural Network model approach explained under the previous sub-title can be followed to determine weights of each activity for the associated student. These data can be within the system so its database and the related codes of using features – functions should be revised. On the other hand, if some activities are done by using external software systems out of the main E-Learning system, their data can be used within again in a regulator Artificial Neural Network in the middle of the whole E-Learning plan. As it is explained under the following sub-title(s), a mathematical fitness function can also be used to do same thing via intelligent optimization algorithms.

Optimization of Academic Success Over Fitness Functions

In intelligent optimization done with Artificial Intelligence based techniques, it is necessary to use a fitness function, which includes the related variables to be optimized. This function is briefly a mathematical model of the objective optimization problem and by using its responses for the given values, optimization

Figure 2. A representative simple scheme for the scenario of optimum content – data providing

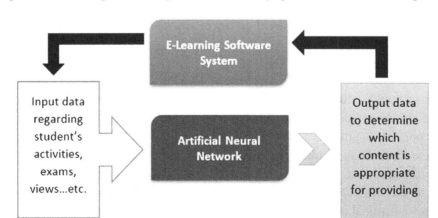

Figure 3. A representative simple scheme for the scenario of optimizing activities students can perform

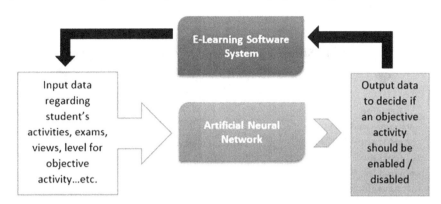

process has been continued. At this point, determining academic success level for students or directing them to specific activities in order to meet the requirements of a specific academic success level, it is possible to form a fitness function and use it within the designed E-Learning plan. The optimization done here is a typical continuous optimization and the fitness function can be formed by collaboration of many experts. The function may include different kind of coefficient, and variables regarding i.e. examinations, course uses, completed tasks – activities. In addition, the optimization problem model can be single-objective by using only one function or provided as in the form of multi-objective optimization by including more than one functions within a relation.

In the literature of Artificial Intelligence, there are many different algorithms – techniques that can perform an optimization process iteratively, according to given inputs. It is important that the source codes of the used E-Learning software systems require to be updated according to complexity of the considered mathematical optimization problem. The related updates can be done according to the structure of the plan as it includes modular software systems or not. Another issue that should be discussed here is the diversity of intelligent optimization techniques. Nowadays, there are many different types of intelligent optimization algorithms – techniques. Even a separate research interest called as 'Swarm Intelligence' has an active flow through the scientific community as including majority of such algorithms – techniques. Some examples of intelligent optimization algorithms are: Particle Swarm Optimization, Artificial Bee Colony, Cuckoo Search, and Genetic Algorithms. Readers are referred to (Bai, 2010; Blum & Li, 2008; Brownlee, 2011; Garnier et al., 2007; Karaboga & Akay, 2009; Reeves, 2009; Yang & Deb, 2010; Wang, 2001; Whitley, 1994) in order to have more information about these algorithms – techniques, the concept of intelligent optimization, and Swarm Intelligence.

Optimum Teaching-Learning Path With Combinatorial Optimization

As different from continuous optimization, task – activity outputs of the used E-Learning software systems can be used to determine a specific teaching-learning path for both teachers and students. According to their performances, it is possible for both teachers and students to find an optimum way of teaching or learning, by using the already provided E-Learning tasks, documents, data, and any other elements having active role in the process. The most important thing to do here is defining a good function, which will evaluate possible teaching-learning paths according to teachers' or students' needs – tasks. In the open

Figure 4. A representative simple scheme for the scenario of optimization of academic success over fitness functions

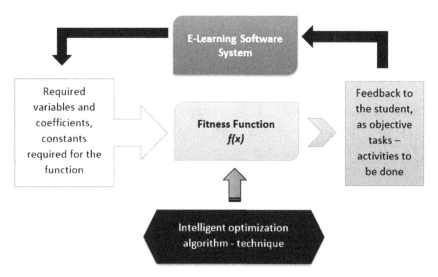

source software systems, it is again needed to update source codes and even it may be required to form new relations, define triggers or procedures according to the current structure of the database included within objective software systems.

Again, Artificial Intelligence comes with specific algorithms – techniques to deal with combinatorial optimization problems. For example, Ant Colony Optimization, Intelligent Water Drops Algorithm, and Algorithmic Reasoning Optimization are some examples of them. Readers are referred to (Blum & Roli, 2003; Dorigo et al., 2006; Kose & Arslan, 2016; Shah-Hosseini, 2009) to have more information about the algorithms and the intelligent combinatorial optimization.

FUTURE RESEARCH DIRECTIONS

Under the previous sections, more consideration was given to the state of currently employed open source E-Learning software solutions and also Artificial Intelligence based optimization ways. It is important that the future has a great potential to move the open source E-Learning to different kinds of application types and maybe transforming it into another revolutionary version of open distance education that we cannot imagine well enough for now. But at this point, it could be also a good start to derive some ideas by thinking about current developments within alternative technologies and also focusing on possible applications of intelligent optimization towards open source E-Learning software systems for at least near future.

By considering the explanations provided under previous sections and also thinking the state of the associated literatures nowadays, some remarkable future research directions can be explained briefly as follows:

Figure 5. A representative simple scheme for the scenario of optimum teaching-learning path with combinatorial optimization

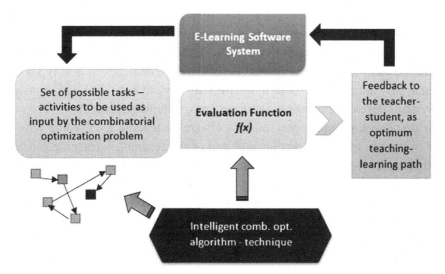

- Although we have thought about continuous and combinatorial optimization while introducing some example scenarios before, near future may have the potential of using more complicated application types of these optimization methods in order to improve open source software systems for E-Learning. It is certain that the literature associated with intelligent optimization techniques is greatly active and because of that, there will be always an open door for new types of optimization scenarios done by i.e. newly introduced optimization algorithms or newly thought optimization problem applications regarding E-Learning processes.

- Artificial Intelligence is not the only supportive technology taking active place in today's E-Learning applications. Considering the open source software structure, it is possible to adapt different types of multimedia technologies for improving E-Learning processes from different sides. For example, Augmented Reality has a great popularity in today's E-Learning applications and because of that there will probably be specific optimization problem settings for open source E-Learning software systems including also Augmented Reality. Readers interested in Augmented Reality are referred to (Azuma, 1997; Azuma et al., 2001; Hainich, 2009; Höllerer & Feiner, 2004; Leighton & Crompton, 2017; Pasaréti et al., 2011; Sánchez-Acevedo et al., 2017; Van Krevelen & Poelman, 2010; Wu et al., 2013) for getting more information about Augmented Reality.

- As indicated under the previous paragraph, Augmented Reality has a remarkable place in the future of education and so an intelligent E-Learning over open source software systems. That may means less use of hardware but it is also important that the Augmented Reality or any other alternative supportive technology within E-Learning can come with alternative types of hardware that can be used by teachers and students. At this point, optimization scenarios regarding optimizing such hardware for better E-Learning experience can be foreseen and thus, possible optimization oriented adjustments between hardware and open source software systems can be considered as under important research directions in the future.

- As it was expressed before, Object Oriented Programming has a valuable place in today's software development processes by including even strong relations with intelligent optimization techniques. But it is not clear that the future will bring us new types of programming approaches with the changed hardware and software technologies and the ways of processing data. So, the future research directions in this manner will always include adaptations to newly introduced programming approaches and directing the current optimization techniques to new types of optimization problems that may appear while designing effective ways of better E-Learning over open source software systems developed thanks to these new programming approaches.

- Since their first developments, open source software systems in E-Learning have become more specific as aiming to solve a particular problem of the teaching – learning process. So, as it is understood from the explanations under this chapter, it has become a common thing to combine different types of software systems for the same E-Learning process. That means hybridization of open software systems will be increasingly popular in the future and research directions will continue to be focused on designing specific optimization scenarios by considering that hybridization factor of E-Learning oriented software systems.

- Scenarios explained under this chapter are some essential types of examples for improving features and functions of open source software systems in order to improve E-Learning experiences in this way. Of course, there can be many different types of optimization problem settings regarding designed E-Learning habitat, code structures of the employed software systems or even data used as input or output for the open source software systems. So, there will be always an active effort on designing alternative ways of optimization scenarios in the future of open source oriented E-Learning.

CONCLUSION

This chapter has focused on open source E-Learning software systems and tried to answer the question of how intelligent optimization scenarios can be employed for improving open source E-Learning systems. In detail, it is important for anyone interested in open source E-Learning software systems to know which types of software oriented approaches are generally followed currently to support E-Learning processes realized by both teachers and students. So, the chapter has firstly provided a brief look at to some examples of open source E-Learning software systems. In the chapter, it was claimed that one effective and efficient way of improving open source software based E-Learning experiences is to employ intelligent solutions within open source software systems. At this point, Artificial Intelligence has been taken into consideration and also more focus was given to intelligent optimization, which is an important research interest of Artificial Intelligence. It is clear that the whole problem solution mechanisms and even naturally occurred dynamics over the world are associated with some optimization processes and because of that they can be formulated or imagined in the form of optimization problems. Moving from that, some example scenarios of optimization for improving using features – functions of the objective open source E-Learning software or just combining more than one system to have more advanced, 'intelligent' E-Learning habitat have been explained briefly under this chapter. The provided scenarios have been some typical theoretical views (but practically applicable) with the use of Swarm Intelligence and Machine Learning techniques to achieve optimization oriented solutions.

It is clear that the scientific developments and improvements have many hidden things waiting for us to be used for designing and developing innovative solutions for real-world based problems. In this context, the field of education has a remarkable popularity for applying innovative applications supported by new technologies. As an important example of them, E-Learning seems to be always active field in even future thanks to employment of new technologies and even scientific approaches, methods, and techniques. Nowadays, employment of Artificial Intelligence is one of the most remarkable factor in achieving positive results within E-Learning processes and at this point, using small steps of solutions has an effective role to get desired educational outputs. As associated with this philosophical view, this chapter has discussed about some examples of intelligent mechanisms, which use optimization for improving the E-Learning experience at the top level by affecting maybe small building blocks of an E-Learning system with open source support. On the other hand, it is important that the chapter has given more emphasis on software coding oriented factors while designing the related optimization scenarios.

REFERENCES

Aghaei, S., Nematbakhsh, M. A., & Farsani, H. K. (2012). Evolution of the world wide web: From WEB 1.0 TO WEB 4.0. *International Journal of Web & Semantic Technology*, *3*(1), 1–10. doi:10.5121/ijwest.2012.3101

Aroyo, L., & Dicheva, D. (2004). The new challenges for e-learning: The educational semantic web. *Journal of Educational Technology & Society*, *7*(4).

Azuma, R., Baillot, Y., Behringer, R., Feiner, S., Julier, S., & MacIntyre, B. (2001). Recent advances in augmented reality. *IEEE Computer Graphics and Applications*, *21*(6), 34–47. doi:10.1109/38.963459

Azuma, R. T. (1997). A survey of augmented reality. *Presence (Cambridge, Mass.)*, *6*(4), 355–385. doi:10.1162/pres.1997.6.4.355

Bai, Q. (2010). Analysis of particle swarm optimization algorithm. *Computer and Information Science*, *3*(1), 180.

Bates, A. T. (2005). *Technology, e-learning and distance education*. Routledge. doi:10.4324/9780203463772

Blum, C., & Li, X. (2008). Swarm intelligence in optimization. In *Swarm Intelligence* (pp. 43–85). Springer Berlin Heidelberg. doi:10.1007/978-3-540-74089-6_2

Blum, C., & Roli, A. (2003). Metaheuristics in combinatorial optimization: Overview and conceptual comparison. *ACM Computing Surveys*, *35*(3), 268–308. doi:10.1145/937503.937505

Brownlee, J. (2011). *Clever algorithms: nature-inspired programming recipes*. Jason Brownlee.

Brusilovsky, P., & Peylo, C. (2003). Adaptive and intelligent web-based educational systems. *International Journal of Artificial Intelligence in Education*, *13*, 159–172.

Burgess, E. O. (2017). *Attrition and Dropouts in the E-learning Environment: Improving Student Success and Retention* (Doctoral dissertation). Northcentral University.

Colchester, K., Hagras, H., Alghazzawi, D., & Aldabbagh, G. (2017). A survey of artificial intelligence techniques employed for adaptive educational systems within E-learning platforms. *Journal of Artificial Intelligence and Soft Computing Research*, 7(1), 47–64. doi:10.1515/jaiscr-2017-0004

Dascalu, M. I., Bodea, C. N., Lytras, M., De Pablos, P. O., & Burlacu, A. (2014). Improving e-learning communities through optimal composition of multidisciplinary learning groups. *Computers in Human Behavior*, 30, 362–371. doi:10.1016/j.chb.2013.01.022

Dorigo, M., Birattari, M., & Stutzle, T. (2006). Ant colony optimization. *IEEE Computational Intelligence Magazine*, 1(4), 28–39. doi:10.1109/MCI.2006.329691

Downes, S. (2005). E-learning 2.0. *E-learn Magazine, 2005*(10), 1.

Ebner, M. (2007). E-Learning 2.0= e-Learning 1.0+ Web 2.0? In *Availability, Reliability and Security, 2007. ARES 2007. The Second International Conference on* (pp. 1235-1239). IEEE.

Garnier, S., Gautrais, J., & Theraulaz, G. (2007). The biological principles of swarm intelligence. *Swarm Intelligence*, 1(1), 3–31. doi:10.1007/s11721-007-0004-y

Hainich, R. R. (2009). *The End of hardware: augmented reality and beyond*. BookSurge.

Hamburg, I., Engert, S., Anke, P., Marin, M., & im IKM Bereich, E. C. A. (2008). Improving e-learning 2.0-based training strategies of SMEs through communities of practice. *Learning, 2*, 610-012.

Herder, E., Sosnovsky, S., & Dimitrova, V. (2017). Adaptive Intelligent Learning Environments. In Technology Enhanced Learning (pp. 109-114). Springer International Publishing. doi:10.1007/978-3-319-02600-8_10

Höllerer, T., & Feiner, S. (2004). *Mobile augmented reality. In Telegeoinformatics: Location-Based Computing and Services* (p. 21). London, UK: Taylor and Francis Books Ltd.

Johnson, R. D., Hornik, S., & Salas, E. (2008). An empirical examination of factors contributing to the creation of successful e-learning environments. *International Journal of Human-Computer Studies*, 66(5), 356–369. doi:10.1016/j.ijhcs.2007.11.003

Kalyuga, S., & Sweller, J. (2005). Rapid dynamic assessment of expertise to improve the efficiency of adaptive e-learning. *Educational Technology Research and Development*, 53(3), 83–93. doi:10.1007/BF02504800

Karaboga, D., & Akay, B. (2009). A comparative study of artificial bee colony algorithm. *Applied Mathematics and Computation*, 214(1), 108–132. doi:10.1016/j.amc.2009.03.090

Kechaou, Z., Ammar, M. B., & Alimi, A. M. (2011). Improving e-learning with sentiment analysis of users' opinions. In *Global Engineering Education Conference* (pp. 1032-1038). IEEE. doi:10.1109/EDUCON.2011.5773275

Klašnja-Milićević, A., Vesin, B., Ivanović, M., Budimac, Z., & Jain, L. C. (2017a). Introduction to E-Learning Systems. In E-Learning Systems (pp. 3-17). Springer International Publishing.

Klašnja-Milićević, A., Vesin, B., Ivanović, M., Budimac, Z., & Jain, L. C. (2017b). Recommender Systems in E-Learning Environments. In E-Learning Systems (pp. 51-75). Springer International Publishing.

Korres, M. P. (2017). The Positive Effect of Evaluation on Improving E-Learning Courses Addressed to Adults: A Case Study on the Evolution of the GSLLLY Courses in Greece over a Decade. *Journal of Education and Training Studies*, *5*(1), 1–11. doi:10.11114/jets.v5i1.1940

Kose, U. (2010). *Web 2.0 Technologies in E-learning. In Free and Open Source Software for E-learning: Issues, Successes and Challenges* (pp. 1–23). Hershey, PA: IGI Global.

Kose, U. (2013). An Artificial Neural Networks Based Software System for Improved Learning Experience. In *Machine Learning and Applications (ICMLA), 2013 12th International Conference on* (Vol. 2, pp. 549-554). IEEE. doi:10.1109/ICMLA.2013.175

Kose, U. (2014). On the State of Free and Open Source E-Learning 2.0 Software. *International Journal of Open Source Software and Processes*, *5*(2), 55–75. doi:10.4018/ijossp.2014040103

Kose, U., & Arslan, A. (2016). Optimization with the idea of algorithmic reasoning. *Journal of Multidisciplinary Developments*, *1*(1), 17–20.

Kose, U., & Arslan, A. (2017). Optimization of self-learning in Computer Engineering courses: An intelligent software system supported by Artificial Neural Network and Vortex Optimization Algorithm. *Computer Applications in Engineering Education*, *25*(1), 142–156. doi:10.1002/cae.21787

Kose, U., & Koc, D. (2014). *Artificial Intelligence Applications in Distance Education*. IGI Global.

Kubat, M. (2015). Artificial neural networks. In *An Introduction to Machine Learning* (pp. 91–111). Springer International Publishing. doi:10.1007/978-3-319-20010-1_5

Leighton, L. J., & Crompton, H. (2017). Augmented Reality in K-12 Education. In Mobile Technologies and Augmented Reality in Open Education (pp. 281-290). IGI Global.

Liaw, S. S. (2008). Investigating students' perceived satisfaction, behavioral intention, and effectiveness of e-learning: A case study of the Blackboard system. *Computers & Education*, *51*(2), 864–873. doi:10.1016/j.compedu.2007.09.005

Macleod, J., & Kefallonitis, E. (2017). Trends Affecting e-Learning Experience Management. In Strategic Innovative Marketing (pp. 753-758). Springer International Publishing. doi:10.1007/978-3-319-33865-1_93

Moore, M. G. (Ed.). (2013). *Handbook of distance education*. Routledge.

Morpus, N. (2016). The Top 6 Free and Open Source School Administration Software. *Capterra – Blog*. Retrieved from http://blog.capterra.com/the-top-6-free-school-administration-software/

Nesbitt, S. (2017). *4 open source tools for sharing files*. Retrieved from https://opensource.com/article/17/3/file-sharing-tools

Pappas, C. (2011). *Top 10 Free and Open Source eLearning Projects to Watch for 2012*. Retrieved from https://www.efrontlearning.com/blog/2011/12/top-10-free-and-open-source-elearning.html

Pappas, C. (2015). *The Top 8 Open Source Learning Management Systems*. Retrieved from https://elearningindustry.com/top-open-source-learning-management-systems

Pappas, C. (2016). *Top 6 Open Source Web Conferencing Software Tools for eLearning Professionals.* Retrieved from https://elearningindustry.com/top-6-open-source-web-conferencing-software-tools-elearning-professionals

Pasaréti, O., Hajdin, H., Matusaka, T., Jambori, A., Molnar, I., & Tucsányi-Szabó, M. (2011). Augmented Reality in education. *INFODIDACT 2011 Informatika Szakmódszertani Konferencia.*

Reeves, C. R. (2009). Genetic algorithms. Encyclopedia of Database Systems, 1224-1227.

Romero, C., & Ventura, S. (Eds.). (2006). *Data mining in e-learning* (Vol. 4). Wit Press. doi:10.2495/1-84564-152-3

Sánchez-Acevedo, M. A., Sabino-Moxo, B. A., & Márquez-Domínguez, J. A. (2017). Mobile Augmented Reality. *Mobile Platforms, Design, and Apps for Social Commerce, 153.*

Schiaffino, S., Garcia, P., & Amandi, A. (2008). eTeacher: Providing personalized assistance to e-learning students. *Computers & Education, 51*(4), 1744–1754. doi:10.1016/j.compedu.2008.05.008

Shah-Hosseini, H. (2009). The intelligent water drops algorithm: A nature-inspired swarm-based optimization algorithm. *International Journal of Bio-inspired Computation, 1*(1-2), 71–79. doi:10.1504/IJBIC.2009.022775

Shen, L., Wang, M., & Shen, R. (2009). Affective e-learning: Using" emotional" data to improve learning in pervasive learning environment. *Journal of Educational Technology & Society, 12*(2), 176.

Song, L., Singleton, E. S., Hill, J. R., & Koh, M. H. (2004). Improving online learning: Student perceptions of useful and challenging characteristics. *The Internet and Higher Education, 7*(1), 59–70. doi:10.1016/j.iheduc.2003.11.003

Sun, P. C., Tsai, R. J., Finger, G., Chen, Y. Y., & Yeh, D. (2008). What drives a successful e-Learning? An empirical investigation of the critical factors influencing learner satisfaction. *Computers & Education, 50*(4), 1183–1202. doi:10.1016/j.compedu.2006.11.007

Tang, T. Y., & McCalla, G. (2003). Smart recommendation for an evolving e-learning system. *Workshop on Technologies for Electronic Documents for Supporting Learning, International Conference on Artificial Intelligence in Education,* 699-710.

Van Eck, R. (2007). Building artificially intelligent learning games. In *Games and simulations in online learning: Research and development frameworks* (pp. 271–307). IGI Global. doi:10.4018/978-1-59904-304-3.ch014

Van Krevelen, D. W. F., & Poelman, R. (2010). A survey of augmented reality technologies, applications and limitations. *International Journal of Virtual Reality, 9*(2), 1.

Villaverde, J. E., Godoy, D., & Amandi, A. (2006). Learning styles' recognition in e-learning environments with feed-forward neural networks. *Journal of Computer Assisted Learning, 22*(3), 197–206. doi:10.1111/j.1365-2729.2006.00169.x

Wang, L. (2001). Intelligent optimization algorithms with applications. Tsinghua University & Springer Press.

Wang, S. C. (2003). Artificial neural network. In Interdisciplinary computing in java programming (pp. 81-100). Springer US. doi:10.1007/978-1-4615-0377-4_5

Web Resources Depot. (2009). *7 Widely-Used and Open Source E-Learning Applications*. Retrieved from https://webresourcesdepot.com/7-widely-used-and-open-source-e-learning-applications/

Welsh, E. T., Wanberg, C. R., Brown, K. G., & Simmering, M. J. (2003). E-learning: emerging uses, empirical results and future directions. *International Journal of Training and Development, 7*(4), 245-258.

Wen-Shung Tai, D., Wu, H. J., & Li, P. H. (2008). Effective e-learning recommendation system based on self-organizing maps and association mining. *The Electronic Library, 26*(3), 329-344.

Wenger, E. (2014). *Artificial intelligence and tutoring systems: computational and cognitive approaches to the communication of knowledge*. Morgan Kaufmann.

Whitley, D. (1994). A genetic algorithm tutorial. *Statistics and Computing, 4*(2), 65–85. doi:10.1007/BF00175354

Woolf, B. P. (2010). *Building intelligent interactive tutors: Student-centered strategies for revolutionizing e-learning*. Morgan Kaufmann.

Wu, H. K., Lee, S. W. Y., Chang, H. Y., & Liang, J. C. (2013). Current status, opportunities and challenges of augmented reality in education. *Computers & Education, 62*, 41–49. doi:10.1016/j.compedu.2012.10.024

Yang, X. S., & Deb, S. (2010). Engineering optimisation by cuckoo search. *International Journal of Mathematical Modelling and Numerical Optimisation, 1*(4), 330–343. doi:10.1504/IJMMNO.2010.035430

Yegnanarayana, B. (2009). *Artificial neural networks*. PHI Learning Pvt. Ltd.

Zhang, D., Zhou, L., Briggs, R. O., & Nunamaker, J. F. Jr. (2006). Instructional video in e-learning: Assessing the impact of interactive video on learning effectiveness. *Information & Management, 43*(1), 15–27. doi:10.1016/j.im.2005.01.004

Zhu, A. (2017). *Artificial Neural Networks. The International Encyclopedia of Geography*. Wiley.

ADDITIONAL READING

Abraham, A. (2005). *Artificial neural networks. Handbook of measuring system design*. Wiley.

Alpaydin, E. (2014). *Introduction to machine learning*. MIT Press.

Arora, J. S., & Baenziger, G. (1986). Uses of artificial intelligence in design optimization. *Computer Methods in Applied Mechanics and Engineering, 54*(3), 303–323. doi:10.1016/0045-7825(86)90108-8

Atkins, D. E., Brown, J. S., & Hammond, A. L. (2007). A review of the open educational resources (OER) movement: Achievements, challenges, and new opportunities (pp. 1-84). Creative common.

Aydin, C. C., & Tirkes, G. (2010). Open source learning management systems in distance learning. TOJET: The Turkish Online Journal of Educational Technology, 9(2).

Azuma, R., Baillot, Y., Behringer, R., Feiner, S., Julier, S., & MacIntyre, B. (2001). Recent advances in augmented reality. *IEEE Computer Graphics and Applications*, *21*(6), 34–47. doi:10.1109/38.963459

Azuma, R. T. (1997). A survey of augmented reality. *Presence (Cambridge, Mass.)*, *6*(4), 355–385. doi:10.1162/pres.1997.6.4.355

Boettcher, S., & Percus, A. (2000). Nature's way of optimizing. *Artificial Intelligence*, *119*(1-2), 275–286. doi:10.1016/S0004-3702(00)00007-2

Bonabeau, E., Dorigo, M., & Theraulaz, G. (1999). *Swarm intelligence: from natural to artificial systems (No. 1)*. Oxford university press.

Braunschweig, B. L., Pantelides, C. C., Britt, H. I., & Sama, S. (2000). Process modeling: The promise of open software architectures. *Chemical Engineering Progress*, *96*(9), 65–76.

Brusilovsky, P. (1999). Adaptive and intelligent technologies for web-based eduction. KI, 13(4), 19-25.

Brusilovsky, P., & Peylo, C. (2003). Adaptive and intelligent web-based educational systems. *International Journal of Artificial Intelligence in Education*, *13*(2), 159–172.

Cavus, N. (2016). Development of an Intellegent Mobile Application for Teaching English Pronunciation. *Procedia Computer Science*, *102*, 365–369. doi:10.1016/j.procs.2016.09.413

Cohen, E., & Nycz, M. (2006). Learning objects and e-learning: An informing science perspective. *Interdisciplinary Journal of E-Learning and Learning Objects*, *2*(1), 23–34.

Coppola, C., & Neelley, E. (2004). Open source-opens learning: Why open source makes sense for education.

Cusumano, M. A. (2004). Reflections on free and open software. *Communications of the ACM*, *47*(10), 25–27. doi:10.1145/1022594.1022615

Dagger, D., O'Connor, A., Lawless, S., Walsh, E., & Wade, V. P. (2007). Service-oriented e-learning platforms: From monolithic systems to flexible services. *IEEE Internet Computing*, *11*(3), 28–35. doi:10.1109/MIC.2007.70

Dalziel, J. (2003). Open standards versus open source in e-learning. *EDUCAUSE Quarterly*, *26*(4), 4–7.

Engelbrecht, A. P. (2006). *Fundamentals of computational swarm intelligence*. John Wiley & Sons.

Evans, J., Jordan, S., & Wolfenden, F. (2016). Developing academics' assessment practices in open, distance and e-learning: an institutional change agenda.

Feller, J., & Fitzgerald, B. (2002). *Understanding open source software development* (pp. 143–159). London: Addison-Wesley.

Fisler, J., & Bleisch, S. (2006). eLML, the eLesson Markup Language: Developing ustainable e-Learning Content Using an Open Source XML Framework. In In WEBIST 2006-International Conference on Web Information Systems and Technologies, April 11th-13th 2006 (Setubal).

Goldszmidt, M., Cohen, I., Fox, A., & Zhang, S. (2005). Three Research Challenges at the Intersection of Machine Learning, Statistical Induction, and Systems. In HotOS.

Graf, S., & List, B. (2005). An evaluation of open source e-learning platforms stressing adaptation issues. In Advanced Learning Technologies, 2005. ICALT 2005. Fifth IEEE International Conference on (pp. 163-165). IEEE. doi:10.1109/ICALT.2005.54

Hauger, D., & Köck, M. (2007). State of the Art of Adaptivity in E-Learning Platforms. In LWA (pp. 355-360).

Hernández-Leo, D., Bote-Lorenzo, M. L., Asensio-Pérez, J. I., Gocmez-Sanchez, E., Villasclaras-Fernández, E. D., Jorrín-Abellán, I. M., & Dimitriadis, Y. A. (2007). Free-and open-source software for a course on network management: Authoring and enactment of scripts based on collaborative learning strategies. *IEEE Transactions on Education*, *50*(4), 292–301. doi:10.1109/TE.2007.904589

Jennings, N. R. (2000). On agent-based software engineering. *Artificial Intelligence*, *117*(2), 277–296. doi:10.1016/S0004-3702(99)00107-1

Keegan, D. (2004). *Foundations of Distance Education*. New York: Routledge.

Kennedy, J. (2006). Swarm intelligence. In Handbook of nature-inspired and innovative computing (pp. 187-219). Springer US.

Kounavis, C. D., Kasimati, A. E., & Zamani, E. D. (2012). Enhancing the tourism experience through mobile augmented reality: Challenges and prospects. *International Journal of Engineering Business Management*, 4.

Kumar, S., Gankotiya, A. K., & Dutta, K. (2011). A comparative study of moodle with other e-learning systems. In Electronics Computer Technology (ICECT), 2011 3rd International Conference on (Vol. 5, pp. 414-418). IEEE. doi:10.1109/ICECTECH.2011.5942032

Kunene, M. F., & Barnes, N. (2017). Perceptions of the Open Distance and E-Learning Model at a South African University. *International Journal of Education and Practice*, *5*(8), 127–137.

Lantz, B. (2015). *Machine learning with R*. Packt Publishing Ltd.

Lee, H., Sin, D., Park, E., Hwang, I., Hong, G., & Shin, D. (2017). Open software platform for companion IoT devices. In Consumer Electronics (ICCE), 2017 IEEE International Conference on (pp. 394-395). IEEE.

Leung, E. W. C., & Li, Q. (2007). An experimental study of a personalized learning environment through open-source software tools. *IEEE Transactions on Education*, *50*(4), 331–337. doi:10.1109/TE.2007.904571

Li, S., Zhang, J., Yu, C., & Chen, L. (2017). Rethinking Distance Tutoring in e-Learning Environments: A Study of the Priority of Roles and Competencies of Open University Tutors in China. *The International Review of Research in Open and Distributed Learning*, *18*(2). doi:10.19173/irrodl.v18i2.2752

Littlejohn, A. (Ed.). (2003). *Reusing online resources: a sustainable approach to e-learning*. Psychology Press.

Lujara, S., Kissaka, M. M., Trojer, L., & Mvungi, N. H. (2007). Introduction of open-source e-learning environment and resources: A novel approach for secondary schools in Tanzania. *The International Journal of Social Sciences (Islamabad)*, *1*(4), 237–241.

Marsland, S. (2015). *Machine learning: an algorithmic perspective*. CRC Press.

Papadimitriou, C. H., & Steiglitz, K. (1998). *Combinatorial optimization: algorithms and complexity*. Courier Corporation.

Pavlicek, R., & Foreword By-Miller, R. (2000). *Embracing insanity: Open source software development*. Sams.

Pawlowski, J. M., Ras, E., Tobias, E., & Snezana, Å. Ä., DÃ3nal, F., Mehigan, T., ... & Moebs, S. (2016). Barriers to open e-learning in public administrations. *Technological Forecasting and Social Change*, *111*(C), 198–208.

Pfenninger, S., DeCarolis, J., Hirth, L., Quoilin, S., & Staffell, I. (2017). The importance of open data and software: Is energy research lagging behind? *Energy Policy*, *101*, 211–215. doi:10.1016/j.enpol.2016.11.046

Prlić, A., & Procter, J. B. (2012). Ten simple rules for the open development of scientific software. *PLoS Computational Biology*, *8*(12), e1002802. doi:10.1371/journal.pcbi.1002802 PMID:23236269

Read, T., Barcena, E., Traxler, J., & Kukulska-Hulme, A. (2017). Toward a Mobile Open and Social Language Learning Paradigm.

Reyes, N. R., Candeas, P. V., Galan, S. G., Viciana, R., Canadas, F., & Reche, P. J. (2009). Comparing open-source e-learning platforms from adaptivity point of view. In *EAEEIE Annual Conference*, 2009 (pp. 1-6). IEEE. doi:10.1109/EAEEIE.2009.5335482

Russell, S. J., Norvig, P., Canny, J. F., Malik, J. M., & Edwards, D. D. (2003). *Artificial intelligence: a modern approach* (Vol. 2). Upper Saddle River: Prentice Hall.

Scacchi, W. (2001). Software development practices in open software development communities: a comparative case study. In Making Sense of the Bazaar: Proceedings of the 1st Workshop on Open Source Software Engineering.

Soman, K. P., Loganathan, R., & Ajay, V. (2009). *Machine learning with SVM and other kernel methods*. PHI Learning Pvt. Ltd.

Stracke, C. M. (2017). Open education and learning quality: The need for changing strategies and learning experiences. In *Global Engineering Education Conference (EDUCON)*, 2017 IEEE (pp. 1049-1053). IEEE. doi:10.1109/EDUCON.2017.7942977

Stracke, C. M. (2017). Why We Need High Drop-Out Rates in MOOCs: New Evaluation and Personalization Strategies for the Quality of Open Education. In Advanced Learning Technologies (ICALT), 2017 IEEE 17th International Conference on (pp. 13-15). IEEE.

Strobl, C., & Neteler, M. (2016). Open Data with Open Software-the EU Copernicus Programme.

Tsolis, D., Stamou, S., Christia, P., Kampana, S., Rapakoulia, T., Skouta, M., & Tsakalidis, A. (2010). An adaptive and personalized open source e-learning platform. *Procedia: Social and Behavioral Sciences, 9,* 38–43. doi:10.1016/j.sbspro.2010.12.112

Wagner, N., Hassanein, K., & Head, M. (2008). Who is responsible for e-learning success in higher education? A stakeholders' analysis. *Journal of Educational Technology & Society, 11*(3).

Woolf, B. P. (2010). *Building intelligent interactive tutors: Student-centered strategies for revolutionizing e-learning.* Morgan Kaufmann.

KEY TERMS AND DEFINITIONS

Artificial Intelligence: (1) Artificial intelligence is a sub-field of computer science dealing with research studies on developing intelligent systems simulating the human-thinking behavior and intelligence or specific mechanisms in nature. (2) Artificial intelligence is a concept used for describing the feature, function, or characteristic of computer systems or machines that are able to simulate human-thinking behavior and intelligence or specific mechanisms from nature.

E-Learning: E-learning is a type of learning activity supported and performed with electronic media sources by directing individuals to experience learning while eliminating limitations caused by time or place.

Intelligent Optimization: Intelligent optimization is a type of optimization that is done by using artificial-intelligence-based approaches, methods, or techniques.

Machine Learning: Machine learning is a sub-field of artificial intelligence, including approaches, methods, and techniques, that has the mechanism of learning from pre-data in order to be trained for dealing effectively with new problem states and solving them.

Open Source (Software): Open source is a type of software system or program of which source codes are freely available to use, change, or adapt.

Optimization: Optimization is the process of finding the most appropriate value or state of a mathematical function or a specific decision variable.

Chapter 6
Unlocking the Unlimited Potentials of Koha OSS/ ILS for Library House- Keeping Functions:
A Global View

Adekunle P. Adesola
Bowen University, Nigeria

Grace Omolara O. Olla
Bowen University, Nigeria

ABSTRACT

Drawing praxis from Bowen University, Nigeria and other libraries worldwide, the chapter unveils the limitless capabilities of Koha ILS to successfully manage core library house-keeping functions—cataloging, acquisitions, circulation control, patrons' management, OPAC, serials, and report generation—in one seamless whole. Web-based features like its flexibility, adaptability, interoperability, MARC, Z39.50, patrons' ability for online logging in, registration, renewal, and many more were revealed. Also, reasons for its global adoptability, benefits, likely challenges, and solutions from practitioners were also highlighted. The chapter concludes that despite the puny but eventually surmounted challenges, Koha holds unlimited potential for libraries of any shape/size by just garnering from the experiences of subsisting users of the software globally.

INTRODUCTION

Faced with growing users' expectations unleashed by current and emerging ICTs and a gradual decline in library revenue, librarians resorted to devising survival strategies to prune down cost and still meet users' expectations. This necessitated a cautious and gradual move towards Open Source Software (OSS)/ Integrated Library Systems (ILS), which has since proved to be a fortuitous move as more libraries are

DOI: 10.4018/978-1-5225-5314-4.ch006

now assuming direct responsibility of anchoring their house-keeping functions and continue to satisfy their growing users' expectations at drastically reduced costs rather than been subjected to the vagaries of software vendors under the proprietary cloud. This has made OSS to become a very popular point of discussion in the library world (Breeding, 2007; Corrado, 2007; Wrosch, 2007). The growing interest among librarians concerning OSS is further reinforced by the fact that the May/June 2007 issue of American Library Association (ALA) TechSource's Library Technology Reports focused on free and OSS (Singh, 2014).

Consequently, this has led to renewed interests, research and experimentations in OSS/ILSs implementation, adoption and use in libraries as demonstrated by an avalanche of research articles on the subject resulting in the gaining of better understanding of the potential uses and capabilities of Open Source Software (OSS) in libraries. Leading the pack of these growing OSS/ILS according to Breeding, (2012) are *Koha* and Evergreen.

As an antecedent to this growing interest in OSS/ILS a lot of libraries worldwide have implemented and are using *Koha* Integrated Library System (ILS) while many more are at varying degrees of adoption and implementation. Some of the reasons for its popularity, acceptance and adoption include being an Open Source Software (OSS), enjoying robust vendor, technical and other supports from community of users (*Koha* Community), its user friendliness, being web based, its support of RSS feeds and social media applications e.g. tagging, its expansiveness (ability to accommodate grown and growing collection), and its interoperability with other databases (Z39.50 allows data import from Library of Congress, Dewey Decimal Classification Scheme, OCLC, etc.), to mention a few.

Moreover, the literature abounds with *Koha* adoption, implementation, utilisation, challenges, comparative advantages over others in its category, checklist for evaluation and every other aspect of its unlimited potentials. Interestingly, Bowen University Library (BUL) is the first library in Nigeria to have fully utilised the whole range of modules (Ojedokun, Olla & Adigun, 2016; ProjektLink, 2010) although not without its attendant challenges which were eventually surmounted, thus giving her a leading edge over other libraries using the software.

Drawing examples from Bowen university and other libraries worldwide, this paper presents time tested and ever increasing potentials of *Koha* OSS/ILS to manage successfully the house-keeping functions of any library.

Objectives

This paper aims to go beyond the theoretical by showcasing the unlimited potentials of *Koha* ILS for library's house-keeping functions of

1. Cataloging
2. Acquisitions
3. Circulation
4. Patrons
5. Serials
6. OPAC
7. Reports

LITERATURE REVIEW

The literature review will highlight different themes pertaining to *Koha* Open Source Software/Integrated Library System (OSS/ILS) as gleaned from over fifty research articles available to the authors. Some of these are its features, adoption, implementation, use, growing popularity globally and among Nigerian libraries, advantages over other library software, challenges faced at various stages of implementation and use and how they were overcome, evaluative and comparative studies, among other issues.

Wikipedia (2012) and Gkoumas and Lazarinis (2015) describe integrated library system (ILS) also referred to as library management system (LMS), as an enterprise resource planning system for a library, used to track items owned, orders made, bills paid and patrons who have borrowed. According to Wikipedia (2012), most of the ILSs are made up of separate modules which are usually integrated with a unified interface. Examples of these modules include Acquisitions, Cataloguing, Circulation, Patrons, Serials and an Online Public Access Catalogue (OPAC). Gkoumas and Lazarinis (2015) added that an ILMS must contain the concept of integrated, i.e. the application must cover all the needs of running a library and using a database and be composed of modules, responsible for cataloging, acquisitions, circulation, serial management, online catalog (OPAC) and interlibrary loan.

In the same vein, ILSs are software applications and hardware that organise, track, and make accessible library information resources. Modules compose the basic architecture of these systems and represent some facet of library operations (Breeding, 2008a in Pruett & Choi, 2013); while Open Source Software (OSS) is a computer software that is released under some free/public license and permits users to study, change and improve the software (Kandar, Mondal & Ray, 2011). "A key aspect of [OSS] is the availability of the source code – the human readable text files used to create the program. Accessing the source code allows anyone to examine the program to see how it works, fix bugs, or change it to suit personal needs. Like freedom of speech, one does not need to use source code to benefit from it" (Pfaffman, 2007).

Koha is one and perhaps, the most widely used of such ILS in libraries. (Adekunle, Olla, Oshiname & Tella, 2015) The name *Koha* comes from a Maori term for a "gift" or "donation. *Koha* is the oldest open source library management software, created in New Zealand by the Horowenua Library Trust and Katipo Communications in 2000 (Wikipedia, 2013). *Koha* has been in the market for more than a decade, has matured greatly and is in use in hundreds of libraries the world over, including the over 40 (and still counting) libraries in Nigeria. (Kari and Baro, 2014; Projektlink Konsult Limited, 2010).

Koha project describes itself on its "About" page thus:

Koha is the first open-source Integrated Library System (ILS). in use worldwide, its development is steered by a growing community of libraries collaborating to achieve their technology goals. Koha's impressive feature set continues to evolve and expand to meet the needs of its user base. In use worldwide in libraries of all sizes, Koha is a true enterprise-class ILS with comprehensive functionality including basic or advanced options. Koha includes modules for circulation, cataloging, acquisitions, serials, reserves, patron management, branch relationships, and more. (Walter & Joann 2010)

Features of *Koha*

Koha is reported to have a range of features including a web based interface, web based Online Public Access Catalogue (OPAC), Cataloguing module, Circulation module, Acquisitions module, Serials module, Reporting module, Copy cataloguing and Z39.50 compliance, MARC21 and UNIMARC for professional cataloguers, ability to manage online and off line resources with the same tool, RSS feed of new acquisitions, ability to e-mail and/or text patron's overdue and other notices, print barcodes, simple and clear search interface for all users, a multi-tasking nature and ability to enable updates of circulation, cataloguing and issues to occur simultaneously (Abboy and Hoskins, 2008; EIFL-FOSS, 2013; Hyoju, 2012; Kushwah, 2008; Lavji and Niraj, 2006; Lopata, 1999; Oduwole, 2005; Okoroma, 2010; Ukachi, Nwachukwu and Onuoha, 2014; Wikipedia, 2011; Zaid, 2004 in Obajemu, Osagie, Akinade and Ekere, 2013).

Consequently, Wikipedia (2012) cited in Uzomba, Oyebola and Izuchukwu (2015) asserts that *Koha* has most of the features that would be expected in an ILS, including various Web 2.0 facilities like tagging, comment, social sharing and RSS feeds, union catalog facility, customisable search, circulation and borrower management, full acquisitions system including budgets and pricing information (including supplier and currency conversion), simple acquisitions system for the smaller library, ability to cope with any number of branches, patrons, patron categories, item categories, items, currencies and other data, serials system for magazines or newspapers among others .All features performing functions as their names imply.

Shafi-Ullah and Qutab (2012) also highlight some *Koha* features as including its simple, clear interface for users, Web 2.0 facilities like tagging and RSS feeds, union catalogue, customised search, strong multi-patron management, etc. Also corroborated by Pruett and Choi (2013), that *Koha*'s OPAC integrates many enhanced content features typical of Web 2.0 including: RSS feeds to notify patrons of new acquisitions in their area of interest, tagging, and comment boxes for search results. Ata-ur-Rehman, Mahmood & Bhatti (2012) added that *Koha* is MARC and z39.50 compliant library system for all types of libraries with a web-based software that has been built on LAMP (Linux, Apache, MySQL, Perl/PHP) platforms.

Pruett & Choi (2013) also emphasise features such as the catalog, OPAC, circulation, acquisitions, serials control, authority control (considered as part of the cataloging module), reporting, and administration modules; but noted the absence of interlibrary loan module.

Koha has been described as a next-generation OPAC for searching the library catalogue, providing two search forms for the users: the simple and the advanced forms. The simple form is a Google-like form available directly from *Koha* home page while the OPAC is a "Social OPAC" or "Web 2.0 OPAC" with many features like tags from patrons, clouds of subject entries and tags, RSS feeds, enriched contents from Amazon, Google, Syndetics Solutions, and LibraryThing, results list sorted by popularity of the items, and dynamic research refinements. (Tajoli, Carassiti, Marchitelli and Valenti, 2011).

Reasons for Adoption

The main reasons for the adoption of, and interest in *Koha* OSS among librarians are the ability to eliminate their dependence on the proprietary service vendors, gain more control over the ILS by customising it to local requirements (Wrosch, 2007), reach lower costs and acquire the flexibility of additional feature development (Eby, 2007). Another reason why an open-source ILS like *Koha* appeals to libraries is its underlying philosophy: "Open source and open access are philosophically linked to intellectual freedom, which is ultimately the mission of libraries." The other two common reasons are cost and functionality (Singh, 2013).

Paul (2010) concurs with the position above and asserts that, *Koha* appears to be the most used perhaps because, adopting *Koha* not only lowers the overall automation costs to a library but, more importantly, it empowers an organisation to take control of the technology and "drive the direction of your integrated library system (ILS) rather than act as a passenger". Furthermore, it is an open-source integrated library system and does not require funds to download and customise (Iroaganachi, Iwu and Esse, 2015). Hence, in a study describing the automation of Adeyemi College of Education Library, Egunjobi and Awoyemi, (2012) observed that using *Koha* ILS will help to solve one of the major problems of library automation in Nigeria which is funding. Additionally, *Koha* has developed different versions, has been translated to over 100 languages, is widespread (implemented in over one thousand libraries worldwide), is readily available and accommodates active participation of both users and developers (Ramzan, 2004, Keep Solutions, 2011; SenthilKumaran and Sreeja, 2017). Hence, Zico (2009) observed that the open source nature of *Koha* makes for easy access to support for developers, users and maintainers.

Earlier, in a paper which focused on the development of an ILS using *Koha*, Zico (2009) stated that the web based nature of *Koha* makes it flexible and portable. According to him *Koha* was installed on a server and was accessed via Internet Protocol (IP) address or its Uniform Resource Locator (URL) thereby eliminating the need to install a third party software like Microsoft Visual Basic to have a complete Library management system. All that is needed is a web browser from which the ILS can be accessed by any computer that is connected to the Internet. He further stated that he was able to customise the *Koha* installation. In his overview of the security system of *Koha* ILS, he reported that the OPAC grants different levels of access to documents on *Koha*. Ogbenege and Adetimirin (2013) also discovered that *Koha* was selected because of integration, ease of use, accessibility and flexibility.

Comparative and Evaluative Studies on *Koha*

A lot of available literature on *Koha* OSS/ILS focused on comparative analysis of *Koha* with other software in its category while others presented an evaluation checklist aimed at helping prospective users decide on which software to adopt based on their strengths and weaknesses

Yang and Hofmann's (2010) comparative study shows that *Koha's* OPAC has six out of the ten compared features for the next-generation catalog, plus two halves. According to them, its full-fledged features include state-of-the-art web interface, enriched content, faceted navigation, a simple keyword search box, user contribution, and RSS feeds. The two halves indicate the existence of a feature that is not fully developed. For instance, "Did you mean . . . ?" in *Koha* does not work the way the next-generation catalog is envisioned. In addition, *Koha* has the capability of linking journal titles to full text via Serials Solutions, while the other two OPACs only display holdings information. Evergreen falls into a distant second position, providing four out of the ten compared features.

Similarly, Singh and Sanaman's (2012) comparative analysis of *Koha* and NewGenLib reveals that both types of software are web-enabled and support library automation but *Koha* has more specific characteristics of open source ILMS, requires very little hardware and is easy to install. Furthermore, *Koha* has advanced database features, supports more formats and standards, provides more user-friendly downloads and a documentation facility.

Macan, Ferna´ndez & Stojanovski (2013) presented an overview of two open source (OS) integrated library systems (ILS) – *Koha* and ABCD (ISIS family), comparing their "next-generation library catalog" functionalities, given comparison of other important features available through ILS modules. A checklist was created for each module: acquisition, cataloging, serials, patron management and circulation, reports and statistics, and administration.

The evaluative study reveals that *Koha* has more functionalities than ABCD, especially those connected with the "next generation library catalog".

Pruett and Choi (2013) also compared select open source and proprietary ILS and find that *Koha* and Evergreen have well developed modules, including circulation, cataloging, the OPAC, authority, administration, reports, and acquisitions that cover all basic technical activities in academic and public libraries. These modules facilitate all major work-flows for library technical services departments and provide the interface for library patrons. As such, library administrators should best consider open source ILS migrations within the context of internal, community, and vendor support. *Koha* and Evergreen have proven adaptable and scalable. The authors concluded that if economics, specialised services, or technical issues necessitate migration to a new integrated library system, open source is a viable alternative to proprietary vendors.

In Singh's (2014) comparison of the technical support-related experiences with the expectations of librarians using open source integrated library systems (ILS), he finds many channels of technical support available to librarians who use open source ILS. Also, these channels of technical support perform at acceptable levels according to the expectations of librarians using open source software.

Madhusudhan and Singh (2016) cited in Sarma (2016) analyse the various features and functions of *Koha*, Libsys, NewGenLib and Virtua with the help of specially designed evaluation checklist and rank them based on features/functions of integrated library management system (ILMS). According to them, the evaluation approach taken is similar to that taken by Singh and Sanaman (2012) and Madhusudhan and Shalini (2014) with minor modifications, comprising 306 features/functions and categorized as ten broad categories. Their findings which evaluated various features and functions of open source (OS) and commercial ILMS reveals that Virtua got the highest score of 218 (77.86 per cent), followed by *Koha* ILMS with 204 score (72.86 per cent) while NewGenLib got the lowest total score, that is, 163 (58.21 per cent) among those evaluated.

Contrary to Madhusudhan and Singh's (2016) findings above, Sarma's (2016) comparative study reveals that *Koha* has fourteen out of the fifteen compared functionalities and comes in the top with NewGenLib coming a far distance behind *Koha*, providing ten out of the fifteen compared functionalities. *Koha*'s full-fledged functionalities include a simple keyword search box, advance search, user contribution through login, and RSS feeds, linking search results with social networking sites and external databases like Google Books and Amazon Books, etc. Evergreen and PhpMyBibli, came in third and fourth, providing eight and seven out of the fifteen functionalities respectively. OpenBiblio supports only two functionalities out of fifteen and comes in last.

From the foregoing therefore, there is no gainsaying that *Koha* is an OSS/ILS with many features and functionalities. It is gaining global acceptability and thus holds a lot of benefits for libraries of all shapes and sizes.

Benefits of *Koha* OSS/ILS

Available literature is replete with numerous benefits of adopting and using *Koha* OSS/ILS. Open source ILS allows libraries to have more control over their software (Breeding and Yelton, 2009a), designing additional functionalities to meet their specific patrons' needs (Genoese and Keith, 2011). *Koha* has additional benefits of customization, flexibility, no vendor lock-in and other OSS-specific advantages (Singh, 2014). In addition, mature open source applications like *Koha* offer a lower total cost of ownership than their commercial counterparts (Surman and Diceman, 2004). Other unique attributes of *Koha* OSS include zero costs of acquisition, ability to use for whatever purpose, ability to adapt to meet local requirements, and ability to distribute changes. Some of the key reasons for OSS low cost are given by Wheeler (2007b) in Amollo (2013), when he asked, "Why Open Source Software/Free Software (OSS/FS)? Look at the Numbers!" According to the author, with *Koha*, no license fees are required, upgrade and maintenance costs are far less due to improved stability and security, OSS can often use older hardware more efficiently than proprietary systems, it yields smaller hardware costs, sometimes eliminating the need for new hardware.

Mace (2015) states that one of the major strengths of *Koha*, which also happens to be one of its limitations, is that it is an open source system. This reduces the library's dependence on a proprietary provider for a business-critical system, and allows greater control over data and software. Thereby, "bringing development closer to the users i.e. the library as well as patrons, who have a greater ability to influence improvements of the system."

Koha, no doubt, has a host of benefits for any library that seeks a user friendly, customisable, cost-effective software with long term vendor and community support, no licensing costs and reduced time of processing library items.

Challenges Associated With OSS

As with other inventions, along with the benefits, there are a number of potential disadvantages associated with adoption and use of OSS. Some of the disadvantages identified with OSS include poor usability, less user-friendly interfaces, a lack of functionality, reliability, security and support, increased costs for purchasing local technical expertise, the lack of guaranteed support or upgrades, lack of technical support during its implementation and the lack of ongoing maintenance of the software (Walls, 2011; Breeding, 2007; Wrosch, 2007; Boss, 2005; Buchanan and Krasnoff, 2005; Cervone, 2003).

However, technical support issues appeared to be a key challenge for librarians who want to adopt OSS or evaluate the feasibility of OSS for their libraries. These issues included installation and configuration (Khan, Zahid & Rafiq, 2016) Also, professionals faced the challenge of choosing where the software was to be installed from such as from its official website, from USB, from DVD or from CD.

Implementation of *Koha* specifically had its challenges, such as poor Internet access, slow speed, low bandwidth, difficulties in installation and maintenance (because of its complex installation procedure), data migration and network problems, erratic power supply, insufficient manpower (Kumar and Jasimudeen, 2012; Omeluzor, Adara, Ezinwayi, Bamidele & Umahi, 2012; Keast, 2011). Walls (2010) notes that the current cataloging interface for *Koha* is considered to be rather awkward, MARC tags are grouped into different tabs, making it difficult to see all the applicable fields in a record at once and *Koha* lacks several important functionalities used in previous ILS before adopting *Koha* such as electronic resources management (ERM) and course reserves.

The experiences of librarians, as stated by Singh (2013), are useful for people who are evaluating open source ILSs, as well as those who are in the process of adoption. This is particularly important because learning from their experiences will help librarians not to reinvent the wheel. The experiences shared in this paper will therefore help the librarians by empowering them with the information they need, and in understanding the current status of *Koha* ILS software.

Daily Challenges in Running and Maintaining *Koha* ILS: Bowen University Experience

Since the adoption of *Koha* in 2007, Bowen University Library (BUL) is yet to experience any major complaints about its versatility. However, there had been some hardware and software challenges, the latter of which can also be experienced on cloud. These include the *Koha* server rebooting, non-connection of client workstation to the server, mounting as read-only, *Koha* allowing duplication of barcode, wrong mapping, indexing problems on *Koha*, uninterrupted sleep by *Koha*, *Koha* not sending mails to patrons, inability of *Koha* to monitor patron transaction, *Koha* not charging/calculating overdue fines, available items showing as 'not loanable', *Koha* double-charging overdue fines, patron identification stamp not on overdue fines payment and system error. In spite of the challenges experienced in running and maintaining *Koha* ILS, there have been gains as better service delivery and development of skilled manpower. There is, however, no doubt that there will be challenges of implementation and of consistently running the ILS, but because of the support available through participation in the open source software ILS user community forum, such challenges can be readily surmounted (Ojedokun, Olla and Adigun, 2016).

Solutions to Technical Issues

Vendor support has been identified as the major solution to technical issues associated with OSS/ILS adoption/implementation. Some developers implemented an alternative business model for OSS where the software source code and licensing are obtained for free by the libraries while charging for installation and training just to ensure a continuous flow of technical support for OSS. Also, commercial companies, like LibLime for *Koha* and Equinox for Evergreen, provide technical support for the adoption, implementation and maintenance of OSS ILS. This accords librarians the benefits of customisation, flexibility, no vendor lock-in and other OSS-specific advantages, while recognising that they also need support for implementing and adopting OSS ILS (Breeding and Yelton, 2009b).

Vendor support option is increasing greatly and has contributed in making OSS/ILS more workable in the library field. According to Breeding (2008b), the proliferation of support options for open source ILS has greatly strengthened its viability for library use, especially for *Koha* and Equinox, and LibLime partnering with Syndetic to extend functionalities (College & Research Libraries News, 2009; Library Journal, 2009a; Library Journal, 2010a; Technology Libraries, 2010a). Cibbarelli (2008) therefore identified different channels to support ILS available for users of OSS ILS such as phone, email, chat and discussion forums. Concluding that technical support is used quite often (almost weekly) by the librarians while paid technical support is commonly accessed by librarians using open source ILS.

Global Adoption and Growing Popularity of *Koha* OSS/ILS

Open-source software (OSS) has become increasingly popular in libraries, and every year more libraries migrate to an open-source integrated library system. There are many discrete open-source applications used by libraries which include *Koha*, Evergreen, and OPALS and have emerged as the most widely implemented and serve as good examples of current state-of-the-art open source ILS. However, the two most popular open-source ILSs in the United States are *Koha* and Evergreen, which are being positioned as alternatives to proprietary ILSs, but a large number of libraries all over the world are using *Koha* ILS for library automation. *Koha* ILS has, as a result, expanded from serving as the integrated library system (ILS) of a single public library in New Zealand to more than one thousand academic, public, and private libraries across the globe (Afroz, 2014; Ata-ur-Rehman, Mahmood and Bhatti, 2012; Randhawa, 2008; Willis, 2010 in Ojedokun, Olla and Adigun, 2016). According to Breeding (2008b) therefore, *Koha* ranks as the first full-featured open-source LMS and serves the most number of libraries, mainly public libraries in the USA.

Karetzky (1998) states that the best sources of reliable information about a particular library application are usually librarians who are currently using it. Singh (2013b) buttresses this by asserting that the experiences of librarians using the software are useful for people who are evaluating open source ILSs, as well as those who are in the process of adoption. Learning from their experiences will help librarians not to reinvent the wheel identified in Ojedokun, Olla and Adigun (2016).

According to Bissels (2008), the first *Koha* implementation experience in the UK, was in 2008 at the CAMLIS library, Royal London Homoeopathic Hospital. Bissels and Chandler (2010) reported that two years after, *Koha* grew into an LMS that supports the wide-ranging needs of a busy and fast-growing specialist library. CAMLIS customised *Koha* by modifying its modules and making additions to meet its needs flexibly, using both UK-based consultancy firms with *Koha* expertise simultaneously.

Walls (2010) details the circumstances, methods and outcomes of the New York University Health Sciences Libraries' (NYUHSL) migration from their previous integrated library system (ILS), Innovative Interfaces, Inc.'s Millennium, to the open-source ILS *Koha*. The study identifies several areas of development for *Koha*, including electronic resource management, course reserves, and cataloging client enhancements and proves that a migration from Millennium to *Koha* could be done very quickly, if the library is properly motivated. New York University Health Sciences Libraries' (NYUHSL) was able to pull off an unprecedented migration with minimal interruption to patron services, despite an aggressive timetable and limited staff resources. In the process, workflows were modified, and some functionality were lost, but the potential for the library to fully control their system and data, and to integrate it with practically any other library system, was well worth the change. Walls concluded that the NYUHSL, having identified some key areas for development, has the potential to be a significant contributor to the international *Koha* community, making *Koha* a better ILS for libraries the world over.

Rafiq and Ameen (2010) in Ata-ur-Rehman, Mahmood, Bhatti (2012) conducted a survey of sixty one (61) university libraries in Pakistan to find the use of free and open source software and found that only three libraries (4.9%) were using *Koha* ILS but as far as the intentions of the library professionals are concerned, 47.8% library professionals said they would adopt *Koha* ILS in future. Consequently, Shafi-Ullah and Qutab (2012) documented the data migration process from LAMP (Library Automation Management Program) to the open source software *Koha*'s (2.2.8 Windows based) in six legislative assembly libraries of Pakistan over the course of three months. The authors reported challenges faced and surmounted with the solutions and support of local consultants and support groups coping with the issues. Thereby concluding that data migration can be done quickly if any support group is properly involved with the library staff.

Furthermore in Pakistan, Khan, Zahid & Rafiq (2016) discussed the process of *Koha* implementation in Government College University (GCU) Library, Lahore in replacing the Library Management Software (LMS) implemented in 1999. The authors address the major technical problems encountered in the implementation of *Koha* and offer solutions, while assuming that other libraries that implemented *Koha* also faced such problems but glossed over the challenges and their solutions. The study also offers valuable insights for Pakistani librarians at large and other libraries in general which are in the process of implementing *Koha* for automation.

Likewise, in Bangladesh, Ahammad (2014) also narrated how the implementation of the *Koha* open-source integrated library system (ILS) at the Independent University Bangladesh (IUB) Library, was carried out with ease and encouraged library professionals to implement *Koha* in their libraries. In Taiwan, bearing testimony to the flexibility, versatility and global acceptability of *Koha* Chang, Tsai and Hopkinson (2010) considered issues of different scripts in the same record when implementing *Koha* (i.e. in MARC21 and Chinese machine-readable cataloguing (CMARC)) and Chinese internal codes i.e. double-byte character set), with a view to promoting the adoption of *Koha* in Taiwan, particularly the contributions from *Koha*-Taiwan and other Asian countries such as China, Japan and Korea

In the same vein, Anuradha, Sivakaminathan and Arun (2011) claim to have made the first implementation enabling the full-text search feature in a library automation software by integrating it into digital library software which enabled full-text search features in the widely used open-source library automation package *Koha*, by integrating it with two open-source digital library software packages, Greenstone Digital Library Software (GSDL) and Fedora Generic Search Service (FGSS), independently. The findings show that full-text searching capability in *Koha* is achieved by integrating either GSDL or FGSS into *Koha* thus confirming its interoperability potentials.

In Australian, where it all started from, Keast (2011) examine the adoption of *Koha* amongst Australian special libraries. According to him, the main reasons given for conversion to *Koha* were practical economic grounds, and the dissatisfaction with conventional library systems. For the libraries, the conversion to *Koha* was reasonably trouble-free and the rate of satisfaction on most aspects of *Koha* performance were "above average" to "good". Library therefore realised their expectations of value for money and overall cost savings.

Furthermore, Amollo (2013) examined the feasibility of the adoption of open source ILS for libraries in Kenya and discovered that out of about ten different types of OSS library systems provided by the respondents as being installed in their libraries, among which are *Koha*, Open Biblio and Winisis, *Koha* seems to have more users compared to the rest. Findings showed that majority had installed *Koha* in their libraries and 67 per cent of the respondents have either worked with or are familiar with *Koha*. The author concluded from the results of findings that there is great potential for OSS in Kenya and OSS has gained sufficient momentum for it to be taken seriously in Kenya's libraries because there is a shift towards open source (*Koha* to be precise) in Kenya's libraries. Also, OSS would be an affordable option at the outset for libraries that wish to automate their processes, having the necessary expertise for installing and implementing due to budgetary constraints in majority of the libraries surveyed.

Also in France, Espiau-Bechetoille, Bernon, Bruley and Mousin (2011) chronicle how three university libraries (Rho^ne-Alpes, France) decided to switch their proprietary software for the Open-ILS *Koha*, with particular focus on how they organised themselves to pool their technical skills, human resources and costs together, thereby providing information for acquiring knowledge and expertise in an Open-ILS, and minimized costs by cooperating.

Among various adoptions and implementations, Stump & Deegan (2013) adopted *Koha* to convert a faculty-created Microsoft Word document of biblical references found within popular films into a searchable database for scholars, at the Albright College, U. S., thus creating a multi-access database called Bible in the Reel World, thereby facilitating faculty research and collaboration with librarians. Also, Afroz (2014) found *Koha* to be the only ILS that satisfies the key functional requirements of a library management system and supports the essential modules, such as cataloguing, circulation, serials, and OPAC that BRAC University library requires. The author learnt that the library could not operate an ILS project without a dedicated systems librarian based in the library itself who will take care of technical issues of installation and customisation.

Librarians in university libraries in Nigerian claim to be using *Koha* for operations such as cataloging, OPAC, serials, acquisitions, circulation, to collate staff research output for the university and manage patron profiles (Kari and Baro, 2014). Thus Awoyemi and Olaniyi's (2012) findings revealed that in ten academic libraries surveyed in Nigeria, cataloging and serials control are embedded in full automation efforts (100%) with the help of *Koha*. Furthermore, *Koha* is used extensively (80% each) in both Patron Management and Selective Dissemination of Information (SDI). Ogbenege and Adetimirin (2013) also discover that *Koha* was selected because of integration, ease of use, accessibility and flexibility. The study concludes that the software was not maximally used in the two universities studied. The results reveal that rate of use in Redeemers University was 49% while Bowen University was 64.3%.

An earlier study by Otunla and Akanmu-Adeyemo (2010) however reported otherwise. Ogbenege and Adetimirin's study ran contrary to Otunla and Akanmu-Adeyemo's study which focused on users' satisfaction with *Koha* application to library operations in Bowen University Library, the first University Library in Nigeria to install and fully utilise *Koha* ILS (Projektlink, 2010; Ojedokun, Olla & Adigun, 2016). Otunla and Akanmu-Adeyemo report that *Koha* was performing to expectations in its first three years of use. The respondents also rated *Koha*'s reliability, Acquisitions module, Cataloguing and Circulations module, OPAC, Patrons' authentication, Report creation, and Interface with internet at 100%, 53%, 73.3%, 73.3%, 93.3%, 66.6% and 100% respectively.

Omeluzor, Adara, Ezinwayi, Bamidele & Umahi (2012) shared Babcock University Library's experience, the attendant challenges and how they were surmounted. Ukachi (2012) also studied 42 Nigerian libraries and reported that only 7 were then using CD/ISIS while 5 others utilise *Koha*. In the space of two years, over 40 Nigerian libraries adopted *Koha* while the number continues to increase. (Projektlink Konsult Limited, 2010).

Similarly, in a survey of factors affecting actual system use, Akinbobola and Adeleke (2013) submitted that usability, supportive management, and computer self-efficacy strongly influenced library personnel's actual use of the *Koha* software system. The findings of the study suggest that the *Koha* software meets library personnel's specifications and has the ability to fulfill their needs effectively and efficiently. The research enumerated overall staff satisfaction for the use of *Koha* ILS, concluding that the use of *Koha* ILS will solve the problem of manual processing and untimely statistics generation.

Also, results of a survey by Kari and Baro (2014) reveal that 24 (66.7%) of university libraries in Nigeria use *Koha*, thus buttressing the findings of an earlier survey by Awoyemi and Olaniyi (2012) that *Koha* was the only open-source software used. This also consolidates the findings of Ogbenege and Adetimirin (2013) that claims that *Koha* was implemented in Bowen and Redeemers University libraries in Nigeria in 2007 and 2011 respectively. Kari and Baro's study further reveals that various software had been in use in various libraries for some time. *Koha* had been in use in a number of university libraries for about ten years, SLAM for about nine years, while VIRTUA for about five years. The authors suggest that those university libraries that had used library software for nine to eleven years must have migrated to *Koha* and SLAM, an indication that these seemed to be the most suitable library software to manage library operations in university libraries in Nigeria.

Akpokodje and Akpokodje's (2015) paper evaluates the adoption of *Koha* ILS for library online registration at the University of Jos, Nigeria. Among other findings, the authors conclude that Open access ILS is more cost effective and aids ease of access to information. Correspondingly, Iroaganachi, Iwu and Esse (2015) discover that *Koha* was the most commonly adopted software and perceived to be most available to academic libraries from South-West Nigeria universities.

Uzomba, et. al (2015) also examine the use of open source integrated library systems in academic libraries in Nigeria in order to highlight the capabilities and potentials of *Koha*, and its practical importance to academic libraries across the globe. The authors report that apart from the fact that it requires little or no cost to operate, it has also proved to be more reliable and effective; and among all the open source software available in the Nigerian market, *Koha* had gained more usability, stability and acceptability in academic libraries.

Functionalities

Almost all the papers reviewed by the authors refer to the functionalities of *Koha* OSS/ILS which contributed to its growing popularity worldwide. However, this section will adopt Pruett and Choi (2013) and Ojedokun, Olla & Adigun, (2016) in discussing the functionalities of *Koha*. Apart from the clear picture painted by Pruett and Choi (2013) and Ojedokun, Olla & Adigun, (2016), the authors of this work are part of the success stories of *Koha* adoption, implementation and ten years of unbroken utilisation in Bowen University library, making it the first and longest running history of *Koha* in Nigeria, and possibly Africa, which has been beautifully captured in Ojedokun, Olla & Adigun (2016).

Koha comprises the cataloging, OPAC, circulation, acquisitions, serials control, authorities control (considered as part of the cataloging module), reports, and administration modules (see Figure 1), however, no interlibrary loan module (manual.Koha-community.org/3.8/en/). Muller (2012) cited in Afroz (2014) ranked *Koha* ILS the most complete FOSS ILS because it performs a number of functions, including routing periodicals, inventory control, authorities, generation of notices to customers, and order tracking

With Koha, access/permission granted is determined by functions to limit/track errors

Acquisitions

The acquisitions module allows librarians to enter information about the library's vendors, including contracts, provides a way to manage suggestions from patrons, manage/track purchases grouped within "baskets" or order; and see information on available funds (see Figures 2 to 8). As asserted by Ojedokun et al, most libraries prefer to manage the acquisitions process manually rather than using the *Koha*

Figure 1. BUL Koha Staff Client

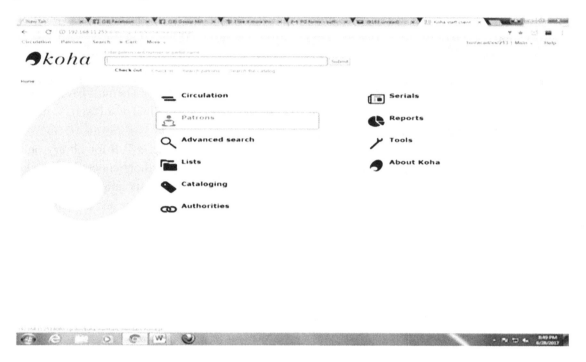

acquisitions module, *Koha* enables a library to acquire library materials, especially through purchases, as well as to set up and track budgets/funds and all materials added to the library database, create suppliers/vendors, manage purchase suggestions, perform acquisitions searches, record orders, place orders, receive ordered items, track late or missing orders, create invoices for ordered items, and claim late orders. The module also makes it possible to perform both "simple" and "full" acquisitions as desired, save money by ascertaining the availability of a material from the database before ordering and eases accounting. Librarians note that the module has great flexibility and is user friendly as it makes selection of item type e.g. books, audio cassettes, CD, DVD, etc., possible while the template displays the fields as appropriate for the chosen type (Ojedokun et al, 2016).

Cataloguing

As seen in Figures 9, 10 and 11, in the *Koha* cataloging module, librarians are able to either create original bibliographic records, or import an existing record from Z39.50, add, search for, and edit authorities, and create full MARC records if needed. Thus, "*Koha*'s simple and advanced search (see Figures 12 and 24) helps in culling out existing records from acquisitions for editing. *Koha* makes use of MARC 21 and UNIMARC standard for cataloguing framework...the cataloguers, working with the acquisitions staff, are able to create new records that do not exist in the database while the use of Z39.50 standard for importing the cataloguing details from remote library server (e.g. Library of Congress) makes editing of records already created faster. *Koha* helps maintenance of database integrity as it allows the cleaning of the database, thus removing the problem of incomplete record and duplicated barcode (accession

Figure 2. Acquisitions Module

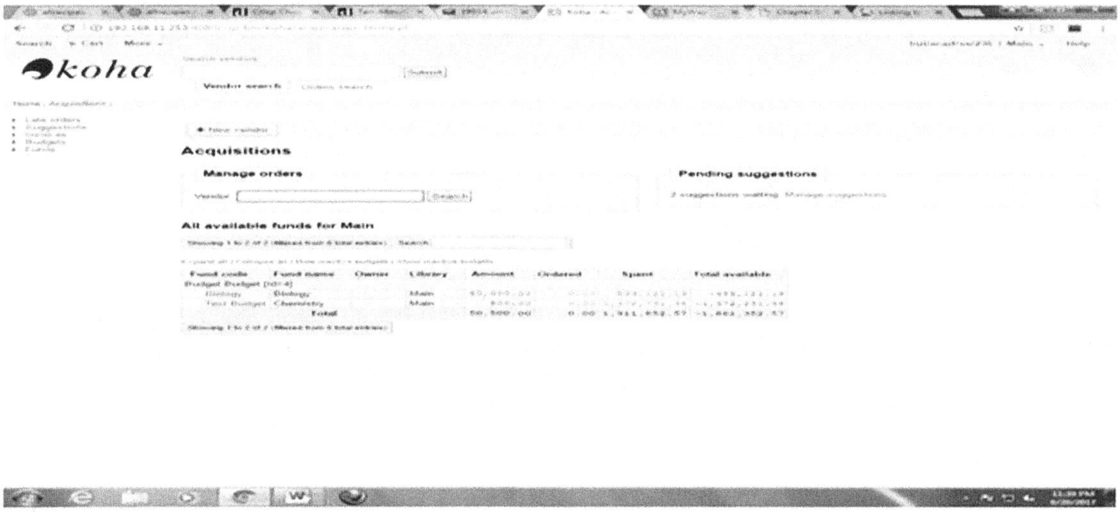

Figure 3. Create new vendor account

number). *Koha* allows batch saving of items, deletion of duplicate records from the database, and time saving in material processing. It permits easy retrieval of items from the database through the use of access points such as barcode, ISBN, title, subject and author." (Ojedokun et al; Pruett and Choi, 2013).

Create new record or item, import new records from Z39.50, edit records or items created earlier either from Acquisitions or through the Cataloguing Module.

With Koha, BUL has been able to edit items in batch instead of individually, attach an already existing item to another with same details, duplicate and edit new items and replace records through Z39.50, thereby saving time.

Figure 4. Manage/claim late orders

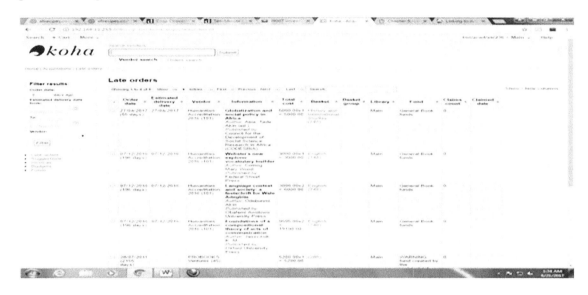

Figure 5. Process patrons' suggestion

Circulation Control

Koha ILS has been reported to ease patron registration through the possibility of online self-registration, thereby ruling out the stress and cumbersome nature of manual registration. Figures 14 to 20 show that in addition to check-outs, check-ins, holds, and patron notices, *Koha* allows librarians to create circulation

Figure 6. Allocate Budgets

Figure 7. Placing Orders

Figure 8. Receiving Shipments/Orders

Figure 9. Cataloging Module

Figure 10.

reports, and track in-house use of library materials, edit/modify account, create private/public reading list(s), tag, secure transaction through self-activated passwords, monitor fine imposition, place items of interest on hold, do self-renewal of items, and suggest useful titles for acquisition at the comfort of the patrons' office/hostel, generation of overdue fines/notices, issuance of notices to defaulting patrons, restriction of patron's account to enforce compliance with library rules, easy deactivation of patrons' account as a result of graduation/disengagement from service, and setting of limit on overdue fine. *Koha* is not susceptible to manipulation, as overdue fines are system generated and cannot be deleted without due permission. *Koha* even has an offline circulation utility, in case of a network or power outage (Ojedukun et al, 2016; Pruett and Choi, 2013).

From the circulation module library staff can search the library catalog, check items in and out, renew and transfer items, perform fast cataloging of new items, set library holding for a particular item and generate circulation reports such as fines, books on hold, transfers etc

Figure 11. Edit Record or Item

Figure 12. Circulation module

Figure 13. Simple search of the catalog from the circulation end

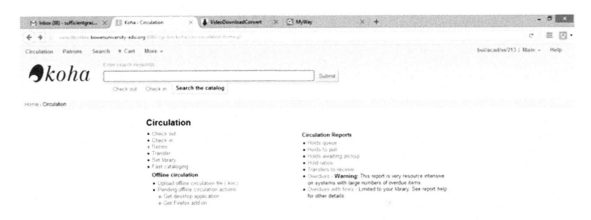

Figure 14. Item check out

Figure 15. Item check in

Figure 16. Item Renewal (Online/Library)

Figure 17. Intra-library Transaction

Figure 18. Patrons management

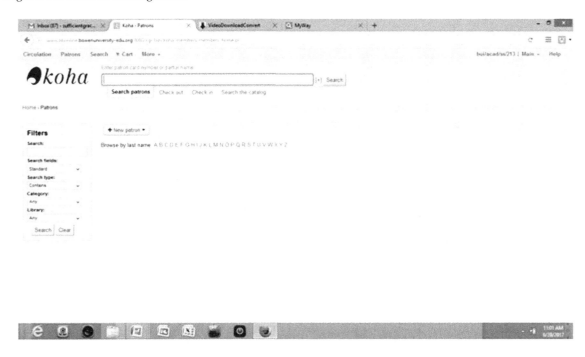

Figure 19. Register new patron

Figure 20. Register new patron by category

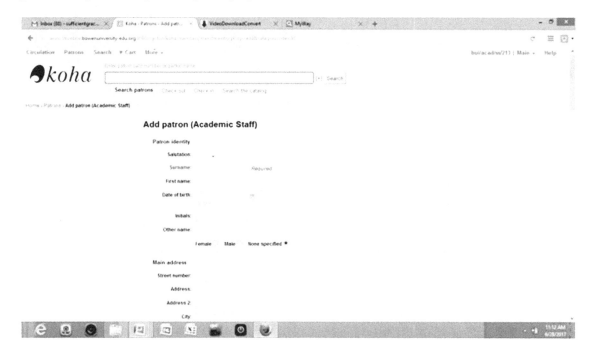

Koha patrons module enables staff to register new patrons, search for existing patrons, browse patrons by last name, check items into and out of patron's account.

Serials Control

The *Koha* serials control module allows librarians to search for, add or and create serials records, create routing lists for branch libraries, track issue regularities and subscription due dates, spot and make claims on late issues as revealed in Figures 21 and 22. Ojedokun et al (2016) reported that with *Koha*, tracking of journals and other materials that come in on a regular schedule is easier, as well as monitoring branch libraries holding specific journal titles. *Koha* has also made multiple receipts and editing of issues simultaneously, possible.

With the serials module, staff can add new subscription, track journal titles/issues, claim late issues, check expiration.

While tracking journals, Koha enables you receive new issues and also view the regularity and history of a title.

OPAC

The OPAC shown in Figure 23 is a very important aspect of *Koha*. It is web-enabled, integrating many enhanced content features typical of Web 2.0 including RSS feeds, tagging, and comment boxes for search results. The simple search interface of OPAC provides 6 access points for searching and links the library user with the library collection and for the advanced searcher and librarian, *Koha* uses the common command language (CCL) (Pruett and Choi, 2013).

Figure 21. Serials Module

Figure 22. Serials Tracking

Reports Generation

Koha's reports module allows librarians to create their own SQL queries, or use the system's pre-determined reports, however, it only displays those reports in tabular format. With *Koha*, report generation is less cumbersome. *Koha* has its own guided report and can also accommodate generation of reports using Structured Query Language (SQL) statements, which makes it compliant with modern day software (Ojedokun et al, 2016).

Figure 23. Bowen University Library OPAC

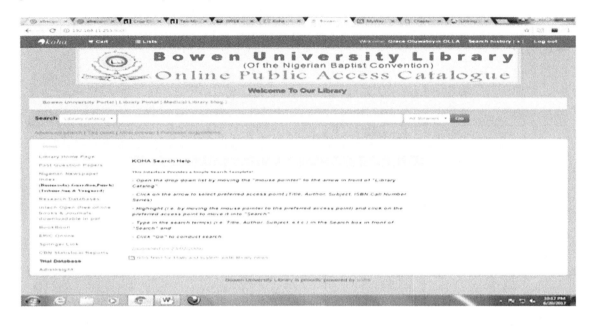

Figure 24. Advanced search

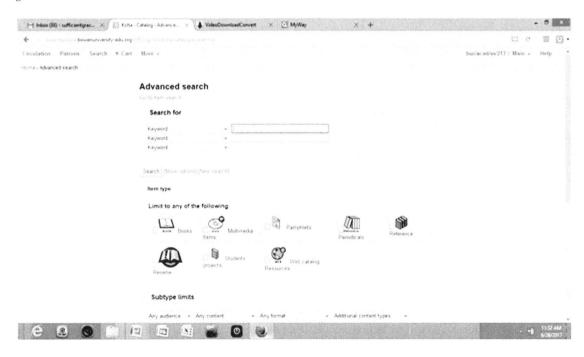

REPORTS GENERATION IN BOWEN UNIVERSITY LIBRARY

Reports generation has become indispensable in libraries to evaluate processes and give summaries of work done. Various Library Management Software are employed in generating reports suiting to the specific needs of libraries. From literature reviewed on various aspects of *Koha* ILS, only Otunla and Akanmu-Adeyemo (2010), Chang, Tsai, and Hopkinson (2010), Keep Solutions (2011), Singh and Sanaman (2012), Hyoju (2012), Akinbobola and Adeleke (2013), Ahammad (2014), Ojedokun, Olla, Adigun (2016), Mama (2016) and SenthilKumaran and Sreeja (2017) made reference to "Reports module" in their studies.

Otunla and Akanmu-Adeyemo's (2010) survey alluded to " report creation, Hyoju's (2012) study referred to "reporting modules" of *Koha* ILS, while Ahammad (2014) and SenthilKumaran and Sreeja (2017) mentioned "report" as one of the modules covered. Chang, Tsai, and Hopkinson (2010) noted that "the report module allows the creation of statistics for all the other modules with the reports generated displayed on the screen. These could also be downloaded as files to be opened with a spreadsheet or text editor. Furthermore, *Koha* has predefined reports, a wizard to create new reports in an easy way, a form to insert SQL queries for creating them and the *Koha* community has a wiki page with many examples of reports from which librarians can find the report they need or ask developers to write new ones. However, they could also create reports from scratch."

Keep Solutions (2011) noted that *Koha* enables the creation and export of reports covering a wide range of indicators and statistics. The system is accompanied by a report wizard that simplifies the creation of reports by non-expert users. Singh and Sanaman (2012) stated that" in *Koha* customised report generation/flexible reporting is integrated ", and Akinbobola and Adeleke's (2013) study concluded that the use of "*Koha* ILS will solve the problem of manual processing and untimely statistics generation".

Ojedokun, et al. (2016) surmise that "with *Koha* the library is able to generate management reports in shorter time than was possible while using the manual process. For example, it now becomes easier for the library to generate lists of holdings for the various departments of the university on demand, take inventory of library holdings, map collection for balanced development as well as produce other statistical reports as and when required". Lastly, Mama (2016) asserts that "the reporting module is the life-saver of the librarians of the said university because of the fast, accurate, and reliable report generation of the system". He added that *Koha* ILS is a big help to the library in terms of the generation of reports because all of the reports can be generated by *Koha* ILS whenever the librarian needs them.

Although *Koha* ILS comes with "Guided Reports" thus making it possible for libraries to generate tailored reports, it also accommodates reports generation using SQL statements. This is corroborated by Boss (2008) that *Koha* came with the original source code used to create it thus allowing libraries to customise it to meet their own needs. Bowen University Library has been able to take advantage of SQL statements to generate required management reports useful for its peculiar needs, thereby making reports generation less cumbersome and as Ojedokun et al noted, easier and faster.

Figure 25 shows some examples of customised *Koha* reports generated in Bowen University Library (BUL) employing SQL statements.

Patron/Circulation Control

Unlike the traditional manual user registration, *Koha* ILS eases patron registration through the possibility of online self-registration. It also allows patrons to edit/modify accounts, create private/public reading

Figure 25. Examples of BUL reports generated using SQL statements

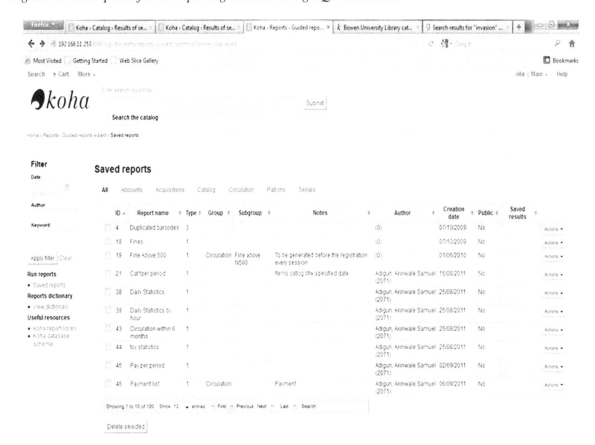

list(s), social tagging, secure transaction through self activated passwords, monitor fine imposition, place items of interest on hold, perform self-renewal of items, and suggest useful titles for acquisition from the comfort of the patrons' office/hostel. *Koha* also allows generation of overdue fines and notices, issuance of notices to defaulting patrons, restriction of patron's account to enforce compliance with library rules, easy de-activation of patrons' account as a result of graduation or disengagement from service, and setting of a limit on overdue fines.

Table 1 highlights *Koha* report module's capacities to generate not only monthly Circulation statistics as shown but daily, weekly, quarterly and annual summaries of activities in a session. From the table, it is possible to determine how many times library items are issued, renewed and returned. As seen also from the table, Patron category of those who are issued library items as well as those who renewed or returned items can be easily determined.

Similarly, Table 2 shows quarterly breakdown of registered library patrons and their categories which can be further broken down to daily, weekly, monthly, quarterly, annually or as desired by individual libraries. The categorisation is crucial as it determines borrowing privileges enjoyed by different categories.

Table 3 is a further breakdown and summation of registered library users across library network. As shown in this example, we have three libraries in the entire network namely the Main, Medical and law libraries.

Table 1. Issues, Renewals and Returns

Patrons Category	Issues				Renewals				Returns			
	Oct	Nov	Dec	Total	Oct	Nov	Dec	Total	Oct	Nov	Dec	Total
Academic Staff	37	36	14	**67**	26	20	25	**71**	35	36	20	**91**
Senior Staff	14	1	11	**26**	13	8	2	**23**	12	12	10	**34**
Junior Staff	6	3	5	**14**	3	7	3	**13**	5	4	3	**12**
Post Graduate	0	3	4	**7**	0	0	0	**0**	0	2	1	**3**
Under Graduate	216	257	33	**506**	76	84	24	**184**	125	238	92	**455**
Total	**273**	**300**	**67**	**640**	**118**	**119**	**54**	**291**	**177**	**292**	**126**	**595**

Table 2. Quarterly breakdown of Users' Registration at a point in time

Patrons Category	Total as at the End of the Previous Quarter	Addition This Quarter	Total as at the End of This Quarter
Academic	273	2	**275**
Senior Staff	112	2	**114**
Junior Staff	30	0	**30**
Postgraduate	13	1	**14**
Undergraduate	6,158	252	**6,410**
Total	**6,586**	**257**	**6,843**

Table 3. Breakdown of Users Registration Across Entire Library Network

Patrons Category	Total as at the End of 1st Quarter	Addition This Quarter				Total as at the End of This Quarter
		Main	Medical	Law	Total	
Academic	273	2	0	0	2	**275**
Senior Staff	112	1	0	1	2	**114**
Junior Staff	30	0	0	0	0	**30**
Postgraduate	13	1	0	0	1	**14**
Undergraduate	6,158	225	16	11	252	**6,410**
Total	**6,586**	**229**	**16**	**12**	**257**	**6,843**

Monthly Breakdown of Overdue Payment

Table 4 is a reflection of monthly summation of overdue payment for a particular library (Main) within the network. As earlier mentioned, overdue fines are system programmed as well as calculated. At the end of desired period (daily, weekly, monthly, etc.) reports module can be used to calculate the amount of overdue fines paid and cleared from the system. Manager ID from the table refers to authorised collector of overdue payments.

Table 4. Overdue Payment for the month of January

Surname	First Name	Card Number	Date	Amount (N)	manager_id	Branch Code
MARK	Joseph Babatunde	REG/SS/010	2016-01-22	-300	2475	MAIN
THOMSON	Theophilus Olatunde	ACAD/SS/004	2016-01-04	-500	2475	MAIN
HENRY	Lucas Adewumi	ACAD/SS/130	2016-01-13	-150	2475	MAIN
JULIUS	AinaAbosede	011/10404	2016-01-13	-10	2475	MAIN
TITUS	Ayotemi Deborah	012/11094	2016-01-22	-20	2475	MAIN
JUDAH	Priscilla Chukwu	012/11499	2016-01-14	-170	2475	MAIN
ISRAEL	Augustina Juwon	012/11524	2016-01-22	-1230	2475	MAIN
PHILIP	AleroLacherie	013/12731	2016-01-22	-160	2475	MAIN
JAMES	PaulMarvelous	014/13444	2016-01-22	-80	2475	MAIN
LOIS	Rachel	015/14499	2016-01-13	-20	2475	MAIN

Acquisitions

Koha acquisitions module has been used by Bowen University Library since 2007 to acquire library materials especially through purchases as well as to track budgets/funds and all materials added to the library database. *Koha* acquisitions module has been used to create vendors and budgets, track budget/ fund, manage purchase suggestions, perform acquisitions searches, place orders, receive ordered items, track all orders including late or missing orders, create invoices for ordered items and claim late orders.

Acquisitions by Purchase

Tables 5 and 6 reflect reports of purchases made in a quarter of a particular session. *Koha* has made it possible to organise these purchases according to vendors, discipline (departments or faculties) and branch libraries.

Acquisitions by Donation

Valuable additions to library collection are constantly received from members of the university community, corporate organisations and others. Table 7 shows donations that were received in a particular quarter, organised by donors and the item location i.e. discipline the donation is meant for.

Additions to the Library Database

Table 8 shows total additions to the library database in a quarter organised by library network and mode of acquisition. From the table, a total of 2 volumes (2 titles), 251 volumes (204 titles) and 479 volumes (305 titles) were added to the Medical, Law and Main libraries respectively. Also, a total of 266 volumes (82 titles) were received by means of donation while 466 volumes (429 titles) were purchased summing up to 732 volumes (511 titles) of books added to the library database.

Table 5. Expenditure on Acquisitions

Invoice Date	Vendor	Department/ Faculty	Titles	Volumes	Total Amount
15/04/2014	**Vendor A**	Humanities	109	113	**39,133.00**
17/04/2014	**Vendor B**	Humanities	112	125	**52,973.00**
28/04/2014	**Vendor C**	Humanities	6	7	**42,000.00**
15/05/2014	**Vendor D**	Humanities	1	1	**4,150.00**
26/05/2014	**Vendor E**	Law	35	47	**79,300.00**
30/05/2014	**Vendor F**	Law	99	99	**40,000.00**
06/06/2014	**Vendor G**	Law	2	5	**85,000.00**
27/06/2014	**Vendor H**	Law	65	69	**39,780.00**
27/06/2014	**Vendor D**	Medical	1	1	**2,350.00**
TOTAL (N)			**429**	**466**	**384,686.00**

Table 6. Expenditure by Branch Library

Library	Quarter		
	Purchase		Amount (N)
	Titles	Volumes	
Medical	1	1	**2,350.00**
Law	201	220	**244,080.00**
Main	227	245	**138,256.00**
Total	**429**	**466**	**384,686.00**

Table 7. Donations

Date	Donor	Item Location	Titles	Volumes
03/04/2014	Donor A	Law	1	1
09/05/2014	Donor B	Humanities	1	4
09/05/2014	Donor C	Humanities	2	2
09/05/2014	Donor D	SMS	1	3
16/05/2014	Donor E	Technology	2	21
16/05/2014	Donor F	Technology	1	18
16/05/2014	Donor G	Technology	2	84
17/06/2014	Donor H	Humanities	14	14
18/06/2014	Donor I	Law	2	30
18/06/2014	Donor J	Medical	1	1
18/06/2014	Donor K	SMS	10	26
18/06/2014	Donor L	SMS	33	35
18/06/2014	Donor M	AGR	12	27
TOTAL			**82**	**266**

Table 8. Additions to the Library database

Library	Quarter		
	Donated	**Purchased**	**Total**
Medical	1(1)	1(1)	**2(2)**
Law	31(3)	220(201)	**251(204)**
Main	234(78)	245(227)	**479(305)**
Total	**266(82)**	**466 (429)**	**732(511)**

* Figures in parentheses represent number of titles

Annual Summary

Table 9 shows quarterly breakdown of acquisitions by purchase in a session for the entire library network. *Koha* reports module makes it possible to query the database indicating a time-frame.

Table 10 shows expenditure on acquisitions for the entire library network organised quarterly in a particular session.

Table 11 is the quarterly breakdown of additions to the Library database in a particular session for the entire library network

Koha also makes it possible to know the total number of items in the library database whenever desired. Table 12 is a reflection of the status of the Library database at the end of a particular session.

Cataloguing and Classification

With the Cataloging framework, the Cataloguers, working with the Acquisitions staff are able to create new records that do not exist in the database while the use of Z39.50 feature make editing of records

Table 9. 2013/2014 Acquisition by Purchase

Library	1st Quarter	2nd Quarter	3rd Quarter	4th Quarter	Grand Total
Medical	0(0)	0(0)	1 (1)	1(1)	**2(2)**
Law	0(0)	0(0)	2 (1)	220(201)	**222(202)**
Main	4(1)	261(115)	211(110)	245(227)	**721(453)**
Total	**4(1)**	**261(115)**	**214 (112)**	**466(429)**	**945(657)**

Table 10. 2013/2014 Expenditure on Acquisitions

Library	1st Quarter	2nd Quarter	3rd Quarter	4th Quarter	Grand Total (N)
	Amount (N)	**Amount (N)**	**Amount (N)**	**Amount (N)**	
Medical	0	0	15,000.00	2,350.00	**17,350.00**
Law	0	0	2,500.00	244,080.00	**246,580.00**
Main	95,000.00	55,200.00	127,615.00	138,256.00	**416,071.00**
Total	**95,000.00**	**55,200.00**	**145,115.00**	**384,686.00**	**680,001.00**

Table 11. Total Additions to Library Collection in a given session

Library	1st Quarter	2nd Quarter	3rd Quarter	4th Quarter	Grand Total
Medical	1(1)	0 (0)	21(2)	2(2)	**24(5)**
Law	1(1)	4(2)	23(4)	251(204)	**279(211)**
Main	507(30)	306(119)	578(246)	479(305)	**1,870(700)**
Total	**509(32)**	**310(121)**	**622(252)**	**732(511)**	**2,173(916)**

* Figures in parentheses represent number of titles

Table 12. Status of the Library database

Item Type	Item Count	Title Count
Books (BK)	20,646	11,729
Multimedia items (MM)	123	52
Periodicals (P)	8,979	663
Pamphlets (PH)	1,210	457
Reference Materials (R)	2,577	882
Students Projects/Thesis (TH)	1,555	1,555
Total	**35,090**	**15,338**

Source: *Koha* Reports Module

already created faster. *Koha*'s simple and advanced search helps tremendously in culling out existing records from acquisitions for editing. Not only is the module simple, it is also flexible and user friendly. *Koha* enhances maintenance of database integrity as it allows the cleaning of the database thus removing problems such as incomplete records and duplicated barcodes (accession numbers). *Koha* allows batch saving of items, deletion of duplicate records from the database, and time saving in materials processing. It permits easy retrieval of items from the database through the use of access points such as barcode, ISBN, title, subject and author.

Table 13 shows item types added to each of the branches in the entire library network in a particular quarter. As shown in the table, *Koha* Reports module specifies item types and their placement in the library network.

The example in Table 14 shows summation of Item types for the entire library network. As shown in the table, a total of 2,307 items were added to the entire library collection during the quarter under review, thus bringing total library collection to 35,090 items at the end of the session.

With *Koha* Reports module, the total number of items in the entire library network can be generated as required. Table 15 shows that total collections in the Medical, Law and Main Libraries stood at 2,522, 3,847 and 28,721 respectively as at end of the session.

Annual Summary

Table 16 is a summation of quarterly additions to the entire library network in a particular session. *Koha* Reports Module also makes this possible.

Table 13. Addition of items to entire Library Network for a given Quarter

Item Type	Item Count as at the Previous Quarter			Additions During the New Quarter			Total
	Medical	Law	Main	Medical	Law	Main	
Books	1,099	845	18, 317	132	144	109	20,646
Multimedia items	6	0	37	0	0	80	123
Periodicals	855	1,620	4,959	181	30	1,334	8,979
Pamphlets	27	12	1,120	0	0	51	1,210
Reference	280	964	1,087	31	88	127	2,577
Students projects	0	0	1,555	0	0	0	1,555
Total	2,267	3,441	27,075	344	262	1,701	35,090

*Source: *Koha* Reports Module

Table 14. Summation of Item types for the entire library network during a particular quarter

Item Type	Item Count as at the End of the Previous Quarter	Additions During the 4th Quarter	Total
Books	20,261	385	20,646
Multimedia items	43	80	123
Periodicals	7,434	1,545	8,979
Pamphlets	1,159	51	1,210
Reference	2,331	246	2,577
Students projects	1,555	0	1,555
Total	32,783	2,307	35,090

Table 15. Breakdown of Item count for Libraries in the entire Network in a particular Session

Item Type	Library			Grand Total
	Medical	Law	Main	
Books	1,295	1,036	18,315	20,646
Multimedia items	12	1	110	123
Periodicals	901	1,784	6,294	8,979
Pamphlets	25	12	1,173	1,210
Reference	289	1,014	1,274	2,577
Students projects	0	0	1,555	1,555
Total	2,522	3,847	28,721	35,090

Table 16. Summation of item type in a particular session

Item Type	Item Count in the Previous Session	Additions During the 1st Quarter	Additions During the 2nd Quarter	Additions During the 3rd Quarter	Additions During the 4th Quarter	Grand Total
Books	18,952	201	182	926	385	**20,646**
Multimedia items	41	2	0	0	80	**123**
Periodicals	4,676	952	178	1,628	1,545	**8,979**
Pamphlets	793	197	39	130	51	**1,210**
Reference	2,182	11	90	48	246	**2,577**
Students projects	1,554	0	0	1	0	**1,555**
Grand Total	**28,198**	**1,363**	**489**	**2,733**	**2,307**	**35,090**

CONCLUSION

Koha translated 'gift' in the original Maori language has indeed been a gift to the World at large, and the Library particularly. With more than twelve years of uninterrupted operations in over three thousand libraries worldwide and without any deprecating instance to any of these libraries, *Koha* has certainly satisfied the aspirations of many libraries/librarians who hitherto, were groaning under the yoke of proprietary software. With a slew of features and benefits- enjoying robust vendor, technical and other supports from community of users (*Koha* Community), user friendliness, being web based, support of RSS feeds and social media applications e.g. tagging, its expansiveness (ability to accommodate grown and growing collection), and its interoperability with other databases (Z39.50 allows data import from Library of Congress, Dewey Decimal Classification Scheme, OCLC, etc.), to mention a few, (Adekunle, Olla, Oshiname & Tella, 2015) *Koha* remains the OSS/ILS to beat.

From the horde of articles reviewed by the authors, there was not a single deprecation of *Koha* and its unlimited potentials other than some puny technical/implementation challenges which were eventually surmounted. Having shown the unlimited potentials of *Koha* as drawn from practical applications worldwide, *Koha* is thus recommended to any library contemplating a cross-over to an OSS/ILS.

REFERENCES

Abboy, I., & Hoskins, R. (2008). The Use of CDS/ISIS Software in Africa. *Innovation*, *36*, 17–37.

Adekunle, P. A., Olla, G. O., Oshiname, R. M., & Tella, A. (2015). Reports Generation with *Koha* Integrated Library System (ILS): Some examples from Bowen University, Nigeria. *International Journal of Digital Library Systems*, *5*(2).

Afroz, H. (2014). Moving Towards the Next-Generation Library: BRAC University experience *World Digital Libraries, 7*(1), 1–14.

Ahammad, N. (2014). Implementing the *Koha* integrated library system at the Independent University, Bangladesh: A practical experience. *The Electronic Library, 32*(5), 642–658. doi:10.1108/EL-04-2012-0036

Akinbobola, O. I., & Adeleke, A. A. (2013). The influence of user efficacy and expectation on actual system use. *Interdisciplinary Journal of Information, Knowledge, and Management, 8,* 43-57. Retrieved June 27, 2016, from http://www.ijikm.org/Volume8/IJIKMV8p043-057Akinbobola0725.pdf

Akpokodje, N.V. & Akpokodje, T. E. (2015). Assessment and evaluation of *Koha* ILS for online library registration at University of Jos, Nigeria. *Asian Journal of Computer and Information Systems.*

Amollo, B. A. (2013). Feasibility of adaptation of open source ILS for libraries in kenya: A practical evaluation. *The Electronic Library, 31*(5), 608–634. doi:10.1108/EL-12-2011-0171

Anuradha, K. T., Sivakaminathan, R., & Arun, P. K. (2011). Open-source tools for enhancing full-text searching of OPACs: Use of *Koha*, Greenstone and Fedora. *Electronic Library and Information Systems, 45*(2), 231–239. doi:10.1108/00330331111129750

Ata-ur-Rehman, M. K., & Bhatti, R. (2012). Free and Open Source Software movement in LIS Profession in Pakistan. Library Philosophy and Practice, 1-20.

Awoyemi, A. R., & Olaniyi, S. T. (2012). A survey of the availability and use of *Koha* open source software by academic libraries in Nigeria. *COCLIN Journal of Library and Information Science, 5*(1/2), 9–29.

Bissels, G. (2008). Implementation of an open source library management system: Experiences with Koha 3.0 at the Royal London Homoeopathic Hospital. *Electronic Library and Information Systems, 42*(3), 303–314. doi:10.1108/00330330810892703

Bissels, G., & Chandler, A. (2010). Two years on: *Koha* 3.0 in use at the CAMLIS library, Royal London Homoeopathic Hospital. *Electronic Library and Information Systems, 44*(3), 283–290. doi:10.1108/00330331011064276

Boss, R. W. (2005). *Open source integrated library system software.* Retrieved from www.ala.org/ala/mgrps/divs/pla/plapublications/platechnotes/opensource 2008.doc

Boss, R. W. (2008). *"Open Source" Integrated Library System Software.* Public Library Association. Retrieved from http://www.ala.org/ala/mgrps/divs/pla/plapublications/platechnotes/ opensourceils.cfm)

Breeding, M. (2007). An update on open source ILS. *Computers in Libraries, 27*(3), 27–29.

Breeding, M. (2008a). *Open source integrated library systems. Library Technology Reports.* Washington, DC: ALA Techsource.

Breeding, M. (2008b). Major Open Source ILS Products. *Library Technology Reports*. Available at: www.techsource.ala.org

Breeding, M. (2012). Automation marketplace 2012: agents of change. *Library Journal, The digital shift*. Retrieved from www.thedigitalshift.com/2012/03/ils/automation-marketplace-2012-agents-of-change/

Breeding, M., & Yelton, A. (2009a). Analyzing comments for themes. *Library Technology Reports*, *47*(4), 9–11.

Breeding, M., & Yelton, A. (2009b). Breaking down the data. *Library Technology Reports*, *47*(4), 12–26.

Buchanan, K., & Krasnoff, B. (2005). Can open source software save school libraries' time and money? *Knowledge Quest*, *33*(3), 32–34.

Cervone, F. (2003). The open source option: Why libraries should and shouldn't be using open source software. *Library Journal*, *128*(12), 8–13.

Chang, N., Tsai, Y., & Hopkinson, A. (2010). An evaluation of implementing *Koha* in a Chinese language environment. *Electronic Library and Information Systems*, *44*(4), 342–356. doi:10.1108/00330331011083239

Cibbarelli, P. R. (2008). Helping you buy ILSs. *Computers in Libraries*, *28*(9), 45–53.

College & Research Libraries News. (2009). Available at: http://crln.acrl.org/content/by/year/2009

Corrado, E. M. (2007). *Libraries and the free and open source software movements*. Paper presented at the Fall Dinner Meeting of the New York Technical Services Librarians Association, New York, NY.

Eby, R. (2007). Open source server applications. *Library Technology Reports*, 48–53.

Egunjobi, R. A., & Awoyemi, R. A. (2012). Library automation with *Koha. Library Hi Tech News*, *29*(3), 12–15. doi:10.1108/07419051211241868

EIFL-FOSS. (2013). *Koha (FOSS Integrated Library System)*. Retrieved from http://www.eifl.net/ koha-fossintegrated-library-system

Espiau-Bechetoille, C., Bernon, J., Bruley, C., & Mousin, S. (2011). An example of inter-university cooperation for implementing *Koha* in libraries Collective approach and institutional needs. *OCLC Systems & Services: International Digital Library Perspectives*, *27*(1), 40–44. doi:10.1108/10650751111106546

Gautam, K. S. (2016). OPAC Module in Open Source Library Management Software: A comparative Study. *DESIDOC Journal of Library and Information Technology*, *36*(1), 56–61. doi:10.14429/djlit.36.1.9223

Genoese, L., & Keith, L. (2011). Jumping ship: One health science library's Voyage from a proprietary ILS to open source. *Journal of Electronic Resources in Medical Libraries*, *8*(2), 126–133. doi:10.1080 /15424065.2011.576605

Gkoumas, G., & Lazarinis, F. (2015). Evaluation and usage scenarios of open source digital library and collection management tools. *Electronic Library and Information Systems*, *49*(3), 226–241. doi:10.1108/ PROG-09-2014-0070

Hyoju, D. (2012). *Pilot of Virtual Union Catalogue (VUC) Using KOHA ILS for Nepali Libraries.* Retrieved January 5, 2016, from www.eifl.net/resources/pilot-virtual-union-catalogue-vuc-using-Koha-ils-nepali-libraries.

Iroaganachi, M. A., Iwu, J. J., & Esse, U. C. (2015). Software Selection and Deployment for Library Co-operation and Resource Sharing Among Academic Libraries in South-West Nigeria. *DESIDOC Journal of Library and Information Technology, 35*(1), 3–8. doi:10.14429/djlit.35.1.6885

Kandar, S., Mondal, S., & Ray, P. (2011). A review of Open Source Software and Open Source movement in developing countries. *International Journal of Computer Science & Informatics, 1*(1), 89–93.

Karetzky, S. (1998). Choosing an Automated System. *Library Journal, 123*(11), 42.

Kari, K. H., & Baro, E. E. (2014). The use of library software in Nigerian University Libraries and challenges. *Library Hi Tech News.* Retrieved from https://www.researchgate.net/publication/263287220

Keast, D. (2011). A survey of *Koha* in Australian special libraries: Open source brings new opportunities to the outback. *OCLC Systems & Services: International Digital Library Perspectives, 27*(1), 23-39.

Khan, M.T., Zahid, A. & Rafiq, M. (2016). Journey from Library management System (LMS) to *KOHA* by Government College University Libraries, Lahore. *Pakistan Journal of Information Management & Libraries, 17,* 184-190.

Kumar, V., & Jasimudeen, S. (2012). Selection and Management of Open Source Software in Libraries. *Annals of Library and Information Studies, 59,* 223–230. Retrieved from http://eprints.rclis.org/18198/1/ALIS%2059%284%29%20223-230.pdf

Kushwah, S. S. (2008). *Library Automation and Open Source Solutions Major Shifts and practices: A Comparative Case Study of Library Automating Systems in India.* International CALIBER.

Lavji, N. Z., & Niraj, R. P. (2006). Application of WINISIS/GENESIS Software in Newspapers Clippings. *DESIDOC Bulletin of Information Technology, 26*(1), 17–26. doi:10.14429/dbit.26.1.3671

Libraries, A. T. (2010a). Equinox announces *Koha* hosting, support services. *Advanced Technology Libraries, 39*(3), 1–12.

Libraries, A. T. (2010b). Nelsonville public chooses ByWater Solutions. *Advanced Technology Libraries, 39*(3), 2.

Library Journal. (2009a). LibLime and syndetic partner on enhanced content. *Library Journal, 134*(10), 19.

Library Journal. (2010a). Equinox to support *Koha* open source ILS. *Library Journal, 135*(5), 17.

Library Journal (2010b). Open source ILS plan for Pennsylvania PLs. *Library Journal, 135*(16), 16.

Lopata, C. (1995). Integrated Library Systems. *ERIC Digest.* Retrieved from http://www. Ericdigest. org/1996-1/library.htm

Macan, B., Ferna'ndez, G. V., & Stojanovski, J. (2013). Open source solutions for libraries: ABCD vs *Koha. Electronic Library and Information Systems, 47*(2), 136–154. doi:10.1108/00330331311313726

Mace, A. H. (2015). *Koha as a local circulation system?* Projekt Summary, January 2015 Stockholm University Library. Retrieved May 23, 2017, from http://www.sub.su.se/media/1114980/Koha-Project-Summary.pdf

Madhusudhan, M., & Shalini, A. (2014). Online public access catalogues of selected university libraries in Delhi: An evaluative study. *World Digital Libraries*, 7(1), 15–42.

Madhusudhan, M., & Singh, V. (2016). Integrated library management systems Comparative analysis of *Koha*, Libsys, NewGenLib, and Virtua. *The Electronic Library*, *34*(2), 223–249. doi:10.1108/EL-08-2014-0127

Mama, A. S. (2016). Perceived Impact on the Adoption of *Koha* on the State University Library's Management System. *International Conference on Research in Social Sciences, Humanities and Education*. Retrieved May 23, 2017, from http://uruae.org/siteadmin/upload/8346UH0516070.pdf

McGinnis, W. and Ransom, J. (2010). Kete and *Koha*: Integration built on open standards. *OCLC Systems & Services: International Digital Library Perspectives, 26*(2), 114-122.

Müller, T. (2012). *How to Choose an Free and Open Source Integrated Library System*. Retrieved from http://eprints.rclis.org/bitstream/10760/15387/1/How%20to%20choose%20an%20open%20source%20ILS.pdf

Obajemu, A. S., Osagie, J. N., Akinade, H. O. J., & Ekere, F. C. (2013). Library software products in Nigeria: A survey of uses and assessment. *International Journal of Library and Information Science*, *5*(5), 113–125.

Oduwole, A. A. (2005). Information Technology Applications to Cataloguing in Nigerian Universities. *The Electronic Library*, *23*(3), 1–2. doi:10.1108/02640470510603688

Ogbenege, J., & Adetimirin, A. (2013). Selection and use of *KOHA* software in two private Nigerian universities. *Library Hi Tech News*, *30*(6), 12–16. doi:10.1108/LHTN-04-2013-0020

Ojedokun, A. A., Olla, G. O., & Adigun, S. A. (2016). Integrated Library System (ILS) implementation: The Bowen University Library experience with *Koha*. *African Journal of Library Archives and Information Science*, *26*(1), 31–42.

Okoroma, F. (2010). Retrospective Conversion in Two Nigerian University Libraries: Comparative Study of Kenneth Dike Library and Obafemi Awolowo University Library. *Library Philosophy and Practice*, 1-26. Retrieved from http://www.Fags.org/periodicals/201005/ 2068075251.html

Omeluzor, S. U., Adara, O., Ezinwayi, M., Bamidele, M. I., & Umahi, F. O. (2012). Implementation of *Koha* Integrated Library Management Software (ILMS): The Babcock University Experience. *Canadian Social Science*, *8*(4).

Otunla, A. O., & Akanmu-Adeyemo, E. A. (2010). Library automation in Nigeria: The Bowen University experience. *African Journal of Library Archives and Information Science*, *20*(2), 93–102.

Paul, O. (2010). *Koha developer wiki: Koha users around the world*. Retrieved March 12, 2013, from http://wiki.Koha.org/doku.php?id_Kohaausers

Pfaffman, J. (2007). It's Time to Consider Open Source Software. *TechTrends, 51*(3), 38–43. doi:10.1007/s11528-007-0040-x

Projektlink Konsult Limited. (2010). *Introducing Koha: An Integrated Library Management System.* Ibadan, Nigeria: Blue Print Concept.

Pruett, J., & Choi, N. (2013). A comparison between select open source and proprietary integrated library systems. *Library Hi Tech, 31*(3), 435–454. doi:10.1108/LHT-01-2013-0003

Rafiq, M., & Ameen, K. (2009). Issues and lessons learned in open source software adoption in Pakistani libraries. *The Electronic Library, 27*(4), 601–610. doi:10.1108/02640470910979561

Rafiq, M., & Ameen, K. (2010). Adoption of open source software in Pakistani libraries: A survey. *Information Age, 4*(3), 35–38.

Ramzan, M. (2004). Levels of IT applications in muslim world libraries. *The Electronic Library, 22*(3), 274–280. doi:10.1108/02640470410541688

Randhawa, S. (2008). *Open source software and libraries.* Retrieved May 23, 2017, from http://eprints.rclis.org/16271/

Sarma, G. K. (2016). OPAC Module in Open Source Library Management Software: A comparative Study. *DESIDOC Journal of Library and Information Technology, 36*(1), 56–61. doi:10.14429/djlit.36.1.9223

SenthilKumaran, P., & Sreeja, K. P. (2017). A Study On Managing *Koha* Open Source Library Management System In the University Library, Central University Of Kerala. *International Journal of Research in Library Science, 3*(1), 91–101.

Shafi-Ullah, F., & Qutab, S. (2012). From LAMP to *Koha*: Case study of the Pakistan legislative Assembly Libraries. *Electronic Library and Information Systems, 46*(1), 43–55. doi:10.1108/00330331211204557

Singh, M., & Sanaman, G. (2012). Open source integrated library management systems: Comparative analysis of *Koha* and NewGenLib. *The Electronic Library, 30*(6), 809–832. doi:10.1108/02640471211282127

Singh, V. (2013). Experiences of Migrating to an Open-Source Integrated Library System. *Information Technology and Libraries, 32*(1), 36. doi:10.6017/ital.v32i1.2268

Singh, V. (2014). Expectations versus experiences: Librarians using open source integrated library systems. *The Electronic Library, 32*(5), 688–709. doi:10.1108/EL-10-2012-0129

Solutions, K. (2011). *Koha Integrated Library Management System.* Retrieved May 23, 2017, from https://www.keep.pt/en/produtos/Koha

Stump, S. L. & Deegan, R. L. (2013). Open Source Opens Doors Repurposing Library Software to Facilitate Faculty Research and Collaboration. *Pennsylvania Libraries: Research & Practice, 1*(2).

Surman, M., & Diceman, J. (2004), *Choosing Open Source: A Decision making Guide for Civil Society Organizations.* The Commons Group. Retrieved from www.commonsgroup.com/docs/opensource-guide_fullversion_v1p0.pdf

Tajoli, Z., Carassiti, A., Marchitelli, A. and Valenti, F. (2011). OSS diffusion in Italian libraries The case of *Koha* by the Consorzio Interuniversitario Lombardo per l'Elaborazione Automatica (CILEA). *OCLC Systems & Services: International Digital Library Perspectives, 27*(1), 45-50.

Ukachi, N. B. (2012). Awareness, availability and utilisation of open source software in Nigerian libraries: the way forward. *International Research Journal of Library, Information and Archival Studies, 1*(1), 1-9.

Ukachi, N. B., Nwachukwu, V. N., & Onuoha, U. D. (2014). Library Automation and Use of Open Source Software to Maximize Library Effectiveness. *Information and Knowledge Management, 3*(4).

Uzomba, E. C., Oyebola, O. J., & Izuchukwu, A. C. (2015). The Use and Application of Open Source Integrated Library System in Academic Libraries in Nigeria: *Koha* Example. *Library Philosophy and Practice,* Paper 1250. Retrieved from http://digitalcommons.unl.edu/libphilprac/1250)

Walls, I. (2010). Migrating from Innovative Interfaces' Millennium to *Koha*: The NYU Health sciences Libraries' experiences. *OCLC Systems & Services: International Digital Library Perspectives, 27*(1), 51-56.

Walter, M., & Joann, R. (2010). Kete and Koha: Integration built on open standards *OCLC Systems & Services. International Digital Library Perspectives, 26*(2), 114–122.

Wheeler, D. A. (2007a). *How to evaluate open source/free software (OSS/FS) programs.* Retrieved July 15, 2016, from www.dwheeler.com/oss_fs_eval.html

Wheeler, D. A. (2007b). *Why open source software/free software (OSS/FS, FLOSS, or FOSS)? Look at the numbers!* Retrieved July 15,2016, from www.dwheeler.com/contactme.html

Wikipedia. (2011). *Integrated Library System.* Retrieved from http://en.Wikipedia.org/wiki/integrated Library System

Wikipedia. (2012). *Web 2.0.* Retrieved from http://en.wikipedia.org/wiki/ Web_2.0#History

Wikipedia. (2013). *Koha (software).* Retrieved from https://en.wikipedia.org/wiki/Koha_%28software%29

Willis, N. (2010). *Koha Community Squares off Against Commercial Fork.* Retrieved from https://lwn.net/articles/386284/

Wrosch, J. (2007). Open source software options for any library. *MLA Forum, 5*(3).

Yang, S. Q., & Hofmann, M. A. (2010). The next generation library catalog: A comparative study of OPACs of *Koha*, Evergreen, and Voyager. *Information Technology and Libraries, 29*(3), 141–150. doi:10.6017/ital.v29i3.3139

Zaid, Y. (2004). Automating Library Records Using GLAS Software: The University of Lagos Experience. *Nigerian Libraries, 38*(1), 55–67.

Zico, M. (2009). *Developing an Integrated Library System (ILS) using open source software KOHA: A Thesis.* Academic Press.

ADDITIONAL READING

Adekunle, P. A., Olla, G. O., Oshiname, R. M., & Tella, A. (2015). Reports Generation with *Koha* Integrated Library System (ILS): Some examples from Bowen University, Nigeria. *International Journal of Digital Library Systems*, *5*(2).

Breeding, M. (2010). Perceptions 2009: an international survey of library automation. Retrieved from www.librarytechnology.org/perceptions2009

Breeding, M. (2010). Public libraries in United States. Retrieved from www.librarytechnology.org/lwc-ils-marketshare.pl?SID1/420100413277801513& Country1/4UnitedþStates&Type1/4Public

Breeding, M. (2011). The new frontier (Cover story). *Library Journal*, *136*(6), 24–34.

Breeding, M., & Yelton, A. (2011). *About the perceptions survey. Library Technology Reports*. Washington, DC: ALA Techsource.

Dalziel, K. (2008). Open source meets turnkey: *Koha* for software, LibLime for support. *PNLA Quarterly*, *72*(3), 6–16.

Hadro, J. (2009b). LibLime's Enterprise *Koha* sets off debate. *Library Journal*, *134*(17), 16–17.

Hadro, J. (2010). New era for *Koha*: PTFS acquires LibLime. *Library Journal*, *135*(2), 15–16.

Helling, J. (2010). Cutting the proprietary cord: A case study of one library's decision to migrate to an open source ILS. *Library Review*, *59*(9), 702–707. doi:10.1108/00242531011087024

Hofmann, M. A., & Yang, S. Q. (2011). How next-gen r u? A review of academic OPACS in the United States and Canada. *Computers in Libraries*, *31*(6).

Rapp, D. (2011). Open source reality check. *Library Journal*, *136*(13), 34–36.

Sadeh, T. (2010). Open products, open interfaces, and Ex Libris open-platform strategy. *Library Review*, *59*(9), 677–689. doi:10.1108/00242531011087006

Webber, D., & Peters, A. (2010). *Integrated Library Systems: Planning, Selecting, and implementing*. Santa Barbara, CA: Libraries Unlimited.

Yeats, D. (2012). *Open-source software development and user-centered design: a study of open-source practices and participants*. Lubbock, TX: Texas Tech University.

KEY TERMS AND DEFINITIONS

Integrated Library System (ILS): An integrated library system is a software program that assists in library planning by tracking books borrowed, bills paid and orders made, patrons registered, etc. with all these separate activities unified as a seamless whole.

Next Generation Catalogs: Are current and emerging discovery tools overlaying existing bibliographic data and repackaging it in displays that differ from the traditional catalog. It is more user-friendly and interactively designed for the next generation of users, hence the name next generation catalogs.

Open Source Software (OSS): Is a software in which the source code is available to the general public for use and/or modification from its original design, free of charge. Open source code is typically created as a collaborative effort in which programmers improve upon the code and share the changes within the community of users.

Proprietary/Commercial Software: Is any software that is copyrighted and bears limits against use, distribution, and modification that are imposed by its publisher, vendor, or developer. Usually fee-based, proprietary software remains the property of its owner/creator and is used by end-users/organisations under predefined conditions.

Source Code: Is the list of human-readable instructions that a programmer writes—often in a word processing program—when s/he is developing a program. The source code is run through a compiler to turn it into machine code, also called object code, that a computer can understand and execute.

Chapter 7
Open Growth:
The Economic Impact of Open Source Software in the USA

Roya Ghafele
OxFirst Ltd., UK

Benjamin Gibert
Independent Researcher, UK

ABSTRACT

Open source software (OSS) is well established in sectors as diverse as aviation, health, telecommunications, finance, publishing, education, and government. As nations increasingly rely on knowledge assets to grow, the adoption of OSS will have profound economic consequences. This chapter identifies the mechanisms inherent to OSS production that help fuel innovation in knowledge-based economies. As a collaborative and open production model, OSS is conceptualized as a prototype of open innovation. OSS-related software development jobs are widely diffused throughout the economy, help build a skilled labour force, and offer wages significantly above the national average. OSS is thus believed to be a strong contributor to growth in high-value employment in the US. The authors also posit that, as industries are exposed to the benefits of OSS as a result of the broad diffusion of OSS-related jobs, open innovation processes outside software development may be adopted through a process of learning and imitation.

INTRODUCTION

The promise of software is as limitless as the human mind. The next era of human achievement will be made possible through a combination of talented minds, software, and the industries that create using these powerful tools. (BSA | the Software Alliance, 2016)

The emergence and evolution of Open Source Software (OSS) has had a dramatic impact on the software industry. While this impact is frequently discussed, its wider influence on innovation and employment growth in other economic sectors is poorly understood. To our knowledge, the impact of OSS on long-

DOI: 10.4018/978-1-5225-5314-4.ch007

term employment in the USA has not yet been evaluated. Our paper is the first of its kind to quantify the impact of OSS on job creation and skill generation at the example of the United States. In doing so, we draw upon new growth theory and theories of learning as developed by scholars like Arora and Arrow.

Knowledge plays a critical role in economic growth and innovation.1 The accumulation of knowledge and the skills of the labour force are increasingly identified as stronger drivers of national growth than the possession of tangible assets (Solow 1957; Lucas 1988; Romer 1986). It is not news that a key variable in economic growth is the efficacy of technology utilization in the economy (Arora, 1995). Yet, the ability to utilize technology efficiently and generate new knowledge is conditioned by the innovation system in which actors are embedded. OSS represents an opportunity to utilize technology efficiently, build high-value skills in the labour force, ensure high software quality and promote innovation diffusion according to a new paradigm founded on openness rather than exclusion. This open system detects and assimilates existing knowledge resources more effectively than closed, proprietary innovation approaches. It also helps individuals to develop IT-related skills and signal technical excellence to employers in diverse industries.

The US lends itself well as a case example as it is the single largest software market in the world and controlled approximately 46% of the global software market in 2008 (OECD STAN Database for Structural Analysis, ed. 2008; cited in BSA 2009). Using official data on employment projections from 2008-2018 for the US, we estimate the impact of OSS on employment throughout the economy. Unlike manufacturing and agricultural industries, high technology industries are less prone to outsourcing concerns and globalization pressures. The US currently enjoys a strong global competitive advantage in high technology products and services. The software sector alone contributed $260 billion to the US economy in 2007, growing at an annual rate of 14% and outpacing growth in other US industries by 12% (OECD STAN Database for Structural Analysis, ed. 2008; cited in BSA 2009). As demand for complex software products increases with the growth of Internet services and the need for businesses to integrate the latest technologies in their production cycles, software development will become an increasingly important component of the economy.

This paper is structured as follows. First, the nature of the OSS phenomenon is briefly outlined. OSS is presented as an open innovation process that leverages the advantages of knowledge exchange and collaboration to fuel innovation in a knowledge economy more effectively than closed organizational structures.

The concept of knowledge is then discussed in order to identify its role in employment creation. Understanding how knowledge is best generated, advanced and transferred helps uncover the link between OSS, skill development, innovation and employment growth and informs out quantitative analysis. We conclude by showing that an analysis of data on US employment projections from 2008 to 2018 suggests that OSS-related jobs have significantly above-average salary levels and will grow rapidly throughout multiple sectors of the US economy over this ten-year period. This process is not restricted to the software publishing industry.

A BRIEF INTRODUCTION TO OPEN SOURCE SOFTWARE

The Free/Libre/Open Source Software (FLOSS) movement is founded on the idea that the open development of software is more effective than its proprietary alternative. Put simply, it is about access to source code and freedom to modify and distribute it (Ajila & Wu, 2007). The distinctions between Free, Libre and Open Source Software models are based on the type of licenses applied to the source code as well as the cost and availability of the final product. Since we are primarily interested in FLOSS as an open production process and its impact on employment, the label Open Source Software (OSS) is applied to all of these activities.

By drawing on a vast pool of diverse expertise, this collaborative approach to soft-ware development is responsive to changes in the needs of its users and highly efficient at fixing software bugs to improve stability. OSS harnesses the power of large and diverse developer communities, proving that 'given enough eyeballs, all bugs are shallow' (Raymond, 1999). The OSS movement is global, self-organizing and can be in spite of a lack of a hierarchical governance structure effective. Authority and management of OSS projects often evolves dynamically (Bitzer, Schrettl, & Schroder, 2007) as decentralized, bottom-up production creates clear hierarchical coordination and decision-making processes that emerge without the support of property rights (Bonaccorsi & Rossi, 2003). OSS has been defined as a complex adaptive system that can deal with changing requirements and accommodate new influences in a manner that renders the software product effective, robust and relatively secure (Benbya & McKelvey, 2006).

From an employment perspective, OSS projects are widely believed to provide programmers with prestige and visibility. Much like in academia, free revealing becomes an investment activity aimed at increasing the signalling quality of human capital (Lerner & Tirole, 2002). Some suggest motivation for projects arises from the need for a currently unavailable software solution (Torvalds & Diamond, 2001) or the intellectual gratification associated with solving complex problems (Bonaccorsi & Rossi, 2003). Regardless, the free revealing of innovations increases their diffusion, stimulating network effects, reputational gains, and the advantages of subsequent innovations revealed by others (Capra et al., 2011), all of which are crucial for dynamic labour markets. While there is a burgeoning literature on the economic underpinning of the OSS phenomenon (David Rullani, 2008; Economides & Katsamakas, 2006; Fitzgerald, 2006; Glass, 2004; Hawkins, 2004; Johnson, 1999; Lerner & Tirole, 2002), these studies only assess the internal dynamics of OSS projects, but they rarely evaluate the broader impact of OSS on employment and skill creation. We thus believe that our study has an important contribution to the academic literature. The codification and exchange of knowledge, as well as the development and signalling of technical excellence, a standard feature of OSS projects, lies at the heart of in-novation processes. And while another string of literature on innovation systems attempts to measure the interaction of institutions and knowledge generation, exchange, and commercialization processes within national economies, (Duesenberry, 1956; Grossman & Helpman, 1990), the precise mechanisms that enable nations to leverage innovation for growth are less well understood. We recognize thus that the process of innovation is embedded in a complex network of values, actors, organizations, and institutions and argue that OSS is an emerging governance structure that positively influences labour markets.

The philosophy of OSS has spawned a mode of production that offers an important contribution to driving innovation in a knowledge-based economy. This is not to say that proprietary innovation is not also important, but the modes of production and the rationale of open innovation that is employed by the OSS movement offers alternative governance structures that bear the potential to activate skills and allow to stay ahead of the curve and not face competition from countries disposing of a low cost labour force. Seen in this light, OSS 'is a functioning, pragmatic demonstration of a production process that is quite distinct from production modes characteristic of the pre-digital era. The difference is not one of degree but one of kind... The open source production process depends upon and uses the Internet to enable not just a more finely grained division of labor, but truly distributed innovation—a revolutionary way of thinking about economic production' (Weber, 2000). Our study shows that this open production process gives way to developing skills in the US labour force that will positively impact employment levels in high-wage jobs and accelerate innovation-based growth in the long-term. Innovation relies in large parts on the skills and knowledge of the labour force. As a decentralized, self-organizing process that helps build software development skills that may prove valuable in competitive labour markets, OSS may have important labour economic benefits that are not yet adequately understood. Offering data describing this phenomenon is thus an important first step towards an alternated research agenda.

OPEN GROWTH

Knowledge Exchange and Learning

Knowledge is the fuel that drives innovation. OSS is a production process that efficiently harnesses this fuel in order to accelerate innovation. Innovation is the process of extracting value from ideas and creativity; it is frequently associated with discontinuous change and a process of creative destruction (Schumpeter, 1942). It is a complex process where new ideas, objects and practices are created, developed or reinvented (Rogers, 1998). The rise of OSS itself can be seen as an innovation, 'a new and revolutionary process of producing soft-ware based on unconstrained access to source code as opposed to the traditional closed and property-based approach of the commercial world' (Bonaccorsi & Rossi, 2003).

Knowledge on the other side can be seen as a public good whose characteristics deeply influence the economics of its exchange. Knowledge is both non-rivalrous in consumption and non-excludable. This means that one person's use of information does not stop another's use of it simultaneously and that it is very difficult to exclude others from the use of this information (Martens 2004). Moreover, knowledge is not subject to the economic constraint of scar-city. A piece of information, such as computer code, can be freely copied and distributed on a huge scale at virtually zero marginal cost. Yet knowledge is not just a product to be traded, it is a social process where exchange can increase output and innovation.

Arrow describes knowledge as 'learning by doing' (1962) and defines technological change as the acquisition of knowledge through the process of learning. Learning occurs when attempting to solve a problem and is therefore bound to activity. Experience, activity and learning are closely linked and technological change relies on adequate mechanisms for these exchanges to be institutionalized (Arrow, 1962). OSS offers just such a mechanism. Learning and skill building in the labour force occurs in a decentralized manner through the active participation of individuals in OSS projects. Digital technologies facilitate and reinforce the circulation of codified and practical knowledge within OSS communities. Adequate codification and organization of knowledge is crucial in order for a wider community to discuss it. In OSS, like in academia, new insights are created by improving transfer, transformation and access to existing stocks of knowledge.

It is hardly surprising that learning is a key process in an economy that is increasingly driven by knowledge. Innovation results from the interaction of various actors and knowledge is the social process that results from this ex-change (Katz & Kahn, 1978). Actors as diverse as firms, users, software developers, suppliers and a multitude of intermediaries can all create a knowledge field (Lundvall and Johnson 2011). Society can be conceived as consisting of networks composed of various actors that can be both humans and machines (Callon, Law, & Rip, 1986; Latour, 1996). These actors do not operate in isolation but are part of a network in which their work is defined and advanced. OSS projects can be conceptualized as networks in which each participant develops skills that both increase the innovative output of the network and signal the quality of human capital that exists within it. Since knowledge production lies at the heart of innovation, the social practices that form the context of knowledge generation are a core element of successful innovation. OSS is both a social practice that provides the context for knowledge generation and a production process founded on the idea of open knowledge exchange. These features of knowledge and innovative learning processes help understand why an open governance structure, such as that of OSS, can have an impact on job creation and skill generation, which we describe as a social practice that strongly differentiates itself from a traditional hierarchical proprietary governance structure.

Open Innovation

Because innovation is not a linear process where inputs translate directly to outputs, the development of an effective framework to extract value from existing knowledge assets is crucial. OSS, as a highly collaborative and open production model that draws its resources from a large group of peers, represents a strong example of an open innovation model that can achieve this. The conceptualization of knowledge as a social process where innovation is accelerated by the open exchange of ideas is the foundation of open innovation strategies. Open innovation focuses on peer production by communities, consumers, lead users, universities or research organizations, and partners from other industries (Enkel, Gassmann, & Chesbrough, 2009). OSS, as an open innovation approach, provides a framework to leverage these diverse knowledge assets and simultaneously signal the quality of human capital available in the labour market to potential employers. These processes are not new and have formed the baseline of academic careers for hundreds of years, yet because of the availability of new technologies they are advancing at a speed not seen before.

Open innovation is based on the idea that knowledge resources are widely diffused in the economy and that a closed innovation model can restrict the resources at an actor's disposal. The defining characteristic of open innovation is the free revealing of knowledge (Von Hippel & Von Krogh, 2003) and the integration of users into the innovation process in order to capitalize on freedom of the early stages of development to understand customers' requirements and integrate users' application knowledge (Gassmann, Enkel, & Chesbrough, 2010). OSS exhibits all of these characteristics. It implements specific license agreements to ensure the openness and diffusion of source code, while capitalizing on the software development benefits of integrating users into the production cycle. This openness can be a vital factor in fuelling productivity gains in a knowledge-based economy. Stallman (1999) remarks how 'the new organizational structure and collaborative nature of open source software development has been hailed as an important organizational innovation. It has broken with a system that divided the public and kept the user helpless.' The various novel economic mechanisms made possible through open source can translate into a more systematic and thorough use of innovation as an engine of growth. At the same time, OSS projects provide a platform to develop increasingly valuable skills within the labour market.

Knowledge generation is a learning experience driven by a combination of existing ideas as well as a radical break with established perspectives. Open access to ideas helps to fuel their cross-fertilization and accelerate innovation at virtually no cost. An efficiency comparison of OSS and closed, profit-driven software development has shown that OSS is superior at accessing the Internet talent pool and utilizing private information in many circumstances (Johnson, 1999). Innovative activities like soft-ware development are affected by the degree of access to diverse knowledge resources; the more diversity and access to these resources, the more a team is able to solve complex technical problems and create novel programs of value to users (Fleming, 2001). In the process of solving these complex technical problems, individuals accumulate and signal skills that are in greater and greater demand throughout the economy.

Open innovation is about using ICT to sustain virtual communities and decentralized innovation processes (Boutellier et al., 1998). Similarly, the OSS model relies on hardware, software and ICT to facilitate the participation and organization (O'Reilly, 1999) of a complex network of actors consisting of diverse human as well electronic artefacts. The Linux project is itself an open innovation model that is built on the recognition of knowledge as a social process. The Linux community has developed a rich set of tools as well as an institutional framework in which the social practice of 'learning by doing' acts both as a provider of new knowledge and an enabler of knowledge spill over effects. Because developers will more likely assimilate knowledge related to their existing field of expertise, similarities across projects can help ease knowledge sharing and transfer among them (Cohen & Levinthal, 1990).

OSS leverages the advantages discussed by open innovation theorists. (Chesbrough 2006) It adapts software production strategy in order to detect and assimilate the knowledge that is widely diffused among a variety of actors using ICT. It recognizes that knowledge has no value in isolation and stimulates self-organizing knowledge networks in order to foster exchange, innovation and skill development. OSS is a production process that exploits the collective intelligence of the community and can match competence with task within a decentralized network (Kogut & Metiu, 2001). As a prominent example of open innovation in a knowledge-based economy, the value created by OSS may also pave the way for the uptake of open strategies in other sectors. It would thus indirectly influence innovation by triggering a diffuse process of learning and imitation.

Openness, Signalling and Skill Development

Openness in production can trigger positive feedback loops that help to improve the user value created by stimulating adoption and fuelling network effects (Shapiro and Varian 1999). The advantages offered by OSS can attract new contributors, which increase the value of OSS output, which in turn attracts more contributors; provided that users are sufficiently qualified and knowledgeable on the subject matter. (Von Hippel, 1988). The free revealing of an innovation can directly benefit the revealer through enhanced reputational gains as well as indirectly through the network effects that spur adoption and by inducing others in the community to reveal their own innovations (Harhoff, Henkel, & von Hippel, 2003). OSS thus bears the potential to leverage positive feedbacks in technology markets: 'like stigmergic organization in insects (Bonabeau et al., 1999), the process is self-reinforcing or autocatalytic (Heylighen, 1999; Heylighen & Gershenson, 2003): the more high quality material is already available on the community site, the more people will be drawn to check it out, and thus the more people are available to improve it further. Thus, open access can profit from a positive feedback cycle that boosts successful projects' (Heylighen, 2006).

Participation in open knowledge exchange helps bolster the innovative capacity of economic actors. It does so by improving their ability to value, assimilate, and apply new knowledge for commercial ends (Cohen & Levinthal, 1990). Similar to the academic process of undergoing through peer review, publishing without expecting to get paid and presenting at conferences, the learning stimulated by participation in OSS projects thus supports the development of valuable skills that make individuals more employable and increases the innovative output of the entire economy. Open innovation paradigms like OSS are feasible for a wide range of industries and goods; 'the main obstacle seems to be that most firms are entrenched in a proprietary attitude and unfamiliar with open-ness' (J. Henkel, 2006). There is an extensive literature detailing the benefits firms derive from contributing to OSS projects (Behlendorf, 1999, Hecker, 1999, Raymond, 1999, Feller & Fitzgerald, 2002, Lerner & Tirole, 2002, Wichmann, 2002, Bonaccorsi & Rossi, 2004, Dahlander & Magnusson, 2005). The production model of OSS is believed to accelerate innovation because it abolishes entry barriers on the supply side, offers identical knowledge-like products and provides the market with perfect information based on signalling mechanisms (Iannacci, 2002). This idea is echoed by Henkel who, among others, suggests that a major benefit of OSS is that it provides a mechanism to signal technical excellence in the labour market (J. Henkel, 2006).

As advanced economies become increasingly dependent on information, analysts predict that most economic value will eventually be produced under an open access approach (Heylighen, 2006). Benkler argues that this networked mode of production provides information goods and services more efficiently than traditional industrial production and reduces financial constraints on innovating firms (Benkler, 2006). The three characteristics of industrial information production - 1) a divide between consumers and producers; 2) one-way, centralized information flow; and 3) high start-up costs – are being replaced by a new reality. Networked production 'inverts the characteristics of industrial information production: consumers are producers, information flows multi-directionally, and production start-up costs are minimal' (Benkler, 2006). This new mode of production bears the potential to leverage human capital inputs more efficiently. Growth fuelled by ICT and open innovation management requires a sufficient supply of skilled workers with diverse levels and fields of expertise to fill new jobs.

Limitations of OSS Governance Structures

Just as development is free and encouraged in open source, it is also not compulsory. Closed source software companies pay salaries to people to develop the software and therefore professional careers are predictable. With OSS there is a risk that it benefits the careers of a small elite, rather than software programmers at large. The newspaper 'Economist' speaks in this context of a Darwinian meritocracy rather than a democracy. The acceptance of contributions can be elitist because not every contribution may get accepted. OSS firms such as MySQL even go as far as only allowing a small core team to advance its software codes. The distinction between proprietary and OSS governance structures seems thus theoretical at many instances.

The open governance structure brings also along issues associated with quality assurance. Projects may get distorted by well- meaning dilettantes or intentional disrupters. Constant self-policing is required to ensure quality and avoid vandalism, prejudice and inaccuracy. (The Economist, 2006) Proprietary software products like that of Microsoft have to the contrary of OSS a track record of reliability, security, choice, manageability and interoperability.

To what extent contributors will remain motivated to advance Codes also needs to be seen. Wiki type platforms have in recent times seen less contributions then before; partly be-cause the novelty effect is cooling down and partially because of significant competition from a multitude of platforms. Another quite important disadvantage to open source software is that as so many developments are going on at the same time it is hard to keep track of which version is the most up to date and who is contributing to which project. Reputational gains and the chance to show one's skills are thus more difficult to obtain then in academia. From a developer point of view, the Mozilla project shows that OSS can be a double-edged sword. On the one hand side it took more than a year to get the first beta out, on the other side it produced a totally new code base. Half of the developers of Mozilla work outside of Netscape. (E.U. Connecta. http://eu.conecta.it/paper/Perceived_disadvantages_ope.html. Last Checked 29.8.2013)

The relationship of OSS to the traditional IP system is still evolving. OSS can be infringing on proprietary software, but it also puts a classical IP system that is based on the notion of single ownership (exceptions are collective marks) upside down. With source code coming from many different contributors, it is hard to discern who the author and thus owner of the copyright should be. On the other side this new mode of handling IP may constitute an opportunity for the IP system to reinvent itself and give way to IP strategies, such as non-exclusive licensing, public interest licensing or geographically limited licensing. Utopists like us also think that the novel models of IP management introduced by OSS may give way to new thinking on logged in debates, such as that on traditional knowledge.

METHODOLOGY

This section applies a quantitative methodology2 to estimate the impact of OSS on employment in the US economy using recent data published by the US Bureau of Labour Statistics. The approach is based on the idea that OSS provides an innovative method for developing IT-related skills and that its use stimulates the broad diffusion of skills with low barriers for skill improvement and deepening. It is supported by the idea that OSS reduces firm costs without outsourcing, in turn generating demand for skilled in-house employment. It is hinged on the fact that employment generation is tied to skill development and that employers greatly value the skills acquired by computer specialists working in the open source sector (Ghosh, 2006). Significantly, any measure of the potential contribution of OSS adoption to job creation in the US economy should consider the cannabilisation of OSS jobs from proprietary software development jobs. Otherwise, job creation from OSS might simply come at the cost of job losses in the proprietary software sector. In doing so, we take salary as a proxy for skill levels and assess the current share of proprietary software, so to discount for it, as well as gather the sectors in which OSS plays a role. We are thus assessing skills and not just mere employment.

In order to understand the amount of OSS-related jobs in the US economy, it is important to distinguish between software development and software support jobs. The job creation potential of OSS is only quantified in relation to software development jobs, since OSS is essentially a software production process. The following occupations are categorized under these two types:

- Occupations falling under 'software development' definition:
  - Computer and information scientists, research
  - Computer programmers
  - Computer software engineers, applications
  - Computer software engineers, systems software
  - Computer systems analysts
- Occupations falling under 'software support' definition:
  - Computer support specialists
  - Database administrators
  - Network and computer systems administrators
  - Network systems and data communication analysis
  - Computer specialists (all other)

The current and projected occupational data is compiled for all software jobs across all industries. Then 'software development' jobs are looked at in greater detail according to occupation and industry. Unfortunately, more recent data was not available on the breakup of the software economy in the US (Table 1). The share of proprietary software licenses in terms of the total value of the software economy is relatively small. It is important to recognize that OSS can effectively be used to develop software in most parts of the software economy and across a broad range of sectors in the US economy.

However, this distribution shows how pack-aged proprietary software actually accounts for a relatively small proportion of the total software market in the US economy. Custom software jobs cannot be cannabilized by OSS from the software publishing industry because it does not involve software license fees, which is the only cost that OSS necessarily eliminates (Ghosh, 2006). OSS could have an important impact on the custom software sector since this sector follows a support and service business model that is entirely compatible with OSS production processes.

In-house software development also cannot really be cannabilized by OSS. Software development in this sector could potentially all become open source because it follows the same principles. Since only one firm is both user and creator, the software is free to use, study, modify, and distribute within that organization. In order to quantify the number of software developers that could be developing OSS throughout the US economy, two estimates are calculated. These two estimates differ only in terms of what sectors are included. OSS1 represents all sectors that could be developing OSS. This includes all sectors except software publishers and computer and electronic product manufacturing. OSS2 represents all sectors that could be developing OSS except computer systems design and related services. This industry, as well as software publishing and computer and electronic product manufacturing industries, are excluded from the OSS2 estimate in order to have a range of how many OSS-related jobs there are across various sectors of the US economy. By taking IDC survey data, which shows the percentage of developers who are using OSS and apply it to U.S. developers who could be developing OSS, we can estimate the number of OSS related software development jobs in the U.S. If we conservatively apply this ratio of OSS to the estimate of total software, we get the number of U.S. software development jobs that are OSS related.

Limitations of the Methodology

The nature of the methodology necessitates caution regarding the final OSS-related employment estimate. The estimate is built on the number of software development jobs in various sectors where OSS development *could* be implemented. The final figure is adjusted ac-cording to survey data of the number of global software developers who *are* developing OSS. While not a direct result of OSS activities, this estimate displays the significant potential of OSS for skill development and employment generation in well-paid salary jobs. The figure is conservative in the sense that the estimate is only applied to software

Table 1. Breakup of US software economy, 2002

Proprietary Software Licenses	Software Services (Development and Customization)	Internal Development
16%	41%	43%

(Source: FISTERA, cited in Ghosh 2006)

development jobs. This focus on employment is useful to quantify OSS-related jobs in the US economy, but it does not quantify the profound impact that OSS will have on industries as diverse as aviation, finance, and health. The broad diffusion of software development jobs in the USA has important implications for its adoption.

CASE STUDY: OPEN SOURCE SOFTWARE AND EMPLOYMENT IN THE U.S.A.

What We Know So Far on U.S. Software Employment Opportunities

The previous sections have shown that knowledge is a social process and that open innovation strategies that stimulate greater knowledge exchange are a powerful means to accelerate innovation and develop skills throughout the labour market. OSS is presented as the proto-typical example of an open innovation strategy that achieves this. While there are drawbacks, the value proposition of OSS extends beyond the software publishing industries. This section shows how software development jobs are broadly diffused in the US economy and enjoy some of the highest growth rates of all occupations. This suggests that diverse economic sectors throughout the economy are in a strong position to adopt OSS and appropriate value from it. It also indicates that OSS may contribute significantly to employment growth in the USA over the long term.

If knowledge is promulgated through activity, experience and practice, the uptake of OSS in diverse industries can act as a key enabler of transformative change in the economy. It is thus highly significant that the employment opportunities for OSS-related jobs in the USA are highly diffuse and growing rapidly. This employment opportunity is quantified according to levels of software development employment across all industries in the USA in 2008 as well as projections for 2018. The results suggest that OSS could become a vital component of US employment growth.

The US Bureau of Labour Statistics expects total employment in the US to increase by 10% from 2008 to 2018, adding a total of 15.3 million jobs (see Figure 1). The employment structure of the US economy will continue to shift in favour of service-providing industries and the jobs created will not be evenly distributed across major industries and occupational groups. Service-providing industries are expected to add 14.5 million wage and salary jobs. Though the healthcare and social assistance industry is anticipated to provide the largest numerical in-crease in jobs (just over 4 million) as a result of demographic shifts in the aging US population, the entire professional and related occupational group is expected to grow the fastest (17% growth rate) and add 5.2 million jobs in total.

Professional, scientific and technical services will add 2.7 million jobs and grow by 34%. Computer systems design and related services will account for nearly one fourth of all jobs in this sector, growing at a rate of 45%. All computer and mathematical science jobs, as a subset of the professional and related occupational group, are one of the fastest growing in the US economy. These occupations are expected to add over 785,000 jobs, growing at twice the average rate for all occupations. Two of the fastest growing occupations are part of the computer specialists occupational group. Network systems and data communications analysts are ranked as the second-fastest growing occupation. Job creation in this occupation is fuelled by increased demand from organizations that must continuously upgrade their techno-logical infrastructure and increasingly rely on wireless networks for their business operations.

Growing at a rate of 30% - much faster than the average for all occupations - computer network, systems and database administrators will add over 286,000 new jobs.

Figure 1. Numeric change in wage and salary employment in service-providing industries, 2008-2018 (projected). (Source: US Bureau of Labour Statistics).

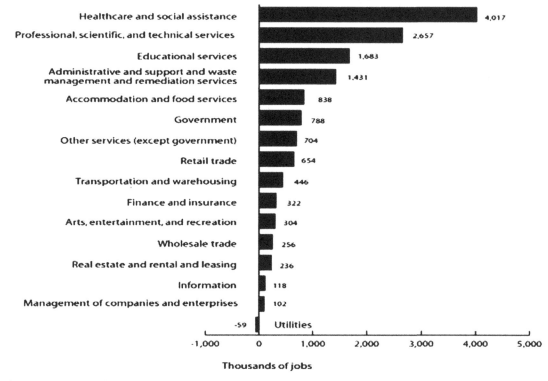

Source: BLS National Employment Matrix

Computer software engineering jobs will also grow much faster than the national average, increasing by 32% and adding over 295,000 jobs between 2008 and 2018 (Table 2). This growth is the result of greater demand for workers who can develop Internet, intranet and web applications. Software engineers and computer programmers are found in a wide range of industries. Software development – an area where OSS-related skills are highly relevant - is a major part of some of the fastest growing of these occupations. The growth rate of this sector compared to all other occupational groups suggests that OSS could be a significant source of skill development and experience in fast-growing and well-paid occupations.

Total Contributions of the Software Industry to the US Economy

A common, but not exhaustive measurement to measure the impact of a certain industry on an economy is to assess the number of jobs directly influenced by the industry as well as the revenue contribution towards the GDP.

Analysing direct contributions of the software industry to the US economy leads to an estimation of the indirect and induced impacts which, by using specific economic multipliers, gives an estimation of the total contributions, and therewith looks beyond the common metrics.

A study carried out by the BSA | the Software Alliance and the Economist Intelligence Unit (EIU) used various multipliers to get these estimations, the multipliers as given by the EIU are: (1) Direct

Table 2. Employment in computer science occupations, 2008-2018 (projected). (Source: US Bureau of Labour Statistics).

Occupation	Employment (in thousands)		Employment Change, 2008-2018		Percent self-employed, 2008	Job openings due to growth and replacement needs, 2008-2018 (in thousands)	2008 Median annual wages (Dollars)	Median annual wages quartile*	Most significant source of postsecondary education or training
	2008	2018	Number (in thousands)	Percent					
Computer software engineers, applications	514.8	689.9	175.1	34.0	2.7	218.4	85,430	VH	Bachelor's degree
Computer software engineers, systems software	394.8	515.0	120.2	30.4	2.7	153.4	92,430	VH	Bachelor's degree
Computer and information scientists, research	28.9	35.9	7.0	24.2	4.6	13.2	97,970	VH	Doctoral degree
Computer systems analysts	532.2	640.3	108.1	20.3	5.7	222.8	75,500	VH	Bachelor's degree
Computer and information systems managers	293.0	342.5	49.5	16.9	3.3	97.1	112,210	VH	Bachelor's or higher degree, plus work experience
Computer support specialists	565.7	643.7	78.0	13.8	1.2	234.6	43,450	H	Associate degree
Computer hardware engineers	74.7	77.5	2.8	3.8	1.3	23.5	97,400	VH	Bachelor's degree
Computer programmers	426.7	414.4	-12.3	-2.9	5.5	80.3	69,620	VH	Bachelor's degree
Computer operators	110.0	89.5	-20.5	-18.6	0.0	12.4	35,600	H	Moderate-term on-the-job training

* VH = Very High; H = High; L = Low; VL = Very Low; n.a. = not available

contributions: the levels of output or employment of the industry in question;(2) Indirect impacts: the inter-industry economic activity resulting from the direct contributions (e.g., purchases of inputs);(3) Induced impacts: the additional economicactivity supported by spending on goods and services by households whose income was affected by the direct contributions and indirect impacts (Source: BSA | The software Alliance, 2016).

The findings of the study prove the significance of the software industry on the economic growth of the United states and the far-reaching impact of the software industry. The term "software industry" includes software based services such as app development or cloud storage services to give an accurate picture of the industry's transformation.

As displayed in Table 3, the software industry influences many jobs in an indirect way, according to the study, in 2014 2.5 million people were directly employed by the software industry and another 7.3 million in supported job sectors, amongst which they count web development, project management and coordination, and accounting. The impact of the software industry on the US economy shows in the contribution towards the Gross Domestic Product; which, according to the study totals an amount of 1.07 trillion US Dollars in 2014, the induced $594.7 billion value added GDP contribution includes

Table 3. Direct and indirect/ induced impacts of the software industry on the US economy, 2014 (Source: BSA | the Software alliance, 2016).

2014	No of Employees (in Millions)	Value Added GDP (in $ Billion)	Average Annual Wages (in $)
Direct	2.5	475.3	108,760
Indirect/ induced	7.3	594.7	-
Total	9.8	1,070	-

factors like tangential job creation as well as investment into research and development. (BSA | The Software Alliance, 2016)

The U.S. Software Labour Economy: Quantifying Its Magnitude

Computer systems design and related services ranks as the top sector for computer specialist employment. However, computer specialist occupations are broadly diffused throughout the US economy (see Appendix tables). In terms of total employment for all computer specialists, proprietary software vendors (software publishing) ranks 10th. Software publishers employ less than 4% of all computer specialists (though this makes up over 50% of employment within the industry). Computer and electronic product manufacturing is another relevant sector for proprietary software. Yet, this sector ranks 11th in terms of computer specialist employment and also only employs less than 4% of all computer specialists. Software development jobs, more specifically, also display a significant degree of diffusion across US sectors (see Tables 4-7).

It is worth noting the balance of software developer employment between 'IT develop-ing'3 and 'IT user'4 sectors.

This distribution of software developer employment by occupation between IT develop-ing sectors and IT user sectors suggests that, in the US, software development skills are widely distributed throughout the economy, putting firms across economy in strong position to adopt OSS. Except for software engineers – where there is a close balance - the majority of software developers are employed in IT User firms.

The difference between average salary paid to developers in software publishing sector and other sectors is an important measure of the skill level of developers in different industries (taking salary level as a proxy for skills). A lack of major salary difference would suggest that software publishers and other firms in IT developing sectors do not have dominant share of highest-skilled employees (although sectoral differences in profit margins will also factor in determining salaries). See Table 8.

Though the software publishing sector is always above average for annual wages paid to developers, the difference is relatively minor (10.5% increase across all industries and software development jobs). A more de-tailed breakup of salary level by industry for each software development occupation (see

appendix) shows there is not a major salary difference across many different sectors; recent statistics of the United States Department of Labor (2017) give the median annual wage for software developers in applications was $100,080 in May 2016 and the one for web developers in system software was $106,860.

The lack of a major difference suggests that development skills are widely distributed outside the proprietary software industry. This data on employment distributions across industries and salary levels suggests that both skills and employees are widely distributed outside the software publishing and IT developing sectors.

Table 4. Computer software engineers: Employment breakup

Sector	2008	2018 Percent of Occupation
IT Developers	52.41	55.87
IT Users	47.59	44.13

Table 5. Computer and information scientists: Employment breakup

Sector	2008	2018 Percent of Occupation
IT Developers	39.10	15.30
IT Users	60.90	84.70

Table 6. Computer programmers: Employment breakup

Sector	2008	2018 Percent of Occupation
IT Developers	42.22	47.51
IT Users	57.78	52.49

Table 7. Computer systems analysts: Employment breakup

Sector	2008	2018 Percent of Occupation
IT Developers	31.76	36.47
IT Users	68.24	63.53

Table 8. Software developers: Employment and salary, May 2010

Occupation	Employment in 000s (AllIndustries)	Annual Wage – Average (All Industries)	Annual Wage – Average (Software Publishing)
Software Developers, Applications	539,580	85,817	94,950
Software Developers, Systems Software	404,160	92,211	100,840
Computer and Information	26,300	103,926	119,950
Research Scientists Computer Programmers	350,040	72,670	81,440
Computer Systems Analysts	504,090	78,993	81,890
TOTAL	1,824,170	86,723	95,814

Given the potential benefits of OSS on innovation efficiency detailed above, it is evident that multiple industries in the US are in a position to leverage OSS to their advantage.

Employment in Software Development

The significant sectors that develop proprietary packaged software are: 1) software publishers (i.e. proprietary software vendors) and 2) computer and electronic product manufacturers. Other than these two sectors (software publishing and a share of developers in computer and electronic product manufacturing), all other sectors *could* be developing OSS. Computer systems design and related services is the top-ranking sector (see appendix) in terms of software developer employment across all occupations. This occupational group is mainly composed of custom software developers, including computing facility management services (i.e. outsourced 'in-house' software developers). As remarked by Ghosh (2006), this sector includes businesses such as IBM, which although producing some proprietary software, primarily design custom software. The custom-software sector is an important sector for OSS-related jobs. Computer systems design and related services is an occupational group that could benefit significantly from OSS adoption. Tables 9-12 provide the estimates on the total amount and share of software developers that *could* be developing OSS by occupation.

These tables show that a significant share of software development jobs in the US could be involved in developing OSS. Though they are not necessarily developing OSS right now, the data illustrates that OSS cannibalization is unlikely to have substantial negative impact on jobs outside the software publishing sector. Also noteworthy is that developers in all other sectors are engaged in developing software more akin to the characteristics of OSS than proprietary software. Table 12 aggregates these figures and provides an estimate of total number of US software developers who *could* be developing OSS.

Total software development jobs in US that could be developing OSS (2008):

- **OSS1 Sector Estimate:** 1,692,100
- **OSS2 Sector Estimate:** 1,129,000

Total software development jobs in US that could be developing OSS (2018):

- **OSS1 Sector Estimate:** 2,081,400
- **OSS2 Sector Estimate:** 1,281,700

IDC data suggests that 71% of global software developers were actively using OSS in 2005 (IDC 2006). If this percentage is applied to the number of developers in the US who could be using OSS (identified by the above methodology), the number of OSS-related software development jobs can be estimated for 2008 and 2018 projections, as seen in Table 14.

OSS-related software development jobs2008:

Table 9. Software Engineers; potential OSS developers

Sector	2008		2018		Percent Change	Employment Change
	Employment (in 000s)	Percent of Occupation	Employment (in 000s)	Percent of Occupation		
OSS1	757.3	83.5	1043.9	86.9	37.8	286.6
OSS2	468.4	51.8	589.4	49.2	25.8	121.0

Table 10. Computer and Information Scientists, Research; potential OSS developers

Sector	2008		2018		Percent Change	Employment Change
	Employment (in 000s)	Percent of Occupation	Employment (in 000s)	Percent of Occupation		
OSS1	25.4	87.6	31.7	88.2	24.8	6.3
OSS2	18.7	64.5	22.1	61.5	18.2	3.4

Table 11. Computer Programmers; potential OSS developers

Sector	2008		2018		Percent change	Employmenthange
	Employment (in 000s)	Percent of occupation	Employment (in000s)	Percent of occupation		
OSS1	401.1	94.1	391.2	94.5	-2.5	-9.9
OSS2	259.9	61.0	232.8	56.2	-10.4	-27.1

Table 12. Computer Systems Analysts; potential OSS developers

Sector	2008		2018		Percentchange	Employmentchange
	Employment(in 000s)	Percent of Occupation	Employment (in000s)	Percent of occupation		
OSS1	508.3	95.5	614.6	96.0	20.9	106.3
OSS2	382.0	71.7	437.4	68.3	14.5	55.4

Table 13. Total Employment in 000s of Software Developers; potential OSS developers

Occupation	2008		2018	
	OSS1 Sector Employment	OSS 2 Sector Employment	OSS1 Sector Employment	OSS 2 SectorEmployment
Software engineers	757.3	468.4	1043.9	589.4
Computer systems analysts	508.3	382	614.6	437.4
Computer programmers	401.1	259.9	391.2	232.8
Computer and information scientists, research	25.4	18.7	31.7	22.1
TOTAL	1692.1	1129	2081.4	1281.7

Table 14. OSS-related software development jobs in 000s, 2008-2018 projected

2008		2018	
OSS1 Sector Employment	OSS2 SectorEmployment	OSS1 SectorEmployment	OSS 2 Sector Employment
1201.391	801.59	1477.794	910.007

- **OSS1 Sector Estimate:** 1,201,391
- **OSS2 Sector Estimate:** 801,590

OSS-related software development jobs 2018:

- **OSS1 Sector Estimate:** 1,477,794
- **OSS2 Sector Estimate:** 910,007

CONCLUSION

While the value of OSS to software development is frequently discussed, the impact its peculiar governance structures has on skill creation and employment generation remains relatively less well understood. This paper attempts to fill this gap by exploring the impact of the broad diffusion of OSS-related software development jobs at the example of the U.S. economy. The wide diffusion of software development jobs throughout the US economy suggests that most sectors are in a strong position to adopt OSS. Computer specialists are one of the fastest growing occupational groups in the US and enjoy an average salary across all industries that is well above the average for all occupations. Software development is a major component of computer specialist occupations and participation in OSS has been shown to be a major source of skill generation and signalling in this field. The number of OSS-related software development jobs is estimated to be between 801,590 and 1,201,391 jobs in 2008. This will grow to between 910,007 and 1,477,794 by 2018. The fact that IT user sectors employ the majority of computer specialists in most software development occupations implies that OSS adoption can be usefully implemented to cut costs, signal technical excellence in the labour force and accelerate innovation in a variety of industries.

Furthermore, as US industries are increasingly exposed to the benefits of OSS, open innovation processes outside software development may be adopted through a process of learning and imitation. The broad diffusion of software development jobs suggests that the adoption of OSS could penetrate all sectors of the US economy, acting as a critical example of an organizational innovation that leverages the characteristics of the knowledge-based economy to ensure sustainable growth. As labour markets in advanced economies are increasingly facing competition from low income countries, open innovation based governance structures as those put forward by OSS offer important opportunities to obtain name recognition among peers and build up the type of social capital that is needed to apply for top jobs. The conceptualization of knowledge as a social process that is best advanced through its exchange helps to understand why OSS has been such an important model for active labour markets. Similar to academia non-remunerated contributions to software creation does not usher in a 'gift economy', but is an important factor in the employment process. As a prototypical example of open innovation, OSS adoption can act as a key enabler of transformative changes in the US economy that will become increasingly reliant on information exchange to generate and appropriate value from innovation in a global economy. Our study is the first of its kind to quantify the economic impact of these novel governance structures. Further research would be needed to assess to what extent the insights we gathered from the U.S. economy also hold for other economies.

REFERENCES

Ajila, S. A., & Wu, D. (2007). Empirical study of the effects of open source adoption on software development economics. *Journal of Systems and Software*, *80*(9), 1517–1529. doi:10.1016/j.jss.2007.01.011

Allen, R. C. (1983). Collective invention. *Journal of Economic Behavior & Organization*, *4*(1), 1–24. doi:10.1016/0167-2681(83)90023-9

Almirall, E., & Casadesus-Masanell, R. (2010). Open versus closed innovation: A model of discovery and divergence. *Academy of Management Review*, *35*(1), 27–47. doi:10.5465/AMR.2010.45577790

Arora, A. (1995). Licensing tacit knowledge: Intellectual property rights and the market for know-how. *Economics of Innovation and New Technology*, *4*(1), 41–60. doi:10.1080/10438599500000013

Arora, A., Fosfuri, A., & Gambardella, A. (2001). Markets for technology and their implications for corporate strategy. *Industrial and Corporate Change*, *10*(2), 419–451. doi:10.1093/icc/10.2.419

Arrow, K. (1962). *Economic welfare and the alloca-tion of resources for invention.* UMI.

Arrow, K. J. (1962). The economic implications of learning by doing. *The Review of Economic Studies,* *29*(3), 155–173. doi:10.2307/2295952

Arthur, W. B. (1989). Competing technologies, increasing returns, and lock-in by historical events. *Economic Journal (London), 99*(394), 116–131. doi:10.2307/2234208

Arthur, W. B. (1994). Positive feedbacks in the economy. *The McKinsey Quarterly,* 81.

Arthur, W. B. (1996). Increasing returns and the new world of business. *Harvard Business Review, 74,* 100–111. PMID:10158472

Arthur, W. B. (2000). Myths and realities of the high-tech economy. In *Talk given at Credit Suisse First Boston Though Leader Forum.* Santa Fe Institute.

Benbya, H., & McKelvey, B. (2006). Toward a com-plexity theory of information systems development. *Information Technology & People, 19*(1), 12–34. doi:10.1108/09593840610649952

Benkler, Y. (2006). *The wealth of networks: How social production transforms markets and freedom.* New Haven, CT: Yale University Press. Retrieved from http://books. google.co.uk/ books?hl=en&lr=&id=McotnvNSjQ 4C&oi=fnd&pg=PR7&dq=benkler+the+wealth+o f+networks &ots=YTsBUfHqy5&sig=bzEONkk7 QTSyFKAZIl3l9NqJC7k

Bergstrom, T., Blume, L., & Varian, H. (1986). On the private provision of public goods. *Journal of Public Economics, 29*(1), 25–49. doi:10.1016/0047-2727(86)90024-1

Bitzer, J., Schrettl, W., & Schroder, P. J. H. (2007). Intrinsic motivation in open source software development. *Journal of Comparative Economics, 35*(1), 160–169. doi:10.1016/j.jce.2006.10.001

Bonaccorsi, A., & Rossi, C. (2003). Why open source software can succeed. *Research Policy, 32*(7), 1243–1258. doi:10.1016/S0048-7333(03)00051-9

BSA | The Software Alliance. (2016). Overview; The Economic Impact of Software. *The Economic Impact Of Software.* Retrieved from http://softwareimpact.bsa.org/pdf/Economic_Impact_of_Software_Overview.pdf

Bureau of Labor Statistics. U.S. Department of Labor. (n.d.). *Occupational Outlook Handbook, 2016-17 Edition, Software Developers.* Retrieved from https://www.bls.gov/ooh/computer-and-information-technology/software-developers.htm

Callon, M., Law, J., & Rip, A. (1986). *Mapping the dynamics of science and technology.* Academic Press.

Campbell-Kelly, M., & Garcia-Swartz, D. D. (2009). Pragmatism, not ideology: Historical perspectives on IBM's adoption of open-source software. *Information Economics and Policy, 21*(3), 229–244. doi:10.1016/j.infoecopol.2009.03.006

Capra, E., Francalanci, C., Merlo, F., & Rossi-Lamastra, C. (2011). Firms' involvement in Open Source projects: A trade-off between software structural quality and popularity. *Journal of Systems and Software, 84*(1), 144–161. doi:.jss.2010.09.00410.1016/j

Chamberlin, J. (1974). Provision of collective goods as a function of group size. *The American Political Science Review*, *68*(2), 707–716. doi:10.1017/S0003055400117496

Chesbrough, H. (2006). *Open business models: How to thrive in the new innovation landscape*. Cambridge, MA: Harvard Business School Press.

Chesbrough, H. W., & Appleyard, M. M. (2007). Open innovation and strategy. *California Management Review*, *50*(1), 57–76. doi:10.2307/41166416

Coase, R. H. (1937). The nature of the firm. *Economica, 4*(16), 386–405. doi:.tb00002.x10.1111/j.1468-0335.1937

Coase, R. H. (2007). The problem of social cost. In *Economic analysis of the law* (pp. 1–13). Blackwell Publishing Ltd.

Cohen, W. M., & Levinthal, D. A. (1990). Absorp-tive capacity: A new perspective on learning and innovation. *Administrative Science Quarterly*, *35*(1), 128–152. doi:10.2307/2393553

David, P. A., & Rullani, F. (2008). Dynamics of innovation in an 'open source' collaboration environment: Lurking, laboring, and launching FLOSS projects on SourceForge. *Industrial and Corporate Change*, *17*(4), 647–710. doi:10.1093/icc/dtn026

de Jong, J. P. J., Kalvet, T., & Vanhaverbeke, W. (2010). Exploring a theoretical framework to structure the public policy implications of open innovation. *Technology Analysis and Strategic Management, 22*(8), 877–896. doi:325.2010.52277110.1080/09537

Duesenberry, J. (1956). Innovation and growth. *The American Economic Review*, *46*(2), 134–14.

Economides, N., & Katsamakas, E. (2006). *Linux vs. windows: A comparison of application and platform innovation incentives for open source and proprietary software platforms. The Economics of Open Source Software Development*. Elsevier Publishers. doi:10.1016/B978-044452769-1/50010-X

Enkel, E., Gassmann, O., & Chesbrough, H. (2009). Open R&D and open innovation: Exploring the phenomenon. *R & D Management*, *39*(4), 311–316. doi:10.1111/j.1467-9310.2009.00570.x

E.U. Connecta. (n.d.). Retrieved from http://eu.conecta.it/paper/Perceived_disadvan-tages_ope.html

Fitzgerald, B. (2006). The transformation of open source software. *Management Information Systems Quarterly*, *30*(3), 587–598.

Gassmann, O., Enkel, E., & Chesbrough, H. (2010). The future of open innovation. *R & D Management*, *40*(3), 213–221. doi:10.1111/j.1467-9310.2010.00605.x

Ghosh, R. (2006). Economic impact of open source software on innovation and competitiveness of the information and communications technologies (ICT) sector in the EU. *Proceedings of the UNU-MERIT prepared for the European Commission*, 1-287.

Glass, R. L. (2004). A look at the economics of open source. *Communications of the ACM*, *47*(2), 25–27. doi:10.1145/966389.966409

Gould, D. M., & Gruben, W. C. (1996). The role of intellectual property rights in economic growth. *Journal of Development Economics, 48*(2), 323–350. doi:10.1016/0304-3878(95)00039-9

Grossman, G. M., & Helpman, E. (1990). Trade, innovation, and growth. *The American Economic Review, 80*(2), 86–91.

Gulati, R. (1995). Does familiarity breed trust? The implications of repeated ties for contractual choice in alliances. *Academy of Management Journal, 38*(1), 85–112. doi:10.2307/256729

Harhoff, D., Henkel, J., & von Hippel, E. (2003). Profiting from voluntary information spillovers: How users benefit by freely revealing their innovations. *Research Policy, 32*(10), 1753–1769. doi:10.1016/S0048-7333(03)00061-1

Hars, A., & Ou, S. (2001). *Working for free? Motivations of participating in open source projects.* Academic Press.

Hawkins, R. E. (2004). The economics of open source software for a competitive firm. *NETNOMICS, 6*(2), 103-117.

Heller, M. A., & Eisenberg, R. S. (1998). Can patents deter innovation? The anticommons in biomedical research. *Science, 280*(5364), 698–701. doi:10.1126/science.280.5364.698 PMID:9563938

Henkel, J. (2006). Selective revealing in open in-novation processes: The case of embedded Linux. *Research Policy, 35*(7), 953–969. doi:.respol.2006.04.01010.1016/j

Hertel, G., Niedner, S., & Herrmann, S. (2003). Motivation of software developers in Open Source projects: An Internet-based survey of contributors to the Linux kernel. *Research Policy, 32*(7), 1159–1177. doi:10.1016/S0048-7333(03)00047-7

Heylighen, F. (2006). *Why is open access development so successful? Stigmergic organization and the economics of information.* Arxiv preprint cs/0612071

Iannacci, F. (2002). The economics of open-source networks. *Communications & Stratégies, 48*(4), 119–138.

Johnson, J. P. (1999). *Economics of open source software.* Unpublished working paper. Massachusetts Institute of Technology.

Katz, D., & Kahn, R. L. (1978). *The social psychology of organizations.* Academic Press.

King, J. L., Gurbaxani, V., Kraemer, K. L., McFarlan, F. W., Raman, K. S., & Yap, C. S. (1994). Institutional factors in information technology innovation. *Information Systems Research, 5*(2), 139–169. doi:10.1287/isre.5.2.139

Kogut, B., & Metiu, A. (2001). Open-source software development and distributed innovation. *Oxford Review of Economic Policy, 17*(2), 248–264. doi:10.1093/oxrep/17.2.248

Latour, B. (1996). On actor-network theory. *Soziale Welt, 47*(4), 369–381.

Lazzarotti, V., & Manzini, R. (2009). Different modes of open innovation: A theoretical framework and an empirical study. *International Journal of Innovation Management, 13*(4), 615–636. doi:10.1142/S1363919609002443

Lerner, J., & Tirole, J. (2002). Some simple economics of open source. *The Journal of Industrial Economics, 50*(2), 197–234. doi:10.1111/1467-6451.00174

Lerner, J., & Tirole, J. (2004). *The economics of technology sharing: Open source and beyond.* National Bureau of Economic Research. doi:10.3386/w10956

Lundvall, B., & Johnson, B. (2011). The learning economy. *Journal of Industry Studies, 1*(2), 23–42. doi:10.1080/13662719400000002

MacCormack, A. D., Rusnak, J., Baldwin, C. Y., & Harvard Business School. Division of Research. (2004). *Exploring the structure of complex software designs: An empirical study of open source and proprietary code.* Citeseer.

Maher, M. (1999). Open source software: The suc-cess of an alternative intellectual property incentive paradigm. *Fordham Intell. Prop. Media & Ent. LJ, 10,* 619.

Merges, R. (1994). Intellectual property rights and bargaining breakdown: The case of blocking patents. *Tennessee Law Review, 62*(1), 74–106.

Millien, R., & Laurie, R. (2008). Meet the middlemen. *Intellectual Asset Management (IAM) Magazine, 28.*

Monk, A. H. B. (2009). The emerging market for intellectual property: Drivers, restrainers, and implications. *Journal of Economic Geography, 9*(4), 469–491. doi:10.1093/jeg/lbp003

Nuvolari, A. (2004). Collective invention during the British industrial revolution: The case of the Cornish pumping engine. *Cambridge Journal of Economics, 28*(3), 347–363. doi:10.1093/cje/28.3.347

O'Reilly, T. (1999). Lessons from open-source soft-ware development: Introduction. *Communications of the ACM, 42*(4), 32–37. doi:10.1145/299157.299164

Osterloh, M., & Rota, S. (2007). Open source software development--Just another case of collective inven-tion? *Research Policy, 36*(2), 157–171. doi:.respol.2006.10.00410.1016/j

Palfrey, T. R., & Rosenthal, H. (1984). Participa-tion and the provision of discrete public goods: A strategic analysis. *Journal of Public Economics, 24*(2), 171–193. doi:10.1016/0047-2727(84)90023-9

Raymond, E. (1999). The cathedral and the bazaar. *Knowledge, Technology & Policy, 12*(3), 23–49. doi:10.1007/s12130-999-1026-0

Reilly, R. F., & Schweihs, R. P. (2004). *The hand-book of business valuation and intellectual property analysis.* McGraw-Hill.

Rogers, M. (1998). *The definition and measurement of innovation.* Melbourne Institute of Applied Economic and Social Research. Retrieved from http://scholar.google.co.uk/scholar.bib?q=info:5oErPpbtQl8J:scholar.google.com/&output=citation&hl=en&as_ sdt=0,5&ct=citation&cd=24

Schumpeter, J. (1942). *Capitalism, socialism and democracy*. New York, NY: Harper.

Shah, S. K. (2006). Motivation, governance, and the viability of hybrid forms in open source software development. *Management Science, 52*(7), 1000–1014. doi:10.1287/mnsc.1060.0553

Singh, P. V., Tan, Y., & Mookerjee, V. (2008). Network effects: The influence of structural social capital on open source project success. *SSRN eLibrary*.

Solow, R. M. (1957). Technical change and the aggre-gate production function. *The Review of Economics and Statistics, 39*(3), 312–320. doi:10.2307/1926047

Spencer, J. W. (2003). Firms' knowledge-sharing strategies in the global innovation system: Empirical evidence from the flat panel display industry. *Strategic Management Journal, 24*(3), 217–233. doi:10.1002/smj.290

The Economist. (2006, March 16). Open source business. Open, but not as usual. *The Economist*, pp. 1-7.

Von Hippel, E. (1988). *The Sources of Innovation* (Vol. 80). Oxford University Press.

Von Hippel, E. (2007). Horizontal innovation net-works—by and for users. *Industrial and Corporate Change, 16*(2), 293–315. doi:10.1093/icc/dtm005

Von Hippel, E., & Von Krogh, G. (2003). Open source software and the 'private-collective' innovation model: Issues for organization science. *Organization Science, 14*(2), 209–223. doi:10.1287/orsc.14.2.209.14992

Weber, S. (2000). *The political economy of open source software*. Retrieved from http://www.escholarship.org/uc/item/3hq916dc

Williamson, O. (1979). Transaction-cost econom-ics: The governance of contractual relations. *The Journal of Law & Economics, 22*(2), 233–261. doi:10.1086/466942

Yu, L. (2008). Self-organization process in open-source software: An empirical study. *Information and Software Technology, 50*(5), 361–374. doi:.infsof.2007.02.01810.1016/j

Ziedonis, R. H. (2004). Don't fence me in: Frag-mented markets for technology and the patent acquisition strategies of firms. *Management Science, 50*(6), 804–820. doi:10.1287/mnsc.1040.0208

ENDNOTES

[1]   The findings of the paper were supposed to be presented at the World Summit on Information Society 2013 and contribute to the recommendations put forward by Academia. However due to illness this was not possible. We would like to thank James Boyle, who is Professor of Law at Duke University School for valuable comments and suggestions. Research Funding was received from the Said Business School of Oxford University and Open Invention Network.

2   For the full rationale underpinning this methodology see: RishabGhosh (2006), 'Economic Impact of Open Source Software on Innovation and Competitiveness of the Information and Communications Technologies (ICT) Sector in the EU', UNU-MERIT prepared for the European Commission, pp. 1-287.

3   IT developing sectors: 'Computer systems design and related services', 'software publishers', 'data processing, host-ing, related services and information services', and 'computer and electronic product manufacturing').

4   All other sectors.

APPENDIX 1

Disclaimer

Funding was received by the Said Business School of Oxford University and by Open Invention Networks. An earlier version of the paper was published under the title Open Growth: The Impact of Open Source Software on Employment in the USA within 5(1), 2014 of the International Journal of Open Source Software and Processes (IJOSSP). This information is provided with the understanding that with respect to the material provided herein OxFirst is providing this paper as a research article This paper should therefore not be used as strategic advice but an independent decision needs to be made with respect to any course of action in connection herewith, as to whether such course of action is appropriate or proper based on your own judgment and your specific circumstances and objectives.

APPENDIX 2

Tables 15-23 were compiled from statistics provided by the US Bureau of Labour Statistics. The raw data from which these tables were aggregated is available from: http://www.bls.gov/emp/ep_table_109.htm See following pages for the tables.

Table 15. Employment by industry, occupation, and percent distribution, 2008 and projected 2018
Computer specialists

(Employment in thousands) Industries with fewer than 50 jobs, confidential data, or poor quality data are not displayed								
Industry	2008			2018			Percentchange	Employmentchange
	Employment	Percentof ind	Percentof occ	Employment	Percentof ind	Percentof occ		
Mining, quarrying, and oil and gas extraction	7.1	0.98	0.21	5.8	0.94	0.14	-18.35	-1.3
Utilities	17.3	3.09	0.50	14.9	2.97	0.36	-13.94	-2.4
Construction	9.8	0.14	0.29	11.8	0.14	0.28	20.95	2.0
Manufacturing, other	133.0	0.94	3.88	126.9	0.94	3.03	-4.16	-5.5
Computer and electronic product manufacturing	133.1	10.67	3.89	110.7	11.00	2.64	-16.85	-22.4
Wholesale trade	173.4	2.91	5.06	171.3	2.75	4.09	-1.22	-2.1
Retail trade	57.5	0.37	1.68	55.6	0.35	1.33	-3.40	-2.0
Transportation and warehousing	23.0	0.51	0.67	24.6	0.50	0.59	6.95	1.6
Software publishers	136.3	51.67	3.98	178.8	52.17	4.27	31.24	42.6
Other publishing, broadcasting and recording industries (except Internet)	39.7	2.89	1.15	39.4	3.08	0.95	-0.76	-0.3
Telecommunications	122.7	12.01	3.58	118.4	12.70	2.83	-3.55	-4.4
Data processing, hosting, related services, and other information services	117.1	29.63	3.42	183.9	32.04	4.39	57.09	66.8
Finance and insurance	294.5	4.90	8.60	321.1	5.07	7.67	9.05	26.6
Real estate and rental and leasing	13.3	0.63	0.39	15.2	0.64	0.36	14.13	1.9
Computer systems design and related services	797.4	54.98	23.29	1187.3	56.36	28.36	48.90	389.9
Other professional, scientific, and technical services (including consulting)	298.6	4.62	8.72	423.5	4.72	10.11	41.80	124.9
Management of companies and enterprises	183.1	9.66	5.35	191.4	9.59	4.57	4.56	8.3
Administrative and support and waste management and remediation services (including employment services)	137.6	1.71	4.02	163.8	1.73	3.91	19.11	26.3
Educational services, public and private	210.3	1.56	6.14	230.3	1.52	5.50	9.51	20.0
Health care and social assistance	86.7	0.51	2.53	111.4	0.53	2.66	28.46	24.7
Arts, entertainment, and recreation	5.0	0.57	0.16	5.7	0.57	0.16	14.00	0.7
Accommodation and food services	2.6	0.02	0.08	2.7	0.02	0.06	5.58	0.1
Other services (except government and private households)	40.5	0.73	1.18	45.2	0.73	1.08	11.56	4.7
Government	228.2	2.07	6.66	246.6	2.09	5.89	8.09	18.5
Other wage and salary employment (agriculture, forestry, fishing, hunting, and private households)	1.3	0.06	0.05	1.1	0.05	0.02	-15.13	-0.2
Self-employed and unpaid family workers, all jobs	154.9	1.32	4.52	198.9	1.61	4.75	28.41	44.0
Total employment, all workers	**3424.0**	**2.27**	**100.00**	**4186.3**	**2.52**	**100.00**	**22.26**	**762.3**

Table 16. Employment by industry, occupation, and percent distribution, 2008 and projected 2018 Computer specialists (Employment in thousands) Industries with fewer than 50 jobs, confidential data, or poor quality data are not displayed

Rank	Industry	2008		2018			2008-2018		
		Employment	Percentof ind	Percentof occ	Employment	Percentof ind	Percentof occ	Percentchange	Employmentchange
1	Computer systems design and related services	797.4	54.98	23.29	1187.3	56.36	28.36	48.9	389.9
2	Other professional, scientific, and technical services (including consulting)	298.6	4.62	8.72	423.5	4.72	10.11	41.8	124.9
3	Finance and insurance	294.5	4.9	8.6	321.1	5.07	7.67	9.05	26.6
4	Government	228.2	2.07	6.66	246.6	2.09	5.89	8.09	18.5
5	Educational services, public and private	210.3	1.56	6.14	230.3	1.52	5.5	9.51	20
6	Management of companies and enterprises	183.1	9.66	5.35	191.4	9.59	4.57	4.56	8.3
7	Wholesale trade	173.4	2.91	5.06	171.3	2.75	4.09	-1.22	-2.1
8	Self-employed and unpaid family workers, all jobs	154.9	1.32	4.52	198.9	1.61	4.75	28.41	44
9	Administrative and support and waste management and remediation services (including employment services)	137.6	1.71	4.02	163.8	1.73	3.91	19.11	26.3
10	Software publishers	136.3	51.67	3.98	178.8	52.17	4.27	31.24	42.6
11	Computer and electronic product manufacturing	133.1	10.67	3.89	110.7	11	2.64	-16.85	-22.4
12	Manufacturing, other	133	0.94	3.88	126.9	0.94	3.03	-4.16	-5.5
13	Telecommunications	122.7	12.01	3.58	118.4	12.7	2.83	-3.55	-4.4
14	Data processing, hosting, related services, and other information services	117.1	29.63	3.42	183.9	32.04	4.39	57.09	66.8
15	Health care and social assistance	86.7	0.51	2.53	111.4	0.53	2.66	28.46	24.7
16	Retail trade	57.5	0.37	1.68	55.6	0.35	1.33	-3.4	-2
17	Other services (except government and private households)	40.5	0.73	1.18	45.2	0.73	1.08	11.56	4.7
18	Other publishing, broadcasting and recording industries (except Internet)	39.7	2.89	1.15	39.4	3.08	0.95	-0.76	-0.3
19	Transportation and warehousing	23	0.51	0.67	24.6	0.5	0.59	6.95	1.6
20	Utilities	17.3	3.09	0.5	14.9	2.97	0.36	-13.94	-2.4
21	Real estate and rental and leasing	13.3	0.63	0.39	15.2	0.64	0.36	14.13	1.9
22	Construction	9.8	0.14	0.29	11.8	0.14	0.28	20.95	2

continued on following page

Table 16. Continued

Rank	Industry	2008			2018			2008-2018		
		Employment	Percentof ind	Percentof occ	Employment	Percentof ind	Percentof occ	Percentchange	Employmentchange
23	Mining, quarrying, and oil and gas extraction	7.1	0.98	0.21	5.8	0.94	0.14	-18.35	-1.3
24	Arts, entertainment, and recreation	5	0.57	0.16	5.7	0.57	0.16	14	0.7
25	Accommod ation and food services	2.6	0.02	0.08	2.7	0.02	0.06	5.58	0.1
26	Other wage and salary employment (agriculture, forestry, fishing, hunting, and private households)	1.3	0.06	0.05	1.1	0.05	0.02	-15.13	-0.2
Total employment, all workers		3424	2.27	100	4186.3	2.52	100	22.26	762.3

Table 17. Employment Totals for all software developers

Occupation	2008		2018	
	FLOSS1 SectorEmployment	FLOSS2 SectorEmployment	FLOSS1 SectorEmployment	FLOSS 2 SectorEmployment
Software engineers	757.3	468.4	1043.9	589.4
Computer systems analysts	508.3	382	614.6	437.4
Computer programmers	401.1	259.9	391.2	232.8
Computer and information scientists, research	25.4	18.7	31.7	22.1
TOTAL	1692.1	1129	2081.4	1281.7
FLOSS-related software development jobs				
IDC Survey - global **developers who use FLOSS:**	71.00%			
	2008		2018	
	FLOSS1 Sector Employment	FLOSS 2 Sector Employment	FLOSS1 Sector Employment	FLOSS 2 Sector Employment
	1,201,391.00	801,590.00	1,477,794.00	910,007.00

Table 18. Employment by industry, occupation, and percent distribution, 2008 and projected 2018
Computer software engineers

(Employment in thousands) Industries with fewer than 50 jobs, confidential data, or poor quality data are not displayed								
Industry	**2008**			**2018**			**Percent change**	**Employment change**
	Employment	**Percent of ind**	**Percent of occ**	**Employment**	**Percent of ind**	**Percent of occ**		
Mining, quarrying, and oil and gas extraction	0.4	0.05	0.04	0.4	0.06	0.03	-10.80	0.0
Utilities	3.3	0.60	0.37	3.1	0.62	0.26	-6.50	-0.2
Construction	1.0	0.01	0.11	1.3	0.02	0.11	34.55	0.3
Manufacturing, other	40.9	0.25	4.48	43.8	0.28	3.64	6.85	2.9
Computer and electronic product manufacturing	84.6	6.78	9.30	73.8	7.33	6.12	-12.83	-10.9
Wholesale trade	44.7	0.75	4.91	47.6	0.77	3.95	6.60	2.9
Retail trade	7.0	0.05	0.77	6.8	0.04	0.56	-2.82	-0.2
Transportation and warehousing	4.2	0.09	0.46	4.9	0.10	0.41	17.25	0.7
Software publishers	65.2	24.71	7.16	84.2	24.58	6.99	29.31	19.1
Other publishing, broadcasting and recording industries (except Internet)	7.0	0.49	0.78	7.6	0.56	0.63	8.57	0.6
Telecommunications	28.3	2.77	3.11	27.6	2.97	2.29	-2.18	-0.6
Data processing, hosting, related services, and other information services	38.2	9.65	4.19	60.6	10.56	5.03	58.86	22.5
Finance and insurance	72.0	1.20	7.91	85.0	1.34	7.06	18.10	13.0
Real estate and rental and leasing	1.2	0.06	0.13	1.5	0.06	0.13	26.96	0.3
Computer systems design and related services	288.9	19.92	1.76	454.5	21.58	37.73	57.35	165.7
Other professional, scientific, and technical services (including consulting)	92.9	1.42	10.22	142.2	1.56	11.80	53.07	49.3
Management of companies and enterprises	37.7	1.99	4.15	43.3	2.17	3.59	14.80	5.6
Administrative and support and waste management and remediation services (including employment services)	23.8	0.30	2.62	31.3	0.33	2.60	31.60	7.5
Educational services, public and private	15.4	0.11	1.70	19.3	0.13	1.60	25.16	3.9
Health care and social assistance	8.8	0.05	0.97	11.3	0.05	0.94	28.29	2.5
Arts, entertainment, and recreation	0.4	0.02	0.04	0.5	0.02	0.04	25.98	0.1
Accommodation and food services	0.1	0.00	0.01	0.1	0.00	0.01	18.45	0.0
Other services (except government and private households)	2.3	0.04	0.26	2.9	0.05	0.24	22.41	0.5
Government	13.9	0.13	1.82	16.6	0.14	1.61	19.28	2.7
Self-employed and unpaid family workers, all jobs	24.9	0.21	2.73	31.7	0.26	2.63	7.34	6.8
Total employment, all workers	**907.1**	**0.60**	**100.00**	**1201.9**	**0.72**	**100.00**	**32.50**	**295.0**
All sectors (except 'software publishers' and 'computer and electronic product manufacturing')	757.3		83.5	1043.9		86.9	37.84	286.6
All sectors (except 'software publishers', 'computer and electronic product manufacturing', and 'computer systems design and related services')	468.4		51.8	589.4		49.2	25.83	121.0

Table 19. Employment by industry, occupation, and percent distribution, 2008 and projected 2018
Computer and information scientists, research

(Employment in thousands) Industries with fewer than 50 jobs, confidential data, or poor quality data are not displayed								
Industry	2008			2018			Percent change	Employment change
	Employment	Percent of ind	Percent of occ	Employment	Percent of ind	Percent of occ		
Manufacturing, other	0.3	0.01	1.02	0.3	0.01	0.84	0.00	0.0
Computer and electronic product manufacturing	0.8	0.06	2.80	0.6	0.06	1.69	-24.81	-0.2
Wholesale trade	1.2	0.02	4.03	1.1	0.02	3.03	-6.45	-0.1
Software publishers	2.8	1.05	9.69	3.6	1.04	10.03	29.31	0.8
Other publishing, broadcasting and recording industries (except Internet)	0.3	0.03	1.02	0.4	0.03	1.11	50.00	0.1
Telecommunications	0.5	0.05	1.73	0.4	0.04	1.11	-12.37	-0.1
Data processing, hosting, related services, and other information services	1.0	0.25	3.46	1.5	0.25	4.18	46.42	0.5
Finance and insurance	0.1	0.00	0.41	0.1	0.00	0.33	2.04	0.0
Computer systems design and related services	6.7	0.46	23.15	9.6	0.45	26.66	43.05	2.9
Other professional, scientific, and technical services (including consulting)	5.6	0.18	19.38	7.0	0.19	19.50	25.00	1.4
Management of companies and enterprises	0.3	0.01	1.02	0.3	0.01	0.80	3.94	0.0
Administrative and support and waste management and remediation services (including employment services)	0.1	0.00	0.35	0.1	0.00	0.29	23.67	0.0
Educational services, public and private	2.0	0.01	6.82	2.2	0.01	6.16	12.15	0.2
Health care and social assistance	0.1	0.00	0.35	0.1	0.00	0.19	14.14	0.0
Government	5.9	0.05	20.41	7.0	0.06	19.50	19.27	1.1
Self-employed and unpaid family workers, all jobs	1.3	0.01	4.49	1.6	0.01	4.46	17.38	0.3
Total employment, all workers	**28.9**	**0.02**	**100.00**	**35.9**	**0.02**	**100.00**	**24.18**	**7.0**
All sectors (except 'software publishers' and 'computer and electronic product manufacturing')	25.4		87.6	31.7		88.2	24.80	6.3
All sectors (except 'software publishers', 'computer and electronic product manufacturing', and 'computer systems design and related services')	18.7		64.5	22.1		61.5	18.18	3.4

Table 20. Employment by industry, occupation, and percent distribution, 2008 and projected 2018
Computer programmers

(Employment in thousands) Industries with fewer than 50 jobs, confidential data, or poor quality data are not displayed	2008			2018			Percent Change	Employment change
Industry	**Employment**	**Percent of ind**	**Percent of occ**	**Employment**	**Percent of ind**	**Percent of occ**		
Mining, quarrying, and oil and gas extraction	0.3	0.04	0.07	0.2	0.03	0.05	-34.86	-0.1
Utilities	1.5	0.28	0.36	1.0	0.20	0.25	-33.85	-0.5
Construction	0.9	0.01	0.21	0.9	0.01	0.22	-0.80	0.0
Manufacturing, other	16.8	0.14	3.96	12.1	0.11	2.93	-27.98	-4.7
Computer and electronic product manufacturing	7.1	0.57	1.66	4.2	0.42	1.01	-40.99	-2.9
Wholesale trade	23.9	0.40	5.61	19.5	0.31	4.70	-18.62	-4.5
Retail trade	8.4	0.05	1.97	6.2	0.04	1.51	-25.62	-2.2
Transportation and warehousing	3.0	0.07	0.71	2.6	0.05	0.62	-15.28	-0.5
Software publishers	18.3	6.94	4.29	18.8	5.48	4.53	2.69	0.5
Other publishing, broadcasting and recording industries (except Internet)	6.2	0.44	1.45	4.8	0.37	1.18	-22.58	-1.4
Telecommunications	6.7	0.66	1.57	4.8	0.51	1.16	-28.46	-1.9
Data processing, hosting, related services, and other information services	13.6	3.43	3.18	15.6	2.71	3.75	14.74	2.0
Finance and insurance	32.3	0.54	7.57	26.2	0.41	6.33	-18.85	-6.1
Real estate and rental and leasing	1.1	0.05	0.26	1.0	0.04	0.25	-5.93	-0.1
Computer systems design and related services	141.2	9.73	33.09	158.4	7.52	38.22	12.19	17.2
Other professional, scientific, and technical services (including consulting)	30.6	0.54	7.18	33.6	0.42	8.11	9.80	3.0
Management of companies and enterprises	17.3	0.91	4.04	14.4	0.72	3.48	-16.49	-2.8
Administrative and support and waste management and remediation services (including employment services)	23.6	0.29	5.53	22.9	0.24	5.53	-2.86	-0.7
Educational services, public and private	19.6	0.15	4.60	17.8	0.12	4.29	-9.45	-1.9
Health care and social assistance	4.8	0.03	1.14	4.4	0.02	1.05	-9.93	-0.5

continued on following page

Table 20. Continued

(Employment in thousands) Industries with fewer than 50 jobs, confidential data, or poor quality data are not displayed								
Industry	**2008**			**2018**			**Percent Change**	**Employment change**
	Employment	**Percent of ind**	**Percent of occ**	**Employment**	**Percent of ind**	**Percent of occ**		
Arts, entertainment, and recreation	0.5	0.02	0.11	0.5	0.02	0.11	-6.38	0.0
Accommodation and food services	0.2	0.00	0.04	0.1	0.00	0.03	-15.00	0.0
Other services (except government and private households)	5.7	0.10	1.34	5.2	0.08	1.26	-9.16	-0.5
Government	18.5	0.17	4.34	16.0	0.14	3.87	-13.42	-2.5
Other wage and salary employment (agriculture, forestry, fishing, hunting, and private households)	0.8	0.04	0.18	0.6	0.03	0.14	-25.64	-0.2
Self-employed and unpaid family workers, all jobs	23.6	0.20	5.54	22.4	0.18	5.42	-5.05	-1.2
Total employment, all workers	**426.5**	**0.28**	**100.00**	**414.2**	**0.25**	**100.00**	**-2.88**	**-12.3**
All sectors (except 'software publishers' and 'computer and electronic product manufacturing')	401.1		94.1	391.2		94.5	-2.47	-9.9
All sectors (except 'software publishers', 'computer and electronic product manufacturing', and 'computer systems design and related services')	259.9		61.0	232.8		56.2	-10.43	-27.1

Table 21. Employment by industry, occupation, and percent distribution, 2008 and projected 2018 Computer systems analysts

(Employment in thousands) Industries with fewer than 50 jobs, confidential data, or poor quality data are not displayed								
Industry	**2008**			**2018**			**Percent change**	**Employment change**
	Employment	**Percent of ind**	**Percent of occ**	**Employment**	**Percent of ind**	**Percent of occ**		
Mining, quarrying, and oil and gas extraction	1.1	0.17	0.21	0.9	0.16	0.14	-18.18	-0.2
Utilities	5.8	1.03	1.08	4.8	0.96	0.75	-16.31	-0.9
Construction	1.0	0.01	0.19	1.2	0.01	0.19	15.60	0.2

continued on following page

Table 21. Continued

(Employment in thousands) Industries with fewer than 50 jobs, confidential data, or poor quality data are not displayed								
Industry	2008			2018			Percent change	Employment change
	Employment	Percent of ind	Percent of occ	Employment	Percent of ind	Percent of occ		
Manufacturing, other	19.0	0.16	3.57	17.3	0.15	2.70	-7.26	-1.7
Computer and electronic product manufacturing	12.5	1.00	2.34	9.4	0.93	1.46	-24.84	-3.1
Wholesale trade	27.2	0.46	5.11	26.4	0.42	4.12	-2.94	-0.8
Retail trade	3.8	0.02	0.71	3.3	0.02	0.51	-13.22	-0.5
Transportation and warehousing	2.6	0.06	0.48	2.8	0.06	0.43	8.01	0.2
Software publishers	11.4	4.34	2.15	16.3	4.75	2.54	42.23	4.8
Other publishing, broadcasting and recording industries (except Internet)	4.0	0.25	0.75	3.7	0.26	0.56	-7.50	-0.3
Telecommunications	12.6	1.24	2.37	11.3	1.21	1.76	-10.61	-1.3
Data processing, hosting, related services, and other information services	18.8	4.75	3.53	30.7	5.36	4.80	63.63	12.0
Finance and insurance	67.9	1.13	12.75	73.4	1.16	11.47	8.20	5.6
Real estate and rental and leasing	1.1	0.05	0.20	1.2	0.05	0.19	15.72	0.2
Computer systems design and related services	126.3	8.71	23.74	177.2	8.41	27.67	40.24	50.8
Other professional, scientific, and technical services (including consulting)	46.8	0.64	8.79	67.5	0.64	10.53	44.23	20.7
Management of companies and enterprises	38.1	2.01	7.16	39.8	1.99	6.21	4.39	1.7
Administrative and support and waste management and remediation services (including employment services)	16.7	0.21	3.13	20.2	0.21	3.16	21.21	3.5
Educational services, public and private	27.3	0.20	5.13	31.1	0.21	4.86	13.83	3.8
Health care and social assistance	17.4	0.10	3.27	22.3	0.11	3.49	28.29	4.9
Arts, entertainment, and recreation	0.4	0.02	0.07	0.4	0.02	0.07	12.96	0.0
Accommodation and food services	0.3	0.00	0.06	0.4	0.00	0.05	6.68	0.0
Other services (except government and private households)	2.0	0.04	0.37	2.2	0.04	0.34	11.75	0.2
Government	37.6	0.34	7.06	40.6	0.34	6.34	7.97	3.0
Other wage and salary employment (agriculture, forestry, fishing, hunting, and private households)	0.2	0.01	0.04	0.2	0.01	0.04	2.14	0.0
Self-employed and unpaid family workers, all jobs	30.3	0.26	5.70	35.7	0.29	5.57	17.49	5.3
Total employment, all workers	**532.2**	**0.35**	**100.00**	**640.3**	**0.39**	**100.00**	**20.31**	**108.1**
All sectors (except 'software publishers' and 'computer and electronic product manufacturing')	508.3		95.47	614.6		95.95	20.91	106.3
All sectors (except 'software publishers', 'computer and electronic product manufacturing', and 'computer systems design and related services')	382.0		71.73	437.4		68.28	14.50	55.4

Table 22. Employment (all software jobs)

SOC Code	Occupation	Employment in 000s (All Industries)	Annual Wage – Average (All Industries)	Annual Wage – Average (Software Publishing)
151132	Software Developers, Applications	539,580	85,817	94,950
151133	Software Developers, Systems Software	404,160	92,211	100,840
151111	Computer and Information Research Scientists	26,300	103,926	119,950
151131	Computer Programmers	350,040	72,670	81,440
151121	Computer Systems Analysts	504,090	78,993	81,890
151141	Database Administrators	105,930	72,356	81,770
151142	Network and Computer Systems Administrators	336,890	70,811	78,800
151150	Computer Support Specialists	600,070	50,049	56,100
151179	Information Security Analysts, Web	247,890	74,414	85,530
	Developers, and Computer Network Architects			
151799	Computer Occupations, All Other	189,940	70,984	85,210
	TOTAL	**3,304,890**	**77,223**	**86,648**
	**EMPLOYMENT (SOFTWARE DEVELOPMENT)**			
SOC Code	Occupation	Employment in 000s (all industries)	Annual Wage - Average (all industries)	Annual Wage - Average (software publishing)
151132	Software Developers, Applications	539,580	85,817	94,950
151133	Software Developers, Systems Software	404,160	92,211	100,840
151111	Computer and Information Research Scientists	26,300	103,926	119,950
151131	Computer Programmers	350,040	72,670	81,440
151121	Computer Systems Analysts	504,090	78,993	81,890
	TOTAL	**1,824,170**	**86,723**	**95,814**
	**EMPLOYMENT (SOFTWARE SUPPORT)**			
SOC Code	Occupation	Employment in 000s (all industries)	Annual Wage - Average (all industries)	Annual Wage - Average (software publishing)
151141	Database Administrators	105,930	72,356	81,770
151142	Network and Computer Systems Administrators	336,890	70,811	78,800
151150	Computer Support Specialists	600,070	50,049	56,100
	Information Security Analysts, Web			
151179	Developers, and Computer Network Architects	247,890	74,414	85,530
151799	Computer Occupations, All Other	189,940	70,984	85,210
	TOTAL	**1,480,720**	**67,723**	**77,482**

Table 23. Average annual wage table (May 2010)

Occ. Code	Occupation Title	Group	Total Employment	Hourly Mean Wage	Annual Mean Wage
00-0000	All Occupations	total	130647610	20.90	43460
15-0000	Computer and mathematical science occupations	major	3303690	36.68	76290.00
15-1011	Computer and information scientists, research		26130	50.66	105370.00
15-1021	Computer programmers		367880	35.91	74690.00
15-1031	Computer software engineers, applications		495500	43.35	90170.00
15-1032	Computer software engineers, systems software		385200	46.45	96620.00
15-1051	Computer systems analysts		512720	38.67	80430.00
15-1041	Computer support specialists		540560	22.77	47360.00
15-1061	Database administrators		108080	35.72	74290.00
15-1071	Network and computer systems administrators		338890	34.10	70930.00
15-1081	Network systems and data communications analysts		226080	36.81	76560.00
15-1099	Computer specialists, all other		195890	37.50	78010.00
15-2011	Actuaries		17940	46.85	97450.00
15-2021	Mathematicians		2770	45.16	93920.00
15-2031	Operations research analysts		60960	36.23	75370.00
15-2041	Statisticians		21370	36.16	75220.00
15-2091	Mathematical technicians		1090	21.27	44230.00
15-2099	Mathematical scientists, all other		2610	29.74	61850.00
All occupations			**$43,460.00**		
Software developers (red occupations)			**$89,456.00**		

Chapter 8
Strategy of Good Software Governance:
FLOSS in the State of Turkey

Hüseyin Tolu
Recep Tayyip Erdogan University, Turkey

ABSTRACT

To chapter concerns emerging cybernetics, which is the school of "meaning to lead" and is particularly associated with the idea of dominations and controls. This chapter initially anatomizes the sociology of software cybernetics into two broad movements—free/libre and open source software (FLOSS) and proprietary close source software (PCSS)—to argue a good software governance approach. This chapter discusses (a) in what matters and (b) for what reasons software governance of Turkey has locked into the ecosystems of PCSS and, in particular, considers causes, effects, and potential outcomes of not utilizing FLOSS in the state of Turkey. The government has continuously stated that there are no compulsory national or international conventions(s) and settlement(s) with the ecosystems of PCSS and that there is no vendor lock-in concern. Nevertheless, the chapter principally argues that Turkey has taken a pragmatic decision-making process of software in the emerging cybernetics that leads and contributes to techno-social externality of PCSS hegemonic stability.

INTRODUCTION

"You never change things by fighting the existing reality. To change something, build a new model that makes the existing model obsolete"; as B. Fuller (1895-1983), believed that in the system of monetary capitalism, it is practically meaningless to fight forces. So, smashing burgeoning technology for putting them out of their particular works is no longer the case of matter in the era of singularity. Nevertheless, this is not meant that the public ought not to have a particular criticism to technological singularity; or at least, no particular ethical concerns about its possible prospective and retrospective memory in the global (capitalist) system. The burgeoning technology is peculiar and mostly irregular, as W. Mossberg states that "why shouldn't a PC work like a refrigerator or a toaster?" Or "I'm an enemy of what I call 'computer

DOI: 10.4018/978-1-5225-5314-4.ch008

theology.' There's a class conflict out there. There's a techno-elite that lives in a different world". These quotations are what makes us concerned about cybernetics which is the school of 'meaning to lead', and particularly associated with the idea of dominations and controls, characteristically regarding criticism against doctrine of technological totalitarianism, existing mechanisms (machines and humans and their commissure), in which known and/or unknown one group control another. So, cybernetic is for the purpose of revealing its orchestrating mechanisms. "It is no longer a question of predicting the future, but of reproducing the present. It is no longer a question of static order, but of a dynamic self-organization" (Tiqqun, 2010, p.18). In this sense, cybernetics refers to an emergent governance of technology, policy and management, in which each element has actual persistence(s) of reality, but when they are merged together, multiplicities of reasonably complex interactions are arisen.

To study concerns of emerging cybernetics, interestingly enough, present software is escalating in order to sell hardware - e.g. present technology has no responsive meaning at all without software applications, such as Operating Systems (OSs) or the Internet. This makes software an interesting but sophisticated phenomenon. It is thereby initially essential to anatomize sociology of software cybernetics into two broad movements: Free/Libre and Open Source Software (FLOSS) and Proprietary Close Source Software (PCSS), to argue how our new technological revolution (e.g. innovations) exposures new concerns of our good governance approach in the capitalist democratic systems. This chapter broadly highlights why not to put technological movements into the same vein at all, because some of burgeoning technology should benefits public as a whole, in the prime imaginable way, as FLOSS movements seek. Then, this chapter compares the sociology of PCSS with those of FLOSS, highlighting their consequences as hegemonic totalitarianism with PCSS versus flexible emancipation with FLOSS. As the "control is as much an effect as a cause, and the idea that control is something you exert is a real handicap to progress" (Grand, 2003). So, it is actually essential to have the core knowledge of sociological of education and technology, in particular neither Utopian nor Luddite approach of Technorealism to conceptualise our new social goods, because

information is the vital element in a 'new' politics and economy that links space, knowledge and capital in networked practices. Freedom is an essential ingredient in this equation if these network practices develop or transform themselves into knowledge cultures. (Peters and Besley, 2008, p.186)

To comprehend these objects, the chapter is organized into seven sections. In the second and third sections, Actor Network Theory (ANT) and then the data collection method are introduced, to begin with, that there is an explicit good governance approach for the current software cybernetics, in particular sociology of education and technology, which crucially anatomizes the movements of FLOSS and PCSS. In this anatomization, the fourth and fifth sections inquire whether or not Turkey has locked-in into the ecosystems of PCSS. If Turkey has been, (a) in what matters and (b) in what reasons has software governance of Turkey locked-in into the ecosystems of PCSS, and in particular it considers causes, effects, potential outcomes for not utilizing FLOSS in the state of Turkey in order to reveal the cybernetics of Turkey. Therefore, the overall aim and contribution of the chapter is to increase an understanding of the underlying socio-political imperatives behind the cybernetics of Turkey in the specific context of PCSS. In the sixth section, it is argued that while the government has constantly stated that there are no compulsory national or international conventions(s) and settlement(s) with the ecosystems of PCSS and there are no vendor lock-in concerns, what does the data analysis principally indicate? Has Turkey actually taken pragmatic decision-making process of software (e.g. de-facto governance) in the emerging cybernetics? And does this negative externality which is certainly driven by state-scapegoatism, builds-in obsolescence and so leads and contributes to PCSS hegemonic stability (e.g. its own dominations and controls) in the era of technological singularity? Before the conclusion remark, the last section particularly focuses on good software governance which is not actually about providing 'correct' decisions, but about the 'best' possible judgment process for developing and implementing these decisions. It is focused that governing current burgeoning technology in specific state structures and regulatory frameworks is crucial for imagining a new sort of 'good software governance' that specific society for the best of the present.

ACTOR NETWORK THEORY

In the literature, ANT is considered as both a theory and a method in which "truth and falsehood. Large and small. Agency and structure. Human and non-human. Before and after. Knowledge and power. Context and content. Materiality and sociality. Activity and passivity. In one way or another all of these divides have been rubbished, in work undertaken in the name of" ANT (Law, 1999, p.3). In spite of this ontological complication, ANT has been applied to many literatures of education and technology. Latour illuminated the motive for ANT popularity as the progression of emerging "an alternative social theory to deal with the new puzzles uncovered after carrying out our fieldwork in science and technology" (2005, p.2). In methodology, the approach of ANT is "through the back door of science in the making, not through the more grandiose entrance of ready made science" (Latour, 1987, p.4) in where technology and science become a reality, for example public and private institutions, labs, etc. ANT's approach is to 'follow actors'. There may be many actors within any obvious network, but some actors may be subsequently excluded or misplaced before the conclusion of the process; the importance of these actors / networks input absence is an unidentified variable (e.g. bureaucrats). So, ANT approach is to highlight the key actors and sub networks, critical to the particular study. ANT, similar to other Science and Technology Studies (STS) approaches, uses 'open black box' technology and science, through evaluating complex associates that might be in presence between various agencies, such as governments, private sectors, etc. Through exploring and highlighting these associates, it becomes clear to realise how and why technology and science harmonize within/between each other; nevertheless,

the actor network is reducible neither to an actor alone nor to a network. Like a network it is composed of a series of heterogeneous elements, animate and inanimate, that have been linked to one another for certain period of time. ... An actor network is simultaneously an actor whose activity is networking heterogeneous elements and a network that is able to redefine and transform what it is made of. (Callon, 1987, p.93)

ANT is taking into consideration of both human and nonhuman actualities as an equilibrium within/ between a particular network(s) (but not necessarily an equally shared power relationship), and symmetrically titled them as an 'actant'. This perspective is called under 'the principle of generalized symmetry' by Callon (1986). ANT approaches human and nonhuman facts as meaningful behaviours, including moral distributed agencies by 'seamless web'. Latour argued that "an 'actor' in ANT is a semiotic definition-an actant-, that is, something that acts or to which activity is granted by others. It implies no special motivation of human individual actors, nor of humans in general. An actant can literally be anything provided it is granted to be the source of an action" (1996, p.373). The important point in ANT is 'follow actors' in order to study mutual and elective associations between actants, because an individual actant has not necessarily and inevitably the acting ability. For semiotic, a 'thing' has a meaning associatively with interactions with other things. ANT approaches both human and nonhuman actants; seeing their identities through their interactive relationships within/between networks.

So materials become resources or constraints; they are said to be passive; to be active only when they are mobilized by flesh and blood actors. But if the social is really materially heterogeneous then this asymmetry doesn't work very well. Yes, there are differences between conversations, texts, techniques and bodies. Of course. But why should we start out by assuming that some of these have no active role to play in social dynamics?" (Callon and Law, 1997, p.168)

ANT scholars highlighted that the network, they would like to seek, is different than traditional technological and sociological disciplines. The approach of ANT is concerned with defining key actors, identifying their roles, and investigating their mobilising roles. For power and connectivity relationships, ANT proposes 'heterogeneous actors' though associations. To do this, ANT does not ask which networks are bigger, wider, longer, faster, etc. than others. Rather, which associations are stronger and powerful than others within/between networks? Actors are not simply stable from one situation to another, rather moving and transforming between practises. For heterogeneous, ANT scholars argue that any social contents are the result of interaction within/between heterogeneous networks. That result may become another effect of the same and/or other heterogeneous networks due to associations within/between heterogeneous networks. ANT scholars perceive the power of social actors from the arisen outcome of actors' interactions. However, for ANT, there is no priority allocation between macro and micro social analyses in actor-networks due to 'the principles of generalised symmetry', which agnostically refuse dichotomies and distinctions. Nevertheless, there are some other concepts that make us think that some networks are more crucial than others; mainly influencing powers of associations that might exist due to various reasons such as, size, nostalgia, legislations, formal/informal structures, etc. The important point is, again, studying how these associations (interactions and connections) are performed.

Literally there is nothing but networks, there is nothing in between them, or, to use a metaphor from the history of physics, there is no aether in which the networks should be immersed. In this sense ANT is a reductionist and relativist theory, but, as I shall demonstrate, this is the first necessary step towards an irreductionist and relationist ontology. (Latour, 1996, p.4)

ANT scholars argue that there are advantages in considering heterogeneous networks in the fields of social science and technology studies. (a) 'The tyranny of distance' is not really a concern anymore. In ANT, there are only networks, which are not defined in terms of proximity between actors, as in geography, but rather meanings of associations between actors within network is the main concern. (b) The concept of networks also solves the distinction between micro and macro scale priorities within networks. (c) And, there are no inclusion/exclusion boundaries, because the concern is whether or not there are interactions and connections, there is no such thing as an outsider.

DATA COLLECTIONS

These key principles of ANT are helpful to begin the construction of establishing good governance approach for the process of planning and implementing software decisions making; because, it is not about constructing 'correct' decisions, but about defining the best imaginable process. Hence, as this chapter argues that the current approach to cybernetics is based on pragmatic techno-sociological perspective (e.g. de-facto governance). Many pragmatist' computer scientists may postulate that pragmatism is essential in the sociology of software cybernetics because it is "a philosophical movement that includes those who claim that an ideology or proposition is true if it works satisfactorily, that the meaning of a proposition is to be found in the practical consequences of accepting it, and that unpractical ideas are to be rejected" (McDermid, 2006). Nevertheless, 'an ideology is true if it works satisfactorily' is not meant that there are no negative outcomes or consequences. More generally, as many economists argue, the related arguments under the title of negative externality in which PCSS might be seen as forms of progress that are not only prone to unavoidably failure (e.g. lock-in), but that also inhibit other, more positive forms of 'Progress' (e.g. collaboration) (Boyle, 2008). And importantly, the philosophy of FLOSS is in an indignation commissure and a powerful phenomenon as artefact and human re-shaped each other to lead a better future (Weber, 2004). Consequently, this study inquires whether or not Governments in Turkey should be guilty of what is analogous to cybernetics, namely the rejection of valid technological knowledge between FLOSS and PCSS since their approaches to cybernetics is based on pragmatic techno-sociological perspective (e.g. de-facto governance), but negative externality of that perspective is certainly driven by state-scapegoatism that builds-in obsolescence.

From this standpoint, the data is obtained from Turkey's public reports, in particular over three hundred parliamentary written and verbal questions and responses reports, five parliamentary investigation proposals reports, thousand minutes of general assembly meeting reports, produced in the years of 2005-2006, 2008-2009 and 2013-2017, as secondary sources and studied by under the principles of ANT. All sources are available in the Grand National Assembly of Turkey (TBMM) website, as typing the basic number (e.g. TBMM, Year, No. 7/1540) in the form of 'written oral questions proposals query'; 'parliament general discussion suggestion query form' and 'parliamentary research proposals inquiry form'. To comprehend the software decision-making process of Ministries or the cybernetics of Turkey, additional documentary sources such as national and international reports were also gathered. Unfortunately, the Prime Ministry and the Minister of Science, Industry and Technology (SIT), which are the highest authorities regarding technological related projects, have not responded to certain questions.

"Documents, both historical and contemporary, are a rich sources of data for education and social research" (Punch, 2009, p.158). Notably, it is impossible to merely demarcate cybernetics as policy, technology and management. To avoid repetition, some of the most significant but repeated concepts are addressed only once. So, the chapter may provide generalizability through collected data since it is simply a snapshot which is not aimed at stating an external truth, but to rather present movements of cybernetics. So, this chapter puts forth a generic argument without focusing on a particular Ministry, since each Ministry has its own characters and settings; this could be useful in the scoping of technology in a particular national-state. The chapter sought to interpret the implementation of different policies of different institutions at different times to illustrate cybernetics of Turkey. Therefore, contemporaneousness, which is the reading of historical information; such as, initiating, remaining or happening in the similar time, does not the limitation of the chapter, is just another signification.

MATTERS OF SOFTWARE GOVERNANCE

Initially, Turkey had an original and innovative Linux project. The Scientific and Technological Research Council of Turkey, Turkish National Academic Network and Information Centre (TUBITAK-ULAKBIM) initiated the Pardus-Linux Project for the purpose of establishing a nationally distributed Linux-Based OSs in 2003, but withdrew its financial and political supports in 2012. Within ten years, the project of Pardus-Linux failed to achieve its targets and intentions defined in 2004 and 2011. Afterwards this failure, TUBITAK has intentionally and hiddenly distorted Pardus-Linux into (forked) Pardus Fraud-Debian within a single day in 2014. Since, it has been claimed that Pardus Fraud-Debian is a sufficient ecosystem of FLOSS in Turkey. There have been many instances where Pardus-Linux has been publicly used as leverage to obtain better fiscal deals from Giants, mostly Microsoft (Tolu, 2016).

Before illustrating (a) in what matters software governance of Turkey has locked-in the ecosystems of PCSS, in particular Microsoft OSs, all these parliamentary concerns (e.g. questions, answers, etc.), have some significant misconceptions that provide an insight into the genetic parliamentary' perspectives upon FLOSS. The critical misconception is the focus of 'national' FLOSS and Pardus-Linux, instead of global FLOSS and Linux (Globalness) as an entire concept. Globalness is the mission, "to preserve, protect and promote the freedom to use, study, copy, modify, and redistribute computer software, and to defend the rights of Free Software users" (Stallman, 2013). In this sense, in the ecosystem of FLOSS, there is no 'national' energy or nationalism, all matter is us. Nevertheless, Ministries and/or Governments of Turkey have mainly postulated Pardus-Linux issues (they see them as issues) rather than evaluating themselves based on FLOSS and Linux. This might be the impulse of not mentioning the real issues of FLOSS in Turkey such as the low level of FLOSS localisation or the failure of Pardus-Linux project, etc.

Technological Mechanism

In the literature of software development, a mechanism is an eco-friendly platform that can be joint with other mechanisms in the same or other computers in a distributed network to perform an application. There are mainly two crucial complexes in the technological mechanisms of particular organizations or systems: (a) compatibility refers studying how well applications function within different OSs and/or Internet browsers and (b) interoperability refers studying how well a system under assessment performs while interacting with something else. In this sense, in Turkey, the Centre of High Performance Computing (Ulusal Yüksek Başarımlı Hesaplama Uygulama ve Araştırma Merkezi) is the only public institution that is mainly based on FLOSS. Other institutions, even TUBITAK itself, have adapted software applications and services derived from Microsoft ecosystems, such as active directory, e-mail, libraries, etc. So, Ministries declared that 'Linux does not support (contribute to) their structural compatibility and interoperability' and additional support services are thereby needed. In this regard, the absurdity is that 'Linux does not support' implies supporting technologies developed by Ministries for Ministries is Linux ecosystem responsibility and accountability. Nevertheless, Ministries should have confessed that the current technologies they operate have not been developed based on recommendations (*OS or browser Agnosticism*) from the Guides of Information Communication Technology (ICT) Project Preparation Annual Reports (since 2005; see the subtitle of software[1] by the State Planning Organization (SPO) in the Prime-Ministry. The guides crucially underline Compatibility and Interoperability to be ensured *Open Standard* and *Avoidance Dependence* which refers *Writes Once and Runs Anywhere*; operating software in different OSs or browsers without rewriting it.

Admittedly, each Ministry has its own priorities and so use various and particular software(s), e.g. the Ministry of Environment and Forestry declared that Computer Assisted Design (CAD) and Geographic Information System (GIS) software are used because they are perceived as more 'useful' and 'functional' for Windows compared to their versions for Linux! (TBMM, 2008, No.7/1727) In 2008, this perspective could have been feasible and reasonable because the primary focus in the Ministry was not technology. However within ten years, there have been so many FLOSS alternative projects for CAD and GIS. If the Ministry were to web search 'FLOSS for CAD and GIS', there are so many Turkish and English academic articles highlighting how to use FLOSS for CAD and GIS in public, or asked an expert in Turkey (e.g. Yener, 2017). In fact, whether or not this information presents a particular response to a particular Ministry's problem depends on a particular cybernetics (e.g. software culture), as argued further. Still, the Ministry had not changed its perspective after four years (TBMM, 2012, No.7/5322) and still argues the same reasons. Panoptically, Ministries should have shifted between FLOSS and PCSS alternatives as their needs and requirements modified to keep up with technological acceleration.

Consequently, the lack of compatibility and interoperability arguments (e.g. Linux does not support) has become an unprofessional misconception of FLOSS due to the fact that the principles of *OS Agnosticism* are already noticed by the authorities.

Platform Dependent

At this juncture of OS or browser Agnosticism, few other Ministries have used Linux/Pardus not only in their personal computers (PCs) but also in their servers. E.g. the Ministry of National Defence (MoND) earlier declared that Pardus-Linux and FLOSS office applications played in 48% of PCs and 84% of servers in 2012 (TBMM, 2012, No.7/5316). Under 'the Turkey's 2016-2019 Cyber Security Strategy and Action Plan', MoND have already had new nine different collaborative protocols with TUBİTAK in order to expand the usage of Pardus and FLOSS (MoND, 2017). Evidently they have overcome the lack of compatibility and incompatibility, but still it does not mean they (e.g. MoND) have solved all issues. Nevertheless, compatibility and interoperability is not FLOSS and Linux's issue but Ministries' issues, such as how to establish technological mechanism. Importantly, Ministries are responsible for shaping their ICT projects and then obtaining all software codes when projects are finalised, so Ministries should have ensured platform independency. There are always Interoperability Framework Guide (IFG) Reports (Version 1 - 2005; Version 2 - 2009 and Version 2.1 – 2012); however, the Prime Minister 2012 E-State: Concept and General Issues Report recognized that IFG Reports are also not followed by most Ministries, not even the Prime-Ministry itself. The current situation is still not changed or improved, since then.

Most Ministries thereby preferred to compare Windows and Linux through the technological infrastructure they currently have. For instance, the Turkish Statistical Institute argued that Microsoft Outlook software is required for exchanging mails elementarily ('trouble-free' and 'full functional') with an institutional email server, e.g. Microsoft Exchange 2010 (TBMM, 2012, 7/5284 and 7/5283). This is an unfortunate reality and internationally problematic issue which has been systematically argued since the Microsoft Antitrust Cases in the USA in 1998 and the EU in 2003-04 (e.g. European Commission, 2004), because Microsoft has not provided complete information (also called interoperability information) that would enable other OSs to interoperate with Windows for exchanging essential data between servers and servers/clients. Concordantly, some Ministries have also complained about office applications issues; even in 2017 there are some interoperability issues between Microsoft Office and LibreOffice. Therefore, Ministries postulated that migrating LibreOffice is 'unnecessary' and 'time-consuming'.

This kind of techno-social mobility may be multiplied in the past decade, and has been extensively argued by the literature of Social-Shaping of Technology Theory, Social Construction of Technology Approach, Socio-Technical Systems, etc., because technology is not, either the only end of its wise choices of techno-social mobility, or essentially just sociologically 'social', it is in fact *both*! Therefore, the relationship between 'compatibility and interoperability' and 'platform independency' is actually an international issue and should be decided upon. Yet, over the past decade, there has been no conclusive global consensus about the definition of *Open Standard* and *Implementation of its Definition.* There are just best practices highlighted by the digital single market strategies (see, the document of 'Open Standard' and 'Against lock-in: building open ICT systems by making better use of standards in public' by European Commission, 2013). Consequently, it is essential either to prepare a new agreed IFG report (definitive enduring solution) or wait PCSS's and so Microsoft's compromise (provisional ephemeral solution). In this sense, Ministries of Turkey have presented the reality, but argued absurdly because it is not logical to protest that Linux ecosystem does not have 100% compatibility and interoperability with Windows ecosystem without presenting (signifying) an argumentation of global IFG report.

Globally, the latest argument of platform independency has been 'Secure-Boot' (also called 'Restricted-Boot') which thought as either provides a *complete* solution of compatibility and interoperability issues or *ensures* that there will be no FLOSS, or at least no Linux, in our own products. "'Secure boot' is a technology described by recent revisions of the [Unified Extensible Firmware Interface] UEFI specification; it offers the prospect of a hardware-verified, malware-free OS bootstrap process that can improve the security of many system deployments. Linux and other open OS will be able to take advantage of secure boot if it is implemented properly in the hardware" (Bottomley & Corbet, 2011). Nevertheless, since 2010, the secure golden key system, such as secure-boot, has not been satisfactorily worked out and leads to new concerns for PCSS ecosystems, such as surveillance (e.g. Hruska, 2016). Besides, there are currently many technological alternatives to overcome these kinds of issues in particular for Linux ecosystems, such as Libreboot, MCUBoot, etc.

Network Effects

In the literature of economic and business, a network effect (also titled network externality) is the effect that one end-user of a good has on the value of that good to other people. More and more end-users who own good, more and more valuable the good is to each owner. As, Robert Kiyosaki states that "the richest people in the world look for and build networks; everyone else looks for work." In this sense, the applications of the Ministry of Justice (MoJ) have been developed through OS agnosticism. Therefore, in the '15th MoJ Coordination and Executive Board Meeting' held in June 2007, it was decided to use Pardus-Linux. It was argued that migrating Pardus-Linux was challenging because installing Pardus-Linux is not sufficient; there are other concerns; authorisations, authentications, etc. (TBMM, 2008, No.7/00731). Without technical supports and consulting services, migration is too difficult for one particular Ministry, even if all software applications are developed as OS agnosticism. Hence, all Ministries protested that in the market, there are insufficient numbers of qualified people and companies specialized in Linux, particularly Pardus-Linux. Although, on the face of OSs, it is free (as freedom) and open to use, taking technical supports and services from these companies are much more 'expensive' than imported OSs. For instance, the Ministry of Environment and Forestry (MoEF) earlier claimed that 800,000 companies across the world and 7,000 companies in Turkey provide Windows products and supports (TBMM,

2008, No.7/1727). It was concluded that this kind of platform in Linux ecosystems is not available and cannot be successfully managed by volunteers. For taking and providing FLOSS supports/services, it is essential to make exact actions by public authorities to ample effective migrations.

In the matter of the belief of suddenly being aphasia (ignorant of ICT), FLOSS literature argues that lack of technical supports and services in Linux ecosystems is a misunderstanding due to an intentional and/or unintentional fear. Nowadays, in FLOSS there are extensive communities who provide instant supports and services. There are thousands of forums, blogs, etc. available online to get appropriate information and formal private support corporations that all depend on a particular strategy (see, the open source observatory community and the open source software strategy 2014-2017 at the EC by the European Commission (2017) or Swedish policy makers want end to IT vendor lock-in (Hillenius, 2017). There might be a lack of on-going technical knowledge in Turkish if technological acceleration is considered, but knowing how to speak English is one of the criteria of ICT specialists in Ministries. So, the question has become how software culture is shaped in the Ministries; what is the Government's responsibility regarding to establishing Linux ecosystems and how should the Government play its role, etc.

The majority of end-users and technical support specialists are familiar with Windows platforms; that is one of the most important obstacles to migrating Linux. Therefore, the use of Linux and FLOSS may cause 'workforce loss!' in Ministries. Besides, for end-users, all service providers offer applications with Windows platforms. So, the Ministry of European Union (MoEU) believed that end-users have access to Windows without requiring any expertise, additional time and effort and end-users can use them with minimal effort (TBMM, 2012, No.7/5212). Nevertheless, what does this information tell us? Most Ministries stated that taking technical specialist preferences, skills and knowledge into consideration, migration to Linux was challenging. The reason for this is because of the criteria for contracting ICT specialist in Ministries; e.g., being a system expert in the Ministry of Science, Industry and Technology (MoSIT), specialists must be Microsoft Certified Technology Specialist, Microsoft Certified Database Administrator, and Microsoft Certified Systems Engineer or have Microsoft Certified IT Professional, etc. Additionally specialists must also have Linux, Unix/BSD and Windows platforms experiences. There is only statement of Linux experience! What does experience mean in there, no specification at all (2017) these requirements are so similar and to be become a sort of informal standard for appointing a public worker in Turkey. Most government apparatus have been using the similar requirements, as they use a 'Copy Policy Strategy', as argued in the following section of software culture.

Nevertheless, if end-users' habits and technical support teams' knowledge and skill are one of the most important obstacles, simply it can be argued how Ministries have decided to use LibreOffice in the Fatih project which is the latest educational technology project in Turkey, and how end-users, who already got familiar with Windows platforms through the history by mainly Ministries training services, will gradually get used to using LibreOffice in schools, even without LibreOffice in-service training and LibreOffice's curriculum in the Ministry of National Education (NoNE, 2014-2017[2]). Thus, Ministries underlined crucial points; knowledge and skill (and so habits); however, the points are unacceptable pretexts, because these are invented by Ministries themselves, so they manipulated the reasoning. Ministries have attempted to minimise their responsibilities to shape *Windows Societies* but the concern should be shaping *Digital Societies* in the *Knowledge-Based Economy* (OECD, 1996). Ministries do not fear of suddenly being ignorant of technology. Sometimes, it is necessary to put law when required, regardless of considering condition of society (e.g. readiness level). Make a law, the law enters into force, and society obeys. Indeed, "writing laws is easy, but governing is difficult." Leo Tolstoy (1828-1910)

The MoEU further instructed that if unwillingness is considered due to average-age and digital-literacy, end-users, who use Windows at home, should be persuaded to use Pardus-Linux at work, by receiving in-service voluntary-based trainings. This however is not the case. When E-Transformation Turkey Project (E-TTP) was launched in 2003, the Government did not ask citizens of Turkey to volunteer. In the project, nearly all public sectors' services have become digitalised and none of them is to be voluntary. Is Information Systems of MoNE (MEBBIS) voluntary for teachers? No! Is using F keyboard voluntary in MoNE? (MoNE, 2001, 2005, 2013) No! So, the discourse of Ministries is that when the concept is nurtured by Government's concerns, it is imperative; on the other hand, others are optional or simply voluntary. Nevertheless, imperative ICT legislations and regulations in Ministries are also problematic because they are not followed by Ministries, such as IFG Reports, F keyboard regulation, etc. Thus, some formal rules have become ineffective and inefficient because of neglecting the role of informal rules due to the fact that pragmatic techno-sociological perspective (e.g. de-facto software governance) has been taken by the relative authorities, as thinking today legal technological practice but not governing its future design! But "He who controls the past controls the future. He who controls the present controls the past" George Orwell (1903-1950). Theoretically, North argued that "we need to know much more about" (informal rules) and "how they interact with formal rules" (1990, p.140) to comprehend the mobility from governing political activities to actual performing activities, "the consequence of small events and chance circumstances can determine solutions that, once they prevail, lead one to a particular path" (ibid, p.4).

Many Ministries believed that if Linux becomes a common OS and developed applications become compatible with Linux, there is no obstacle to migrate to Linux. The absurd discourse of Ministries emphasized one reality in the Linux ecosystem, but they have deliberately ignored the main responsibility of the Governments, and their contributions for this outcome such as tender specifications, planning ICT projects, etc. In this sense, the MoEU has become a Microsoft spokesperson because it simply expects Linux to be Windows and to make FLOSS and Linux a scapegoat.

Sublation of FLOSS

The term of sublation has been clarified as abolish, cancel, preserve, and transcend. In the literature of philosophy, 'aufheben' was used by Hegel to illuminate what occurs when a thesis and antithesis relate, and in this sense is interpreted primarily as "sublate". As in the concept of FLOSS, Turkey has been constantly confusing what FLOSS is and what FLOSS is not. The Ministry of Development (MoD) stated that the aim of Pardus project should be transformed from the project supported by TUBITAK to competitive and sustainable OSs. To expand the use and development of FLOSS, the aim is to establish a Pardus-Linux ecosystem that would increasingly meet the demands of public and private sectors. Therefore, Pardus-Linux should be supported until developing a certain level of maturity. After this level, various services such as maintenance, sustainable technical support etc., should be given to commercial firms within the frame of a business plan for establishing Pardus Solution Partners (PSP) (TBMM, 2012, 7/5284 and 7/5283), since the concept of matters are the same[3]. Nevertheless, this business plan contradicts with Linux's philosophy because FLOSS is not a pure business, is also fun and science driven mainly by voluntaries. Ministries understood that today, making Pardus-Linux and office application obligatory for all public institutions and organizations is not 'practicable' because it is needed to be sure that TUBITAK, universities and private sectors should provide education and support activities, otherwise creating an ecosystem is not 'plausible'. However, there is no particular Ministry which is responsible for preparing these related projects.

Currently in Turkey, there is lack of available technical and vocational qualifications and ICT occupational standards. The Professional Competency Board in the Ministry of Labour and the Social Security Department has just developed these standards since 2013[4]. So, why would TUBITAK and Ministries (2008-2012-2017) claim there would be technical standards for PSP?[5] Throughout history, ICT markets and its international standards (Career-Space, SIFA, NWCET, European SOCs, etc.) have controlled ICT occupational standards in Turkey and many other nations. So, the MoD is either mistaken or intentionally misguiding the general public. The related literature is argued under the title of *Glocalization* which is a portmanteau of *Globalisation* and *Localisation*[6]. There are so many national and international bodies that offer standards through Windows ecosystem based on local language, norms etc. The European Centre for the Development of Vocational Training earlier stated that

The ICT sector provides a particular example of task and technology-related certificates and licences. They are in most cases awarded by multinational companies (Apple, Cisco, Microsoft, Oracle, Sun) and exemplify the role of private companies in certifying skills and competences. We also find ICT certification developed outside multinational companies. The European computer driving licence (ECDL) is currently the best known and widely used of these. (2012, p.16)

The aims of the Pardus-Linux project were declared by the MoD in 2012. Yet, these aims are not new. They have been declared repeatedly by TUBITAK since 2005. So, it can be asked whether or not TUBITAK appropriately supported the Pardus project since TUBITAK stated that political decision making is not included in the duties and authorities of TUBITAK (TBMM, 2008, No.7/00731 and No.7/1368). In TUBITAK, while Pardus-Linux was used in all PCs, but not in the intranet system. TUBITAK declared that there are some applications developed for various purposes, and Pardus-Linux migration plans had been prepared and conversion studies had been continuing. After completing all these studies, TUBITAK would use Pardus-Linux in all hardware, and then recommend using Pardus-Linux to all public sectors. Interestingly, the development of Pardus-Linux was started in 2003, in 2008-12, 2012-2017, TUBITAK has not defined and clarified its position. According to Akgül who is an academician and president of Internet Technologies Association (INETD),

Everyone looks positively on FLOSS; however the use of FLOSS is negligible.... So nearly all public talk about the intention of Pardus' usage, but none of them use it. Migration to FLOSS relies on being ready for change by a social leader. In Turkey, I cannot say that Turkey has a study of leadership. TUBITAK, which funds the Pardus project, does not use Pardus appropriately. E.g., in one period, the licence cost of office applications was very costly and TUBITAK was not willing to pay it. When they were just migrating to StartOffice/OpenOffice, Microsoft let the software free of charge. Instantly TUBITAK returned to Microsoft Office. (2008, p.36-37)

After ten years past, Akgül restates that

State wants to use Pardus as a national OS, but Information and Communication Technologies Authority (BTK)... does not mention (recommend) Pardus to public at all, why in this world! (2017[7])

Admittedly, TUBITAK should not be locked-in to one particular PCSS application, because its R&D centre is in charge of keeping up to date with technological acceleration. Notably, commercial 'gift giving' (free of charge) at this financial level, would be recognized as illegal in global competition law: that, however still academically and/or non-academically disputable[8].

REASONS OF SOFTWARE GOVERNANCE

Due to these above four matters of FLOSS, it can be claimed that Turkey does not misapply FLOSS; in reality it does not apply FLOSS whatsoever that has governed (resulted in) unfair competition and barriers to entry, but there are further reasons of software governance.

Total Cost of Ownership (TCO)

"The only thing more expensive than commercial software is free software" Microsoft[9]

The State Planning Organization (SPO) in the Prime-Ministry which is one of the highest level public institutions declared that there is no delimitative agreement and/or protocol between Microsoft and Governments in the matter of software (TBMM, 2008, No.7/1779). While SPO's point might be accurate and acceptable, each Ministry however has its own method of handling ICT projects that is also problematic because Ministries would not acted in harmony, (e.g. in MoNE, there have been Microsoft Partners in Learning Protocols (MPLPs); 2004/2009). For instance, since 2015, the General Directorate of Lifelong Learning in the MoNE and Microsoft has just launched a Business Association Project (BAP) aimed at developing the technology skills of young people in Turkey in line with the requirements of the 21st century (MoNE, 2015). The perspective of SPO is that individual-national states make strategic collaborations with international corporations for different reasons, including the reduction of license fees. These agreements should only be considered with regard to their duration and scope. Nevertheless and evidently, since MPLPs and BAP are not only covered for purchasing Windows licences, what do the protocols and projects actually mean? No particular information is introduced or elucidated.

In terms of software, Ministries desire either annual agreements or whole sale tenders and these agreements include free updates and important basic training. Most Ministries declared that when training cost is taken into consideration, TCO of purchased software is generally and relatively cheaper than other options. Comparing hardware and OS licence costs for each device, the institutional license is significantly lower. So, Ministries prefer bundle tenders or what is also called turn-key solution. Thus, SPO declared that making regulation for the use of Linux OSs as 'imperative' in all public institutions is not considered in a short period because it is noticed as 'nonenforceable' (TBMM, 2008, No.7/1779). The turn-key solution has still been preferred by Ministries based on irrational pretexts for ensuring interoperability instead of separating budgets according to software and hardware. However that preference has evidently become an inconsistency with the Circular Letters of 1998 & 2008 'Use of Licensed Software' by the Prime Ministry which strictly compel public institutions to separate their software purchasing budges as software and hardware. So, Ministries have accomplished *a legally illegal act* with the Prime Ministry itself; and, their accomplishments have become *legally invalid* or at least *in legal conflict of interest*. Nevertheless, that leads unfair competitions for FLOSS's and even PCSS's sectors as we (who analyses the decision-making process) do not have a particular information about what they (e.g. Ministries) do inconsistently. Ministries purchased software which is mainly provided by hardware vendors. So, individual-national software corporations have been forced to be in line with international software and hardware corporations. Since 1993, the Word Bank advised Governments in Turkey against software 'barriers to entry and competition' and hardware vendors are willing to create their own propriety software systems that result in unfair competition on the market. However even until now, the purchasing process is still in the same inconsistency.

IBM was by far the leading player on the market. Clearly, hardware vendors provide a significant transfer of know-how to the software industry through training, quality standards and procedures, and exposure to best international practice. However, these benefits need to be balanced against the barriers to entry and competition that hardware vendors often create through proprietary software and systems. (World Bank, 1993, p.65)

Disinformation and Misinformation

In the software governance, there are many disinformation and misinformation stated by the Government apparatuses. Disinformation refers to intended information that is wrong, with a deceiving approach behind its wrongness and misinformation is modest information that is unintentionally wrong, or incorrect. Under the reason of TCO, most Ministries stated that if TCO is considered, Linux, which is thought at no cost, is a mistake and inaccurate. In servers, the issue of 'sustainability' and 'supportability' is essential to use OS which already provides 'interoperability' guarantee from server manufacturers to ensure 'smooth' and 'reliable' operation. The MoEU postulated that almost all serious Linux versions supported by server manufacturers are commercial-based, and for versions used in public institutions, there are paid supports and update services on yearly basis (TBMM, 2012, No.7/5212). Preference for Linux, which is less costly, is a decision that must be taken on account of TCO duration in whole projects cycles (infrastructure). The MoEF also claimed that international independent supervision and research institutions such as Gartner, Forrester, Yankee, IDC have revealed that TCO of Linux is much more than TCO of Windows (TBMM, 2008, No:7/1727). The perspective of the Ministries is misleading and misdirect because the literature has shown that comparing Linux to Windows in the sense of TCO is not considered useful and advisable that it all depends on strategic plan(s) (e.g. Russo, 2009, Rentocchini, 2010, Wheeler, 2014). So, no endorsed conclusion can be made based on such assertion due to nature of technology. Thus, Ministries provided their perspectives without providing an appropriate argumentation scheme that would also submit their further un-professionalism and so disinformation. This is the case of, "politically protected monopoly rents are at the heart of profitability in the most advanced sectors of the global neo-liberal economy. Profitability for everyone from Big Pharma and their proprietary drugs to Microsoft and its monopoly on Windows depends on gaining and maintaining monopoly control over intangible assets, which can be achieved only by political means" (Evans, 2008, p.278).

Regarding un-professionalism, the MoD also argued that public institutions have been migrated onto Linux because they are either in the process of renewing their own ICT infrastructures or establishing new additional ICT infrastructure in the direction of expanding their FLOSS's policy (e.g. MoND, the Radio and Television High Council- TBMM, 2012, 7/5284 and 7/5283). From the Ministry's perspective, it is not a logical expectation from institutions which have already established stable and continuing ICT infrastructures, to migrate totally onto different systems due to TCO. This is indeed a wise and admirable perspective; however, it is not an exact case. According to the 23(8) of Directive 2004/18/EC which is consolidated by the European Court of Justice's (ECJ) jurisprudence on the matter, it indicates that "technical specifications shall not refer to a specific make or source, or a particular process, or to trademarks, patents, types or a specific origin or production with the effect of favouring or eliminating certain undertakings or certain products"[10]. Nevertheless, Ministries of Turkey have already ill-guided the relevant arguments.

One-Size-Fits-All-Software

Due to various parliamentary questions, Ministries and Governments presented over three hundreds parliamentary reports and all other hundred formal documents. However, none of them states Free Libre Open Source Software, all of them rather state Open Source Software and/or National Software. In this regard, Free is translated in Turkish as *Özgür-Freedom*, so there is no confusion in Turkish as in English as Stallman (2002) elucidates that 'free as in free speech, not as in free beer'. Therefore, *Freedom* in FLOSS has not been elucidated appropriately in Turkey.

On the subject of PCSS philosophies, the MoEF believed that Linux software applications are still in the development process. Providing such considerable effort and letting this software free of charge as a public good (General Public Licence) is still controversial (TBMM, 2008, No.7/1727); but, the Ministry is misleading and/or being misled because of PCSS (see more the discussion of European Union Public Licence (EUPL)[11]. The literature argues why OS should be signified as a public good because it has a feature of an intellectual good and PCSS model intentionally controlled (e.g. restrained) the potential for innovation and invention. Admittedly there is a crucial distinction between *innovation* and *invention*. This distinction actually generates more arguments than it solves. For instance, what kind of world are we living in if we agree (to some extent) that technologies are some sort of phenomenology, as such a *digital good*, or at least a *knowledge development cycle*? Menell anticipates that "patent protection would lead to an overinvestment in research and development that could result in discoveries that fell within the patent domain, wastefully diverting resources from more appropriate endeavours"(1999, p.132). In the sociology of technology, Proprietary OS actually contradicts itself; because, "it is impossible to keep them secret anyway. The source code--the original lines of text written by the programmers--can be kept secret. But an OS as a whole is a collection of small subroutines that do very specific, very clearly defined jobs. … It is the fate of operating systems to become free" (Stephenson, 2004, p.19-20).

It appears Ministers neither support nor appreciate philosophy of FLOSS. The Ministry of Agriculture and Rural Affairs stated that it is crucial to perceive that not all Linux-based software are 'reliable' and 'costless' (TBMM, 2008, No.7/1727). This is a valid perspective, and acceptable. The Ministry believed that the methods of software licensing are independent of OS and yet various. Here the important point is: it should be known that there is no such 'free' software which presents 24/7 guarantees for uninterrupted service and provides necessary supports. Interestingly, the discourse of the Ministry is so aggressive and protective that it gives a lesson to MPs who asked the parliamentary questions such as MoEU (2012, No.7/5212). The Ministry clearly puts its pragmatic perspective as a Microsoft Spokesman and protests against FLOSS as a kind of (*negative*) social movement, as being voluntary-based and being not viable in ICT sectors. However, contrary to what is believed in Ministries, software and by extension, FLOSS and PCSS platforms are not simply an artefact. Evidently, each of these has its own technological, political, economical, philosophical and even cultural powers to shape societies or shaped by societies (see, the literature of Social-Shaping of Technology Theory), but the question is to where (*Linux-Societies* versus *Windows-Societies*), as Alice asks 'would you tell me, please, which way I ought to go from here?' Cheshire cat answers 'that depends a good deal on where you want to get to,' crucially, the sophistry of PCSS perception ultimately seeks to keep controlling societies without a tipping point! We cannot be free at all unless we can control our destiny and realise our own power or the power of our capacities. If we signify the sociology of technology, we readjust techno-human interactions and then we may remedy the division between one and another which could be end-users' interests or giant corporations' interests, but in FLOSS, everything is all about our common interests without controlling one to another. The key point is thereby the Freedom of End-Users.

Due to technological promises, services of public and private sectors (e.g. communication channels) have been digitized in recent times. Currently, all digital services in any institution entirely rely upon ICT in which there are four concepts: *infrastructure, hardware, software* and *format* that are all compatibly integrated (interpretability) into each other. Since OS is an essential part in these mechanisms, used computing mechanism cannot stand-alone, rather complex system mechanisms. In this sense, most Ministries highlighted that one particular OS (Linux), which stably works, is not, in principle, sufficient for public institutions' needs and requirements. Ministries postulated that they should have used the 'same' and 'common' technologies with the 'same' and 'common' language to ensure 'integrity' and 'cohesion', and to establish 'proper' and 'suitable' ICT mechanisms. The postulations of sameness and commonness have been still argued by Ministries; such as, see discourse of the 25th Meeting of the High Council of Science and Technology by TUBITAK, 2013. If any institution has an intention of migrating to Linux platforms, they have to modify all their ICT mechanisms, including the incumbent ICT-culture. Consequently, all Ministries have denied Linux migration studies and declared their unwillingness to risk the possibility of 'interruption' and 'disputation' of the current ICT mechanisms.

The above discourse is indeed a *one-size-fits-all-software-system* as a *Procrustean bed system* (identical and pure technological-determination). Nonetheless, certainly a one-size-fits-all-software-system cannot be *realistic* and *useful* for ICT, and is not *the solution* in ICT mechanisms because in reality, there can be no one-size-fits-all in ICT. It is obviously *unsteady* and *uncontrollable*; dissimilar software may work better in dissimilar mechanisms, and there are always lock-in issues, see the 'Guide for the Procurement of Standards based ICT Elements of Good Practice by the Commission of the European Union, 2017'. In particular, FLOSS is not a one-size-fits-all system. It would be agreeable for all these needs and requirements, yet the 'sameness' and 'commonness' of technological platforms (insensible singleness, oneness and/or one-sidedness) cannot constantly assure *integrity* and *cohesion* into public and private institutions without precise on-going interoperability reports, like the European Interoperability Framework (EIF) Version 1.0. (2004-2009). Nonetheless, technology improves from variety of areas for various purposes, so there are always accessible technologies to overcome interoperability issues, such as software and hardware virtualizations, rather than simply locked-in.

Hypengyophobic Software Culture

If there is no comprehensible ICT Policy, Software Policy and so FLOSS Policy, there is one crucial thing left– software culture! The MoNE summarised software culture explicitly and similarly for all Ministries,

The basic principle of the Ministry is to integrate hardware and software technologies, which have demonstrated their reliability at national and international level, into educational practices with being an independent on a particular product and service. This basic principle is avoidance of monopolization in public and private sectors with creating competitive market environments. In line with this principle, in the Ministry, either in central institutions or other sub-institutions, the best and most consistent technology is under consideration from national and/or international corporations, which have the most common technical service networks, within the lowest prices, as the widest range of different platforms. So, the Ministry do intentional consistency. Whilst ICT market changes rapidly, the main principle is to present the most excellent ICT culture to students, with maintaining Open Source Software (OSS) solution as equilibrium to likely the extent. Despite the fact that Windows platforms are being used in the Ministry, there are continuing activities to support improving Linux's usage in some other institutions, to support OSS. The main principle of these activities is the achievement of OSS culture for not only students but also staff in the Ministry. (TBMM, 2012, No.7/5313; 2008, No.7/1540 and No.7/1315).

Whether the software is stable, reliable, supported, and updated might be arguable because of the nature of ICT. However, being under the guarantee of compatibility and providing solutions for all compatibility and interoperability, FLOSS cannot answer and meet the software culture in Ministries. For FLOSS and Linux, end-users initially should know that FLOSS is not PCSS, and shall not be. With regard to initiatives of Ministries, a fact, or simply, a matter of fact might be understood as just happening because of our needs and requirements. On the other hand, for others (e.g. FLOSS supporters) it might be a threat (e.g. surveillance) and even the reason of something else, as in this instance negative externality (e.g. locked-in). Agreeably, the purposes of ICT projects should not be in the centre for all Ministries; however, the outcomes of the ways of accomplishing these purposes should be anticipated by a particular Ministry due to unintended consequences. The Ministries have underestimated software culture. There is always lock-in, and national security issues. We should remember that "a computer will do what you tell it to do, but that may be much different from what you had in mind" Joseph Weizenbaum (1923-2008)

The MoNE clearly underlined the best and most reliable products with the best price regarding OSS (not FLOSS) in the balance of creating software culture for all, the same as other Ministries that may be called as 'copy policy strategy'. However, FLOSS is never perceived as a real alternative to PCSS. According to MP Erdal Aksünger, in 2012, the strange bureaucratic chain of command is the first main obstacle for the Pardus-Linux development. In his speech in the parliament, he stated that bureaucrats are interrupting to use Pardus-Linux in institutions because of their own un-acceptance and anxiety. In public procurement authority, bureaucrats perceive PCSS as a *commodity* and FLOSS as a *service* only. Ministries, as other state apparatus (e.g. public bodies and authorities) are bound to pursue certain rules whilst procuring goods, services and works. This procurement process should also apply to the procurement of software. For instance, the Article 5 of Public Procurement Law in Turkey compels that "in tenders to be conducted in accordance with this Law, the contracting authorities are liable for ensuring transparency, competition, equal treatment, reliability, confidentiality, public supervision, and fulfilment of needs appropriately, promptly, and efficient use of resources" (issued in January 2012, p.16). These are governing principles of public procurement and the main pillars of the decision-making process. Considering the fact that failing to respect these principles of procurement could result in administrative/ criminal liability. Also, institutions may delay their preference for ICT mechanisms which if they are unfamiliar and require a substantial upgrading before implementation can be justified from the public policy or legal perspective. "'If your attitude to IT is 'Who do I sue when things go wrong?' the document concludes, then perhaps" [FLOSS] "is not for you." (International Development Association, 2003) This is unfortunately replicable from other developed nations, such as in the UK,

We have standardised on Company X's Products; we therefore purchase from Company X; and we have a long term licensing agreement with Company X – and will adapt our own business logic and standards

to fit their application. Within such arrangements, government is purchasing (technology) inputs rather than (service) outputs, and it becomes locked in to proprietary standards and processes controlled by the supplier, with whom it occupies a correspondingly weak commercial position. [12]

In Turkey, there have been studies carried out by private and public sectors, to develop Linux-based OSs, e.g. the Pardus-Linux project. While such studies are seen with appreciation by most Ministries, based on Laws of Ministries, it is not considered that constituting ICT and so software policy, in particular FLOSS is within the jurisdiction of Ministries. In this sense, there is no particular Ministry that takes *responsibility* and *obligation* for FLOSS, except TUBITAK which is not a Ministry and has no political power to recommend or criticise Governments and Ministries. Besides, 'bestness', 'mostness', 'cheapestness', as declared by Ministries are sensitive to providing uninterrupted service to 80 million citizens. This perspective might be disputable through comparative studies between FLOSS and PSCC; and Linux and Windows in terms of technological point of view. However, more importantly, it is simply intriguing to fathom how Ministries take a hypengyophobic software culture, and solely relied on Windows platforms to provide their services (e.g. 'the document management system in MoNE has crashed, so there is no paperwork' while 'RedHack hacked the presidency of telecommunication, communication'). There are several websites on Google representing these crashes and hacks. Thus, purchasing variable 'X-NESS' is clearly not eligible and desirable for promising to provide uninterrupted services. Software culture which is based on factors such as lifelong learning, knowing how to know for problem solving and on-going knowledge management, and so forth should be formed by/within Ministries. It must be emphasised that while software culture can be argued with the literature, yet, an analysis of these arguments is beyond the scope of this study. So, software culture should be that "today's technological transformations hinge on each country's ability to unleash the creativity of its people, enabling them to understand and master technology, to INNOVATE and to ADAPT technology to their own needs and opportunities" (United Nations, 2001, p.29), because "the world of the future will be an even more demanding struggle against the limitations of our intelligence, not a comfortable hammock in which we can lie down to be waited upon by our robot slaves." (Wiener, 1950)

GOOD SOFTWARE GOVERNANCE

[1] the power of the state depends upon the scapegoat, whose presence is necessary to disguise and diffuse the conflicts, corruption, and contradictions that underlie all political systems. ... [2] The scapegoat need not be innocent of any wrongdoing. It is only essential that the substitute be seen as a wrongdoer, and that his or her role not be attributed to any established institutional interests. (Shaffer, 2012)

Although, in the 63. State action plan, September 2014, or 2015-2018 Information Society Strategy and Action Plan, March 2015, it was constantly re-announced that FLOSS and Pardus-Linux will be used in public institutions in future (MoD, 2017), as history indicates that there are so many *however* and *nevertheless* (mostly pretexts), as realised from the beginner to end of this paper, as a great precedent for state-scapegoatism. Nearly all Ministries claim the principles of Ministries are 'effective' and 'efficient' in terms of using state's public resources. Ministries have interoperated with national software corporations, except OSs, system security, and some other software applications. The discourse signifies that national techno-social economy is one of the main concerns for Ministries, but for another concerns, there is no choice for them. When Pardus-Linux reaches a sufficient level of development, it can be thought as a *useable OS*, because continuity and maintenance is crucial to provide services without interruptions and distractions.

In specific, the MoD has clarified the satisfactory level as; to use Pardus-Linux in servers; (1) services of database, application server, web and virtualization become entirely stable and easy management tools added into the package repository; (2) migration tools developed for database and application server and educational videos prepared; (3) 24/7 technical support unit established by TUBITAK; and (4) educational programs are prepared and implemented. Nevertheless, there are other Linux distros that can meet these requirements. Besides, Pardus Debian might also now meet these requirements in terms of a technological point of view. To use Pardus-Linux in PCs; (1) Wine software which is a FLOSS compatibility level software application to allow applications considered for Microsoft, is improved for maintaining continuity of current ad-hoc software; (2) technical software, such as process management (activity - business process management platform), remote sensing/geographical information system, data mining, engineering, CAD are added into the package repository; (3) conversion problems in LibreOffice are solved (TBMM, 2012, No.7/5284 and No.7/528). Technologically, there is no issue because it depends on how the migration plan is prepared. However, interestingly, migrating Linux is considered if and only if there are no *interoperability* and *sustainability* issues with Windows platforms. Ministries' approaches to FLOSS, in particular Linux platforms, are a *mirror/clone* of PCSS, in particular Windows platforms. In other words, the Ministries' argument indicates that Ministries should initially establish Windows platforms, to migrate Linux. Regarding these, what does it mean if Pardus-Linux can answer all requirements and needs of institutions? If it is the initial point, Ministries should not use Linux because it will not answer what Ministries are seeking for. Being a part of the FLOSS community means that we exercise responsibility and accountability.

If the aim is full control of cybernetics, has Governments of Turkey issued scapegoatism to cover their failures? We are in the imagination world of knowledge-based economy, which is significantly different from a tradition-based economy. However, the majority of Ministries who frequently responded to parliamentary questions either based on 'article (x) of the questions above is concerned with Ministry/ Institutions, so it is approved to answer the question(s) as follows' and ignoring the other questions and/ or 'article (y) of the questions above is not concerned with the Ministry/Institutions, so it is not approved to answer the question(s)'. So, there is a broad definition of *transparency* among Ministries even though there is no *responsibility* and *accountability* engaged by Ministries. Transparency is important for the Government; however, the decision making process should also be applied and shared. Consequently, for Ministries, FLOSS and Linux can/cannot answer all needs and requirements but the question is that should Ministries consider FLOSS, if so how? To answer this question, there are some examples, such as the Turkey Radio and Television Corporation (TRT), which has used different Linux options for different purposes. For instance, regarding OSs, Debian, Redhat and Fedora OSs based on Linux, AIX OS based on UNIX are used. To shape ICT mechanisms in the direction of unpredictable technological changes, there is only one thing left -*Written Policies*. However, Turkey has failed to govern written ICT Policies and to ascertain pervasive and trustworthy (flexible) ICT ecosystems which identify either a balanced progress between FLOSS and PCSS or a FLOSS favourable system (Tolu, 2013). FLOSS should be interiorised due to the rationalist desideratum of cybernetics, because "when you simply have power – in potentia – nothing happens and you are powerless; when you exert power – in actu – others are performing the action and not you. ... Power is not something you may possess and hoard. Either you have it in practice and you do not have it –others have- or you simply have it in theory and you do not have it" (Latour, 1986, p.264).

According to the FSFeurope, governments should adapt FLOSS due to three fundamental justifications. The first is the *viral effect* which is proclivity to press citizens to use the same software and platform as the government use. The usage of FLOSS within government applications provides avoidance of proprietary monopoly and lock-in issue. The second is the *squandered resource* which is the lack of local government connections, and their low possibility of obtaining mass information. Any large scale issues at local level could be solved in a similar way through FLOSS. The third is the *role model* which is to illustrate the government's position. FLOSS creates social and cultural values to establish and support the brand equity in the software market (2003). When governments take the side of FLOSS, PCSS's corporations are inevitably affected. However, fourth, government is the most significant influencer upon the software market, the biggest software consumer. Fifth, government and universities can cooperatively develop their own software solution in R&D centres. Sixth, in developing countries, especially governments are responsible to obtain new revolutions of information technologies. Seventh, indisputably, decision-makers have responsibility of eliminating lock-in issue, (*PCSS's hegemony*, and particularly *Microsoft's monopoly*) and finding the best way of spending public money, because

the market has no inherent tendency to 'self-regulation'. Markets in fact generate inequality and encourage competition instead of co-operation as the central structuring norm of the community. In this sense, while markets are an important mechanism for the efficient performance and growth of the economic lives of individuals and communities, they must in their own right be regulated and controlled by the state. (Olssen, et al. 2004)

CONCLUSİVE REMARKS

"Policymaking is best seen as an interactive process in which different actors exchange resources in a series of trust-based relationships in order to achieve their goals" (Daugbjerg, 2011, p.4). For cybernetics, the concepts are more than *trust-based* relationships; these are techno-politically supported *PCSS' hegemony*, particularly *Microsoft's monopoly*. Consequently, the current approach to technology (*de-facto governance*) is certainly driven by *state-scapegoatism* that builds-in *obsolescence* (invisible of market forces), so it has become covertly unfeasible now and in the future. Turkey's pragmatic technological vision on cybernetics and its inconsistencies between needs and requirements of cybernetics and its acknowledgment of locked-in confirms us where the misconceptions and discriminations are. Perhaps, it has become seemingly unfeasible in meeting present and future needs. Indeed, someone may still postulate that Turkey never wants to be *a controller of her cybernetics* (adapters) and remain *a pure controlled* (adopter), as many other similar individual-nations. However, cybernetics is not just for Turkey, it is a global archaic provision and the similar for many developed and developing nations. For instance, the failure and/or success of Government Open Source Policies can be globally achieved from the literature (see, Lewis, 2010, Redhat, 2010). In this regards, OpenForum Europe Procurement Monitoring Report states that "engaging in a more comprehensive and global analysis of the EU's procurement market would show that the use of discriminatory technical specifications is a widespread practice within the EU" (2013, p.1).

Ever since each generation in a particular society has its own particular faith, beliefs, and agreements with its own particular notices, it has to look its own unique issues and efforts, and even its own impasses. Nevertheless, what is clear is that a new cybernetics is urgently needed. According to Yücel 'there is no solution other than the enlargement of the FLOSS ecosystem in Turkey, considering that TÜBİTAK or Pardus is alone limited to doing it alone' (2017). Yet, PCSS' interests are globally protected from *No-National-Law Concept* by PCSS's hegemony and governments' patronages within flagrant injustices; e.g., by approving exclusive rights to offer PCSS only, there is no global dirigisme for software that speaks of an illusionist legal egalitarianism to wit '*Let me issue and control a nation's money and I care not who writes the law*' by Mayer Amschel Rothschild. In this sense, '*give someone (giants) control of global technology, and no one cares that it controls all of us*' (modern libertarianism and clandestine control) (e.g. Bogard, 1996).

To elaborate, by going back to the introductory question, *movements of cybernetics* have philosophically become a '*phenomenon*' (a fact and/or an observable circumstance), as the opposite of '*naumenon*' (incapable of being known and/or inobservable circumstance), in which there is no *democratic-decision making process*, there is indeed techno-politically supported *PCSS' hegemony*. This negative externality certainly driven by state-scapegoatism, builds-in obsolescence and so leads and contributes to PCSS hegemonic stability (e.g. its own dominations and controls) in the era of technological singularity. Hegemonic stability is international system, more likely to remain stable when a particular PCSS ecosystem is the dominant world power, or hegemon. According to Tiemann, there is a powerful and rising global FLOSS's economy, but "18% of all IT projects are abandoned before production while 55% of all IT projects are "challenged" (late, broken, or both)"; also, "proprietary software model destroys 85% of the global innovation potential" (2010). Consequently, there is an *adventurous legal liaison* between Governments and PCSS, while many connexionists from PCSS may dispute differently! Ultimately, there is a *negative externality of cybernetics* (tragedy of the commons- unsustainable development without any reasonable elucidation) especially when "a decision can be rational without being right and right without being rational" (Peterson, 2009, p.4), and "one of the penalties for refusing to participate in politics is that you end up being governed by your inferiors" Plato.

REFERENCES

Akgül, M. (2008). Özgür Yazılım Dünyası Ne İster? *Bilisim ve Hukuk Dergisi*. Retrieved 25/06/2017 from http://www.ankarabarosu.org.tr/Siteler/1944-2010/Dergiler/BilisimveHukukDergisi/2008-4.pdf

Aksünger, E. (2012). Türkiye Büyük Millet Meclisi (TBMM) Genel Kurul Tutanağı; 24. Dönem 2. Yasama Yılı 68. Birleşim; 2012, February 21. *TBMM*. Retrieved 25/06/2017 from https://www.tbmm. gov.tr/develop/owa/tutanak_sd.birlesim_baslangic?P4=21133&P5=B&page1=65&page2=65&w eb_user_id=14953822

Bottomley, J., & Corbet, J. (2011). Making UEFI Secure Boot Work With Open Platforms. *The Linux Foundation*. Retrieved 25/06/2017 from https://www.linuxfoundation.org/sites/main/files/lf_uefi_se-cure_boot_open_platforms.pdf

Boyle, J. (2008). *The Public Domain: Enclosing of the Commons of the Mind*. Yale University Press.

Callon, M. (1987). Society in the Making: The Study of Technology as a Tool For Sociological Analysis. In W. Bijker, T. Hughes, & T. Pinch (Eds.), *The Social Construction of Technological Systems*. Cambridge, MA: MIT Press.

Callon, M., & Law, J. (1997). After the Individual in Society: Lessons on Collectivity from Science, Technology and Society. *Canadian Journal of Sociology*, 22(2), 165–182. doi:10.2307/3341747

Daugbjerg, C. (2001). *Governance Theory And The Question of Power: Lesson Drawing from The Governance Network Analysis Schools*. Paper to the 61st Political Studies Association Annual Conference, London, UK.

European Centre for the Development of Vocational Training (Cedefop). (2012). *International Qualifications*. Luxembourg: Publications Office of the European Union.

European Commission. (2004). *Commission concludes on Microsoft investigation, imposes conduct remedies and a fine*. Retrieved 25/06/2017 from http://europa.eu/rapid/press-release_IP-04-382_en.htm

European Commission. (2009). *European Interoperability Framework for pan-European eGovernment services, the European Interoperability Framework (EIF) Version 1.0*. Retrieved 25/06/2017 from http://ec.europa.eu/idabc/en/document/2319/5644.html

European Commission. (2013a). *Against lock-in: building open ICT systems by making better use of standards in public*. Retrieved 25/06/2017 from http://cordis.europa.eu/fp7/ict/ssai/docs/study-action23/d3-guidelines-finaldraft2012-03-22.pdf

European Commission. (2013b). *Open Standard*. Retrieved 25/06/2017 from http://ec.europa.eu/digital-agenda/en/open-standards

European Commission. (2017). *Strategy for internal use of OSS*. Retrieved 25/06/2017 from http://ec.europa.eu/dgs/informatics/oss_tech/index_en.htm

Evans, P. (2008). Is an Alternative Globalization Possible? *Politics & Society*, *36*(2), 271–305. doi:10.1177/0032329208316570

Grand, S. (2003). *Creation: Life and How to Make It*. Harvard University Press.

Hillenius, G. (2017). Swedish policy makers want end to IT vendor lock-in. *Joinup*. Retrieved 25/06/2017 from https://joinup.ec.europa.eu/community/osor/news/swedish-policy-makers-want-end-it-vendor-lock

Hruska, J. (2016). Microsoft leaks Secure Boot credentials, shows why backdoor 'golden keys' can't work. *Extremetech*. Retrieved 25/06/2017 from https://www.extremetech.com/computing/233400-microsoft-leaks-secure-boot-credentials-demonstrates-why-backdoor-golden-keys-cant-work

International Development Association (IDA). (2003). *IDA issues Open Source Migration Guidelines*. Retrieved 25/06/2017 from http://ec.europa.eu/idabc/en/document/1921.html

Law, J. (1999). After ANT: Complexity, Naming and Topology. In J. Hassard & J. Law (Eds.), *Actor-Network Theory and After*. Oxford, UK: Blackwell Publishers. doi:10.1111/j.1467-954X.1999.tb03479.x

Latour, B. (1986). The Powers of Association. In J. Law (Ed.), *Power, Action and Belief: A New Sociology of Knowledge* (pp. 264–280). London: Routledge & Kegan Paul.

Latour, B. (1996). On Actor-Network Theory: A Few Clarifications. *Soziale Welt*, 369–381.

Latour, B. (2005). *Reassembling the Social: An Introduction to Actor -Network Theory*. New York: Oxford University Press.

McDermid, D. (2006). *Pragmatism*. Retrieved 25/06/2017 from http://www.iep.utm.edu/pragmati/

Menell, P. S. (1999). *Intellectual Property: General Theories*. Berkeley Center for Law and Technology University of California at Berkeley.

Ministry of Science, Industry and Technology (MoSIT). (2017). *T.C. Bilim, Sanayi ve Teknoloji Bakanlığı Sözleşmeli Bilişim Personeli Alım İlanı*. Retrieved 25/06/2017 from http://bid.sanayi.gov.tr/Dokuman-GetHandler.ashx?dokumanId=2071cce7-3a6d-48a9-a59d-fad83972c9eb

Minister of Development. (2017). *2015-2018 Bilgi Toplumu Stratejisi ve Eylem Planı*. retrieved 25/06/2017 from http://www.kalkinma.gov.tr/Pages/EylemVeDigerPlanlar.aspx

Ministry of National Education (MoNE). (2001, 2001, 2005, 2013). *Standart Türk Klavyesi*. Retrieved 25/06/2017 from http://www.resmigazete.gov.tr/eskiler/2013/12/20131210-9.htm

Ministry of National Education (MoNE). (2015). *MEB ile Microsoft Türkiye'den iş birliği projesi*. Retrieved 25/06/2017 from http://www.meb.gov.tr/meb-ile-microsoft-turkiyeden-is-birligi-projesi/haber/8695/tr

North, D. C. (1990). *Institutional Change, and Economic Performance*. Cambridge, UK: Cambridge University Press. doi:10.1017/CBO9780511808678

Olssen, M., Codd, J., & O'Neill, A. (2004). *Education Policy: Globalization, Citizenship and Democracy*. Thousand Oaks, CA: Sage.

OpenForum Europe. (2013). *OFE Procurement Monitoring Report 2013 – 1st Snapshot*. Retrieved 25/06/2017 http://www.openforumeurope.org/library/ofe-procurement-monitoring-report-2013-1st-snapshot/

Organisation for Economic Co-operation and Development (OECD). (1996). *The Knowledge Based Economy*. Paris: Author.

Peters, M. A., & Besley, T. (2008). *Building Knowledge Cultures: Education and Development in the Age of Knowledge Capitalism*. Rowman & Littlefield Publishers.

Peterson, P. (2009). *An Introduction to Decision Theory*. Cambridge University Press. doi:10.1017/CBO9780511800917

Punch, K. (2009). *Introduction to Research Methods in Education*. London: Sage.

Minister, P. (2012). *E-Devlet: Kavram ve Genel Sorunlar* [E-State: Concept and General Issues Report]. Retrieved 25/06/2017 from https://www.tbmm.gov.tr/arastirma_komisyonlari/bilisim_internet/docs/sunumlar/Koordinasyon_Calismasi_Sunum-ea_06062012_1045.pdff

Public Procurement Authority of Turkey. (2012). *Public Procurement Law*. Retrieved 25/06/2017 from, http://www2.ihale.gov.tr/english/4734_English.pdf

Shaffer, B. (2012). The Importance of Free Minds. *Lewrockwell*. retrieved 25/06/2017 from http://archive. lewrockwell.com/shaffer/shaffer250.html

Sondakika News. (2013). *E Okul VBS girişi çöktü MEB sitesine girilmiyor*. Retrieved 25/06/2017 from, http://www.ihlassondakika.com/haber/E-Okul-VBS-girisi-coktu-MEB-sitesine-girilmiyor_568692.html#

Stallman, R. (2002). *Free Software, Free Society: Selected Essays of Richard M. Stallman*. Retrieved 25/06/2017 from http://www.gnu.org/philosophy/fsfs/rms-essays.pdf

Stallman, R. (2013). FLOSS and FOSS. *Free Software Foundation*. Retrieved 25/06/2017 from https:// www.gnu.org/philosophy/floss-and-foss.en.html

Stephenson, N. (2004). *In the Beginning was the Command Line*. Retrieved 25/06/2017 from http:// introcs.cs.princeton.edu/java/15inout/command.txt

Scientific and Technological Research Council of Turkey (TUBITAK). (2013). *25th Meeting of the High Council of Science and Technology Report*. Retrieved 25/06/2017 from http://www.tubitak.gov.tr/sites/ default/files/btyk25_yeni_kararlar_toplu.pdf

Rentocchini, F., & Tartari, D. (2010). An Analysis of the Adoption of Open Source Software by Local Public Administrations: Evidence from the Emilia-Romagna Region of Italy. *International Journal of Open Source Software and Processes*, *2*(3), 1–29. doi:10.4018/jossp.2010070101

Russo, B., & Succi, G. (2009). A Cost Model of Open Source Software Adoption. *International Journal of Open Source Software and Processes*, *1*(3), 60–82. doi:10.4018/jossp.2009070105

Tiemann, T. (2010). *Growing an Open Source Economy With Competence at the Centre*. Open Source Initiative Vice President, Open Source Affairs, Red Hat Inc.

Tiqqun. (2010). *The Cybernetic Hypothesis*. The Anarchist Library Anti-Copyright.

Tolu, H. (2013). Expendable 'Written' ICT Policies in a Digital Era, No Broken Promise. *International Free and Open Source Software Law Review*, *5*(2), 79–104. doi:10.5033/ifosslr.v5i2.86

Tolu, H. (2016). Techno-Social Policy of Free Open Source Software in Turkey, A Case Study on Pardus. *Journal of Software*, *11*(3), 287–311. doi:10.17706/jsw.11.3.287-311

United Nations. (2001). *Human Development Report*. Retrieved 25/06/2017 from http://hdr.undp.org/ en/reports/global/hdr2001/chapters/

Weber, S. (2004). *The Success of Open Source*. Cambridge, MA: Harvard University Press.

Wiener, N. (1950). *The Human Use Of Human Beings: Cybernetics And Society*. Houghton Mifflin.

Wheeler, A. D. (2014). *Why Open Source Software / Free Software (OSS/FS)? Look at the Numbers!* Retrieved 25/06/2017 from http://www.dwheeler.com/oss_fs_why.html

World Bank. (1993). *Turkey: Informatics and Economic Modernization, A World Bank Country Study*. The World Bank. Retrieved 25/06/2017 from http://www-wds.worldbank.org/external/default/WD-SContentServer/IW3P/IB/1993/03/01/000009265_3970128104047/Rendered/INDEX/multi0page.txt

Yener, D. (2017). *Handbook of Research on Geographic Information Systems Applications and Advancements*. IGI Global.

Yücel, N. (2017). *Pardus: Dünü Bugünü*. Retrieved 25/06/2017 from http://www.pardus.org.tr/forum/t/pardus-dunu-bugunu/1592

ENDNOTES

[1]   http://www.bilgitoplumu.gov.tr/yayinlar/.

[2]   http://fatihprojesi.meb.gov.tr/.

[3]   http://www.pardus.org.tr/#.

[4]   See, professional competency board, at http://www.myk.gov.tr/index.php/en/ulusal-meslek-standard-ana.

[5]   Notably, since 2015, the Pardus team has just released two books; (a) Pardus OS and (b) Pardus (Linux Professional Institute) Certification.

[6]   See, 2016 European inventory on national qualifications frameworks, retrieved 25/06/2017 from http://www.cedefop.europa.eu/en/news-and-press/news/2016-european-inventory-national-qualifications-frameworks-just-released.

[7]   Akgül, M. (2017) twitted that "Devlet, Pardus'u Milli İşletim sistemi olarak kullanmak istiyor, ama BTK, US yurttaşlara önerilerinde Pardus'dan bahsetmiyor. Niye acaba" retrieved 25/06/2017 from https://twitter.com/akgul/status/864489144407425029.

[8]   To obtain the on-going argumentation, see, Journal of International Free and Open Source Software Law Review, at http://www.ifosslr.org/ifosslr or the Reports of the Global Competition Review, at http://globalcompetitionreview.com/.

[9]   Cited in Friedman, T. (2005) *The World Is Flat: A Brief History of the Twenty-First Century,* Farrar, Straus and Giroux Hardcover. See, p.21.

[10]   Cf. Cases C-359/93 Commission of the European Communities v. Kingdom of the Netherlands (UNIX) [1995] ECR I-157 and C-59/00 Bent Mousten Vestergaard v. Spøttrup Boligselskab [2001] ECR I-9505.

[11]   https://joinup.ec.europa.eu/community/eupl/og_page/eupl.

[12]   Cited in Thompson, M. (2014). Open standards are about the business model, not the technology ComputerWeekly.com, retrieved 25/06/2017 from http://www.computerweekly.com/opinion/Open-standards-are-about-the-business-model-not-the-technology.

Chapter 9
Towards Sustainable Development Through Open Source Software in the Arab World

Manar Abu Talib
University of Sharjah, UAE

ABSTRACT

A literature survey study was conducted to explore the state-of-the-art of open source software and the opportunities and challenges faced by this segment of the software industry in seven Arab countries: Tunisia, Egypt, Jordan, Saudi Arabia, Qatar, Oman, and UAE. A framework and road map for OSS is derived and presented from interviews conducted in the UAE with at least four experts from each of the following categories: governments and ministries, IT companies, universities, and IT enthusiasts. This is the first study of its kind in this part of the world and is expected to make a significant contribution to the direction for open source software in the region and beyond.

INTRODUCTION

According to Fitzgerald (2009), "Open source software (OSS) has elicited a great deal of research interest across a range of disciplines since the term was introduced in 1998. Much of this research, however, has focused inward on the phenomenon itself, studying the motivations of individual developers to contribute to OSS projects, or investigating the characteristics of specific OSS products and projects" (Fitzgerald, 2009). He also reports that the need for rigorous research into this process is important for several reasons: 1) recent estimates suggest widespread adoption of OSS: A survey of public administrations in 13 European countries reported that 78% were using open source. 2) A large-scale survey in the US estimated that 87% of organizations were using open source software (Fitzgerald, 2009).

DOI: 10.4018/978-1-5225-5314-4.ch009

Many Arab countries now possess the most technologically advanced telecommunications infrastructure including access to the multitude of communication technologies available in Western countries. The Global Information Technology Report 2014 a recent survey by the World Economic Forum, reports that in terms of IT spending many Arab countries rank among the highest in the world (The Global Information Technology Report, 2014)

A 2009 survey conducted by International Data Corporation (IDC) found that the Open Source Software (OSS) market experienced a strong boost from the prevailing economic downturn, with worldwide revenues expected to grow at a compound annual growth rate of 22.4%, reaching $8.1 billion by 2013 (Jaspersoft, 2010). The increased quality, reliability, and support services supplied by OSS providers has no doubt contributed to this growth. In a downturn economy, and IT departments under increased scrutiny and pressure to reduce costs many have turned to these providers.

Abu Talib et al. report (2014), as elsewhere in the world, many information systems in the Arab World are proprietary, requiring extensive customization that only a specific vendor can perform due to copyright, licensing, and patent constraints. This demands that organizations allocate a substantial amount of time and money to software debugging, and maintenance. Faced with shrinking financial resources, some academic and research organizations have turned to OSS for fulfilling their information and technological needs. In addition, in order to meet the intrinsically stringent security and privacy requirements, OSS has also proved beneficial for research and development in law enforcement agencies, and in defense, legal and justice departments according to Webopedia (2015).

According to Radtke et al., "there have been attempts to identify factors that influence FLOSS. These have ranged from pure speculation to surveys of developers to case studies using data mined from SourceForge" (Radtke, 2009). Open source developed in the technological community is a response to proprietary software owned by corporations. Our literature survey revealed that, in developing countries, there was no substantial OSS development or deployment strategy in place comparable to that found in developed countries. According to Abu Talib et al. (2014), the developing countries deploy OSS because of the following reasons:

- Valuable way to gain independence from single suppliers.
- Introducing diversity into the software code reduces the possibility of catastrophic failures due to viruses that attack a monoculture of code.
- Edgar Villanueva, a Congressman from Peru sent a letter to Microsoft Peru, he stressed that, in order to ensure the free access for citizens to public information, it is essential that data coding and treatment should not be tied to a particular supplier.
- Essentially, countries must be capable of relying on systems without elements controlled by foreign providers in order to ensure their national security.
- Intellectual property: OSS is "cracked to start with".
- Opens the door for developing country users to customize applications according to the local market specifications.
- Can support developing countries' sustainability.
- An insight into the proprietary software development process and a chance to improve community skills.

On the other hand, to apply the balanced view, there are many advantages on proprietary software (Closed Source Software, CSS) such as

- There are reliable, professional support and training available.
- Packaged, comprehensive, modular formats.
- regularly and easily updated.
- Provides the vendor a guaranteed income.
- Developed according to the customer needs.
- Mature and user-oriented product.

In this paper, we examined OSS usage in the Arab World which is different from other developing countries. According to Naama, K. (2006), there are several leading areas for the application of strategies of information and communications technology development in the region including: initiatives for building technologies, the establishment of R&D institutions, and increasing awareness about ICT among Arab governments. For example, gulf countries have the advantages of small populations and a wealth of resources, which they have used to improve national communication networks and to catch up with the rest of the world. Other Arab countries, such as Egypt, Morocco, Jordan, Lebanon and Syria, have increased their budget allocations for the ICT sector (Naama, 2006). In this research paper, a literature survey study was conducted to explore the state-of-the-art of Open Source Software and the opportunities and challenges faced by this segment of the software industry in seven Arabic countries — Tunisia, Egypt, Jordan, KSA, Qatar, Oman and UAE. A framework and road map for OSS is presented derived from interviews conducted in the UAE with at least four experts from each of the following categories: governments and ministries, IT companies, universities and IT enthusiasts. This is the first study of its kind in this part of the world and is expected to make a significant contribution to the direction for Open Source Software in the region and beyond.

BACKGROUND

Originally developed as a pragmatic alternative to the ideology of Free Software, Open Source Software (OSS) is increasingly viewed as a new approach to developing commercial software applications and doing business on the net. Whereas the role of firms is clear for commercial OS projects, further investigation is needed for projects based in communities (Capra, Francalancia, Merloa & Rossi-Lamastrab, 2011). The success of Linux and Apache has strengthened the view that the open source paradigm is one of the most promising strategies for enhancing the maturity, quality, and efficiency of software development activities (Fuggetta, 2003). According to Elpem et al. (2009),

Yet the reality is that most computer users interact with open source technologies every day as Google, Yahoo and eBay all utilize open source software. Open source is a key component of the most dynamic segment of computing, the Internet. Almost 70% of Web page accesses are provided via the over 40 million Apache™ servers. This is a market share two and half times greater than the nearest commercial technology.

Van Reijswoud et al. report that

Leading organizations in the software and ICT consulting industry have embraced FOSS at a rapid speed. IBM is now the major champion of FOSS, and in 2002 IBM announced the receipt of approxi-

mately US$1 billion in revenue from the sale of Linux-based software, hardware, and services. Other technology leaders, including Hewlett-Packard, Motorola, Dell, Oracle, Intel, and Sun Microsystems, have also made major commitments to FOSS. The major player objecting the FOSS paradigm at the moment is Microsoft Corporation. (Van Reijswoud, 2012)

Defined as software where the source code is available to all users free of charge, OSS is frequently developed in a public, collaborative manner, motivated by an altruistic desire to improve society at large that puts society first and individual commercial interests a distant second. "The promise of open source is better quality, higher reliability, more flexibility, lower cost and an end to predatory vendor lock-in (Open Source Initiative, 2015). An empirical study of the effects of OSS component reuse on software development economics by (Ajila & Wub, 2007) found that "OSS components are of highest quality and that the open source community is not setting a bad example (contrary to some opinion) so far as 'good practices' are concerned." In the Arab World, OSS promises to be a valuable approach to avoid total dependence on a single supplier or on foreign providers, opening the door to customized applications designed to develop information systems that best fit the needs of the organization, while enhancing national security (Abu Talib, AbuOdeh, lmansoori & AlNauimi, 2014). Moreover, OSS can provide significant opportunity for Arab World undergraduate/graduate students, researchers, and developers to improve their programming skills, support innovation and therefore enhance regional sustainability (Abu Talib et al., 2014). As well, improvements in cost-effectiveness and increased access to knowledge that OSS provides are important strategic goals many countries strive for. OSS is well established in sectors as diverse as aviation, health, telecommunications, finance, publishing, education, and government (Ghafele, 2014). With OSS, managers can experiment with the suitability of business solutions without the cost of license fees, a significant concern for commercial software. Many managers have already turned to enterprise OSS applications as viable sourcing alternatives for databases, data warehouses, and enterprise-grade software applications (such as ERP) to reduce costs and increase competitive advantage (Abu Talib et al., 2014). OSS also eliminates the concept of "cracking" software as this term has no meaning in the OSS community (Abu Talib et al., 2014). Amrollahi et al. report that (2014)

Development in ICT is an essential and fundamental aspect of development which has been increasingly emphasized in research and international guidelines for public and private sectors. While the rate of ICT failure in developing countries is estimated to be about 50% and there is a need for huge amount of investment in software infrastructures usually hinder the progress of projects, researchers and practitioners are motivated in finding new ways of ICT development to remove these barriers".

According to Bakar et al. (2014),

In Africa, where the social economic barrier, imbalance of economic policies and lack of financial resources are the major problems due to more opportunities obtained in comparison with the challenges, OSS technology has triggered many of its countries to adopt it in their private and even in public organizations.

OSS is not limited to particular research tools, experimental toolkits, or visualization plug-ins. A wide spectrum of system and application software is envisaged, including programming languages, databases, information rendering and visualization tools, operating systems, applets, business applications, digital forensic tools, simulation tools, and privacy and security toolkits, all designed to run on tiny mobile phones, enterprise-level database servers, and intrusion detection systems (Abu Talib et al., 2014). Many commercial projects are now using open-source applications or components (Ullah, 2015) with more companies releasing their proprietary software as open source, forming a software ecosystem of related development projects complemented with a social ecosystem of community members (Kilamo, Hammouda, Mikkonen, T. & Aaltonen, 2012).

Our literature review indicates a number of quality OSS initiatives already under way in the Arab region. For example, the ITU Arab Regional Office (2015) reports the following OSS initiatives:

- The Free and Open Source Software Center (FOSS) was established with ITU support in Tunisia in 2012.
- A regional network of FOSS Centers has been established which aims to disseminate free open-source software and manage a portal that will provide a link to related resources and relevant news in Arabic.
- A FOSS regional network website designed and launched in April 2015 will be kindly hosted and run by the MCIT of Egypt.
- Current stakeholders include, Egypt, Oman, Tunis, Palestine and Lebanon as well as academia and private sector members from the region.

However, the research literature references little about the state-of-the- art of Open Source Software in the Arab World. We take a close look at OSS usage in the Arab World and Figure 1 shows the methodical planning for the research conducted in this paper following Kitchenham 's procedures for performing systematic reviews (Kitchenham, 2004).

LITERATURE SURVEY

According to Chahal et al. (2016), "There is need to put the whole body of work at one place to make it easy to understand for researchers as well as practitioners in the field. Otherwise the plenitude of studies in the domain may create confusion". In this paper we summarized data collected on OSS state-of-the-art from seven Arabic countries to create a comprehensive reference. According to a survey carried out by the ITU Arab Regional Office (2015), seven countries (Tunisia, Egypt, Jordan, Oman, Qatar, Saudi

Figure 1. Methodical planning

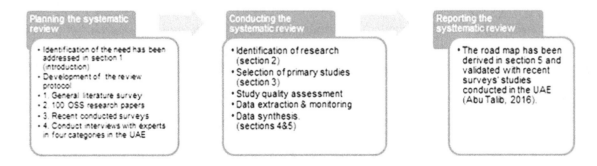

Arabia and the United Arab Emirates) are interested in participating in a network to support OSS, and Saudi Arabia and Oman have already started national programs.

Tunisia

In the field of Information Technology and Communication, the Tunisian strategy dedicated a special interest to Open Source Software as a technical and technological alternative to be considered in new or in redesigning system projects (Lewis, 2010; UNESCO, 2008; opensource.tn, 2015). In July 2001 the Government of Tunisia defined a Free and Open Source Software (FOSS) policy (Lewis, 2010). The objectives encourage migration to FOSS, including FOSS in school curricula, providing incentives to FOSS company start-ups, and ensuring that public procurement policies are not biased against FOSS (Lewis, 2010). According to UNISCO (2008), the Tunisian commitment adopted in 2005, recommends the development of applications based on open and interoperable standards, and the utilization of technologies developed under open-source and free modalities. The Tunisian commitment also encourages and fosters collaborative development, inter-operative platforms and free and open-source software (UNESCO, 2008). The Tunisian agenda for the Information Society, also adopted in 2005, reiterates the support for the development of software that renders itself easily to localization, and enables users to choose appropriate solutions from different software models including open-source, free and proprietary software (UNESCO, 2008).

The Ministŕy of Communication Technologies is also involved in establishing several initiatives, conventions, frameworks, and a number of agreements including (Tunisian Open Source Software Unit. Ministry of Communication Technologies, 2015):

- An agreement with the International Telecommunication Union (ITU) to create the first OSS center in the Arab world, to be based in Tunisia. This was successfully created in 2012.
- An agreement with Marseille-Provence Technopole at Chateau Gombert in France, aimed at benefiting enterprises operating with Open Source Software.
- An agreement with the competitiveness cluster SYSTEM@TIC PARIS-REGION in France to facilitate extension of OSS company activities in both countries.

Figure 2 shows the OSS statistics for Tunisia (Tunisian Open Source Software Unit. Ministry of Communication Technologies, 2015).

1. Proportion of public entities with an OSS infrastructure.
2. Number of public sector technical sector trained in OSS.
3. Proportion of public entities with technical officers trained in OSS.

Egypt

Rizk et al. (2010) published the first academic study on open source software in Egypt in early 2010. A further study by Rizk appeared in 2012. In June 2011, a joint workshop titled 'Toward an Open Source Strategy for Egypt' was held between Arab Digital Expression Foundation (ADEF) and the Access to Knowledge for Development Center (A2K4D) at AUC. At the workshop, the team brought together the open source community to eventually establish "Open Egypt," an NGO dedicated to open source software

Figure 2. The OSS statistics in Tunisia (Lewis, J.A., 2010)

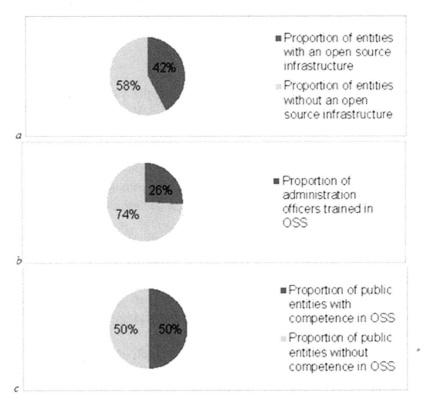

(Government Launches Open Software Strategy Drafted by A2K4D, 2015). The opinions and views expressed in the workshop to establish a national strategy resulted from different rounds of discussions of committee members, as well as from the multiple phases of consultations with a multi-stakeholder committee, the ministry, civil society and the private sector to ensure that the strategy reflects the opinions and interests of all (Government Launches Open Software Strategy Drafted by A2K4D, 2015).

The Ministry of Communication and Information Technology (MCIT) issued a national strategy for the adoption of open source software in March 2014, in parallel with efforts to promote proprietary software innovation models (Open software becomes a national strategy in Egypt, 2015; Blind, Pohlmann, Ramel & Wunsch-Vincent, 2014) MCIT relied on the Software Engineering Competence Center (SECC) as a focal point to coordinate the efforts of all stakeholders to activate the FOSS strategy (Blind et al., 2014). In this strategy, open software is advocated as a vehicle for development with a focus on human capital, since OSS runs on a pool of skilled developers. It is also advocated as a means to decentralize and democratize knowledge, which is otherwise limited to large corporations developing proprietary digital solutions (Open software becomes a national strategy in Egypt, 2015; Blind et al., 2014). Actions made to activate the strategy include representation of FOSS experts on the SECC Board of Trustees, forming a working group of specialists to design and follow-up on applying related initiatives and programs in coordination with the participating bodies (Blind et al., 2014). The Center has already begun to design and implement FOSS training programs in the field of cloud computing and mobile applications in cooperation with the Technology Innovation and Entrepreneurship Center (TIEC) (Blind et al., 2014). The strategy works to achieve eight main objectives deemed "the effective value of this kind of software" (Blind et al., 2014). These are: 1) delivering knowledge to citizens at the lowest cost, 2) improving transparency and effectiveness of the governmental sector, 3) supporting the development of the ICT sector and maximizing competitiveness for the benefit of the user, 4) supporting the rational budgeting and reducing unexplained cost on technology solutions, 5) achieving technological independence, 6) building a sustainable knowledge-society including users and developers, boosting micro and small companies, 7) raising society awareness about available solutions and 8) promoting the culture of FOSS in different sectors of the society.

Jordan

In 2008, Jordan's Ministry of Information and Communications Technology announced that the government is officially neutral toward Open Source. Jordan Open Source Association, a non-profit association, was founded in 2008 to support OSS, open Web, open content, open source hardware and open governance (Jordan Open Source Association, 2015). In 2010, the Ministry of Information and Communications Technology (MOICT) signed an MOU with open source data management company, Ingres, aimed at raising awareness and creating an understanding among government agency leaders about the value of open source software especially as it allows IT systems to be built without expensive up front investments in license fees without compromising the critical needs for privacy, security, and reliability crucial to Jordanian government agencies (ITP.net, 2015; Business Wire, 2015). Initial focus was on universities in Jordan, with the establishment of an open source laboratory in a Jordanian university, and boot camps and free training to certify individuals in open source (ITP.net, 2015; Business Wire, 2015). Arabic language training was provided by Ingres' partner Duroob (ITP.net, 2015) According to Roger Burkhardt, CEO of Ingres "Government agencies are always looking for the best way to quickly deliver quality services for their citizens using advanced technologies, but they also have an obligation to taxpayers to drive down their IT procurement costs. The open source model delivers cost savings through a subscription model that provides excellent support with a cost that is aligned to the value delivered and totally eliminates the expense of proprietary license fees" (ITP.net, 2015).

Another notable OSS initiative in Jordan was organizing the first international conference on Open source software computing in September 2015 (OSSCOM, 2015). Sponsored by IEEE, it was meant to be an international forum for experts, professionals, researchers, and students to promote, share, and discuss Open-Source Software (OSS) services, resources, applications, products, and tools. Researchers and professionals from all over the world were invited to submit proposals for tutorials and workshops as well as papers in areas related to open-source software (OSSCOM, 2015).

Oman

Information Technology Authority (ITA) of Oman held the first symposium on Free and Open Source Software (FOSS) in March 2010 to shed light on the national initiative to promote and support the use of FOSS. This initiative was aligned with Oman's strategic direction to play a neutral role towards promoting different technologies (Information Technology Authority Oman, 2015). As a result, a national program was launched with ITA shouldering the responsibility of the initiative in cooperation with concerned governmental institutions such as Higher Education institutions, the Research Council, private institutions, etc. (Omanuna, 2015). The aim was to "spread awareness about free and open software within community, build qualified employees in this field through training, encourage developing solutions and applications that depend on FOSS, provide technical support needed through finding a way to improve the solutions and applications of FOSS, apply FOSS in governmental entities, support research, development plans and innovative ideas on FOSS, raise awareness about intellectual property rights by encouraging people to use FOSS instead of unauthorized software and encourage developers to improve and use FOSS by launching Oman Summer of Code competition (Omanuna, 2015)". ITA also adopted a national youth program to provide youth an opportunity, over a three-month period, to work on various projects using Free and Open Source software to develop applications functional in different work environments (Omanuna, 2015). The competition is announced in the middle of May each year and is open for 2 weeks (Omanuna, 2015).

In addition, the Free and Open Source Software Conference (FOSSC Oman) on Free and Open Source Software (FOSS), jointly organized by the Communication and Information Research Center (CIRC) at Sultan Qaboos University (SQU) and the Information Technology Authority (ITA) (FOSSC Oman, 2015), is scheduled every two years. The first one was in 2013 and the following one is scheduled for 2015 (FOSSC Oman, 2015).

Qatar

The Ministry of Information and Communications Technology (ictQATAR) was established to be an extension of the Supreme Council of Information and Communication Technology established in 2004. ictQatar is committed to growing an open source developer community in Qatar and supports digital openness in general. In 2011, ictQATAR and Creative Commons Qatar (CC Qatar) hosted an Open Source Developers Workshop with participation by many entrepreneurs, students, educators, public and private sector employees (Ministry of Transport and Communications, 2015).

As part of the workshop, participants worked on three tangible open source projects. The first was to develop an open Arabic font for the web. Working through a project on the Open Font Library, participants developed and uploaded a new font and provided feedback on existing Arabic web fonts. A second project was developing a Wiki for children's stories in Arabic. Using MediaWiki, a free open source software originally used for Wikipedia, participants developed a platform where anyone could contribute their own children's story and share it with others, with users being able to edit or remix existing stories under a Creative Commons license. The third project was the translation of academic paper abstracts into Arabic on Acawiki, an open platform for academic publications (Ministry of Transport and Communications, 2015).

Saudi Arabia and United Arab Emirates

According to Abu Talib (2015), there are significant OSS efforts in the UAE and KSA, but the vision for OSS in the GCC region is not yet clear. According to interviewees as well as survey participants from both countries, OSS is widely used in many organizations and companies. However, there is no official authority or organizing body to unite these efforts—even though, as shown by the OSS opportunities presented in the paper, such efforts could contribute significantly to sustainable development in the region. Nevertheless, according to the survey results, adoption of open source is improving, and the challenges should diminish over time. According to Alarifi (2013) more than two thirds of the Saudi Community are not aware of OSS technologies. Consequently, work to develop the core of the OSS ecosystem in Saudi Arabia is now underway including the following action items (Alarifi, 2013):

- National OSS Strategy
- Government to adopt OSS solutions
- Several pilot projects
- Development of useful OSS software
- Joining the global community to enhance OSS solutions.

Table 1 summarizes the OSS initiatives in the UAE & KSA (Abu Talib, 2015).

Other Arab Countries

It is worth mentioning that there are promising OSS initiatives in other Arab countries. For example, Ma3bar is the Arab Support Center for FOSS located in Lebanon (Walid, 2010). Since its inception by UNDPICTDAR, UNESCO and the University of Balamand, the center strives to disseminate FOSS as a philosophy and culture in academia and Arab societies (Walid, 2010). Meant to increase awareness

Table 1. Summary of OSS survey study in the UAE & KSA (Abu Talib, 2015)

Survey Question	UAE	KSA
How did you learn about OSS? *checkbox* *Total Respondents*	88% online resources /tutorials 60% trial and error 56% online user group 49% reading a manual 41% seminars 36% colleague or friend *170*	61% trial and error 56% online resources /tutorials 35% online user group 33% colleague or friend 29% reading a manual 19% seminars *296*
Are you a member of any online OSS user group? *Total Respondents*	27% yes 73% no *170*	37% yes 63% no *296*
I have knowledge about the country's initiatives in open source programming. *Total Respondents*	8% strongly agree 33% agree 43% neutral 4% disagree 12% strongly disagree 266	17% strongly agree 33% agree 31% neutral 10% disagree 9% strongly disagree 269
Why do you use open source programs? *checkbox* *Total Respondents*	81% less cost 36% easier to use 36% not controlled by licenses 26% vendor independency 18% high quality 17% was advised to use 14% safe 11% less bug fix/ updates 7% my company supports them *170*	49% less cost 40% easier to use 30% not controlled by licenses 28% high quality 26% less bug fix/ updates 25% safe 20% vendor independency 20% was advised to use 10% my company supports them *296*
What are the challenges that you faced when using open source programs? *checkbox* *Total Respondents*	55% little technical support 28% requires training 25% not safe 18% not flexible 14% not available in Arabic 7% low quality 5% hard *170*	35% little technical support 32% low quality 30% requires training 26% not available in Arabic 22% not safe 17% hard 14% not flexible *296*

in public and private institutions in universities, colleges, schools and scientific and research centers (Walid, 2010), Ma3bar also raises awareness among government agencies and the public sector including central and local government departments, municipalities, military forces and police bodies (Walid, 2010). The center also provides training programs, courses and sessions on FOSS. Moreover, the Open Source Lebanese Movement, as part of the Open Source Initiative (OSI) and member of Free software foundation (FSF), is a non-profit online organization with global scope formed to educate about and advocate for the benefit of open source and to build bridges among different constituencies in the open source community (The Open Source Lebanese Movement'2015). The Open Source Lebanese Movement strategy is designed to (The Open Source Lebanese Movement'2015):

- Create a network among different stakeholders.
- Build local, regional and international links to share best practices.
- Work closely with government.
- Organize conferences, workshops and panels to disseminate awareness among new audiences and overcome challenges related to the change.
- Carry out research and studies, in academic institutions, to influence decision making.
- Provide training and technical support.
- Organize campaigns to mobilize public opinion and promote regulations and procedures.
- Invite leaders and policy makers to play a positive role in promoting FOSS.
- Have local, regional and international partners.

In Sudan, the Nile Center Technology Research (NCTR) considers Open Source to be a strategic goal (Nile Center Technology Research', 2015). This strategy considers Open Source to be the first source for ICT application, and aims to promote and settle open source software in the country (Nile Center Technology Research', 2015). The vision of NCTR is to establish an open source community so as to develop local skills and knowledge of open source; to build a nation competitive in software applications development, hence, capable of sharing knowledge with others, and contributing to the global knowledge and literature in IT applications (Nile Center Technology Research', 2015).

In Kuwait, there are different software models that foster access to information. In governmental institutions and private sector companies, the trend is to use copyrighted software that allows greater content management, deals with a larger quantity of information, and can be safely linked to these institutions and other establishments that are transactional in nature. Individual sites, sites belonging to NGOs, or sites dedicated to awareness campaigns or SMEs, rely on open source software, or low cost and average performance software (ESCWA, 2007).

In 2006 Bahrain's Ministry of Social Development (MOSD) became the first ministry in the Kingdom and in the Middle East to base its entire IT infrastructure on open source technology (Lewis, 2010). Reasons for the migration included lower cost, simplified IT management, the ability for modular scalability, and improved security and space efficiency (Lewis, 2010).

RESULTS

As discussed in Section 3, there are significant OSS efforts and a few national programs in the Arab region. Table 2 summarizes OSS initiatives in the Arab world reviewed in our study. It shows slow but

Table 2. Summary of OSS initiatives in the Arab World

Country	OSS Initiatives
Tunis	**2001** the government defined FOSS policy **2005** fostered collaborative development, inter-operative platforms and FOSS **2012** established first FOSS center in the Arab World
Egypt	**2010** first academic study about OSS in Egypt **2011** workshop at AUC titled towards OSS in Egypt **2012** extended OSS study **2014** launched national strategy by MCIT
Jordan	**2008** Ministry is officially neutral toward Open Source **2008** established Jordan Open Source Association **2010** MOU between government and Ingres **2015** 1st conference on Open Source Software Computing
Lebanon	**2010** established Ma3bar, the Arab Support Center for FOSS **2011** The Open Source Lebanese Movement **2016** 2nd conference on Open Source Software Computing
Sudan	**2007** Nile Center Technology Research (NCTR) considers FOSS **2010** launched SUDAFOSS, a volunteering Sudanese society
Oman	**2010** ITA held the first symposium on FOSS **2010** launched national program by government **2010** launched national youth program by government **2013** 1st conference on FOSS **2015** 2nd conference on FOSS **2017** 3rd conference on FOSS
Bahrain	**2006** Open Source Infrastructure for Ministry of Social Development
Qatar	**2011** ictQatar &CC Qatar hosted OSS workshop
Saudi Arabia	**2013** launched national program by KACST
United Arab Emirates	**2016** launched OpenUAE by Telecommunications Regulatory Authority (TRA) and University of Sharjah (UoS)

sure movement to increased OSS initiatives with increasing OSS awareness and activity in more recent years. However, there are still large areas for usage, research and deployment of OSS in the Arab World.

Government and OSS Policies in Arab World

There remain few Arab countries that have a clear vision for OSS research and deployment. Although Tunisia, Egypt, Jordan, Lebanon, Oman and KSA have established an OSS center and promote a few national programs for OSS, the state-of-the-art lacks many resources and clear knowledge of a successful OSS business model. The valuable efforts and research achieved so far are still recent in the Arab region.

Software practitioners and researchers need to study the impact of OSS deployment in several sectors and clarify the set of software metrics for different types of OSS. In this way, Arab countries can efficiently contribute to OSS in the same way as in the developed countries.

OSS in Higher Education in Arab World

There are many studies on deploying OSS in Higher Education in the Arab World (Khelifi, Abu Talib, Farouk & Hamam, 2009; Sahraoui, 2009; Albarrak, Aboalsamh & Abouzahra, 2010; Hammouda, Laine

& Peltonen, 2010; Barry, 2009; Khan, 2013; Al-Badi & Al-Badi, 2014). OSS can make a vital contribution to the improvement of technologies designed to support learning and knowledge development. The Open University project (OUP), presented in (Khelifi et al. 2009), is aimed at providing a complete OSS platform that meets user requirements in the Higher Education sector and promotes the use of such products in the UAE. The OUP can considerably reduce the IT costs of any academic institution, if funds are invested appropriately. Moreover, rapid and sustained economic and social development can be achieved by using affordable and effective open-source solutions to bridge the digital divide between north and south in the Higher Education sector (Khelifi et al., 2009).

Another notable research effort in the Arab region was presented in (Sahraoui, 2009) where the governance conundrum faced by open source adoption in developing countries was illustrated through a detailed case study of an open source project failure at GNU, an American-style university in the Gulf region (Sahraoui, 2009). The rise and fall of the GNU open source project was discussed within a general framework of ICT and open source governance in the higher education sector of developing countries. Lessons were drawn from the case to recommend a FOSS strategy for development (Sahraoui, 2009).

OSS Conferences and Publications in Arab World

As shown in Section 3, there have been number of FOSS conferences and workshops showing there is high awareness of OSS in many Arab countries. Between 2000 and 2015, there were significant number of OSS publications. After surveying 100 OSS publications, we discovered there were many studies on deploying OSS in Higher Education. 25% of publications discussed international OSS experience in conferences hosted by Arab countries (excluding the FOSS conferences). Even so, there remain many research opportunities in this sector of the software industry.

OSS Groups in Arab World

There are large numbers of enthusiastic OSS groups such as the GNU/Linux users Groups in Egypt, Jordan, Palestine, Lebanon, Qatar and Kuwait (QGLUG), the Digital Free Software Association in Tunisia, the Jordan Open Source Association, Open Source communities in UAE, Kuwait, Bahrain, Lebanon and Palestine. However, many of them are not active as communities in the developed countries. Figure 3 shows one of the OSS group meeting. The Arab world is less active compared to other countries.

Figure 3. One of OSS groups' meeting

OSS Framework and Road Map for the Arab World

The OSS framework and road map introduced in this section is derived from interviews conducted in the UAE with at least four experts from each category from the following: governments and ministries, IT companies, universities and IT enthusiasts. The interview lasted for 1-2 hours. Here are some of the interview questions that have been discussed with these experts and their answers have been recorded and notes have been taken by the research assistants: What are the challenges that face the use of Open Source Software (OSS)? What are the advantages of OSS in your opinion? Are you aware of the role of some institutions to encourage the use of OSS? Mention some of these institutes and their roles? Do you expect an increase in the use of OSS in the next five years, and in what percentage? Is there a complete absence of OSS in government institutions? What are the open source applications that you may use for your institute? What are your suggestions to increase the awareness of OSS? In which level is UAE in developing OSS? Do you look for experience in OSS when hiring employees and give them priority? Is the focus in training on the proprietary software or is there attention to OSS as well? Is OSS a "goal" or a "tool" at the current time? Did you hear of or used any network for information exchange for Arab developers? Mention some. What would you like to see from these networks? Is it important to use forums and groups to enrich the OSS society? Why? etc. Table 3 summarizes the experts' answers. Hence, the OSS framework and road map is derived for the Arab world (Figure 4).

Table 3.OSS Framework & Road Map for the Arab World

Category	Action Items
Government & Ministries	- promote national programs that have clear vision, agenda, guidelines and milestones. - promote national youth programs toward OSS that consist of coding camps, competitions, events, school projects, conferences, workshops… etc. To be connected to schools and universities. - form an evaluation committee that evaluates and recommends OSS applications based on specific software metrics. To be connected with research groups and centers. - support forums for IT Companies, Academia and IT enthusiasts to discuss the latest OSS updates and enrich the collaboration among different parties.
IT Companies	- provide in house training sessions in both closed software and open source software. - use channels of suggestions that belongs to the government and other companies to increase the awareness of open source. - showcase real and successful examples and capabilities of OSS. - consider OSS skills while hiring employees. - provide consultation in OSS. - explore how international technology providers that deal with Open Source technology are impacting the region. Are they investing this technology in the country and are they willing to share their infrastructure with the region? - define the relation between the open source service providers and industries. - propose solutions to OSS challenges.
Academia	- enhance the education system through OSS tools and applications. They can be part of many courses such as mobile computing, cloud computing, software engineering, operating systems, ..etc. - establish OSS labs in the universities for innovation, excellency and creativity. - connect with Entrepreneurship centers through OSS usage in establishing small companies. - provide OSS training and organize conferences and workshops that targets all stakeholders. - should be updated to the market needs and trends and support OSS more to produce aware graduates. - provide consultation in OSS. - approach other departments and push faculty members such as Mechanical engineering and business to use open source software that is equivalent to the commercial ones. - provide a portal for universities (What are the software related to faculty members research and post it in the portal)
IT Enthusiasts	- allow the young generation to get involved and develop OSS applications which will increase the use of OSS and enhance the education system in the region. - participate in forums, hackathons, start up, competitions, ..etc. - work for this community as they are working for their real work, they have to be serious, dedicated, smart and creative. They also have to make a balance between working as volunteers and working as professionals.

Figure 4. OSS Roadmap for Arab World

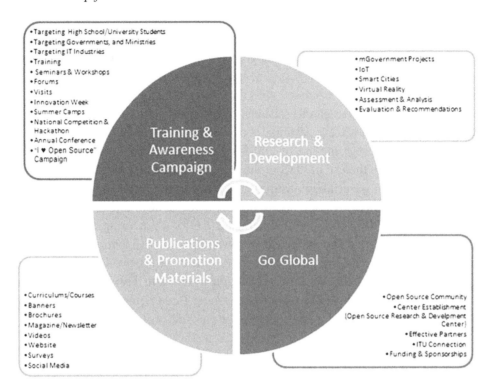

In interviews with participants from ministries and government institutions, most knew of no network or forum for exchanging information about OSS in the UAE. Expectations for such a community included: providing expertise in the use of OSS, managing and effectively controlling OSS in the country, putting high priority on security, targeting university students, presenting successful case studies of OSS applications to demonstrate the advantages of OSS, establishing procedures and rules to protect the rights of OSS users in the UAE and, finally, working for this community as they engage in their day-to-day professional activities.

Interviews with participants from IT companies suggested having an organizing body that would lead the open-source movement in the UAE and could organize educational events and marketing campaigns. This organizing body should target decision makers and vendors to help them understand the effects of OSS technology on companies and the market and to show how international technology providers that deal with Open Source technology are impacting the UAE. One interviewee comment on this issue was revealing: "I don't think the awareness in the coming years will need such huge organizing bodies, because awareness will happen by itself with time, and 30-40% of organizations are using open source products even without knowing it." A valuable research study by Kilamo et al. (2012) studied the problem of building open-source communities for industrial software originally developed as closed-source. In this research study, supporting processes, guidelines and best practices were discussed and illustrated through an industrial case study.

Interviewees from academia offered a number of suggestions such as beginning with the education sector by educating students about OSS, developing a top-down approach, having a platform to refer to, and closing the gap between academia and industry. According to interviewees in this group, OSS use is more prevalent in the Western world than in the Arab world because of the lack of skilled and trained professionals who are fully aware of OSS features and advantages. Software testing and security approval procedures are also needed.

Interviewees from the IT enthusiasts category said they were not aware of any network for OSS information exchange for Arab developers. They also agreed that it is important to use forums and groups to enrich the OSS community. They would like to see efforts in raising awareness, holding seminars and workshops, incorporating OSS applications, providing alternatives to replace CSS, and providing opportunities for the younger generation to become involved. In using OSS, interviewees in the IT enthusiast group stated their role is to explore OSS and use it as a tool to enhance applications. They reported using OSS for university projects or personal use.

In summary, all participants from all categories agreed on the importance of having an OSS community in the country for developers and users. The community role should include improving applications and tools, and being very supportive, active and always available.

When the outcomes of these interviews are compared with other OSS studies in other countries in Arab World (as it is also shown in section 2), the conclusion is the same in terms of OSS opportunities, challenges and recommendations. Figure 4 gives the big picture about open source roadmap for this region in the world.

UAE APPLIED CASE STUDY

OpenUAE is the officially supported Open Source initiative in the UAE. There are already successful case studies of organizations in the UAE that have been able to create successful platforms based on open source software. Open source software has been proven to cut IT expenses in the UAE, while at the same time improving productivity. 81% of organizations, that have used open source software in the UAE, have positive attitudes to it.

OpenUAE is established to achieve the following:

- Build a self-sustainable community, dedicated to creating and promoting open source software in the UAE and spreading open-source knowledge and capabilities in the UAE.
- Engage the open source community through various initiatives and activities (e.g. competitions, trainings, seminars …).
- Encourage open source collaboration by creating a git repository with projects and libraries from across the UAE.
- Lead research and development of open source in the UAE.
- Ensure the global positioning of the community.

OpenUAE has expanded in a relatively short span of time to include ambassadors from 23 universities and more than 30 diverse industries/governments at the bachelor, master and PhD levels. There are currently about 200 members who delivered more than 20 trainings/seminars to more than 400 university students. Around 38 projects (150 university students) participated in OpenUAE Competition from 11 Universities. OpenUAE is providing training with more than 150 videos and onsite workshops. Once OpenUAE research outcomes are shared with the Regional ITU in Arab States through the UAE representative (TRA), it will reach the International ITU (Figure 5). ITU is the United Nations specialized agency for information and communication technologies – ICTs. They allocate global radio spectrum and satellite orbits, develop the technical standards that ensure networks and technologies seamlessly interconnect, and strive to improve access to ICTs to underserved communities worldwide. ITU is committed to connecting all the world's people – wherever they live and whatever their means. Through our work, we protect and support everyone's fundamental right to communicate. Their website is http://www.itu.int/en/about/Pages/default.aspx.

CONCLUSION

There is lack of resources and journals about OSS in the Arab world. The Arab world has a combined population of around 422 million people in 22 countries. Therefore, this paper introduces detailed case study and unites the OSS efforts done in the Arab world and gives clear guidelines, recommendations and road map that can set as a valuable reference for the reader. In this research paper, we explored the state-of-the-art of OSS in the Arab World which ranged from countries that have national programs and government policies to countries with high awareness but without official authority to represent its OSS efforts. This study comprehensively collected an overview of OSS, including opportunities and challenges, in many Arab countries, for decision makers as well as software practitioners and researchers

Figure 5. Global Positioning of OpenUAE

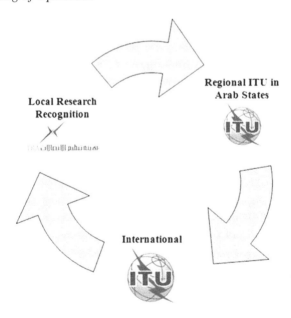

to know the areas of OSS for investigation and improvement. It is hoped that this study can serve as an important reference in the research literature as it paves the way for future work towards OSS deployment and development of OSS quality metrics. The promising results of this study point to three main avenues for future research: 1) Encouraging researchers in other countries to conduct similar studies. 2) Encouraging other researchers in the Gulf and Arab countries to conduct comparison research studies. 3) Collaborating with research teams within and outside the UAE to unite their efforts towards OSS development in the region.

ACKNOWLEDGMENT

The author wishes to thank the Graduate Studies Office at the University of Sharjah and the Center of Digital Innovation (CoDI) at TRA for its generous funding of this research project. We are also grateful to Anfal Hassan, Balsam Alkouz, Randa AbuAli and Arwa Yahya, research assistants from the University of Sharjah, for their valuable contribution in the survey study as well as for their help in conducting the interviews.

REFERENCES

Abu Talib, M. (2015). *Towards Sustainable Development through Open Source Software in GCC*. The 2015 IEEE International Symposium on Signal Processing and Information Technology (ISSPIT), Abu Dhabi, UAE.

Abu Talib, M. (2016). Open Source Software in the UAE: Opportunities. *Challenges and Recommendations*.

Abu Talib, M., AbuOdeh, M., Almansoori, A., & AlNauimi, A. (2014). Enhancing Social Science Research in the UAE: An Open Source Software Solution University of Sharjah (UOS) Case Study. *Journal of Computer Science, 11*, 98-108. DOI: 10.3844/jcssp.2015.98.108

Ajilaa, S. A., & Wub, D. (2007). Empirical study of the effects of open source adoption on software development economics. *Journal of Systems and Software, 80*, 1517-1529. DOI: 10.1016/j.jss.2007.01.011

Alarifi, A. (2013). *National Program for Free and Open Source Technologies Saudi Arabia. King Abdulaziz City for Science and Technology*. KACST.

Albarrak, A. I., Aboalsamh, H. A., & Abouzahra, M. (2010). Evaluating learning management systems for University medical education. *International Conference on Education and Management Technology (ICEMT)*, Cairo, Egypt. doi:10.1109/ICEMT.2010.5657569

Amrollahi, A., Khansari, M., & Manian, A. (2014). Success of Open Source in Developing Countries: The Case of Iran. *International Journal of Open Source Software and Processes, 5*(1), 50–65. doi:10.4018/ijossp.2014010103

Bakar, A. D., Sultan, A. B., Zulzalil, H., & Din, J. (2014). Open Source Software Adaptation in Africa: Is a Matter of Inferior or Cheap is Not Quality? *International Journal of Open Source Software and Processes, 5*(1), 1–15. doi:10.4018/ijossp.2014010101

Barry, B. I. A. (2009). Using Open Source Software in Education in Developing Countries: The Sudan as an Example. *International Conference on Computational Intelligence and Software Engineering*, Wuhan, China. doi:10.1109/CISE.2009.5364872

Blind, K., Pohlmann, T., Ramel, F., & Wunsch-Vincent, S. (2014). *The Egyptian Information Technology Sector and the Role of Intellectual Property: Economic Assessment and Recommendations*. WIPO Economics & Statistics Series.

Capra, E., Francalancia, C., Merloa, F., & Rossi-Lamastrab, C. (2011). Firms' involvement in Open Source projects: A trade-off between software structural quality and popularity. *Journal of Systems and Software, 84*, 144-161. DOI: 10.1016/j.jss.2010.09.004

CC Qatar and ictQATAR Qatar Hold Open Source Workshop. (n.d.). Retrieved from http://www.ictqatar. qa/en/news-events/news/cc-qatar-and-ictqatar-qatar-hold-open-source-workshop

Chahal, K. K., & Saini, M. (2016). Open Source Software Evolution: A Systematic Literature Review (Part 1). *International Journal of Open Source Software and Processes, 7*(1), 1–27. doi:10.4018/ IJOSSP.2016010101

Elpern, J., & Dascalu, S. (2009). A Framework for Understanding the Open Source Revolution. *International Journal of Open Source Software and Processes, 1*(3), 1–16. doi:10.4018/jossp.2009070101

ESCWA. (2007). *Economic and Social Commission for Western Asia: National Profil of the Information Society in Kuwait*. United Nations.

Fitzgerald, B. (2009). Open Source Software Adoption: Anatomy of Success and Failure. *International Journal of Open Source Software and Processes, 1*(1), 1–23. doi:10.4018/jossp.2009010101

Fuggetta, A. (2003). Open source software—An evaluation. *Journal of Systems and Software, 66*, 77-90. DOI: 10.1016/S0164-1212(02)00065-1

Ghafele, R., & Gibert, B. (2014). Open Growth: The Impact of Open Source Software on Employment in the USA. *International Journal of Open Source Software and Processes, 5*(1), 16–49. doi:10.4018/ ijossp.2014010102

Government Launches Open Software Strategy Drafted by A2K4D. (n.d.). Retrieved from http://www. aucegypt.edu/business/newsroom/Pages/story.aspx?eid=107

Government of Jordan Selects Ingres to Drive Open Source Adoption Across the Country. (n.d.). Retrieved from http://www.businesswire.com/news/home/20100112005382/en/Government-Jordan-Selects-Ingres-Drive-Open-Source#.VZ1LGflViko

Hammouda, I., Laine, R., & Peltonen, J. (2010). *Transfer of Educational Methods through Open Sourcing of Learning Management Systems*. 2010 IEEE 10th International Conference Advanced Learning Technologies (ICALT), Sousse, France. doi:10.1109/ICALT.2010.185

International Conference on Open Source Software Computing (OSSCOM 2015). (n.d.). Retrieved from http://osscom2015.osscom.org/

ITA of Oman: The First Symposium on Free Source. (n.d.). Retrieved from http://www.ita.gov.om/ITAPortal/MediaCenter/NewsDetail.aspx?NID=302

ITU Arab Regional Office. (2015). *Establishment of a network to support open-source software*. Retrieved from https://itunews.itu.int/en/2334-Establishment-of-a-network-to-support-open-source-software.note.aspx

Jaspersoft. (2010). T*he State of Enterprise Open Source Software After the Oracle Acquisition of Sun Microsystems*. Jaspersoft Report. Retrieved from http://www.jaspersoft.com/sites/default/files/Jaspersoft_Survey-Oracle_Java_White_Paper.pdf

Jordan Open Source Association. (n.d.). Retrieved from http://www.jordanopensource.org/

KACST. (2013). *Enhancing Innovations through Free/Open Source Software in KSA*. King Abdulaziz City for Science and Technology.

Khan, M. A., & Urrehman, F. (2013). *An Extendable OpenSource Architecture of E-Learning System*. Fourth International Conference on e-Learning "Best Practices in Management, Design and Development of e-Courses: Standards of Excellence and Creativity", Manama. doi:10.1109/ECONF.2013.51

Khelifi, A., Abu Talib, M., Farouk, M., & Hamam, H. (2009, July-September). Developing an Initial Open Source Platform for the Higher Education Sector: A Case Study: ALHOSN University. *IEEE Transactions on Learning Technologies*, 2(3), 239–248. doi:10.1109/TLT.2009.13

Kilamo, T., Hammouda, I., Mikkonen, T., & Aaltonen, T. (2012). From proprietary to open source—Growing an open source ecosystem. *Journal of Systems and Software, 85*, 1467-1478. DOI: 10.1016/j.jss.2011.06.071

Kitchenham, B. (2004). *Procedures for Performing Systematic Reviews*. Joint Technical Report between Keele University and NICTA.

Lewis, J. A. (2010). *Government Open Source Policies*. Retrieved from http://csis.org/publication/government-open-source-policies-0

Naama, K. (2006). *The State of Information Technology in the Arab World*. University of Veliko Turnovo.

Nile Center Technology Research. (n.d.). Retrieved from http://www.nctr.sd/en/index.php/nctr-opensource/foss.html

Oman Government. Free and Open Source Initiative. (n.d.). Retrieved from http://www.oman.om/

Open software becomes a national strategy in Egypt. (n.d.). Retrieved from http://www.madamasr.com/news/open-software-becomes-national-strategy-egypt

Open Source Initiative. (n.d.). Retrieved from http://opensource.org/

Radtke, N. P., Janssen, M. A., & Collofello, J. S. (2009). What Makes Free/Libre Open Source Software (FLOSS) Projects Successful? An Agent-Based Model of FLOSS Projects. *International Journal of Open Source Software and Processes*, 1(2), 1–13. doi:10.4018/jossp.2009040101

Rizk, N. (2012). Free and open source software (FOSS) as a vehicle for human development in Egypt: Some evidence and insights. *Int. J. Technological Learning. Innovation and Development, 5*(3), 221.

Rizk, N., & El-Kassas, S. (2010). The software industry in Egypt: What role for open source? In Access to Knowledge in Egypt, New Research on 64 Intellectual Property, Innovation, and Development. Bloomsbury.

Sahraoui, S. M. (2009). ICT governance in higher education: Case study of the rise and fall of open source in a Gulf university. *International Conference on Information and Communication Technologies and Development (ICTD)*. IEEE. doi:10.1109/ICTD.2009.5426692

The Free and Open Source Software Conference (FOSSC Oman). (n.d.). Retrieved from http://fossc. om/2015/

The Government of Jordan and open source database management company Ingres have signed an MOU to promote open source software adoption in the country. (n.d.). Retrieved from http://www.itp. net/578825-jordan-information-ministry-signs-deal-on-open-source

The Open Source Lebanese Movement. (n.d.). Retrieved from http://oslm.cofares.net/p/open-source-lebanese-movement.html

Tunisian Open Source Software Unit. Ministry of Communication Technologies. (n.d.). Retrieved from http://www.opensource.tn/open-source/accueil/

Ullah, N. (2015). A method for predicting open source software residual defects. *Software Quality Journal, 23*, 55-76. DOI: 10.1007/s11219-014-9229-3

UNESCO. (2008). *Intergovernmental Council for the Information for All Programme (IFAP) Fifth Session*. UNESCO.

Van Reijswoud, V., & Mulo, E. (2012). Evaluating the Potential of Free and Open Source Software in the Developing World. *International Journal of Open Source Software and Processes, 4*(3), 38–51. doi:10.4018/ijossp.2012070104

Walid, K. (2010). Open Source Software in the Arab Region. *The Third International Symposium on Web Services*. Zayed University.

Webopedia. (n.d.). Retrieved from http://www.webopedia.com/TERM/O/open_source.html

World Economic Forum. (2014). *The Global Information Technology Report 2014*. Retrieved from http:// www3.weforum.org/docs/WEF_GlobalInformationTechnology_Report_2014.pdf

Related References

To continue our tradition of advancing information science and technology research, we have compiled a list of recommended IGI Global readings. These references will provide additional information and guidance to further enrich your knowledge and assist you with your own research and future publications.

Aalmink, J., von der Dovenmühle, T., & Gómez, J. M. (2013). Enterprise tomography: Maintenance and root-cause-analysis of federated erp in enterprise clouds. In P. Ordóñez de Pablos, H. Nigro, R. Tennyson, S. Gonzalez Cisaro, & W. Karwowski (Eds.), *Advancing information management through semantic web concepts and ontologies* (pp. 133–153). Hershey, PA: IGI Global. doi:10.4018/978-1-4666-2494-8.ch007

Abu, S. T., & Tsuji, M. (2011). The development of ICT for envisioning cloud computing and innovation in South Asia. *International Journal of Innovation in the Digital Economy*, 2(1), 61–72. doi:10.4018/jide.2011010105

Abu, S. T., & Tsuji, M. (2012). The development of ICT for envisioning cloud computing and innovation in South Asia. In *Grid and cloud computing: Concepts, methodologies, tools and applications* (pp. 453–465). Hershey, PA: IGI Global. doi:10.4018/978-1-4666-0879-5.ch207

Abu, S. T., & Tsuji, M. (2013). The development of ICT for envisioning cloud computing and innovation in South Asia. In I. Oncioiu (Ed.), *Business innovation, development, and advancement in the digital economy* (pp. 35–47). Hershey, PA: IGI Global. doi:10.4018/978-1-4666-2934-9.ch003

Adams, R. (2013). The emergence of cloud storage and the need for a new digital forensic process model. In K. Ruan (Ed.), *Cybercrime and cloud forensics: Applications for investigation processes* (pp. 79–104). Hershey, PA: IGI Global. doi:10.4018/978-1-4666-2662-1.ch004

Adeyeye, M. (2013). Provisioning converged applications and services via the cloud. In D. Kanellopoulos (Ed.), *Intelligent multimedia technologies for networking applications: Techniques and tools* (pp. 248–269). Hershey, PA: IGI Global. doi:10.4018/978-1-4666-2833-5.ch010

Aggarwal, A. (2013). A systems approach to cloud computing services. In A. Bento & A. Aggarwal (Eds.), *Cloud computing service and deployment models: Layers and management* (pp. 124–136). Hershey, PA: IGI Global. doi:10.4018/978-1-4666-2187-9.ch006

Ahmed, K., Hussain, A., & Gregory, M. A. (2013). An efficient, robust, and secure SSO architecture for cloud computing implemented in a service oriented architecture. In X. Yang & L. Liu (Eds.), *Principles, methodologies, and service-oriented approaches for cloud computing* (pp. 259–282). Hershey, PA: IGI Global. doi:10.4018/978-1-4666-2854-0.ch011

Ahuja, S. P., & Mani, S. (2013). Empirical performance analysis of HPC benchmarks across variations in cloud computing. *International Journal of Cloud Applications and Computing*, 3(1), 13–26. doi:10.4018/ijcac.2013010102

Ahuja, S. P., & Rolli, A. C. (2011). Survey of the state-of-the-art of cloud computing. *International Journal of Cloud Applications and Computing*, 1(4), 34–43. doi:10.4018/ijcac.2011100103

Ahuja, S. P., & Rolli, A. C. (2013). Survey of the state-of-the-art of cloud computing. In S. Aljawarneh (Ed.), *Cloud computing advancements in design, implementation, and technologies* (pp. 252–262). Hershey, PA: IGI Global. doi:10.4018/978-1-4666-1879-4.ch018

Ahuja, S. P., & Sridharan, S. (2012). Performance evaluation of hypervisors for cloud computing. *International Journal of Cloud Applications and Computing*, 2(3), 26–67. doi:10.4018/ijcac.2012070102

Akyuz, G. A., & Rehan, M. (2013). A generic, cloud-based representation for supply chains (SC's). *International Journal of Cloud Applications and Computing*, 3(2), 12–20. doi:10.4018/ijcac.2013040102

Al-Aqrabi, H., & Liu, L. (2013). IT security and governance compliant service oriented computing in cloud computing environments. In X. Yang & L. Liu (Eds.), *Principles, methodologies, and service-oriented approaches for cloud computing* (pp. 143–163). Hershey, PA: IGI Global. doi:10.4018/978-1-4666-2854-0.ch006

Al-Zoube, M., & Wyne, M. F. (2012). Building integrated e-learning environment using cloud services and social networking sites. In Q. Jin (Ed.), *Intelligent learning systems and advancements in computer-aided instruction: Emerging studies* (pp. 214–233). Hershey, PA: IGI Global. doi:10.4018/978-1-61350-483-3.ch013

Alam, N., & Karmakar, R. (2014). Cloud computing and its application to information centre. In S. Dhamdhere (Ed.), *Cloud computing and virtualization technologies in libraries* (pp. 63–76). Hershey, PA: IGI Global. doi:10.4018/978-1-4666-4631-5.ch004

Alhaj, A., Aljawarneh, S., Masadeh, S., & Abu-Taieh, E. (2013). A secure data transmission mechanism for cloud outsourced data. *International Journal of Cloud Applications and Computing*, 3(1), 34–43. doi:10.4018/ijcac.2013010104

Alharbi, S. T. (2012). Users' acceptance of cloud computing in Saudi Arabia: An extension of technology acceptance model. *International Journal of Cloud Applications and Computing*, 2(2), 1–11. doi:10.4018/ijcac.2012040101

Ali, S. S., & Khan, M. N. (2013). ICT infrastructure framework for microfinance institutions and banks in Pakistan: An optimized approach. *International Journal of Online Marketing*, 3(2), 75–86. doi:10.4018/ijom.2013040105

Aljawarneh, S. (2011). Cloud security engineering: Avoiding security threats the right way. *International Journal of Cloud Applications and Computing*, *1*(2), 64–70. doi:10.4018/ijcac.2011040105

Aljawarneh, S. (2013). Cloud security engineering: Avoiding security threats the right way. In S. Aljawarneh (Ed.), *Cloud computing advancements in design, implementation, and technologies* (pp. 147–153). Hershey, PA: IGI Global. doi:10.4018/978-1-4666-1879-4.ch010

Alshattnawi, S. (2013). Utilizing cloud computing in developing a mobile location-aware tourist guide system. *International Journal of Advanced Pervasive and Ubiquitous Computing*, *5*(2), 9–18. doi:10.4018/japuc.2013040102

Alsmadi, I. (2013). Software development methodologies for cloud computing. In K. Buragga & N. Zaman (Eds.), *Software development techniques for constructive information systems design* (pp. 110–117). Hershey, PA: IGI Global. doi:10.4018/978-1-4666-3679-8.ch006

Anand, V. (2013). Survivable mapping of virtual networks onto a shared substrate network. In X. Yang & L. Liu (Eds.), *Principles, methodologies, and service-oriented approaches for cloud computing* (pp. 325–343). Hershey, PA: IGI Global. doi:10.4018/978-1-4666-2854-0.ch014

Antonova, A. (2013). Green, sustainable, or clean: What type of IT/IS technologies will we need in the future? In P. Ordóñez de Pablos (Ed.), *Green technologies and business practices: An IT approach* (pp. 151–162). Hershey, PA: IGI Global. doi:10.4018/978-1-4666-1972-2.ch008

Ardissono, L., Bosio, G., Goy, A., Petrone, G., Segnan, M., & Torretta, F. (2011). Collaboration support for activity management in a personal cloud environment. *International Journal of Distributed Systems and Technologies*, *2*(4), 30–43. doi:10.4018/jdst.2011100103

Ardissono, L., Bosio, G., Goy, A., Petrone, G., Segnan, M., & Torretta, F. (2013). Collaboration support for activity management in a personal cloud environment. In N. Bessis (Ed.), *Development of distributed systems from design to application and maintenance* (pp. 199–212). Hershey, PA: IGI Global. doi:10.4018/978-1-4666-2647-8.ch012

Argiolas, M., Atzori, M., Dessì, N., & Pes, B. (2012). Dataspaces enhancing decision support systems in clouds. *International Journal of Web Portals*, *4*(2), 35–55. doi:10.4018/jwp.2012040103

Arinze, B., & Anandarajan, M. (2012). Factors that determine the adoption of cloud computing: A global perspective. In M. Tavana (Ed.), *Enterprise Information Systems and Advancing Business Solutions: Emerging Models* (pp. 210–223). Hershey, PA: IGI Global. doi:10.4018/978-1-4666-1761-2.ch012

Arinze, B., & Sylla, C. (2012). Conducting research in the cloud. In L. Chao (Ed.), *Cloud computing for teaching and learning: Strategies for design and implementation* (pp. 50–63). Hershey, PA: IGI Global. doi:10.4018/978-1-4666-0957-0.ch004

Arshad, J., Townend, P., & Xu, J. (2011). An abstract model for integrated intrusion detection and severity analysis for clouds. *International Journal of Cloud Applications and Computing*, *1*(1), 1–16. doi:10.4018/ijcac.2011010101

Arshad, J., Townend, P., & Xu, J. (2013). An abstract model for integrated intrusion detection and severity analysis for clouds. In S. Aljawarneh (Ed.), *Cloud computing advancements in design, implementation, and technologies* (pp. 1–17). Hershey, PA: IGI Global. doi:10.4018/978-1-4666-1879-4.ch001

Arshad, J., Townend, P., Xu, J., & Jie, W. (2012). Cloud computing security: Opportunities and pitfalls. *International Journal of Grid and High Performance Computing*, *4*(1), 52–66. doi:10.4018/jghpc.2012010104

Baars, T., & Spruit, M. (2012). Designing a secure cloud architecture: The SeCA model. *International Journal of Information Security and Privacy*, *6*(1), 14–32. doi:10.4018/jisp.2012010102

Bai, X., Gao, J. Z., & Tsai, W. (2013). Cloud scalability measurement and testing. In S. Tilley & T. Parveen (Eds.), *Software testing in the cloud: Perspectives on an emerging discipline* (pp. 356–381). Hershey, PA: IGI Global. doi:10.4018/978-1-4666-2536-5.ch017

Baldini, G., & Stirparo, P. (2014). A cognitive access framework for security and privacy protection in mobile cloud computing. In J. Rodrigues, K. Lin, & J. Lloret (Eds.), *Mobile networks and cloud computing convergence for progressive services and applications* (pp. 92–117). Hershey, PA: IGI Global. doi:10.4018/978-1-4666-4781-7.ch006

Balduf, S., Balke, T., & Eymann, T. (2012). Cultural differences in managing cloud computing service level agreements. In *Grid and cloud computing: Concepts, methodologies, tools and applications* (pp. 1237–1263). Hershey, PA: IGI Global. doi:10.4018/978-1-4666-0879-5.ch512

Banerjee, S., Sing, T. Y., Chowdhury, A. R., & Anwar, H. (2013). Motivations to adopt green ICT: A tale of two organizations. *International Journal of Green Computing*, *4*(2), 1–11. doi:10.4018/jgc.2013070101

Barreto, J., Di Sanzo, P., Palmieri, R., & Romano, P. (2013). Cloud-TM: An elastic, self-tuning transactional store for the cloud. In D. Kyriazis, A. Voulodimos, S. Gogouvitis, & T. Varvarigou (Eds.), *Data intensive storage services for cloud environments* (pp. 192–224). Hershey, PA: IGI Global. doi:10.4018/978-1-4666-3934-8.ch013

Belalem, G., & Limam, S. (2011). Fault tolerant architecture to cloud computing using adaptive checkpoint. *International Journal of Cloud Applications and Computing*, *1*(4), 60–69. doi:10.4018/ijcac.2011100105

Belalem, G., & Limam, S. (2013). Fault tolerant architecture to cloud computing using adaptive checkpoint. In S. Aljawarneh (Ed.), *Cloud computing advancements in design, implementation, and technologies* (pp. 280–289). Hershey, PA: IGI Global. doi:10.4018/978-1-4666-1879-4.ch020

Ben Belgacem, M., Abdennadher, N., & Niinimaki, M. (2012). Virtual EZ grid: A volunteer computing infrastructure for scientific medical applications. *International Journal of Handheld Computing Research*, *3*(1), 74–85. doi:10.4018/jhcr.2012010105

Bhatt, S., Chaudhary, S., & Bhise, M. (2013). Migration of data between cloud and non-cloud datastores. In A. Ionita, M. Litoiu, & G. Lewis (Eds.), *Migrating legacy applications: Challenges in service oriented architecture and cloud computing environments* (pp. 206–225). Hershey, PA: IGI Global. doi:10.4018/978-1-4666-2488-7.ch009

Biancofiore, G., & Leone, S. (2014). Google apps as a cloud computing solution in Italian municipalities: Technological features and implications. In S. Leone (Ed.), *Synergic integration of formal and informal e-learning environments for adult lifelong learners* (pp. 244–274). Hershey, PA: IGI Global. doi:10.4018/978-1-4666-4655-1.ch012

Bibi, S., Katsaros, D., & Bozanis, P. (2012). How to choose the right cloud. In *Grid and cloud computing: Concepts, methodologies, tools and applications* (pp. 1530–1552). Hershey, PA: IGI Global. doi:10.4018/978-1-4666-0879-5.ch701

Bibi, S., Katsaros, D., & Bozanis, P. (2012). How to choose the right cloud. In X. Liu & Y. Li (Eds.), *Advanced design approaches to emerging software systems: Principles, methodologies and tools* (pp. 219–240). Hershey, PA: IGI Global. doi:10.4018/978-1-60960-735-7.ch010

Bitam, S., Batouche, M., & Talbi, E. (2012). A bees life algorithm for cloud computing services selection. In S. Ali, N. Abbadeni, & M. Batouche (Eds.), *Multidisciplinary computational intelligence techniques: Applications in business, engineering, and medicine* (pp. 31–46). Hershey, PA: IGI Global. doi:10.4018/978-1-4666-1830-5.ch003

Bittencourt, L. F., Madeira, E. R., & da Fonseca, N. L. (2014). Communication aspects of resource management in hybrid clouds. In H. Mouftah & B. Kantarci (Eds.), *Communication infrastructures for cloud computing* (pp. 409–433). Hershey, PA: IGI Global. doi:10.4018/978-1-4666-4522-6.ch018

Bonelli, L., Giudicianni, L., Immediata, A., & Luzzi, A. (2013). Compliance in the cloud. In D. Kyriazis, A. Voulodimos, S. Gogouvitis, & T. Varvarigou (Eds.), *Data intensive storage services for cloud environments* (pp. 109–131). Hershey, PA: IGI Global. doi:10.4018/978-1-4666-3934-8.ch008

Boniface, M., Nasser, B., Surridge, M., & Oliveros, E. (2012). Securing real-time interactive applications in federated clouds. In *Grid and cloud computing: Concepts, methodologies, tools and applications* (pp. 1822–1835). Hershey, PA: IGI Global. doi:10.4018/978-1-4666-0879-5.ch806

Boukhobza, J. (2013). Flashing in the cloud: Shedding some light on NAND flash memory storage systems. In D. Kyriazis, A. Voulodimos, S. Gogouvitis, & T. Varvarigou (Eds.), *Data intensive storage services for cloud environments* (pp. 241–266). Hershey, PA: IGI Global. doi:10.4018/978-1-4666-3934-8.ch015

Bracci, F., Corradi, A., & Foschini, L. (2014). Cloud standards: Security and interoperability issues. In H. Mouftah & B. Kantarci (Eds.), *Communication infrastructures for cloud computing* (pp. 465–495). Hershey, PA: IGI Global. doi:10.4018/978-1-4666-4522-6.ch020

Brown, A. W. (2013). Experiences with cloud technology to realize software testing factories. In S. Tilley & T. Parveen (Eds.), *Software testing in the cloud: Perspectives on an emerging discipline* (pp. 1–27). Hershey, PA: IGI Global. doi:10.4018/978-1-4666-2536-5.ch001

Calcavecchia, N. M., Celesti, A., & Di Nitto, E. (2012). Understanding decentralized and dynamic brokerage in federated cloud environments. In M. Villari, I. Brandic, & F. Tusa (Eds.), *Achieving federated and self-manageable cloud infrastructures: Theory and practice* (pp. 36–56). Hershey, PA: IGI Global. doi:10.4018/978-1-4666-1631-8.ch003

Calero, J. M., König, B., & Kirschnick, J. (2012). Cross-layer monitoring in cloud computing. In H. Rashvand & Y. Kavian (Eds.), *Using cross-layer techniques for communication systems* (pp. 328–348). Hershey, PA: IGI Global. doi:10.4018/978-1-4666-0960-0.ch014

Cardellini, V., Casalicchio, E., & Silvestri, L. (2012). Service level provisioning for cloud-based applications service level provisioning for cloud-based applications. In A. Pathan, M. Pathan, & H. Lee (Eds.), *Advancements in distributed computing and internet technologies: Trends and issues* (pp. 363–385). Hershey, PA: IGI Global. doi:10.4018/978-1-61350-110-8.ch017

Cardellini, V., Casalicchio, E., & Silvestri, L. (2012). Service level provisioning for cloud-based applications service level provisioning for cloud-based applications. In *Grid and cloud computing: Concepts, methodologies, tools and applications* (pp. 1479–1500). Hershey, PA: IGI Global. doi:10.4018/978-1-4666-0879-5.ch611

Carlin, S., & Curran, K. (2013). Cloud computing security. In K. Curran (Ed.), *Pervasive and ubiquitous technology innovations for ambient intelligence environments* (pp. 12–17). Hershey, PA: IGI Global. doi:10.4018/978-1-4666-2041-4.ch002

Carlton, G. H., & Zhou, H. (2011). A survey of cloud computing challenges from a digital forensics perspective. *International Journal of Interdisciplinary Telecommunications and Networking, 3*(4), 1–16. doi:10.4018/jitn.2011100101

Carlton, G. H., & Zhou, H. (2012). A survey of cloud computing challenges from a digital forensics perspective. In *Grid and cloud computing: Concepts, methodologies, tools and applications* (pp. 1221–1236). Hershey, PA: IGI Global. doi:10.4018/978-1-4666-0879-5.ch511

Carlton, G. H., & Zhou, H. (2013). A survey of cloud computing challenges from a digital forensics perspective. In M. Bartolacci & S. Powell (Eds.), *Advancements and innovations in wireless communications and network technologies* (pp. 213–228). Hershey, PA: IGI Global. doi:10.4018/978-1-4666-2154-1.ch016

Carpen-Amarie, A., Costan, A., Leordeanu, C., Basescu, C., & Antoniu, G. (2012). Towards a generic security framework for cloud data management environments. *International Journal of Distributed Systems and Technologies, 3*(1), 17–34. doi:10.4018/jdst.2012010102

Casola, V., Cuomo, A., Villano, U., & Rak, M. (2012). Access control in federated clouds: The cloud-grid case study. In M. Villari, I. Brandic, & F. Tusa (Eds.), *Achieving Federated and Self-Manageable Cloud Infrastructures: Theory and Practice* (pp. 395–417). Hershey, PA: IGI Global. doi:10.4018/978-1-4666-1631-8.ch020

Casola, V., Cuomo, A., Villano, U., & Rak, M. (2013). Access control in federated clouds: The cloudgrid case study. In *IT policy and ethics: Concepts, methodologies, tools, and applications* (pp. 148–169). Hershey, PA: IGI Global. doi:10.4018/978-1-4666-2919-6.ch008

Celesti, A., Tusa, F., & Villari, M. (2012). Toward cloud federation: Concepts and challenges. In M. Villari, I. Brandic, & F. Tusa (Eds.), *Achieving federated and self-manageable cloud infrastructures: Theory and practice* (pp. 1–17). Hershey, PA: IGI Global. doi:10.4018/978-1-4666-1631-8.ch001

Chaka, C. (2013). Virtualization and cloud computing: Business models in the virtual cloud. In A. Loo (Ed.), *Distributed computing innovations for business, engineering, and science* (pp. 176–190). Hershey, PA: IGI Global. doi:10.4018/978-1-4666-2533-4.ch009

Chang, J. (2011). A framework for analysing the impact of cloud computing on local government in the UK. *International Journal of Cloud Applications and Computing, 1*(4), 25–33. doi:10.4018/ijcac.2011100102

Chang, J. (2013). A framework for analysing the impact of cloud computing on local government in the UK. In S. Aljawarneh (Ed.), *Cloud computing advancements in design, implementation, and technologies* (pp. 243–251). Hershey, PA: IGI Global. doi:10.4018/978-1-4666-1879-4.ch017

Chang, J., & Johnston, M. (2012). Cloud computing in local government: From the perspective of four London borough councils. *International Journal of Cloud Applications and Computing*, 2(4), 1–15. doi:10.4018/ijcac.2012100101

Chang, K., & Wang, K. (2012). Efficient support of streaming videos through patching proxies in the cloud. *International Journal of Grid and High Performance Computing*, 4(4), 22–36. doi:10.4018/jghpc.2012100102

Chang, R., Liao, C., & Liu, C. (2013). Choosing clouds for an enterprise: Modeling and evaluation. *International Journal of E-Entrepreneurship and Innovation*, 4(2), 38–53. doi:10.4018/ijeei.2013040103

Chang, V., De Roure, D., Wills, G., & Walters, R. J. (2011). Case studies and organisational sustainability modelling presented by cloud computing business framework. *International Journal of Web Services Research*, 8(3), 26–53. doi:10.4018/JWSR.2011070102

Chang, V., Li, C., De Roure, D., Wills, G., Walters, R. J., & Chee, C. (2011). The financial clouds review. *International Journal of Cloud Applications and Computing*, 1(2), 41–63. doi:10.4018/ijcac.2011040104

Chang, V., Li, C., De Roure, D., Wills, G., Walters, R. J., & Chee, C. (2013). The financial clouds review. In S. Aljawarneh (Ed.), *Cloud computing advancements in design, implementation, and technologies* (pp. 125–146). Hershey, PA: IGI Global. doi:10.4018/978-1-4666-1879-4.ch009

Chang, V., Walters, R. J., & Wills, G. (2012). Business integration as a service. *International Journal of Cloud Applications and Computing*, 2(1), 16–40. doi:10.4018/ijcac.2012010102

Chang, V., & Wills, G. (2013). A University of Greenwich case study of cloud computing: Education as a service. In D. Graham, I. Manikas, & D. Folinas (Eds.), *E-logistics and e-supply chain management: Applications for evolving business* (pp. 232–253). Hershey, PA: IGI Global. doi:10.4018/978-1-4666-3914-0.ch013

Chang, V., Wills, G., Walters, R. J., & Currie, W. (2012). Towards a structured cloud ROI: The University of Southampton cost-saving and user satisfaction case studies. In W. Hu & N. Kaabouch (Eds.), *Sustainable ICTs and management systems for green computing* (pp. 179–200). Hershey, PA: IGI Global. doi:10.4018/978-1-4666-1839-8.ch008

Chang, Y., Lee, Y., Juang, T., & Yen, J. (2013). Cost evaluation on building and operating cloud platform. *International Journal of Grid and High Performance Computing*, 5(2), 43–53. doi:10.4018/jghpc.2013040103

Chao, L. (2012). Cloud computing solution for internet based teaching and learning. In L. Chao (Ed.), *Cloud computing for teaching and learning: Strategies for design and implementation* (pp. 210–235). Hershey, PA: IGI Global. doi:10.4018/978-1-4666-0957-0.ch015

Chao, L. (2012). Overview of cloud computing and its application in e-learning. In L. Chao (Ed.), *Cloud computing for teaching and learning: Strategies for design and implementation* (pp. 1–16). Hershey, PA: IGI Global. doi:10.4018/978-1-4666-0957-0.ch001

Chauhan, S., Raman, A., & Singh, N. (2013). A comparative cost analysis of on premises IT infrastructure and cloud-based email services in an Indian business school. *International Journal of Cloud Applications and Computing*, *3*(2), 21–34. doi:10.4018/ijcac.2013040103

Chen, C., Chao, H., Wu, T., Fan, C., Chen, J., Chen, Y., & Hsu, J. (2011). IoT-IMS communication platform for future internet. *International Journal of Adaptive, Resilient and Autonomic Systems*, *2*(4), 74–94. doi:10.4018/jaras.2011100105

Chen, C., Chao, H., Wu, T., Fan, C., Chen, J., Chen, Y., & Hsu, J. (2013). IoT-IMS communication platform for future internet. In V. De Florio (Ed.), *Innovations and approaches for resilient and adaptive systems* (pp. 68–86). Hershey, PA: IGI Global. doi:10.4018/978-1-4666-2056-8.ch004

Chen, C. C. (2013). Cloud computing in case-based pedagogy: An information systems success perspective. *International Journal of Dependable and Trustworthy Information Systems*, *2*(3), 1–16. doi:10.4018/jdtis.2011070101

Cheney, A. W., Riedl, R. E., Sanders, R., & Tashner, J. H. (2012). The new company water cooler: Use of 3D virtual immersive worlds to promote networking and professional learning in organizations. In Organizational learning and knowledge: Concepts, methodologies, tools and applications (pp. 2848-2861). Hershey, PA: IGI Global. doi:10.4018/978-1-60960-783-8.ch801

Chiang, C., & Yu, S. (2013). Cloud-enabled software testing based on program understanding. In S. Tilley & T. Parveen (Eds.), *Software testing in the cloud: Perspectives on an emerging discipline* (pp. 54–67). Hershey, PA: IGI Global. doi:10.4018/978-1-4666-2536-5.ch003

Chou, Y., & Oetting, J. (2011). Risk assessment for cloud-based IT systems. *International Journal of Grid and High Performance Computing*, *3*(2), 1–13. doi:10.4018/jghpc.2011040101

Chou, Y., & Oetting, J. (2012). Risk assessment for cloud-based IT systems. In *Grid and cloud computing: Concepts, methodologies, tools and applications* (pp. 272–285). Hershey, PA: IGI Global. doi:10.4018/978-1-4666-0879-5.ch113

Chou, Y., & Oetting, J. (2013). Risk assessment for cloud-based IT systems. In E. Udoh (Ed.), *Applications and developments in grid, cloud, and high performance computing* (pp. 1–14). Hershey, PA: IGI Global. doi:10.4018/978-1-4666-2065-0.ch001

Cohen, F. (2013). Challenges to digital forensic evidence in the cloud. In K. Ruan (Ed.), *Cybercrime and cloud forensics: Applications for investigation processes* (pp. 59–78). Hershey, PA: IGI Global. doi:10.4018/978-1-4666-2662-1.ch003

Cossu, R., Di Giulio, C., Brito, F., & Petcu, D. (2013). Cloud computing for earth observation. In D. Kyriazis, A. Voulodimos, S. Gogouvitis, & T. Varvarigou (Eds.), *Data intensive storage services for cloud environments* (pp. 166–191). Hershey, PA: IGI Global. doi:10.4018/978-1-4666-3934-8.ch012

Costa, J. E., & Rodrigues, J. J. (2014). Mobile cloud computing: Technologies, services, and applications. In J. Rodrigues, K. Lin, & J. Lloret (Eds.), *Mobile networks and cloud computing convergence for progressive services and applications* (pp. 1–17). Hershey, PA: IGI Global. doi:10.4018/978-1-4666-4781-7.ch001

Creaner, G., & Pahl, C. (2013). Flexible coordination techniques for dynamic cloud service collaboration. In G. Ortiz & J. Cubo (Eds.), *Adaptive web services for modular and reusable software development: Tactics and solutions* (pp. 239–252). Hershey, PA: IGI Global. doi:10.4018/978-1-4666-2089-6.ch009

Crosbie, M. (2013). Hack the cloud: Ethical hacking and cloud forensics. In K. Ruan (Ed.), *Cybercrime and cloud forensics: Applications for investigation processes* (pp. 42–58). Hershey, PA: IGI Global. doi:10.4018/978-1-4666-2662-1.ch002

Curran, K., Carlin, S., & Adams, M. (2012). Security issues in cloud computing. In L. Chao (Ed.), *Cloud computing for teaching and learning: Strategies for design and implementation* (pp. 200–208). Hershey, PA: IGI Global. doi:10.4018/978-1-4666-0957-0.ch014

Dahbur, K., & Mohammad, B. (2011). Toward understanding the challenges and countermeasures in computer anti-forensics. *International Journal of Cloud Applications and Computing*, *1*(3), 22–35. doi:10.4018/ijcac.2011070103

Dahbur, K., Mohammad, B., & Tarakji, A. B. (2011). Security issues in cloud computing: A survey of risks, threats and vulnerabilities. *International Journal of Cloud Applications and Computing*, *1*(3), 1–11. doi:10.4018/ijcac.2011070101

Dahbur, K., Mohammad, B., & Tarakji, A. B. (2012). Security issues in cloud computing: A survey of risks, threats and vulnerabilities. In *Grid and cloud computing: Concepts, methodologies, tools and applications* (pp. 1644–1655). Hershey, PA: IGI Global. doi:10.4018/978-1-4666-0879-5.ch707

Dahbur, K., Mohammad, B., & Tarakji, A. B. (2013). Security issues in cloud computing: A survey of risks, threats and vulnerabilities. In S. Aljawarneh (Ed.), *Cloud computing advancements in design, implementation, and technologies* (pp. 154–165). Hershey, PA: IGI Global. doi:10.4018/978-1-4666-1879-4.ch011

Daim, T., Britton, M., Subramanian, G., Brenden, R., & Intarode, N. (2012). Adopting and integrating cloud computing. In E. Eyob & E. Tetteh (Eds.), *Customer-oriented global supply chains: Concepts for effective management* (pp. 175–197). Hershey, PA: IGI Global. doi:10.4018/978-1-4666-0246-5.ch011

Davis, M., & Sedsman, A. (2012). Grey areas: The legal dimensions of cloud computing. In C. Li & A. Ho (Eds.), *Crime prevention technologies and applications for advancing criminal investigation* (pp. 263–273). Hershey, PA: IGI Global. doi:10.4018/978-1-4666-1758-2.ch017

De Coster, R., & Albesher, A. (2013). The development of mobile service applications for consumers and intelligent networks. In I. Lee (Ed.), *Mobile services industries, technologies, and applications in the global economy* (pp. 273–289). Hershey, PA: IGI Global. doi:10.4018/978-1-4666-1981-4.ch017

De Filippi, P. (2014). Ubiquitous computing in the cloud: User empowerment vs. user obsequity. In J. Pelet & P. Papadopoulou (Eds.), *User behavior in ubiquitous online environments* (pp. 44–63). Hershey, PA: IGI Global. doi:10.4018/978-1-4666-4566-0.ch003

De Silva, S. (2013). Key legal issues with cloud computing: A UK law perspective. In A. Bento & A. Aggarwal (Eds.), *Cloud computing service and deployment models: Layers and management* (pp. 242–256). Hershey, PA: IGI Global. doi:10.4018/978-1-4666-2187-9.ch013

Deed, C., & Cragg, P. (2013). Business impacts of cloud computing. In A. Bento & A. Aggarwal (Eds.), *Cloud computing service and deployment models: Layers and management* (pp. 274–288). Hershey, PA: IGI Global. doi:10.4018/978-1-4666-2187-9.ch015

Deng, M., Petkovic, M., Nalin, M., & Baroni, I. (2013). Home healthcare in cloud computing. In M. Cruz-Cunha, I. Miranda, & P. Gonçalves (Eds.), *Handbook of research on ICTs and management systems for improving efficiency in healthcare and social care* (pp. 614–634). Hershey, PA: IGI Global. doi:10.4018/978-1-4666-3990-4.ch032

Desai, A. M., & Mock, K. (2013). Security in cloud computing. In A. Bento & A. Aggarwal (Eds.), *Cloud computing service and deployment models: Layers and management* (pp. 208–221). Hershey, PA: IGI Global. doi:10.4018/978-1-4666-2187-9.ch011

Deshpande, R. M., Patle, B. V., & Bhoskar, R. D. (2014). Planning and implementation of cloud computing in NIT's in India: Special reference to VNIT. In S. Dhamdhere (Ed.), *Cloud computing and virtualization technologies in libraries* (pp. 90–106). Hershey, PA: IGI Global. doi:10.4018/978-1-4666-4631-5.ch006

Dhamdhere, S. N., & Lihitkar, R. (2014). The university cloud library model and the role of the cloud librarian. In S. Dhamdhere (Ed.), *Cloud computing and virtualization technologies in libraries* (pp. 150–161). Hershey, PA: IGI Global. doi:10.4018/978-1-4666-4631-5.ch009

Di Martino, S., Ferrucci, F., Maggio, V., & Sarro, F. (2013). Towards migrating genetic algorithms for test data generation to the cloud. In S. Tilley & T. Parveen (Eds.), *Software testing in the cloud: Perspectives on an emerging discipline* (pp. 113–135). Hershey, PA: IGI Global. doi:10.4018/978-1-4666-2536-5.ch006

Di Sano, M., Di Stefano, A., Morana, G., & Zito, D. (2013). FSaaS: Configuring policies for managing shared files among cooperating, distributed applications. *International Journal of Web Portals*, 5(1), 1–14. doi:10.4018/jwp.2013010101

Dippl, S., Jaeger, M. C., Luhn, A., Shulman-Peleg, A., & Vernik, G. (2013). Towards federation and interoperability of cloud storage systems. In D. Kyriazis, A. Voulodimos, S. Gogouvitis, & T. Varvarigou (Eds.), *Data intensive storage services for cloud environments* (pp. 60–71). Hershey, PA: IGI Global. doi:10.4018/978-1-4666-3934-8.ch005

Distefano, S., & Puliafito, A. (2012). The cloud@home volunteer and interoperable cloud through the future internet. In M. Villari, I. Brandic, & F. Tusa (Eds.), *Achieving federated and self-manageable cloud infrastructures: Theory and practice* (pp. 79–96). Hershey, PA: IGI Global. doi:10.4018/978-1-4666-1631-8.ch005

Djoleto, W. (2013). Cloud computing and ecommerce or ebusiness: "The now it way" – An overview. In *Electronic commerce and organizational leadership: perspectives and methodologies* (pp. 239–254). Hershey, PA: IGI Global. doi:10.4018/978-1-4666-2982-0.ch010

Dollmann, T. J., Loos, P., Fellmann, M., Thomas, O., Hoheisel, A., Katranuschkov, P., & Scherer, R. (2011). Design and usage of a process-centric collaboration methodology for virtual organizations in hybrid environments. *International Journal of Intelligent Information Technologies*, 7(1), 45–64. doi:10.4018/jiit.2011010104

Dollmann, T. J., Loos, P., Fellmann, M., Thomas, O., Hoheisel, A., Katranuschkov, P., & Scherer, R. (2013). Design and usage of a process-centric collaboration methodology for virtual organizations in hybrid environments. In V. Sugumaran (Ed.), *Organizational efficiency through intelligent information technologies* (pp. 45–64). Hershey, PA: IGI Global. doi:10.4018/978-1-4666-2047-6.ch004

Dreher, P., & Vouk, M. (2012). Utilizing open source cloud computing environments to provide cost effective support for university education and research. In L. Chao (Ed.), *Cloud computing for teaching and learning: Strategies for design and implementation* (pp. 32–49). Hershey, PA: IGI Global. doi:10.4018/978-1-4666-0957-0.ch003

Drum, D., Becker, D., & Fish, M. (2013). Technology adoption in troubled times: A cloud computing case study. *Journal of Cases on Information Technology*, *15*(2), 57–71. doi:10.4018/jcit.2013040104

Dunaway, D. M. (2013). Creating virtual collaborative learning experiences for aspiring teachers. In R. Hartshorne, T. Heafner, & T. Petty (Eds.), *Teacher education programs and online learning tools: Innovations in teacher preparation* (pp. 167–180). Hershey, PA: IGI Global. doi:10.4018/978-1-4666-1906-7.ch009

Dykstra, J. (2013). Seizing electronic evidence from cloud computing environments. In K. Ruan (Ed.), *Cybercrime and cloud forensics: Applications for investigation processes* (pp. 156–185). Hershey, PA: IGI Global. doi:10.4018/978-1-4666-2662-1.ch007

El-Refaey, M., & Rimal, B. P. (2012). Grid, SOA and cloud computing: On-demand computing models. In *Grid and cloud computing: Concepts, methodologies, tools and applications* (pp. 12–51). Hershey, PA: IGI Global. doi:10.4018/978-1-4666-0879-5.ch102

El-Refaey, M., & Rimal, B. P. (2012). Grid, SOA and cloud computing: On-demand computing models. In N. Preve (Ed.), *Computational and data grids: Principles, applications and design* (pp. 45–85). Hershey, PA: IGI Global. doi:10.4018/978-1-61350-113-9.ch003

Elnaffar, S., Maamar, Z., & Sheng, Q. Z. (2013). When clouds start socializing: The sky model. *International Journal of E-Business Research*, *9*(2), 1–7. doi:10.4018/jebr.2013040101

Elwood, S., & Keengwe, J. (2012). Microbursts: A design format for mobile cloud computing. *International Journal of Information and Communication Technology Education*, *8*(2), 102–110. doi:10.4018/jicte.2012040109

Emeakaroha, V. C., Netto, M. A., Calheiros, R. N., & De Rose, C. A. (2012). Achieving flexible SLA and resource management in clouds. In M. Villari, I. Brandic, & F. Tusa (Eds.), *Achieving federated and self-manageable cloud infrastructures: Theory and practice* (pp. 266–287). Hershey, PA: IGI Global. doi:10.4018/978-1-4666-1631-8.ch014

Etro, F. (2013). The economics of cloud computing. In A. Bento & A. Aggarwal (Eds.), *Cloud computing service and deployment models: Layers and management* (pp. 296–309). Hershey, PA: IGI Global. doi:10.4018/978-1-4666-2187-9.ch017

Ezugwu, A. E., Buhari, S. M., & Junaidu, S. B. (2013). Virtual machine allocation in cloud computing environment. *International Journal of Cloud Applications and Computing*, *3*(2), 47–60. doi:10.4018/ijcac.2013040105

Fauzi, A. H., & Taylor, H. (2013). Secure community trust stores for peer-to-peer e-commerce applications using cloud services. *International Journal of E-Entrepreneurship and Innovation*, *4*(1), 1–15. doi:10.4018/jeei.2013010101

Ferguson-Boucher, K., & Endicott-Popovsky, B. (2013). Forensic readiness in the cloud (FRC): Integrating records management and digital forensics. In K. Ruan (Ed.), *Cybercrime and cloud forensics: Applications for investigation processes* (pp. 105–128). Hershey, PA: IGI Global. doi:10.4018/978-1-4666-2662-1.ch005

Ferraro de Souza, R., Westphall, C. B., dos Santos, D. R., & Westphall, C. M. (2013). A review of PACS on cloud for archiving secure medical images. *International Journal of Privacy and Health Information Management*, *1*(1), 53–62. doi:10.4018/ijphim.2013010104

Firdhous, M., Hassan, S., & Ghazali, O. (2013). Statistically enhanced multi-dimensional trust computing mechanism for cloud computing. *International Journal of Mobile Computing and Multimedia Communications*, *5*(2), 1–17. doi:10.4018/jmcmc.2013040101

Formisano, C., Bonelli, L., Balraj, K. R., & Shulman-Peleg, A. (2013). Cloud access control mechanisms. In D. Kyriazis, A. Voulodimos, S. Gogouvitis, & T. Varvarigou (Eds.), *Data intensive storage services for cloud environments* (pp. 94–108). Hershey, PA: IGI Global. doi:10.4018/978-1-4666-3934-8.ch007

Frank, H., & Mesentean, S. (2012). Efficient communication interfaces for distributed energy resources. In E. Udoh (Ed.), *Evolving developments in grid and cloud computing: Advancing research* (pp. 185–196). Hershey, PA: IGI Global. doi:10.4018/978-1-4666-0056-0.ch013

Gallina, B., & Guelfi, N. (2012). Reusing transaction models for dependable cloud computing. In H. Yang & X. Liu (Eds.), *Software reuse in the emerging cloud computing era* (pp. 248–277). Hershey, PA: IGI Global. doi:10.4018/978-1-4666-0897-9.ch011

Garofalo, D. A. (2013). Empires of the future: Libraries, technology, and the academic environment. In E. Iglesias (Ed.), *Robots in academic libraries: Advancements in library automation* (pp. 180–206). Hershey, PA: IGI Global. doi:10.4018/978-1-4666-3938-6.ch010

Gebremeskel, G. B., He, Z., & Jing, X. (2013). Semantic integrating for intelligent cloud data mining platform and cloud based business intelligence for optimization of mobile social networks. In V. Bhatnagar (Ed.), *Data mining in dynamic social networks and fuzzy systems* (pp. 173–211). Hershey, PA: IGI Global. doi:10.4018/978-1-4666-4213-3.ch009

Gentleman, W. M. (2013). Using the cloud for testing NOT adjunct to development. In S. Tilley & T. Parveen (Eds.), *Software testing in the cloud: Perspectives on an emerging discipline* (pp. 216–230). Hershey, PA: IGI Global. doi:10.4018/978-1-4666-2536-5.ch010

Ghafoor, K. Z., Mohammed, M. A., Abu Bakar, K., Sadiq, A. S., & Lloret, J. (2014). Vehicular cloud computing: Trends and challenges. In J. Rodrigues, K. Lin, & J. Lloret (Eds.), *Mobile networks and cloud computing convergence for progressive services and applications* (pp. 262–274). Hershey, PA: IGI Global. doi:10.4018/978-1-4666-4781-7.ch014

Giannakaki, M. (2012). The "right to be forgotten" in the era of social media and cloud computing. In C. Akrivopoulou & N. Garipidis (Eds.), *Human rights and risks in the digital era: Globalization and the effects of information technologies* (pp. 10–24). Hershey, PA: IGI Global. doi:10.4018/978-1-4666-0891-7.ch002

Gillam, L., Li, B., & O'Loughlin, J. (2012). Teaching clouds: Lessons taught and lessons learnt. In L. Chao (Ed.), *Cloud computing for teaching and learning: Strategies for design and implementation* (pp. 82–94). Hershey, PA: IGI Global. doi:10.4018/978-1-4666-0957-0.ch006

Gonsowski, D. (2013). Compliance in the cloud and the implications on electronic discovery. In K. Ruan (Ed.), *Cybercrime and cloud forensics: Applications for investigation processes* (pp. 230–250). Hershey, PA: IGI Global. doi:10.4018/978-1-4666-2662-1.ch009

Gonzalez-Sanchez, J., Conley, Q., Chavez-Echeagaray, M., & Atkinson, R. K. (2012). Supporting the assembly process by leveraging augmented reality, cloud computing, and mobile devices. *International Journal of Cyber Behavior, Psychology and Learning*, 2(3), 86–102. doi:10.4018/ijcbpl.2012070107

Gopinath, R., & Geetha, B. (2013). An e-learning system based on secure data storage services in cloud computing. *International Journal of Information Technology and Web Engineering*, 8(2), 1–17. doi:10.4018/jitwe.2013040101

Gossin, P. C., & LaBrie, R. C. (2013). Data center waste management. In P. Ordóñez de Pablos (Ed.), *Green technologies and business practices: An IT approach* (pp. 226–235). Hershey, PA: IGI Global. doi:10.4018/978-1-4666-1972-2.ch014

Goswami, V., Patra, S. S., & Mund, G. B. (2012). Performance analysis of cloud computing centers for bulk services. *International Journal of Cloud Applications and Computing*, 2(4), 53–65. doi:10.4018/ijcac.2012100104

Goswami, V., & Sahoo, C. N. (2013). Optimal resource usage in multi-cloud computing environment. *International Journal of Cloud Applications and Computing*, 3(1), 44–57. doi:10.4018/ijcac.2013010105

Gräuler, M., Teuteberg, F., Mahmoud, T., & Gómez, J. M. (2013). Requirements prioritization and design considerations for the next generation of corporate environmental management information systems: A foundation for innovation. *International Journal of Information Technologies and Systems Approach*, 6(1), 98–116. doi:10.4018/jitsa.2013010106

Grieve, G. P., & Heston, K. (2012). Finding liquid salvation: Using the cardean ethnographic method to document second life residents and religious cloud communities. In N. Zagalo, L. Morgado, & A. Boa-Ventura (Eds.), *Virtual worlds and metaverse platforms: New communication and identity paradigms* (pp. 288–305). Hershey, PA: IGI Global. doi:10.4018/978-1-60960-854-5.ch019

Grispos, G., Storer, T., & Glisson, W. B. (2012). Calm before the storm: The challenges of cloud computing in digital forensics. *International Journal of Digital Crime and Forensics*, 4(2), 28–48. doi:10.4018/jdcf.2012040103

Grispos, G., Storer, T., & Glisson, W. B. (2013). Calm before the storm: The challenges of cloud computing in digital forensics. In C. Li (Ed.), *Emerging digital forensics applications for crime detection, prevention, and security* (pp. 211–233). Hershey, PA: IGI Global. doi:10.4018/978-1-4666-4006-1.ch015

Guster, D., & Lee, O. F. (2011). Enhancing the disaster recovery plan through virtualization. *Journal of Information Technology Research*, *4*(4), 18–40. doi:10.4018/jitr.2011100102

Hanawa, T., & Sato, M. (2013). D-Cloud: Software testing environment for dependable distributed systems using cloud computing technology. In S. Tilley & T. Parveen (Eds.), *Software testing in the cloud: Perspectives on an emerging discipline* (pp. 340–355). Hershey, PA: IGI Global. doi:10.4018/978-1-4666-2536-5.ch016

Hardy, J., Liu, L., Lei, C., & Li, J. (2013). Internet-based virtual computing infrastructure for cloud computing. In X. Yang & L. Liu (Eds.), *Principles, methodologies, and service-oriented approaches for cloud computing* (pp. 371–389). Hershey, PA: IGI Global. doi:10.4018/978-1-4666-2854-0.ch016

Hashizume, K., Yoshioka, N., & Fernandez, E. B. (2013). Three misuse patterns for cloud computing. In D. Rosado, D. Mellado, E. Fernandez-Medina, & M. Piattini (Eds.), *Security engineering for cloud computing: Approaches and tools* (pp. 36–53). Hershey, PA: IGI Global. doi:10.4018/978-1-4666-2125-1.ch003

Hassan, Q. F., Riad, A. M., & Hassan, A. E. (2012). Understanding cloud computing. In H. Yang & X. Liu (Eds.), *Software reuse in the emerging cloud computing era* (pp. 204–227). Hershey, PA: IGI Global. doi:10.4018/978-1-4666-0897-9.ch009

Hasselmeyer, P., Katsaros, G., Koller, B., & Wieder, P. (2012). Cloud monitoring. In M. Villari, I. Brandic, & F. Tusa (Eds.), *Achieving federated and self-manageable cloud infrastructures: Theory and practice* (pp. 97–116). Hershey, PA: IGI Global. doi:10.4018/978-1-4666-1631-8.ch006

Hertzler, B. T., Frost, E., Bressler, G. H., & Goehring, C. (2011). Experience report: Using a cloud computing environment during Haiti and Exercise. *International Journal of Information Systems for Crisis Response and Management*, *3*(1), 50–64. doi:10.4018/jiscrm.2011010104

Hertzler, B. T., Frost, E., Bressler, G. H., & Goehring, C. (2013). Experience report: Using a cloud computing environment during Haiti and Exercise24. In M. Jennex (Ed.), *Using social and information technologies for disaster and crisis management* (pp. 52–66). Hershey, PA: IGI Global. doi:10.4018/978-1-4666-2788-8.ch004

Ho, R. (2013). Cloud computing and enterprise migration strategies. In A. Loo (Ed.), *Distributed computing innovations for business, engineering, and science* (pp. 156–175). Hershey, PA: IGI Global. doi:10.4018/978-1-4666-2533-4.ch008

Hobona, G., Jackson, M., & Anand, S. (2012). Implementing geospatial web services for cloud computing. In *Grid and cloud computing: Concepts, methodologies, tools and applications* (pp. 615–636). Hershey, PA: IGI Global. doi:10.4018/978-1-4666-0879-5.ch305

Hochstein, L., Schott, B., & Graybill, R. B. (2011). Computational engineering in the cloud: Benefits and challenges. *Journal of Organizational and End User Computing*, *23*(4), 31–50. doi:10.4018/joeuc.2011100103

Hochstein, L., Schott, B., & Graybill, R. B. (2013). Computational engineering in the cloud: Benefits and challenges. In A. Dwivedi & S. Clarke (Eds.), *Innovative strategies and approaches for end-user computing advancements* (pp. 314–332). Hershey, PA: IGI Global. doi:10.4018/978-1-4666-2059-9.ch017

Honarvar, A. R. (2013). Developing an elastic cloud computing application through multi-agent systems. *International Journal of Cloud Applications and Computing, 3*(1), 58–64. doi:10.4018/ijcac.2013010106

Hossain, S. (2013). Cloud computing terms, definitions, and taxonomy. In A. Bento & A. Aggarwal (Eds.), *Cloud computing service and deployment models: Layers and management* (pp. 1–25). Hershey, PA: IGI Global. doi:10.4018/978-1-4666-2187-9.ch001

Hudzia, B., Sinclair, J., & Lindner, M. (2013). Deploying and running enterprise grade applications in a federated cloud. In *Supply chain management: Concepts, methodologies, tools, and applications* (pp. 1350–1370). Hershey, PA: IGI Global. doi:10.4018/978-1-4666-2625-6.ch080

Hung, S., Shieh, J., & Lee, C. (2011). Migrating android applications to the cloud. *International Journal of Grid and High Performance Computing, 3*(2), 14–28. doi:10.4018/jghpc.2011040102

Hung, S., Shieh, J., & Lee, C. (2013). Migrating android applications to the cloud. In E. Udoh (Ed.), *Applications and developments in grid, cloud, and high performance computing* (pp. 307–322). Hershey, PA: IGI Global. doi:10.4018/978-1-4666-2065-0.ch020

Islam, S., Mouratidis, H., & Weippl, E. R. (2013). A goal-driven risk management approach to support security and privacy analysis of cloud-based system. In D. Rosado, D. Mellado, E. Fernandez-Medina, & M. Piattini (Eds.), *Security engineering for cloud computing: Approaches and tools* (pp. 97–122). Hershey, PA: IGI Global. doi:10.4018/978-1-4666-2125-1.ch006

Itani, W., Kayssi, A., & Chehab, A. (2013). Hardware-based security for ensuring data privacy in the cloud. In D. Rosado, D. Mellado, E. Fernandez-Medina, & M. Piattini (Eds.), *Security engineering for cloud computing: Approaches and tools* (pp. 147–170). Hershey, PA: IGI Global. doi:10.4018/978-1-4666-2125-1.ch008

Jackson, A., & Weiland, M. (2013). Cloud computing for scientific simulation and high performance computing. In X. Yang & L. Liu (Eds.), *Principles, methodologies, and service-oriented approaches for cloud computing* (pp. 51–70). Hershey, PA: IGI Global. doi:10.4018/978-1-4666-2854-0.ch003

Jaeger, M. C., & Hohenstein, U. (2013). Content centric storage and current storage systems. In D. Kyriazis, A. Voulodimos, S. Gogouvitis, & T. Varvarigou (Eds.), *Data intensive storage services for cloud environments* (pp. 27–46). Hershey, PA: IGI Global. doi:10.4018/978-1-4666-3934-8.ch003

James, J. I., Shosha, A. F., & Gladyshev, P. (2013). Digital forensic investigation and cloud computing. In K. Ruan (Ed.), *Cybercrime and cloud forensics: Applications for investigation processes* (pp. 1–41). Hershey, PA: IGI Global. doi:10.4018/978-1-4666-2662-1.ch001

Jena, R. K. (2013). Green computing to green business. In P. Ordóñez de Pablos (Ed.), *Green technologies and business practices: An IT approach* (pp. 138–150). Hershey, PA: IGI Global. doi:10.4018/978-1-4666-1972-2.ch007

Jeyarani, R., & Nagaveni, N. (2012). A heuristic meta scheduler for optimal resource utilization and improved QoS in cloud computing environment. *International Journal of Cloud Applications and Computing, 2*(1), 41–52. doi:10.4018/ijcac.2012010103

Jeyarani, R., Nagaveni, N., & Ram, R. V. (2011). Self adaptive particle swarm optimization for efficient virtual machine provisioning in cloud. *International Journal of Intelligent Information Technologies*, *7*(2), 25–44. doi:10.4018/jiit.2011040102

Jeyarani, R., Nagaveni, N., & Ram, R. V. (2013). Self adaptive particle swarm optimization for efficient virtual machine provisioning in cloud. In V. Sugumaran (Ed.), *Organizational efficiency through intelligent information technologies* (pp. 88–107). Hershey, PA: IGI Global. doi:10.4018/978-1-4666-2047-6.ch006

Jeyarani, R., Nagaveni, N., Sadasivam, S. K., & Rajarathinam, V. R. (2011). Power aware meta scheduler for adaptive VM provisioning in IaaS cloud. *International Journal of Cloud Applications and Computing*, *1*(3), 36–51. doi:10.4018/ijcac.2011070104

Jeyarani, R., Nagaveni, N., Sadasivam, S. K., & Rajarathinam, V. R. (2013). Power aware meta scheduler for adaptive VM provisioning in IaaS cloud. In S. Aljawarneh (Ed.), *Cloud computing advancements in design, implementation, and technologies* (pp. 190–204). Hershey, PA: IGI Global. doi:10.4018/978-1-4666-1879-4.ch014

Jiang, J., Huang, X., Wu, Y., & Yang, G. (2013). Campus cloud storage and preservation: From distributed file system to data sharing service. In X. Yang & L. Liu (Eds.), *Principles, methodologies, and service-oriented approaches for cloud computing* (pp. 284–301). Hershey, PA: IGI Global. doi:10.4018/978-1-4666-2854-0.ch012

Jing, S. (2012). The application exploration of cloud computing in information technology teaching. *International Journal of Advanced Pervasive and Ubiquitous Computing*, *4*(4), 23–27. doi:10.4018/japuc.2012100104

Johansson, D., & Wiberg, M. (2012). Conceptually advancing "application mobility" towards design: Applying a concept-driven approach to the design of mobile IT for home care service groups. *International Journal of Ambient Computing and Intelligence*, *4*(3), 20–32. doi:10.4018/jaci.2012070102

Jorda, J., & M'zoughi, A. (2013). Securing cloud storage. In D. Rosado, D. Mellado, E. Fernandez-Medina, & M. Piattini (Eds.), *Security engineering for cloud computing: Approaches and tools* (pp. 171–190). Hershey, PA: IGI Global. doi:10.4018/978-1-4666-2125-1.ch009

Juiz, C., & Alexander de Pous, V. (2014). Cloud computing: IT governance, legal, and public policy aspects. In I. Portela & F. Almeida (Eds.), *Organizational, legal, and technological dimensions of information system administration* (pp. 139–166). Hershey, PA: IGI Global. doi:10.4018/978-1-4666-4526-4.ch009

Kaisler, S. H., Money, W., & Cohen, S. J. (2013). Cloud computing: A decision framework for small businesses. In A. Bento & A. Aggarwal (Eds.), *Cloud computing service and deployment models: Layers and management* (pp. 151–172). Hershey, PA: IGI Global. doi:10.4018/978-1-4666-2187-9.ch008

Kanamori, Y., & Yen, M. Y. (2013). Cloud computing security and risk management. In A. Bento & A. Aggarwal (Eds.), *Cloud computing service and deployment models: Layers and management* (pp. 222–240). Hershey, PA: IGI Global. doi:10.4018/978-1-4666-2187-9.ch012

Karadsheh, L., & Alhawari, S. (2011). Applying security policies in small business utilizing cloud computing technologies. *International Journal of Cloud Applications and Computing*, *1*(2), 29–40. doi:10.4018/ijcac.2011040103

Karadsheh, L., & Alhawari, S. (2013). Applying security policies in small business utilizing cloud computing technologies. In S. Aljawarneh (Ed.), *Cloud computing advancements in design, implementation, and technologies* (pp. 112–124). Hershey, PA: IGI Global. doi:10.4018/978-1-4666-1879-4.ch008

Kaupins, G. (2012). Laws associated with mobile computing in the cloud. *International Journal of Wireless Networks and Broadband Technologies*, 2(3), 1–9. doi:10.4018/ijwnbt.2012070101

Kemp, M. L., Robb, S., & Deans, P. C. (2013). The legal implications of cloud computing. In A. Bento & A. Aggarwal (Eds.), *Cloud computing service and deployment models: Layers and management* (pp. 257–272). Hershey, PA: IGI Global. doi:10.4018/978-1-4666-2187-9.ch014

Khan, N., Ahmad, N., Herawan, T., & Inayat, Z. (2012). Cloud computing: Locally sub-clouds instead of globally one cloud. *International Journal of Cloud Applications and Computing*, 2(3), 68–85. doi:10.4018/ijcac.2012070103

Khan, N., Noraziah, A., Ismail, E. I., Deris, M. M., & Herawan, T. (2012). Cloud computing: Analysis of various platforms. *International Journal of E-Entrepreneurship and Innovation*, 3(2), 51–59. doi:10.4018/jeei.2012040104

Khansa, L., Forcade, J., Nambari, G., Parasuraman, S., & Cox, P. (2012). Proposing an intelligent cloud-based electronic health record system. *International Journal of Business Data Communications and Networking*, 8(3), 57–71. doi:10.4018/jbdcn.2012070104

Kierkegaard, S. (2012). Not every cloud brings rain: Legal risks on the horizon. In M. Gupta, J. Walp, & R. Sharman (Eds.), *Strategic and practical approaches for information security governance: Technologies and applied solutions* (pp. 181–194). Hershey, PA: IGI Global. doi:10.4018/978-1-4666-0197-0.ch011

Kifayat, K., Shamsa, T. B., Mackay, M., Merabti, M., & Shi, Q. (2013). Real time risk management in cloud computation. In D. Rosado, D. Mellado, E. Fernandez-Medina, & M. Piattini (Eds.), *Security engineering for cloud computing: Approaches and tools* (pp. 123–145). Hershey, PA: IGI Global. doi:10.4018/978-1-4666-2125-1.ch007

King, T. M., Ganti, A. S., & Froslie, D. (2013). Towards improving the testability of cloud application services. In S. Tilley & T. Parveen (Eds.), *Software testing in the cloud: Perspectives on an emerging discipline* (pp. 322–339). Hershey, PA: IGI Global. doi:10.4018/978-1-4666-2536-5.ch015

Kipp, A., Schneider, R., & Schubert, L. (2013). Encapsulation of complex HPC services. In C. Rückemann (Ed.), *Integrated information and computing systems for natural, spatial, and social sciences* (pp. 153–176). Hershey, PA: IGI Global. doi:10.4018/978-1-4666-2190-9.ch008

Kldiashvili, E. (2012). The cloud computing as the tool for implementation of virtual organization technology for ehealth. *Journal of Information Technology Research*, 5(1), 18–34. doi:10.4018/jitr.2012010102

Kldiashvili, E. (2013). Implementation of telecytology in georgia for quality assurance programs. *Journal of Information Technology Research*, 6(2), 24–45. doi:10.4018/jitr.2013040102

Kosmatov, N. (2013). Concolic test generation and the cloud: deployment and verification perspectives. In S. Tilley & T. Parveen (Eds.), *Software testing in the cloud: Perspectives on an emerging discipline* (pp. 231–251). Hershey, PA: IGI Global. doi:10.4018/978-1-4666-2536-5.ch011

Kotamarti, R. M., Thornton, M. A., & Dunham, M. H. (2012). Quantum computing approach for alignment-free sequence search and classification. In S. Ali, N. Abbadeni, & M. Batouche (Eds.), *Multidisciplinary computational intelligence techniques: Applications in business, engineering, and medicine* (pp. 279–300). Hershey, PA: IGI Global. doi:10.4018/978-1-4666-1830-5.ch017

Kremmydas, D., Petsakos, A., & Rozakis, S. (2012). Parametric optimization of linear and non-linear models via parallel computing to enhance web-spatial DSS interactivity. *International Journal of Decision Support System Technology*, *4*(1), 14–29. doi:10.4018/jdsst.2012010102

Krishnadas, N., & Pillai, R. R. (2013). Cloud computing diagnosis: A comprehensive study. In X. Yang & L. Liu (Eds.), *Principles, methodologies, and service-oriented approaches for cloud computing* (pp. 1–18). Hershey, PA: IGI Global. doi:10.4018/978-1-4666-2854-0.ch001

Kübert, R., & Katsaros, G. (2011). Using free software for elastic web hosting on a private cloud. *International Journal of Cloud Applications and Computing*, *1*(2), 14–28. doi:10.4018/ijcac.2011040102

Kübert, R., & Katsaros, G. (2013). Using free software for elastic web hosting on a private cloud. In S. Aljawarneh (Ed.), *Cloud computing advancements in design, implementation, and technologies* (pp. 97–111). Hershey, PA: IGI Global. doi:10.4018/978-1-4666-1879-4.ch007

Kumar, P. S., Ashok, M. S., & Subramanian, R. (2012). A publicly verifiable dynamic secret sharing protocol for secure and dependable data storage in cloud computing. *International Journal of Cloud Applications and Computing*, *2*(3), 1–25. doi:10.4018/ijcac.2012070101

Lasluisa, S., Rodero, I., & Parashar, M. (2013). Software design for passing sarbanes-oxley in cloud computing. In C. Rückemann (Ed.), *Integrated information and computing systems for natural, spatial, and social sciences* (pp. 27–42). Hershey, PA: IGI Global. doi:10.4018/978-1-4666-2190-9.ch002

Lasluisa, S., Rodero, I., & Parashar, M. (2014). Software design for passing sarbanes-oxley in cloud computing. In *Software design and development: Concepts, methodologies, tools, and applications* (pp. 1659–1674). Hershey, PA: IGI Global. doi:10.4018/978-1-4666-4301-7.ch080

Lee, W. N. (2013). An economic analysis of cloud: "Software as a service" (saas) computing and "virtual desktop infrastructure" (VDI) models. In A. Bento & A. Aggarwal (Eds.), *Cloud computing service and deployment models: Layers and management* (pp. 289–295). Hershey, PA: IGI Global. doi:10.4018/978-1-4666-2187-9.ch016

Levine, K., & White, B. A. (2011). A crisis at hafford furniture: Cloud computing case study. *Journal of Cases on Information Technology*, *13*(1), 57–71. doi:10.4018/jcit.2011010104

Levine, K., & White, B. A. (2013). A crisis at Hafford furniture: Cloud computing case study. In M. Khosrow-Pour (Ed.), *Cases on emerging information technology research and applications* (pp. 70–87). Hershey, PA: IGI Global. doi:10.4018/978-1-4666-3619-4.ch004

Li, J., Meng, L., Zhu, Z., Li, X., Huai, J., & Liu, L. (2013). CloudRank: A cloud service ranking method based on both user feedback and service testing. In X. Yang & L. Liu (Eds.), *Principles, methodologies, and service-oriented approaches for cloud computing* (pp. 230–258). Hershey, PA: IGI Global. doi:10.4018/978-1-4666-2854-0.ch010

Liang, T., Lu, F., & Chiu, J. (2012). A hybrid resource reservation method for workflows in clouds. *International Journal of Grid and High Performance Computing*, *4*(4), 1–21. doi:10.4018/jghpc.2012100101

Lorenz, M., Rath-Wiggins, L., Runde, W., Messina, A., Sunna, P., Dimino, G., & Borgotallo, R. et al. (2013). Media convergence and cloud technologies: Smart storage, better workflows. In D. Kyriazis, A. Voulodimos, S. Gogouvitis, & T. Varvarigou (Eds.), *Data intensive storage services for cloud environments* (pp. 132–144). Hershey, PA: IGI Global. doi:10.4018/978-1-4666-3934-8.ch009

M., S. G., & G., S. K. (2012). An enterprise mashup integration service framework for clouds. *International Journal of Cloud Applications and Computing*, *2*(2), 31-40. doi:10.4018/ijcac.2012040103

Maharana, S. K., Mali, P. B., Prabhakar, G. J. S., & Kumar, V. (2011). Cloud computing applied for numerical study of thermal characteristics of SIP. *International Journal of Cloud Applications and Computing*, *1*(3), 12–21. doi:10.4018/ijcac.2011070102

Maharana, S. K., Mali, P. B., Prabhakar, G. J. S., & Kumar, V. (2013). Cloud computing applied for numerical study of thermal characteristics of SIP. In S. Aljawarneh (Ed.), *Cloud computing advancements in design, implementation, and technologies* (pp. 166–175). Hershey, PA: IGI Global. doi:10.4018/978-1-4666-1879-4.ch012

Maharana, S. K., P, G. P., & Bhati, A. (2012). A study of cloud computing for retinal image processing through MATLAB. *International Journal of Cloud Applications and Computing*, *2*(2), 59–69. doi:10.4018/ijcac.2012040106

Maharana, S. K., Prabhakar, P. G., & Bhati, A. (2013). A study of cloud computing for retinal image processing through MATLAB. In *Image processing: Concepts, methodologies, tools, and applications* (pp. 101–111). Hershey, PA: IGI Global. doi:10.4018/978-1-4666-3994-2.ch006

Mahesh, S., Landry, B. J., Sridhar, T., & Walsh, K. R. (2011). A decision table for the cloud computing decision in small business. *Information Resources Management Journal*, *24*(3), 9–25. doi:10.4018/irmj.2011070102

Mahesh, S., Landry, B. J., Sridhar, T., & Walsh, K. R. (2013). A decision table for the cloud computing decision in small business. In M. Khosrow-Pour (Ed.), *Managing information resources and technology: Emerging Applications and theories* (pp. 159–176). Hershey, PA: IGI Global. doi:10.4018/978-1-4666-3616-3.ch012

Marquezan, C. C., Metzger, A., Pohl, K., Engen, V., Boniface, M., Phillips, S. C., & Zlatev, Z. (2013). Adaptive future internet applications: Opportunities and challenges for adaptive web services technology. In G. Ortiz & J. Cubo (Eds.), *Adaptive web services for modular and reusable software development: Tactics and solutions* (pp. 333–353). Hershey, PA: IGI Global. doi:10.4018/978-1-4666-2089-6.ch014

Marshall, P. J. (2012). Cloud computing: Next generation education. In L. Chao (Ed.), *Cloud computing for teaching and learning: Strategies for design and implementation* (pp. 180–185). Hershey, PA: IGI Global. doi:10.4018/978-1-4666-0957-0.ch012

Martinez-Ortiz, A. (2012). Open cloud technologies. In L. Vaquero, J. Cáceres, & J. Hierro (Eds.), *Open source cloud computing systems: Practices and paradigms* (pp. 1–17). Hershey, PA: IGI Global. doi:10.4018/978-1-4666-0098-0.ch001

Massonet, P., Michot, A., Naqvi, S., Villari, M., & Latanicki, J. (2013). Securing the external interfaces of a federated infrastructure cloud. In *IT policy and ethics: Concepts, methodologies, tools, and applications* (pp. 1876–1903). Hershey, PA: IGI Global. doi:10.4018/978-1-4666-2919-6.ch082

Mavrogeorgi, N., Gogouvitis, S. V., Voulodimos, A., & Alexandrou, V. (2013). SLA management in storage clouds. In D. Kyriazis, A. Voulodimos, S. Gogouvitis, & T. Varvarigou (Eds.), *Data intensive storage services for cloud environments* (pp. 72–93). Hershey, PA: IGI Global. doi:10.4018/978-1-4666-3934-8.ch006

Mehta, H. K. (2013). Cloud selection for e-business a parameter based solution. In K. Tarnay, S. Imre, & L. Xu (Eds.), *Research and development in e-business through service-oriented solutions* (pp. 199–207). Hershey, PA: IGI Global. doi:10.4018/978-1-4666-4181-5.ch009

Mehta, H. K., & Gupta, E. (2013). Economy based resource allocation in IaaS cloud. *International Journal of Cloud Applications and Computing*, *3*(2), 1–11. doi:10.4018/ijcac.2013040101

Miah, S. J. (2012). Cloud-based intelligent DSS design for emergency professionals. In S. Ali, N. Abbadeni, & M. Batouche (Eds.), *Multidisciplinary computational intelligence techniques: Applications in business, engineering, and medicine* (pp. 47–60). Hershey, PA: IGI Global. doi:10.4018/978-1-4666-1830-5.ch004

Miah, S. J. (2013). Cloud-based intelligent DSS design for emergency professionals. In *Data mining: Concepts, methodologies, tools, and applications* (pp. 991–1003). Hershey, PA: IGI Global. doi:10.4018/978-1-4666-2455-9.ch050

Mikkilineni, R. (2012). Architectural resiliency in distributed computing. *International Journal of Grid and High Performance Computing*, *4*(4), 37–51. doi:10.4018/jghpc.2012100103

Millham, R. (2012). Software asset re-use: Migration of data-intensive legacy system to the cloud computing paradigm. In H. Yang & X. Liu (Eds.), *Software reuse in the emerging cloud computing era* (pp. 1–27). Hershey, PA: IGI Global. doi:10.4018/978-1-4666-0897-9.ch001

Mircea, M. (2011). Building the agile enterprise with service-oriented architecture, business process management and decision management. *International Journal of E-Entrepreneurship and Innovation*, *2*(4), 32–48. doi:10.4018/jeei.2011100103

Modares, H., Lloret, J., Moravejosharieh, A., & Salleh, R. (2014). Security in mobile cloud computing. In J. Rodrigues, K. Lin, & J. Lloret (Eds.), *Mobile networks and cloud computing convergence for progressive services and applications* (pp. 79–91). Hershey, PA: IGI Global. doi:10.4018/978-1-4666-4781-7.ch005

Moedjiono, S., & Mas'at, A. (2012). Cloud computing implementation strategy for information dissemination on meteorology, climatology, air quality, and geophysics (MKKuG). *Journal of Information Technology Research*, *5*(3), 71–84. doi:10.4018/jitr.2012070104

Moiny, J. (2012). Cloud based social network sites: Under whose control? In A. Dudley, J. Braman, & G. Vincenti (Eds.), *Investigating cyber law and cyber ethics: Issues, impacts and practices* (pp. 147–219). Hershey, PA: IGI Global. doi:10.4018/978-1-61350-132-0.ch009

Moreno, I. S., & Xu, J. (2011). Energy-efficiency in cloud computing environments: Towards energy savings without performance degradation. *International Journal of Cloud Applications and Computing*, *1*(1), 17–33. doi:10.4018/ijcac.2011010102

Moreno, I. S., & Xu, J. (2013). Energy-efficiency in cloud computing environments: Towards energy savings without performance degradation. In S. Aljawarneh (Ed.), *Cloud computing advancements in design, implementation, and technologies* (pp. 18–36). Hershey, PA: IGI Global. doi:10.4018/978-1-4666-1879-4.ch002

Muñoz, A., Maña, A., & González, J. (2013). Dynamic security properties monitoring architecture for cloud computing. In D. Rosado, D. Mellado, E. Fernandez-Medina, & M. Piattini (Eds.), *Security engineering for cloud computing: Approaches and tools* (pp. 1–18). Hershey, PA: IGI Global. doi:10.4018/978-1-4666-2125-1.ch001

Mvelase, P., Dlodlo, N., Williams, Q., & Adigun, M. O. (2011). Custom-made cloud enterprise architecture for small medium and micro enterprises. *International Journal of Cloud Applications and Computing*, *1*(3), 52–63. doi:10.4018/ijcac.2011070105

Mvelase, P., Dlodlo, N., Williams, Q., & Adigun, M. O. (2012). Custom-made cloud enterprise architecture for small medium and micro enterprises. In *Grid and cloud computing: Concepts, methodologies, tools and applications* (pp. 589–601). Hershey, PA: IGI Global. doi:10.4018/978-1-4666-0879-5.ch303

Mvelase, P., Dlodlo, N., Williams, Q., & Adigun, M. O. (2013). Custom-made cloud enterprise architecture for small medium and micro enterprises. In S. Aljawarneh (Ed.), *Cloud computing advancements in design, implementation, and technologies* (pp. 205–217). Hershey, PA: IGI Global. doi:10.4018/978-1-4666-1879-4.ch015

Naeem, M. A., Dobbie, G., & Weber, G. (2014). Big data management in the context of real-time data warehousing. In W. Hu & N. Kaabouch (Eds.), *Big data management, technologies, and applications* (pp. 150–176). Hershey, PA: IGI Global. doi:10.4018/978-1-4666-4699-5.ch007

Ofosu, W. K., & Saliah-Hassane, H. (2013). Cloud computing in the education environment for developing nations. *International Journal of Interdisciplinary Telecommunications and Networking*, *5*(3), 54–62. doi:10.4018/jitn.2013070106

Oliveros, E., Cucinotta, T., Phillips, S. C., Yang, X., Middleton, S., & Voith, T. (2012). Monitoring and metering in the cloud. In D. Kyriazis, T. Varvarigou, & K. Konstanteli (Eds.), *Achieving real-time in distributed computing: From grids to clouds* (pp. 94–114). Hershey, PA: IGI Global. doi:10.4018/978-1-60960-827-9.ch006

Orton, I., Alva, A., & Endicott-Popovsky, B. (2013). Legal process and requirements for cloud forensic investigations. In K. Ruan (Ed.), *Cybercrime and cloud forensics: Applications for investigation processes* (pp. 186–229). Hershey, PA: IGI Global. doi:10.4018/978-1-4666-2662-1.ch008

Pakhira, A., & Andras, P. (2013). Leveraging the cloud for large-scale software testing – A case study: Google Chrome on Amazon. In S. Tilley & T. Parveen (Eds.), *Software testing in the cloud: Perspectives on an emerging discipline* (pp. 252–279). Hershey, PA: IGI Global. doi:10.4018/978-1-4666-2536-5.ch012

Pal, K., & Karakostas, B. (2013). The use of cloud computing in shipping logistics. In D. Graham, I. Manikas, & D. Folinas (Eds.), *E-logistics and e-supply chain management: Applications for evolving business* (pp. 104–124). Hershey, PA: IGI Global. doi:10.4018/978-1-4666-3914-0.ch006

Pal, S. (2013). Cloud computing: Security concerns and issues. In A. Bento & A. Aggarwal (Eds.), *Cloud computing service and deployment models: Layers and management* (pp. 191–207). Hershey, PA: IGI Global. doi:10.4018/978-1-4666-2187-9.ch010

Pal, S. (2013). Storage security and technical challenges of cloud computing. In D. Kyriazis, A. Voulodimos, S. Gogouvitis, & T. Varvarigou (Eds.), *Data intensive storage services for cloud environments* (pp. 225–240). Hershey, PA: IGI Global. doi:10.4018/978-1-4666-3934-8.ch014

Palanivel, K., & Kuppuswami, S. (2014). A cloud-oriented reference architecture to digital library systems. In S. Dhamdhere (Ed.), *Cloud computing and virtualization technologies in libraries* (pp. 230–254). Hershey, PA: IGI Global. doi:10.4018/978-1-4666-4631-5.ch014

Paletta, M. (2012). Intelligent clouds: By means of using multi-agent systems environments. In L. Chao (Ed.), *Cloud computing for teaching and learning: Strategies for design and implementation* (pp. 254–279). Hershey, PA: IGI Global. doi:10.4018/978-1-4666-0957-0.ch017

Pallot, M., Le Marc, C., Richir, S., Schmidt, C., & Mathieu, J. (2012). Innovation gaming: An immersive experience environment enabling co-creation. In M. Cruz-Cunha (Ed.), *Handbook of research on serious games as educational, business and research tools* (pp. 1–24). Hershey, PA: IGI Global. doi:10.4018/978-1-4666-0149-9.ch001

Pankowska, M. (2011). Information technology resources virtualization for sustainable development. *International Journal of Applied Logistics*, 2(2), 35–48. doi:10.4018/jal.2011040103

Pankowska, M. (2013). Information technology resources virtualization for sustainable development. In Z. Luo (Ed.), *Technological solutions for modern logistics and supply chain management* (pp. 248–262). Hershey, PA: IGI Global. doi:10.4018/978-1-4666-2773-4.ch016

Parappallil, J. J., Zarvic, N., & Thomas, O. (2012). A context and content reflection on business-IT alignment research. *International Journal of IT/Business Alignment and Governance*, 3(2), 21–37. doi:10.4018/jitbag.2012070102

Parashar, V., Vishwakarma, M. L., & Parashar, R. (2014). A new framework for building academic library through cloud computing. In S. Dhamdhere (Ed.), *Cloud computing and virtualization technologies in libraries* (pp. 107–123). Hershey, PA: IGI Global. doi:10.4018/978-1-4666-4631-5.ch007

Pendyala, V. S., & Holliday, J. (2012). Cloud as a computer. In X. Liu & Y. Li (Eds.), *Advanced design approaches to emerging software systems: Principles, methodologies and tools* (pp. 241–249). Hershey, PA: IGI Global. doi:10.4018/978-1-60960-735-7.ch011

Petruch, K., Tamm, G., & Stantchev, V. (2012). Deriving in-depth knowledge from IT-performance data simulations. *International Journal of Knowledge Society Research*, 3(2), 13–29. doi:10.4018/jksr.2012040102

Philipson, G. (2011). A framework for green computing. *International Journal of Green Computing*, *2*(1), 12–26. doi:10.4018/jgc.2011010102

Philipson, G. (2013). A framework for green computing. In K. Ganesh & S. Anbuudayasankar (Eds.), *International and interdisciplinary studies in green computing* (pp. 12–26). Hershey, PA: IGI Global. doi:10.4018/978-1-4666-2646-1.ch002

Phythian, M. (2013). The 'cloud' of unknowing – What a government cloud may and may not offer: A practitioner perspective. *International Journal of Technoethics*, *4*(1), 1–10. doi:10.4018/jte.2013010101

Pym, D., & Sadler, M. (2012). Information stewardship in cloud computing. In *Grid and cloud computing: Concepts, methodologies, tools and applications* (pp. 185–202). Hershey, PA: IGI Global. doi:10.4018/978-1-4666-0879-5.ch109

Pym, D., & Sadler, M. (2012). Information stewardship in cloud computing. In S. Galup (Ed.), *Technological applications and advancements in service science, management, and engineering* (pp. 52–69). Hershey, PA: IGI Global. doi:10.4018/978-1-4666-1583-0.ch004

Qiu, J., Ekanayake, J., Gunarathne, T., Choi, J. Y., Bae, S., & Ruan, Y. … Tang, H. (2013). Data intensive computing for bioinformatics. In Bioinformatics: Concepts, methodologies, tools, and applications (pp. 287-321). Hershey, PA: IGI Global. doi:10.4018/978-1-4666-3604-0.ch016

Rabaey, M. (2012). A public economics approach to enabling enterprise architecture with the government cloud in Belgium. In P. Saha (Ed.), *Enterprise architecture for connected e-government: Practices and innovations* (pp. 467–493). Hershey, PA: IGI Global. doi:10.4018/978-1-4666-1824-4.ch020

Rabaey, M. (2013). A complex adaptive system thinking approach of government e-procurement in a cloud computing environment. In P. Ordóñez de Pablos, J. Lovelle, J. Gayo, & R. Tennyson (Eds.), *E-procurement management for successful electronic government systems* (pp. 193–219). Hershey, PA: IGI Global. doi:10.4018/978-1-4666-2119-0.ch013

Rabaey, M. (2013). Holistic investment framework for cloud computing: A management-philosophical approach based on complex adaptive systems. In A. Bento & A. Aggarwal (Eds.), *Cloud computing service and deployment models: Layers and management* (pp. 94–122). Hershey, PA: IGI Global. doi:10.4018/978-1-4666-2187-9.ch005

Rak, M., Ficco, M., Luna, J., Ghani, H., Suri, N., Panica, S., & Petcu, D. (2012). Security issues in cloud federations. In M. Villari, I. Brandic, & F. Tusa (Eds.), *Achieving federated and self-manageable cloud infrastructures: Theory and practice* (pp. 176–194). Hershey, PA: IGI Global. doi:10.4018/978-1-4666-1631-8.ch010

Ramanathan, R. (2013). Extending service-driven architectural approaches to the cloud. In R. Ramanathan & K. Raja (Eds.), *Service-driven approaches to architecture and enterprise integration* (pp. 334–359). Hershey, PA: IGI Global. doi:10.4018/978-1-4666-4193-8.ch013

Ramírez, M., Gutiérrez, A., Monguet, J. M., & Muñoz, C. (2012). An internet cost model, assignment of costs based on actual network use. *International Journal of Web Portals*, *4*(4), 19–34. doi:10.4018/jwp.2012100102

Rashid, A., Wang, W. Y., & Tan, F. B. (2013). Value co-creation in cloud services. In A. Lin, J. Foster, & P. Scifleet (Eds.), *Consumer information systems and relationship management: Design, implementation, and use* (pp. 74–91). Hershey, PA: IGI Global. doi:10.4018/978-1-4666-4082-5.ch005

Ratten, V. (2012). Cloud computing services: Theoretical foundations of ethical and entrepreneurial adoption behaviour. *International Journal of Cloud Applications and Computing*, 2(2), 48–58. doi:10.4018/ijcac.2012040105

Ratten, V. (2013). Exploring behaviors and perceptions affecting the adoption of cloud computing. *International Journal of Innovation in the Digital Economy*, 4(3), 51–68. doi:10.4018/jide.2013070104

Ravi, V. (2012). Cloud computing paradigm for indian education sector. *International Journal of Cloud Applications and Computing*, 2(2), 41–47. doi:10.4018/ijcac.2012040104

Rawat, A., Kapoor, P., & Sushil, R. (2014). Application of cloud computing in library information service sector. In S. Dhamdhere (Ed.), *Cloud computing and virtualization technologies in libraries* (pp. 77–89). Hershey, PA: IGI Global. doi:10.4018/978-1-4666-4631-5.ch005

Reich, C., Hübner, S., & Kuijs, H. (2012). Cloud computing for on-demand virtual desktops and labs. In L. Chao (Ed.), *Cloud computing for teaching and learning: strategies for design and implementation* (pp. 111–125). Hershey, PA: IGI Global. doi:10.4018/978-1-4666-0957-0.ch008

Rice, R. W. (2013). Testing in the cloud: Balancing the value and risks of cloud computing. In S. Tilley & T. Parveen (Eds.), *Software testing in the cloud: Perspectives on an emerging discipline* (pp. 404–416). Hershey, PA: IGI Global. doi:10.4018/978-1-4666-2536-5.ch019

Ruan, K. (2013). Designing a forensic-enabling cloud ecosystem. In K. Ruan (Ed.), *Cybercrime and cloud forensics: Applications for investigation processes* (pp. 331–344). Hershey, PA: IGI Global. doi:10.4018/978-1-4666-2662-1.ch014

Sabetzadeh, F., & Tsui, E. (2011). Delivering knowledge services in the cloud. *International Journal of Knowledge and Systems Science*, 2(4), 14–20. doi:10.4018/jkss.2011100102

Sabetzadeh, F., & Tsui, E. (2013). Delivering knowledge services in the cloud. In G. Yang (Ed.), *Multidisciplinary studies in knowledge and systems science* (pp. 247–254). Hershey, PA: IGI Global. doi:10.4018/978-1-4666-3998-0.ch017

Saedi, A., & Iahad, N. A. (2013). Future research on cloud computing adoption by small and medium-sized enterprises: A critical analysis of relevant theories. *International Journal of Actor-Network Theory and Technological Innovation*, 5(2), 1–16. doi:10.4018/jantti.2013040101

Saha, D., & Sridhar, V. (2011). Emerging areas of research in business data communications. *International Journal of Business Data Communications and Networking*, 7(4), 52–59. doi:10.4018/IJBDCN.2011100104

Saha, D., & Sridhar, V. (2013). Platform on platform (PoP) model for meta-networking: A new paradigm for networks of the future. *International Journal of Business Data Communications and Networking*, 9(1), 1–10. doi:10.4018/jbdcn.2013010101

Sahlin, J. P. (2013). Cloud computing: Past, present, and future. In X. Yang & L. Liu (Eds.), *Principles, methodologies, and service-oriented approaches for cloud computing* (pp. 19–50). Hershey, PA: IGI Global. doi:10.4018/978-1-4666-2854-0.ch002

Salama, M., & Shawish, A. (2012). Libraries: From the classical to cloud-based era. *International Journal of Digital Library Systems*, 3(3), 14–32. doi:10.4018/jdls.2012070102

Sánchez, C. M., Molina, D., Vozmediano, R. M., Montero, R. S., & Llorente, I. M. (2012). On the use of the hybrid cloud computing paradigm. In M. Villari, I. Brandic, & F. Tusa (Eds.), *Achieving federated and self-manageable cloud infrastructures: Theory and practice* (pp. 196–218). Hershey, PA: IGI Global. doi:10.4018/978-1-4666-1631-8.ch011

Sasikala, P. (2011). Architectural strategies for green cloud computing: Environments, infrastructure and resources. *International Journal of Cloud Applications and Computing*, 1(4), 1–24. doi:10.4018/ijcac.2011100101

Sasikala, P. (2011). Cloud computing in higher education: Opportunities and issues. *International Journal of Cloud Applications and Computing*, 1(2), 1–13. doi:10.4018/ijcac.2011040101

Sasikala, P. (2011). Cloud computing towards technological convergence. *International Journal of Cloud Applications and Computing*, 1(4), 44–59. doi:10.4018/ijcac.2011100104

Sasikala, P. (2012). Cloud computing and e-governance: Advances, opportunities and challenges. *International Journal of Cloud Applications and Computing*, 2(4), 32–52. doi:10.4018/ijcac.2012100103

Sasikala, P. (2012). Cloud computing in higher education: Opportunities and issues. In *Grid and cloud computing: Concepts, methodologies, tools and applications* (pp. 1672–1685). Hershey, PA: IGI Global. doi:10.4018/978-1-4666-0879-5.ch709

Sasikala, P. (2012). Cloud computing towards technological convergence. In *Grid and cloud computing: Concepts, methodologies, tools and applications* (pp. 1576–1592). Hershey, PA: IGI Global. doi:10.4018/978-1-4666-0879-5.ch703

Sasikala, P. (2013). Architectural strategies for green cloud computing: Environments, infrastructure and resources. In S. Aljawarneh (Ed.), *Cloud computing advancements in design, implementation, and technologies* (pp. 218–242). Hershey, PA: IGI Global. doi:10.4018/978-1-4666-1879-4.ch016

Sasikala, P. (2013). Cloud computing in higher education: Opportunities and issues. In S. Aljawarneh (Ed.), *Cloud computing advancements in design, implementation, and technologies* (pp. 83–96). Hershey, PA: IGI Global. doi:10.4018/978-1-4666-1879-4.ch006

Sasikala, P. (2013). Cloud computing towards technological convergence. In S. Aljawarneh (Ed.), *Cloud computing advancements in design, implementation, and technologies* (pp. 263–279). Hershey, PA: IGI Global. doi:10.4018/978-1-4666-1879-4.ch019

Sasikala, P. (2013). New media cloud computing: Opportunities and challenges. *International Journal of Cloud Applications and Computing*, 3(2), 61–72. doi:10.4018/ijcac.2013040106

Schrödl, H., & Wind, S. (2013). Requirements engineering for cloud application development. In A. Bento & A. Aggarwal (Eds.), *Cloud computing service and deployment models: Layers and management* (pp. 137–150). Hershey, PA: IGI Global. doi:10.4018/978-1-4666-2187-9.ch007

Sclater, N. (2012). Legal and contractual issues of cloud computing for educational institutions. In L. Chao (Ed.), *Cloud computing for teaching and learning: Strategies for design and implementation* (pp. 186–199). Hershey, PA: IGI Global. doi:10.4018/978-1-4666-0957-0.ch013

Sen, J. (2014). Security and privacy issues in cloud computing. In A. Ruiz-Martinez, R. Marin-Lopez, & F. Pereniguez-Garcia (Eds.), *Architectures and protocols for secure information technology infrastructures* (pp. 1–45). Hershey, PA: IGI Global. doi:10.4018/978-1-4666-4514-1.ch001

Shah, B. (2013). Cloud environment controls assessment framework. In *IT policy and ethics: Concepts, methodologies, tools, and applications* (pp. 1822–1847). Hershey, PA: IGI Global. doi:10.4018/978-1-4666-2919-6.ch080

Shah, B. (2013). Cloud environment controls assessment framework. In S. Tilley & T. Parveen (Eds.), *Software testing in the cloud: Perspectives on an emerging discipline* (pp. 28–53). Hershey, PA: IGI Global. doi:10.4018/978-1-4666-2536-5.ch002

Shang, X., Zhang, R., & Chen, Y. (2012). Internet of things (IoT) service architecture and its application in e-commerce. *Journal of Electronic Commerce in Organizations*, *10*(3), 44–55. doi:10.4018/jeco.2012070104

Shankararaman, V., & Kit, L. E. (2013). Integrating the cloud scenarios and solutions. In A. Bento & A. Aggarwal (Eds.), *Cloud computing service and deployment models: Layers and management* (pp. 173–189). Hershey, PA: IGI Global. doi:10.4018/978-1-4666-2187-9.ch009

Sharma, A., & Maurer, F. (2013). A roadmap for software engineering for the cloud: Results of a systematic review. In X. Wang, N. Ali, I. Ramos, & R. Vidgen (Eds.), *Agile and lean service-oriented development: Foundations, theory, and practice* (pp. 48–63). Hershey, PA: IGI Global. doi:10.4018/978-1-4666-2503-7.ch003

Sharma, A., & Maurer, F. (2014). A roadmap for software engineering for the cloud: Results of a systematic review. In *Software design and development: Concepts, methodologies, tools, and applications* (pp. 1–16). Hershey, PA: IGI Global. doi:10.4018/978-1-4666-4301-7.ch001

Sharma, S. C., & Bagoria, H. (2014). Libraries and cloud computing models: A changing paradigm. In S. Dhamdhere (Ed.), *Cloud computing and virtualization technologies in libraries* (pp. 124–149). Hershey, PA: IGI Global. doi:10.4018/978-1-4666-4631-5.ch008

Shawish, A., & Salama, M. (2013). Cloud computing in academia, governments, and industry. In X. Yang & L. Liu (Eds.), *Principles, methodologies, and service-oriented approaches for cloud computing* (pp. 71–114). Hershey, PA: IGI Global. doi:10.4018/978-1-4666-2854-0.ch004

Shebanow, A., Perez, R., & Howard, C. (2012). The effect of firewall testing types on cloud security policies. *International Journal of Strategic Information Technology and Applications*, *3*(3), 60–68. doi:10.4018/jsita.2012070105

Sheikhalishahi, M., Devare, M., Grandinetti, L., & Incutti, M. C. (2012). A complementary approach to grid and cloud distributed computing paradigms. In *Grid and cloud computing: Concepts, methodologies, tools and applications* (pp. 1929–1942). Hershey, PA: IGI Global. doi:10.4018/978-1-4666-0879-5.ch811

Sheikhalishahi, M., Devare, M., Grandinetti, L., & Incutti, M. C. (2012). A complementary approach to grid and cloud distributed computing paradigms. In N. Preve (Ed.), *Computational and data grids: Principles, applications and design* (pp. 31–44). Hershey, PA: IGI Global. doi:10.4018/978-1-61350-113-9.ch002

Shen, Y., Li, Y., Wu, L., Liu, S., & Wen, Q. (2014). Cloud computing overview. In Y. Shen, Y. Li, L. Wu, S. Liu, & Q. Wen (Eds.), *Enabling the new era of cloud computing: Data security, transfer, and management* (pp. 1–24). Hershey, PA: IGI Global. doi:10.4018/978-1-4666-4801-2.ch001

Shen, Y., Li, Y., Wu, L., Liu, S., & Wen, Q. (2014). Main components of cloud computing. In Y. Shen, Y. Li, L. Wu, S. Liu, & Q. Wen (Eds.), *Enabling the new era of cloud computing: Data security, transfer, and management* (pp. 25–50). Hershey, PA: IGI Global. doi:10.4018/978-1-4666-4801-2.ch002

Shen, Y., Yang, J., & Keskin, T. (2014). Impact of cultural differences on the cloud computing ecosystems in the USA and China. In Y. Shen, Y. Li, L. Wu, S. Liu, & Q. Wen (Eds.), *Enabling the new era of cloud computing: Data security, transfer, and management* (pp. 269–283). Hershey, PA: IGI Global. doi:10.4018/978-1-4666-4801-2.ch014

Shetty, S., & Rawat, D. B. (2013). Cloud computing based cognitive radio networking. In N. Meghanathan & Y. Reddy (Eds.), *Cognitive radio technology applications for wireless and mobile ad hoc networks* (pp. 153–164). Hershey, PA: IGI Global. doi:10.4018/978-1-4666-4221-8.ch008

Shi, Z., & Beard, C. (2014). QoS in the mobile cloud computing environment. In J. Rodrigues, K. Lin, & J. Lloret (Eds.), *Mobile networks and cloud computing convergence for progressive services and applications* (pp. 200–217). Hershey, PA: IGI Global. doi:10.4018/978-1-4666-4781-7.ch011

Shuster, L. (2013). Enterprise integration: Challenges and solution architecture. In R. Ramanathan & K. Raja (Eds.), *Service-driven approaches to architecture and enterprise integration* (pp. 43–66). Hershey, PA: IGI Global. doi:10.4018/978-1-4666-4193-8.ch002

Siahos, Y., Papanagiotou, I., Georgopoulos, A., Tsamis, F., & Papaioannou, I. (2012). An architecture paradigm for providing cloud services in school labs based on open source software to enhance ICT in education. *International Journal of Cyber Ethics in Education*, 2(1), 44–57. doi:10.4018/ijcee.2012010105

Simon, E., & Estublier, J. (2013). Model driven integration of heterogeneous software artifacts in service oriented computing. In A. Ionita, M. Litoiu, & G. Lewis (Eds.), *Migrating legacy applications: Challenges in service oriented architecture and cloud computing environments* (pp. 332–360). Hershey, PA: IGI Global. doi:10.4018/978-1-4666-2488-7.ch014

Singh, J., & Kumar, V. (2013). Compliance and regulatory standards for cloud computing. In R. Khurana & R. Aggarwal (Eds.), *Interdisciplinary perspectives on business convergence, computing, and legality* (pp. 54–64). Hershey, PA: IGI Global. doi:10.4018/978-1-4666-4209-6.ch006

Singh, V. V. (2012). Software development using service syndication based on API handshake approach between cloud-based and SOA-based reusable services. In H. Yang & X. Liu (Eds.), *Software reuse in the emerging cloud computing era* (pp. 136–157). Hershey, PA: IGI Global. doi:10.4018/978-1-4666-0897-9.ch006

Smeitink, M., & Spruit, M. (2013). Maturity for sustainability in IT: Introducing the MITS. *International Journal of Information Technologies and Systems Approach*, 6(1), 39–56. doi:10.4018/jitsa.2013010103

Smith, P. A., & Cockburn, T. (2013). Socio-digital technologies. In *Dynamic leadership models for global business: Enhancing digitally connected environments* (pp. 142–168). Hershey, PA: IGI Global. doi:10.4018/978-1-4666-2836-6.ch006

Sneed, H. M. (2013). Testing web services in the cloud. In S. Tilley & T. Parveen (Eds.), *Software testing in the cloud: Perspectives on an emerging discipline* (pp. 136–173). Hershey, PA: IGI Global. doi:10.4018/978-1-4666-2536-5.ch007

Solomon, B., Ionescu, D., Gadea, C., & Litoiu, M. (2013). Geographically distributed cloud-based collaborative application. In A. Ionita, M. Litoiu, & G. Lewis (Eds.), *Migrating legacy applications: Challenges in service oriented architecture and cloud computing environments* (pp. 248–274). Hershey, PA: IGI Global. doi:10.4018/978-1-4666-2488-7.ch011

Song, W., & Xiao, Z. (2013). An infrastructure-as-a-service cloud: On-demand resource provisioning. In X. Yang & L. Liu (Eds.), *Principles, methodologies, and service-oriented approaches for cloud computing* (pp. 302–324). Hershey, PA: IGI Global. doi:10.4018/978-1-4666-2854-0.ch013

Sood, S. K. (2013). A value based dynamic resource provisioning model in cloud. *International Journal of Cloud Applications and Computing*, 3(1), 1–12. doi:10.4018/ijcac.2013010101

Sotiriadis, S., Bessis, N., & Antonopoulos, N. (2012). Exploring inter-cloud load balancing by utilizing historical service submission records. *International Journal of Distributed Systems and Technologies*, 3(3), 72–81. doi:10.4018/jdst.2012070106

Soyata, T., Ba, H., Heinzelman, W., Kwon, M., & Shi, J. (2014). Accelerating mobile-cloud computing: A survey. In H. Mouftah & B. Kantarci (Eds.), *Communication infrastructures for cloud computing* (pp. 175–197). Hershey, PA: IGI Global. doi:10.4018/978-1-4666-4522-6.ch008

Spyridopoulos, T., & Katos, V. (2011). Requirements for a forensically ready cloud storage service. *International Journal of Digital Crime and Forensics*, 3(3), 19–36. doi:10.4018/jdcf.2011070102

Spyridopoulos, T., & Katos, V. (2013). Data recovery strategies for cloud environments. In K. Ruan (Ed.), *Cybercrime and cloud forensics: Applications for investigation processes* (pp. 251–265). Hershey, PA: IGI Global. doi:10.4018/978-1-4666-2662-1.ch010

Srinivasa, K. G., S, H. R. C., H, M. K. S., & Venkatesh, N. (2012). MeghaOS: A framework for scalable, interoperable cloud based operating system. *International Journal of Cloud Applications and Computing*, 2(1), 53–70. doi:10.4018/ijcac.2012010104

Stantchev, V., & Stantcheva, L. (2012). Extending traditional IT-governance knowledge towards SOA and cloud governance. *International Journal of Knowledge Society Research*, *3*(2), 30–43. doi:10.4018/jksr.2012040103

Stantchev, V., & Tamm, G. (2012). Reducing information asymmetry in cloud marketplaces. *International Journal of Human Capital and Information Technology Professionals*, *3*(4), 1–10. doi:10.4018/jhcitp.2012100101

Steinbuß, S., & Weißenberg, N. (2013). Service design and process design for the logistics mall cloud. In X. Yang & L. Liu (Eds.), *Principles, methodologies, and service-oriented approaches for cloud computing* (pp. 186–206). Hershey, PA: IGI Global. doi:10.4018/978-1-4666-2854-0.ch008

Stender, J., Berlin, M., & Reinefeld, A. (2013). XtreemFS: A file system for the cloud. In D. Kyriazis, A. Voulodimos, S. Gogouvitis, & T. Varvarigou (Eds.), *Data intensive storage services for cloud environments* (pp. 267–285). Hershey, PA: IGI Global. doi:10.4018/978-1-4666-3934-8.ch016

Sticklen, D. J., & Issa, T. (2011). An initial examination of free and proprietary software-selection in organizations. *International Journal of Web Portals*, *3*(4), 27–43. doi:10.4018/jwp.2011100103

Sun, Y., White, J., Gray, J., & Gokhale, A. (2012). Model-driven automated error recovery in cloud computing. In *Grid and cloud computing: Concepts, methodologies, tools and applications* (pp. 680–700). Hershey, PA: IGI Global. doi:10.4018/978-1-4666-0879-5.ch308

Sun, Z., Yang, Y., Zhou, Y., & Cruickshank, H. (2014). Agent-based resource management for mobile cloud. In J. Rodrigues, K. Lin, & J. Lloret (Eds.), *Mobile networks and cloud computing convergence for progressive services and applications* (pp. 118–134). Hershey, PA: IGI Global. doi:10.4018/978-1-4666-4781-7.ch007

Sutherland, S. (2013). Convergence of interoperability of cloud computing, service oriented architecture and enterprise architecture. *International Journal of E-Entrepreneurship and Innovation*, *4*(1), 43–51. doi:10.4018/jeei.2013010104

Takabi, H., & Joshi, J. B. (2013). Policy management in cloud: Challenges and approaches. In D. Rosado, D. Mellado, E. Fernandez-Medina, & M. Piattini (Eds.), *Security engineering for cloud computing: Approaches and tools* (pp. 191–211). Hershey, PA: IGI Global. doi:10.4018/978-1-4666-2125-1.ch010

Takabi, H., & Joshi, J. B. (2013). Policy management in cloud: Challenges and approaches. In *IT policy and ethics: Concepts, methodologies, tools, and applications* (pp. 814–834). Hershey, PA: IGI Global. doi:10.4018/978-1-4666-2919-6.ch037

Takabi, H., Joshi, J. B., & Ahn, G. (2013). Security and privacy in cloud computing: Towards a comprehensive framework. In X. Yang & L. Liu (Eds.), *Principles, methodologies, and service-oriented approaches for cloud computing* (pp. 164–184). Hershey, PA: IGI Global. doi:10.4018/978-1-4666-2854-0.ch007

Takabi, H., Zargar, S. T., & Joshi, J. B. (2014). Mobile cloud computing and its security and privacy challenges. In D. Rawat, B. Bista, & G. Yan (Eds.), *Security, privacy, trust, and resource management in mobile and wireless communications* (pp. 384–407). Hershey, PA: IGI Global. doi:10.4018/978-1-4666-4691-9.ch016

Teixeira, C., Pinto, J. S., Ferreira, F., Oliveira, A., Teixeira, A., & Pereira, C. (2013). Cloud computing enhanced service development architecture for the living usability lab. In R. Martinho, R. Rijo, M. Cruz-Cunha, & J. Varajão (Eds.), *Information systems and technologies for enhancing health and social care* (pp. 33–53). Hershey, PA: IGI Global. doi:10.4018/978-1-4666-3667-5.ch003

Thimm, H. (2012). Cloud-based collaborative decision making: Design considerations and architecture of the GRUPO-MOD system. *International Journal of Decision Support System Technology*, *4*(4), 39–59. doi:10.4018/jdsst.2012100103

Thomas, P. (2012). Harnessing the potential of cloud computing to transform higher education. In L. Chao (Ed.), *Cloud computing for teaching and learning: Strategies for design and implementation* (pp. 147–158). Hershey, PA: IGI Global. doi:10.4018/978-1-4666-0957-0.ch010

Toka, A., Aivazidou, E., Antoniou, A., & Arvanitopoulos-Darginis, K. (2013). Cloud computing in supply chain management: An overview. In D. Graham, I. Manikas, & D. Folinas (Eds.), *E-logistics and e-supply chain management: Applications for evolving business* (pp. 218–231). Hershey, PA: IGI Global. doi:10.4018/978-1-4666-3914-0.ch012

Torrealba, S. M., Morales, P. M., Campos, J. M., & Meza, S. M. (2013). A software tool to support risks analysis about what should or should not go to the cloud. In D. Rosado, D. Mellado, E. Fernandez-Medina, & M. Piattini (Eds.), *Security engineering for cloud computing: Approaches and tools* (pp. 72–96). Hershey, PA: IGI Global. doi:10.4018/978-1-4666-2125-1.ch005

Trivedi, M., & Suthar, V. (2013). Cloud computing: A feasible platform for ICT enabled health science libraries in India. *International Journal of User-Driven Healthcare*, *3*(2), 69–77. doi:10.4018/ijudh.2013040108

Truong, H., Pham, T., Thoai, N., & Dustdar, S. (2012). Cloud computing for education and research in developing countries. In L. Chao (Ed.), *Cloud computing for teaching and learning: Strategies for design and implementation* (pp. 64–80). Hershey, PA: IGI Global. doi:10.4018/978-1-4666-0957-0.ch005

Tsirmpas, C., Giokas, K., Iliopoulou, D., & Koutsouris, D. (2012). Magnetic resonance imaging and magnetic resonance spectroscopy cloud computing framework. *International Journal of Reliable and Quality E-Healthcare*, *1*(4), 1–12. doi:10.4018/ijrqeh.2012100101

Turner, H., White, J., Reed, J., Galindo, J., Porter, A., Marathe, M., & Gokhale, A. et al. (2013). Building a cloud-based mobile application testbed. In *IT policy and ethics: Concepts, methodologies, tools, and applications* (pp. 879–899). Hershey, PA: IGI Global. doi:10.4018/978-1-4666-2919-6.ch040

Turner, H., White, J., Reed, J., Galindo, J., Porter, A., Marathe, M., & Gokhale, A. et al. (2013). Building a cloud-based mobile application testbed. In S. Tilley & T. Parveen (Eds.), *Software testing in the cloud: Perspectives on an emerging discipline* (pp. 382–403). Hershey, PA: IGI Global. doi:10.4018/978-1-4666-2536-5.ch018

Tusa, F., Paone, M., & Villari, M. (2012). CLEVER: A cloud middleware beyond the federation. In M. Villari, I. Brandic, & F. Tusa (Eds.), *Achieving federated and self-manageable cloud infrastructures: Theory and practice* (pp. 219–241). Hershey, PA: IGI Global. doi:10.4018/978-1-4666-1631-8.ch012

Udoh, E. (2012). Technology acceptance model applied to the adoption of grid and cloud technology. *International Journal of Grid and High Performance Computing*, *4*(1), 1–20. doi:10.4018/jghpc.2012010101

Vannoy, S. A. (2011). A structured content analytic assessment of business services advertisements in the cloud-based web services marketplace. *International Journal of Dependable and Trustworthy Information Systems*, *2*(1), 18–49. doi:10.4018/jdtis.2011010102

Vaquero, L. M., Cáceres, J., & Morán, D. (2011). The challenge of service level scalability for the cloud. *International Journal of Cloud Applications and Computing*, *1*(1), 34–44. doi:10.4018/ijcac.2011010103

Vaquero, L. M., Cáceres, J., & Morán, D. (2013). The challenge of service level scalability for the cloud. In S. Aljawarneh (Ed.), *Cloud computing advancements in design, implementation, and technologies* (pp. 37–48). Hershey, PA: IGI Global. doi:10.4018/978-1-4666-1879-4.ch003

Venkatraman, R., Venkatraman, S., & Asaithambi, S. P. (2013). A practical cloud services implementation framework for e-businesses. In K. Tarnay, S. Imre, & L. Xu (Eds.), *Research and development in e-business through service-oriented solutions* (pp. 167–198). Hershey, PA: IGI Global. doi:10.4018/978-1-4666-4181-5.ch008

Venkatraman, S. (2013). Software engineering research gaps in the cloud. *Journal of Information Technology Research*, *6*(1), 1–19. doi:10.4018/jitr.2013010101

Vijaykumar, S., Rajkarthick, K. S., & Priya, J. (2012). Innovative business opportunities and smart business management techniques from green cloud TPS. *International Journal of Asian Business and Information Management*, *3*(4), 62–72. doi:10.4018/jabim.2012100107

Wang, C., Lam, K. T., & Ma, K. R. K. (2012). A computation migration approach to elasticity of cloud computing. In J. Abawajy, M. Pathan, M. Rahman, A. Pathan, & M. Deris (Eds.) Network and traffic engineering in emerging distributed computing applications (pp. 145-178). Hershey, PA: IGI Global. doi:10.4018/978-1-4666-1888-6.ch007

Wang, D., & Wu, J. (2014). Carrier-grade distributed cloud computing: Demands, challenges, designs, and future perspectives. In H. Mouftah & B. Kantarci (Eds.), *Communication infrastructures for cloud computing* (pp. 264–281). Hershey, PA: IGI Global. doi:10.4018/978-1-4666-4522-6.ch012

Wang, H., & Philips, D. (2012). Implement virtual programming lab with cloud computing for web-based distance education. In L. Chao (Ed.), *Cloud computing for teaching and learning: Strategies for design and implementation* (pp. 95–110). Hershey, PA: IGI Global. doi:10.4018/978-1-4666-0957-0.ch007

Warneke, D. (2013). Ad-hoc parallel data processing on pay-as-you-go clouds with nephele. In A. Loo (Ed.), *Distributed computing innovations for business, engineering, and science* (pp. 191–218). Hershey, PA: IGI Global. doi:10.4018/978-1-4666-2533-4.ch010

Wei, Y., & Blake, M. B. (2013). Adaptive web services monitoring in cloud environments. *International Journal of Web Portals*, *5*(1), 15–27. doi:10.4018/jwp.2013010102

White, S. C., Sedigh, S., & Hurson, A. R. (2013). Security concepts for cloud computing. In X. Yang & L. Liu (Eds.), *Principles, methodologies, and service-oriented approaches for cloud computing* (pp. 116–142). Hershey, PA: IGI Global. doi:10.4018/978-1-4666-2854-0.ch005

Williams, A. J. (2013). The role of emerging technologies in developing and sustaining diverse suppliers in competitive markets. In *Enterprise resource planning: Concepts, methodologies, tools, and applications* (pp. 1550–1560). Hershey, PA: IGI Global. doi:10.4018/978-1-4666-4153-2.ch082

Williams, A. J. (2013). The role of emerging technologies in developing and sustaining diverse suppliers in competitive markets. In J. Lewis, A. Green, & D. Surry (Eds.), *Technology as a tool for diversity leadership: Implementation and future implications* (pp. 95–105). Hershey, PA: IGI Global. doi:10.4018/978-1-4666-2668-3.ch007

Wilson, L., Goh, T. T., & Wang, W. Y. (2012). Big data management challenges in a meteorological organisation. *International Journal of E-Adoption*, *4*(2), 1–14. doi:10.4018/jea.2012040101

Wu, R., Ahn, G., & Hu, H. (2012). Towards HIPAA-compliant healthcare systems in cloud computing. *International Journal of Computational Models and Algorithms in Medicine*, *3*(2), 1–22. doi:10.4018/jcmam.2012040101

Xiao, J., Wang, M., Wang, L., & Zhu, X. (2013). Design and implementation of C-iLearning: A cloud-based intelligent learning system. *International Journal of Distance Education Technologies*, *11*(3), 79–97. doi:10.4018/jdet.2013070106

Xing, R., Wang, Z., & Peterson, R. L. (2011). Redefining the information technology in the 21st century. *International Journal of Strategic Information Technology and Applications*, *2*(1), 1–10. doi:10.4018/jsita.2011010101

Xu, L., Huang, D., Tsai, W., & Atkinson, R. K. (2012). V-lab: A mobile, cloud-based virtual laboratory platform for hands-on networking courses. *International Journal of Cyber Behavior, Psychology and Learning*, *2*(3), 73–85. doi:10.4018/ijcbpl.2012070106

Xu, Y., & Mao, S. (2014). Mobile cloud media: State of the art and outlook. In J. Rodrigues, K. Lin, & J. Lloret (Eds.), *Mobile networks and cloud computing convergence for progressive services and applications* (pp. 18–38). Hershey, PA: IGI Global. doi:10.4018/978-1-4666-4781-7.ch002

Xu, Z., Yan, B., & Zou, Y. (2013). Beyond hadoop: Recent directions in data computing for internet services. In S. Aljawarneh (Ed.), *Cloud computing advancements in design, implementation, and technologies* (pp. 49–66). Hershey, PA: IGI Global. doi:10.4018/978-1-4666-1879-4.ch004

Yan, Z. (2014). Trust management in mobile cloud computing. In *Trust management in mobile environments: Autonomic and usable models* (pp. 54–93). Hershey, PA: IGI Global. doi:10.4018/978-1-4666-4765-7.ch004

Yang, D. X. (2012). QoS-oriented service computing: Bringing SOA into cloud environment. In X. Liu & Y. Li (Eds.), *Advanced design approaches to emerging software systems: Principles, methodologies and tools* (pp. 274–296). Hershey, PA: IGI Global. doi:10.4018/978-1-60960-735-7.ch013

Yang, H., Huff, S. L., & Tate, M. (2013). Managing the cloud for information systems agility. In A. Bento & A. Aggarwal (Eds.), *Cloud computing service and deployment models: Layers and management* (pp. 70–93). Hershey, PA: IGI Global. doi:10.4018/978-1-4666-2187-9.ch004

Yang, M., Kuo, C., & Yeh, Y. (2011). Dynamic rightsizing with quality-controlled algorithms in virtualization environments. *International Journal of Grid and High Performance Computing*, 3(2), 29–43. doi:10.4018/jghpc.2011040103

Yang, X. (2012). QoS-oriented service computing: Bringing SOA into cloud environment. In *Grid and cloud computing: Concepts, methodologies, tools and applications* (pp. 1621–1643). Hershey, PA: IGI Global. doi:10.4018/978-1-4666-0879-5.ch706

Yang, Y., Chen, J., & Hu, H. (2012). The convergence between cloud computing and cable TV. *International Journal of Technology Diffusion*, 3(2), 1–11. doi:10.4018/jtd.2012040101

Yassein, M. O., Khamayseh, Y. M., & Hatamleh, A. M. (2013). Intelligent randomize round robin for cloud computing. *International Journal of Cloud Applications and Computing*, 3(1), 27–33. doi:10.4018/ijcac.2013010103

Yau, S. S., An, H. G., & Buduru, A. B. (2012). An approach to data confidentiality protection in cloud environments. *International Journal of Web Services Research*, 9(3), 67–83. doi:10.4018/jwsr.2012070104

Yu, W. D., Adiga, A. S., Rao, S., & Panakkel, M. J. (2012). A SOA based system development methodology for cloud computing environment: Using uhealthcare as practice. *International Journal of E-Health and Medical Communications*, 3(4), 42–63. doi:10.4018/jehmc.2012100104

Yu, W. D., & Bhagwat, R. (2011). Modeling emergency and telemedicine heath support system: A service oriented architecture approach using cloud computing. *International Journal of E-Health and Medical Communications*, 2(3), 63–88. doi:10.4018/jehmc.2011070104

Yu, W. D., & Bhagwat, R. (2013). Modeling emergency and telemedicine health support system: A service oriented architecture approach using cloud computing. In J. Rodrigues (Ed.), *Digital advances in medicine, e-health, and communication technologies* (pp. 187–213). Hershey, PA: IGI Global. doi:10.4018/978-1-4666-2794-9.ch011

Yuan, D., Lewandowski, C., & Zhong, J. (2012). Developing a private cloud based IP telephony laboratory and curriculum. In L. Chao (Ed.), *Cloud computing for teaching and learning: Strategies for design and implementation* (pp. 126–145). Hershey, PA: IGI Global. doi:10.4018/978-1-4666-0957-0.ch009

Yuvaraj, M. (2014). Cloud libraries: Issues and challenges. In S. Dhamdhere (Ed.), *Cloud computing and virtualization technologies in libraries* (pp. 316–338). Hershey, PA: IGI Global. doi:10.4018/978-1-4666-4631-5.ch018

Zaman, M., Simmers, C. A., & Anandarajan, M. (2013). Using an ethical framework to examine linkages between "going green" in research practices and information and communication technologies. In B. Medlin (Ed.), *Integrations of technology utilization and social dynamics in organizations* (pp. 243–262). Hershey, PA: IGI Global. doi:10.4018/978-1-4666-1948-7.ch015

Zapata, B. C., & Alemán, J. L. (2013). Security risks in cloud computing: An analysis of the main vulnerabilities. In D. Rosado, D. Mellado, E. Fernandez-Medina, & M. Piattini (Eds.), *Security engineering for cloud computing: Approaches and tools* (pp. 55–71). Hershey, PA: IGI Global. doi:10.4018/978-1-4666-2125-1.ch004

Zapata, B. C., & Alemán, J. L. (2014). Security risks in cloud computing: An analysis of the main vulnerabilities. In *Software design and development: Concepts, methodologies, tools, and applications* (pp. 936–952). Hershey, PA: IGI Global. doi:10.4018/978-1-4666-4301-7.ch045

Zardari, S., Faniyi, F., & Bahsoon, R. (2013). Using obstacles for systematically modeling, analysing, and mitigating risks in cloud adoption. In I. Mistrik, A. Tang, R. Bahsoon, & J. Stafford (Eds.), *Aligning enterprise, system, and software architectures* (pp. 275–296). Hershey, PA: IGI Global. doi:10.4018/978-1-4666-2199-2.ch014

Zech, P., Kalb, P., Felderer, M., & Breu, R. (2013). Threatening the cloud: Securing services and data by continuous, model-driven negative security testing. In S. Tilley & T. Parveen (Eds.), *Software testing in the cloud: Perspectives on an emerging discipline* (pp. 280–304). Hershey, PA: IGI Global. doi:10.4018/978-1-4666-2536-5.ch013

Zhang, F., Cao, J., Cai, H., & Wu, C. (2011). Provisioning virtual resources adaptively in elastic compute cloud platforms. *International Journal of Web Services Research*, 8(3), 54–69. doi:10.4018/jwsr.2011070103

Zhang, G., Li, C., Xue, S., Liu, Y., Zhang, Y., & Xing, C. (2012). A new electronic commerce architecture in the cloud. *Journal of Electronic Commerce in Organizations*, 10(4), 42–56. doi:10.4018/jeco.2012100104

Zhang, J., Yao, J., Chen, S., & Levy, D. (2011). Facilitating biodefense research with mobile-cloud computing. *International Journal of Systems and Service-Oriented Engineering*, 2(3), 18–31. doi:10.4018/jssoe.2011070102

Zhang, J., Yao, J., Chen, S., & Levy, D. (2013). Facilitating biodefense research with mobile-cloud computing. In D. Chiu (Ed.), *Mobile and web innovations in systems and service-oriented engineering* (pp. 318–332). Hershey, PA: IGI Global. doi:10.4018/978-1-4666-2470-2.ch017

Zheng, S., Chen, F., Yang, H., & Li, J. (2013). An approach to evolving legacy software system into cloud computing environment. In X. Yang & L. Liu (Eds.), *Principles, methodologies, and service-oriented approaches for cloud computing* (pp. 207–229). Hershey, PA: IGI Global. doi:10.4018/978-1-4666-2854-0.ch009

Zhou, J., Athukorala, K., Gilman, E., Riekki, J., & Ylianttila, M. (2012). Cloud architecture for dynamic service composition. *International Journal of Grid and High Performance Computing*, 4(2), 17–31. doi:10.4018/jghpc.2012040102

Compilation of References

Abboy, I., & Hoskins, R. (2008). The Use of CDS/ISIS Software in Africa. *Innovation, 36*, 17–37.

Abd-El-Hafiz, S. (2004). *An Information Theory Approach to Studying Software Evolution. Alexandria Engineering Journal, 43*(2), 275–284.

Abu Talib, M. (2015). *Towards Sustainable Development through Open Source Software in GCC.* The 2015 IEEE International Symposium on Signal Processing and Information Technology (ISSPIT), Abu Dhabi, UAE.

Abu Talib, M., AbuOdeh, M., Almansoori, A., & AlNauimi, A. (2014). Enhancing Social Science Research in the UAE: An Open Source Software Solution University of Sharjah (UOS) Case Study. *Journal of Computer Science, 11*, 98-108. DOI: 10.3844/jcssp.2015.98.108

Abu Talib, M. (2016). Open Source Software in the UAE: Opportunities. *Challenges and Recommendations.*

Adams, B., De Schutter, K., Tromp, H., & De Meuter, W. (2008). The evolution of the Linux build system. *Electronic Communications of the EASST, 8.*

Adekunle, P. A., Olla, G. O., Oshiname, R. M., & Tella, A. (2015). Reports Generation with *Koha* Integrated Library System (ILS): Some examples from Bowen University, Nigeria. *International Journal of Digital Library Systems, 5*(2).

Afroz, H. (2014). Moving Towards the Next-Generation Library: BRAC University experience *World Digital Libraries, 7*(1), 1–14.

Aghaei, S., Nematbakhsh, M. A., & Farsani, H. K. (2012). Evolution of the world wide web: From WEB 1.0 TO WEB 4.0. *International Journal of Web & Semantic Technology, 3*(1), 1–10. doi:10.5121/ijwest.2012.3101

Agrawal, K., Amreen, S., & Mockus, A. (2015). Commit quality in five high performance computing projects. In *International Workshop on Software Engineering for High Performance Computing in Science* (pp. 24-29). IEEE Press. doi:10.1109/SE4HPCS.2015.11

Ahammad, N. (2014). Implementing the *Koha* integrated library system at the Independent University, Bangladesh: A practical experience. *The Electronic Library, 32*(5), 642–658. doi:10.1108/EL-04-2012-0036

Ahmed, I., Mannan, U., Gopinath, R., & Jensen, C. (2015). An Empirical Study of Design Degradation: How Software Projects Get Worse over Time. *Proceedings of the 2015 ACM/IEEE International Symposium on Empirical Software Engineering and Measurement*, 1 – 10. doi:10.1109/ESEM.2015.7321186

Ajila, S. A., & Wu, D. (2007). Empirical study of the effects of open source adoption on software develop-ment economics. *Journal of Systems and Software, 80*(9), 1517–1529. doi:10.1016/j.jss.2007.01.011

Akgül, M. (2008). Özgür Yazılım Dünyası Ne İster? *Bilisim ve Hukuk Dergisi.* Retrieved 25/06/2017 from http://www.ankarabarosu.org.tr/Siteler/1944-2010/Dergiler/BilisimveHukukDergisi/2008-4.pdf

Akinbobola, O. I., & Adeleke, A. A. (2013). The influence of user efficacy and expectation on actual system use. *Interdisciplinary Journal of Information, Knowledge, and Management, 8,* 43-57. Retrieved June 27, 2016, from http://www.ijikm.org/Volume8/IJIKMV8p043-057Akinbobola0725.pdf

Akpokodje, N.V. & Akpokodje, T. E. (2015). Assessment and evaluation of *Koha* ILS for online library registration at University of Jos, Nigeria. *Asian Journal of Computer and Information Systems.*

Aksünger, E. (2012). Türkiye Büyük Millet Meclisi (TBMM) Genel Kurul Tutanağı; 24. Dönem 2. Yasama Yılı 68. Birleşim; 2012, February 21. *TBMM.* Retrieved 25/06/2017 from https://www.tbmm.gov.tr/develop/owa/tutanak_sd.birlesim_baslangic?P4=21133&P5=B&page1=65&page2=65&web_user_id=14953822

Alali, A., Kagdi, H., & Maletic, J. (2008). What's a Typical Commit? A Characterization of Open Source Software Repositories. In *Proceedings of the 16th International Conference on Program Comprehension* (pp. 182-191). IEEE. doi:10.1109/ICPC.2008.24

Alarifi, A. (2013). *National Program for Free and Open Source Technologies Saudi Arabia. King Abdulaziz City for Science and Technology.* KACST.

Albarrak, A. I., Aboalsamh, H. A., & Abouzahra, M. (2010). Evaluating learning management systems for University medical education. *International Conference on Education and Management Technology (ICEMT)*, Cairo, Egypt. doi:10.1109/ICEMT.2010.5657569

Alenezi, M., & Khellah, F. (2015). Architectural Stability Evolution in Open-Source Systems. In *Proceedings of the International Conference on Engineering & MIS 2015 (ICEMIS '15).* ACM. doi:10.1145/2832987.2833014

Alenezi, M., & Zarour, M. (2015). Modularity Measurement and Evolution in Object-Oriented OpenSource Projects. In *Proceedings of the International Conference on Engineering & MIS (ICEMIS '15).* doi:10.1145/2832987.2833013

Ali, S., & Maqbool, O. (2009). Monitoring Software Evolution Using Multiple Types of Changes. In *Proceedings of the 2009 International Conference on Emerging Technologies* (pp. 410-415). IEEE. doi:10.1109/ICET.2009.5353135

Allen, R. C. (1983). Collective invention. *Journal of Economic Behavior & Organization, 4*(1), 1–24. doi:10.1016/0167-2681(83)90023-9

Almeida, M. D., & Matwin, S. (1999). Machine learning method for software quality model building. *International symposium on methodologies for intelligent systems*, 565-573.

Almirall, E., & Casadesus-Masanell, R. (2010). Open versus closed innovation: A model of discovery and divergence. *Academy of Management Review, 35*(1), 27–47. doi:10.5465/AMR.2010.45577790

Amollo, B. A. (2013). Feasibility of adaptation of open source ILS for libraries in kenya: A practical evaluation. *The Electronic Library, 31*(5), 608–634. doi:10.1108/EL-12-2011-0171

Amrollahi, A., Khansari, M., & Manian, A. (2014). Success of Open Source in Developing Countries: The Case of Iran. *International Journal of Open Source Software and Processes, 5*(1), 50–65. doi:10.4018/ijossp.2014010103

Antoniol, G., Casazza, G., Penta, M., & Merlo, E. (2001). Modeling Clones Evolution through Time Series. In *Proceedings of the IEEE International Conference on Software Maintenance* (pp. 273-280). IEEE.

Anuradha, K. T., Sivakaminathan, R., & Arun, P. K. (2011). Open-source tools for enhancing full-text searching of OPACs: Use of *Koha*, Greenstone and Fedora. *Electronic Library and Information Systems, 45*(2), 231–239. doi:10.1108/00330331111129750

Apache Cloudstack. (n.d.). Retrieved March 18, 2016, from https://cloudstack.apache.org/ downloads.html

Apache Tomcat. (n.d.). Retrieved March 16, 2016, from https://tomcat.apache.org/download-80.cgi

Arbuckle, T. (2009). Measure Software and its Evolution-using Information Content. In *Proceedings of the joint international and annual ERCIM workshops on Principles of Software Evolution (IWPSE) and Software Evolution (Evol) Workshops* (pp. 129-134). ACM. doi:10.1145/1595808.1595831

Arbuckle, T. (2011). Studying Software Evolution using Artifacts Shared Information Content. *Science of Computer Programming*, *76*(12), 1078–1097. doi:10.1016/j.scico.2010.11.005

Arora, A. (1995). Licensing tacit knowledge: Intellectual property rights and the market for know-how. *Economics of Innovation and New Technology*, *4*(1), 41–60. doi:10.1080/10438599500000013

Arora, A., Fosfuri, A., & Gambardella, A. (2001). Markets for technology and their implications for corporate strategy. *Industrial and Corporate Change*, *10*(2), 419–451. doi:10.1093/icc/10.2.419

Aroyo, L., & Dicheva, D. (2004). The new challenges for e-learning: The educational semantic web. *Journal of Educational Technology & Society*, *7*(4).

Arrow, K. (1962). *Economic welfare and the alloca-tion of resources for invention*. UMI.

Arrow, K. J. (1962). The economic implications of learning by doing. *The Review of Economic Studies*, *29*(3), 155–173. doi:10.2307/2295952

Arthur, W. B. (2000). Myths and realities of the high-tech economy. In *Talk given at Credit Suisse First Boston Though Leader Forum*. Santa Fe Institute.

Arthur, W. B. (1989). Competing technologies, increasing returns, and lock-in by historical events. *Economic Journal (London)*, *99*(394), 116–131. doi:10.2307/2234208

Arthur, W. B. (1994). Positive feedbacks in the economy. *The McKinsey Quarterly*, 81.

Arthur, W. B. (1996). Increasing returns and the new world of business. *Harvard Business Review*, *74*, 100–111. PMID:10158472

Askari, M., & Holt, R. (2006). Information theoretic evaluation of change prediction models for large-scale software. *International workshop on Mining software repositories*, 126–132. doi:10.1145/1137983.1138013

Ata-ur-Rehman, M. K., & Bhatti, R. (2012). Free and Open Source Software movement in LIS Profession in Pakistan. Library Philosophy and Practice, 1-20.

Atkins, D., Ball, T., Graves, T., & Mockus, A. (1999). Using version control data to evaluate the impact of software tools. *International Conference on Software Engineering*, 324-333. doi:10.1145/302405.302649

Awoyemi, A. R., & Olaniyi, S. T. (2012). A survey of the availability and use of *Koha* open source software by academic libraries in Nigeria. *COCLIN Journal of Library and Information Science*, *5*(1/2), 9–29.

Azuma, R. T. (1997). A survey of augmented reality. *Presence (Cambridge, Mass.)*, *6*(4), 355–385. doi:10.1162/pres.1997.6.4.355

Azuma, R., Baillot, Y., Behringer, R., Feiner, S., Julier, S., & MacIntyre, B. (2001). Recent advances in augmented reality. *IEEE Computer Graphics and Applications*, *21*(6), 34–47. doi:10.1109/38.963459

Bai, Q. (2010). Analysis of particle swarm optimization algorithm. *Computer and Information Science*, *3*(1), 180.

Bakar, A. D., Sultan, A. B., Zulzalil, H., & Din, J. (2014). Open Source Software Adaptation in Africa: Is a Matter of Inferior or Cheap is Not Quality? *International Journal of Open Source Software and Processes*, *5*(1), 1–15. doi:10.4018/ijossp.2014010101

Barry, B. I. A. (2009). Using Open Source Software in Education in Developing Countries: The Sudan as an Example. *International Conference on Computational Intelligence and Software Engineering*, Wuhan, China. doi:10.1109/CISE.2009.5364872

Barry, E., Kemerer, C., & Slaughter, S. (2003). On the Uniformity of Software Evolution Patterns. *Proceedings of the 25th International Conference on Software Engineering*, 106-113. doi:10.1109/ICSE.2003.1201192

Barua, A., Thomas, S. W., & Hassan, A. E. (2014). What are developers talking about? an analysis of topics and trends in stack overflow. *Empirical Software Engineering*, *19*(3), 619–654. doi:10.1007/s10664-012-9231-y

Bates, A. T. (2005). *Technology, e-learning and distance education*. Routledge. doi:10.4324/9780203463772

Bauer, A., & Pizka, M. (2003). The Contribution of Free Software to Software Evolution. In *Proceedings of the Sixth International Workshop on Principles of Software Evolution* (pp. 170-179). IEEE. doi:10.1109/IWPSE.2003.1231224

Beaton, W. (n.d.). *Eclipse Corner Article*. Retrieved March 12, 2016, from https://www.eclipse.org/articles/article.php?file=Article-JavaCodeManipulation

Beecham, S., Baddoo, N., Hall, T., Robinson, H., & Sharp, H. (2008). Motivation in software engineering: A systematic literature review. *Information and Software Technology*, *50*(9-10), 860–878. doi:10.1016/j.infsof.2007.09.004

Bell, R., Ostrand, T., & Weyuker, E. (2006). Looking for bugs in all the right places. Intl Symp. Software Testing and Analysis, 61–72.

Benbya, H., & McKelvey, B. (2006). Toward a com-plexity theory of information systems development. *Information Technology & People*, *19*(1), 12–34. doi:10.1108/09593840610649952

Benkler, Y. (2006). *The wealth of networks: How social production transforms markets and freedom*. New Haven, CT: Yale University Press. Retrieved from http://books. google.co.uk/books?hl=en&lr=&id=McotnvNSjQ 4C&oi=fnd &pg=PR7&dq=benkler+the+wealth+o f+networks&ots=YTsBUfHqy5&sig=bzEONkk7 QTSyFKAZIl3l9NqJC7k

Bergstrom, T., Blume, L., & Varian, H. (1986). On the private provision of public goods. *Journal of Public Economics*, *29*(1), 25–49. doi:10.1016/0047-2727(86)90024-1

Bettenburg, N., & Hassan, A. (2010). Studying the impact of social structures on software quality. *International Conference on Program Comprehension*, 124–133. doi:10.1109/ICPC.2010.46

Bevan, J., Whitehead, E. Jr, Kim, S., & Godfrey, M. (2005). Facilitating Software Evolution Research with Kenyon. *Software Engineering Notes*, *30*(5), 177–186. doi:10.1145/1095430.1081736

Bhattacharya, P., & Neamtiu, I. (2011). Assessing Programming Language Impact on Development and Maintenance: A Study on C and C++. In *Proceedings of the 33rd International Conference on Software Engineering (ICSE)* (pp. 171-180). IEEE. doi:10.1145/1985793.1985817

Biçer, S., Basar, A., & Çaglayan, B. (2011). Defect prediction using social network analysis on issue repositories. *International Conference on Software and Systems Process*, 63-71.

Bird, C., Nagappan, N., Gall, H., Murphy, B., & Devanbu, P. (2009). *Putting it all together: Using socio-technical networks to predict failures*. Intl Symp. Software Reliability Eng.

Bissels, G. (2008). Implementation of an open source library management system: Experiences with Koha 3.0 at the Royal London Homoeopathic Hospital. *Electronic Library and Information Systems*, *42*(3), 303–314. doi:10.1108/00330330810892703

Bissels, G., & Chandler, A. (2010). Two years on: *Koha* 3.0 in use at the CAMLIS library, Royal London Homoeopathic Hospital. *Electronic Library and Information Systems*, *44*(3), 283–290. doi:10.1108/00330331011064276

Bitzer, J., Schrettl, W., & Schroder, P. J. H. (2007). Intrinsic motivation in open source software devel-opment. *Journal of Comparative Economics*, *35*(1), 160–169. doi:10.1016/j.jce.2006.10.001

Blei, D. M., Ng, A. Y., & Jordan, M. I. (2003). Latent dirichlet allocation. *The Journal of Machine Learning Research*, *3*, 993-1022.

Blind, K., Pohlmann, T., Ramel, F., & Wunsch-Vincent, S. (2014). *The Egyptian Information Technology Sector and the Role of Intellectual Property: Economic Assessment and Recommendations*. WIPO Economics & Statistics Series.

Blum, C., & Li, X. (2008). Swarm intelligence in optimization. In *Swarm Intelligence* (pp. 43–85). Springer Berlin Heidelberg. doi:10.1007/978-3-540-74089-6_2

Blum, C., & Roli, A. (2003). Metaheuristics in combinatorial optimization: Overview and conceptual comparison. *ACM Computing Surveys*, *35*(3), 268–308. doi:10.1145/937503.937505

Boldyreff, C., Beecher, K., & Capiluppi, A. (2009). Identifying exogenous drivers and evolutionary stages in Floss projects. *Journal of Systems and Software, 82*(5), 739–750.

Bonaccorsi, A., & Rossi, C. (2003). Why open source software can succeed. *Research Policy*, *32*(7), 1243–1258. doi:10.1016/S0048-7333(03)00051-9

Boss, R. W. (2005). *Open source integrated library system software*. Retrieved from www.ala.org/ala/mgrps/divs/pla/plapublications/platechnotes/opensource 2008.doc

Boss, R. W. (2008). *"Open Source" Integrated Library System Software*. Public Library Association. Retrieved from http://www.ala.org/ala/mgrps/divs/pla/plapublications/platechnotes/ opensourceils.cfm)

Bottomley, J., & Corbet, J. (2011). Making UEFI Secure Boot Work With Open Platforms. *The Linux Foundation*. Retrieved 25/06/2017 from https://www.linuxfoundation.org/sites/main/files/lf_uefi_secure_boot_open_platforms.pdf

Boyle, J. (2008). *The Public Domain: Enclosing of the Commons of the Mind*. Yale University Press.

Breeding, M. (2008b). Major Open Source ILS Products. *Library Technology Reports*. Available at: www.techsource.ala.org

Breeding, M. (2012). Automation marketplace 2012: agents of change. *Library Journal, The digital shift*. Retrieved from www.thedigitalshift.com/2012/03/ils/automation-marketplace-2012-agents-of-change/

Breeding, M. (2007). An update on open source ILS. *Computers in Libraries*, *27*(3), 27–29.

Breeding, M. (2008a). *Open source integrated library systems. Library Technology Reports*. Washington, DC: ALA Techsource.

Breeding, M., & Yelton, A. (2009a). Analyzing comments for themes. *Library Technology Reports*, *47*(4), 9–11.

Breeding, M., & Yelton, A. (2009b). Breaking down the data. *Library Technology Reports*, *47*(4), 12–26.

Breese, J. S., Heckerman, D., & Kadie, C. (1998, July). Empirical analysis of predictive algorithms for collaborative filtering. In *Proceedings of the Fourteenth conference on Uncertainty in artificial intelligence* (pp. 43-52). Morgan Kaufmann Publishers Inc.

Breivold, H., Chauhan, M., & Babar, M. (2010) A Systematic Review of Studies of Open Source Software Evolution. *Proceedings of the 17th Asia Pacific Software Engineering Conference (APSEC)*, 356-365. doi:10.1109/APSEC.2010.48

Brereton, P., Kitchenham, B. A., Budgen, D., Turner, M., & Khalil, M. (2007). Lessons from applying the systematic literature review process within the software engineering domain. *Journal of Systems and Software*, *80*(4), 571–583. doi:10.1016/j.jss.2006.07.009

Brownlee, J. (2011). *Clever algorithms: nature-inspired programming recipes*. Jason Brownlee.

Brusilovsky, P., & Peylo, C. (2003). Adaptive and intelligent web-based educational systems. *International Journal of Artificial Intelligence in Education*, *13*, 159–172.

BSA | The Software Alliance. (2016). Overview; The Economic Impact of Software. *The Economic Impact Of Software*. Retrieved from http://softwareimpact.bsa.org/pdf/Economic_Impact_of_Software_Overview.pdf

Buchanan, K., & Krasnoff, B. (2005). Can open source software save school libraries' time and money? *Knowledge Quest*, *33*(3), 32–34.

Bureau of Labor Statistics. U.S. Department of Labor. (n.d.). *Occupational Outlook Handbook, 2016-17 Edition, Software Developers*. Retrieved from https://www.bls.gov/ooh/computer-and-information-technology/software-developers.htm

Burgess, E. O. (2017). *Attrition and Dropouts in the E-learning Environment: Improving Student Success and Retention* (Doctoral dissertation). Northcentral University.

Caglayan, B., Bener, A., & Koch, S. (2009). Merits of using repository metrics in defect prediction for open source projects. *CSE Workshop Emerging Trends in Free/Libre/Open Source Software Research and Development*, 31–36. doi:10.1109/FLOSS.2009.5071357

Callon, M., Law, J., & Rip, A. (1986). *Mapping the dynamics of science and technology*. Academic Press.

Callon, M. (1987). Society in the Making: The Study of Technology as a Tool For Sociological Analysis. In W. Bijker, T. Hughes, & T. Pinch (Eds.), *The Social Construction of Technological Systems*. Cambridge, MA: MIT Press.

Callon, M., & Law, J. (1997). After the Individual in Society: Lessons on Collectivity from Science, Technology and Society. *Canadian Journal of Sociology*, *22*(2), 165–182. doi:10.2307/3341747

Campbell-Kelly, M., & Garcia-Swartz, D. D. (2009). Pragmatism, not ideology: Historical perspectives on IBM's adoption of open-source software. *Information Economics and Policy*, *21*(3), 229–244. doi:10.1016/j.infoecopol.2009.03.006

Capiluppi, A. (2009). Domain Drivers in the Modularization of FLOSS Systems. Open Source EcoSystems: Diverse Communities Interacting. In C. Boldyreff, K. Crownston, B. Lundell et al. (Eds.), *Proceedings of the 5th IFIP WG 2.13 International Conference on Open Source Systems OSS '09*. Skovde, Sweden: Springer. doi:10.1007/978-3-642-02032-2_3

Capiluppi, A. (2003). Models for the Evolution of OS Projects. In *Proceedings of International Conference on Software Maintenance (ICSM)*. IEEE. doi:10.1109/ICSM.2003.1235407

Capiluppi, A., & Adams, P. J. (2009). Reassessing brooks law for the free software community. *IFIP Advances in Information and Communication Technology*, *299*, 274–283. doi:10.1007/978-3-642-02032-2_24

Capiluppi, A., Morisio, M., & Ramil, J. (2004a). The Evolution of Source folder structure in actively evolved Open Source Systems. In *Proceedings of the 10th International Symposium on Software metrics (METRICS '04)* (pp. 2-13). IEEE Computer Society, doi:10.1109/METRIC.2004.1357886

Capiluppi, A., Morisio, M., & Ramil, J. (2004b). Structural Evolution of an Open Source System: A case study. *Proceedings of the International Workshop on Program Comprehension*. doi:10.1109/WPC.2004.1311059

Capra, E., Francalanci, C., Merlo, F., & Rossi-Lamastra, C. (2011). Firms' involvement in Open Source projects: A trade-off between software structural quality and popularity. *Journal of Systems and Software, 84*(1), 144–161. doi:. jss.2010.09.00410.1016/j

Capra, E., Francalancia, C., Merloa, F., & Rossi-Lamastrab, C. (2011). Firms' involvement in Open Source projects: A trade-off between software structural quality and popularity. *Journal of Systems and Software, 84*, 144-161. DOI: 10.1016/j.jss.2010.09.004

Capra, E. (2006). Mining Open Source web repositories to measure the cost of Evolutionary reuse. In *Proceedings of the 1st International Conference on Digital Information Management* (pp. 496-503). IEEE.

Caprio, F., Casazza, G., Penta, M., & Villano, U. (2001). Measuring and predicting the Linux kernel Evolution. *Proceedings of the Seventh Workshop on Empirical Studies of Software Maintenance*, 77.

Catala, C., Sevima, U., & Diri, B. (2011). Practical development of an Eclipse-based software fault prediction tool using Naive Bayes algorithm. *Expert Systems with Applications*, *38*(3), 2347–2353. doi:10.1016/j.eswa.2010.08.022

Catal, C. (2011). Software fault prediction: A literature review and current trends. *Expert Systems with Applications*, *38*(4), 4626–4636. doi:10.1016/j.eswa.2010.10.024

Catal, C., & Diri, B. (2009). A systematic review of software fault prediction studies. *Expert Systems with Applications*, *36*(4), 7346–7354. doi:10.1016/j.eswa.2008.10.027

CC Qatar and ictQATAR Qatar Hold Open Source Workshop. (n.d.). Retrieved from http://www.ictqatar.qa/en/news-events/news/cc-qatar-and-ictqatar-qatar-hold-open-source-workshop

Cervone, F. (2003). The open source option: Why libraries should and shouldn't be using open source software. *Library Journal*, *128*(12), 8–13.

Chahal, K. K., & Saini, M. (2016a). Open Source Software Evolution: A Systematic Literature Review (Part 1). *International Journal of Open Source Software and Processes*, *7*(1), 1–27. doi:10.4018/IJOSSP.2016010101

Chahal, K. K., & Saini, M. (2016b). Open Source Software Evolution: A Systematic Literature Review (Part 2). *International Journal of Open Source Software and Processes*, *7*(1), 28–48. doi:10.4018/IJOSSP.2016010102

Chaikalis, T., & Chatzigeorgiou, A. (2015). Forecasting Java Software Evolution Trends Employing Network Models. *IEEE Transactions on Software Engineering*, *41*(6), 582–602. doi:10.1109/TSE.2014.2381249

Chamberlin, J. (1974). Provision of collective goods as a function of group size. *The American Political Science Review*, *68*(2), 707–716. doi:10.1017/S0003055400117496

Chang, N., Tsai, Y., & Hopkinson, A. (2010). An evaluation of implementing *Koha* in a Chinese language environment. *Electronic Library and Information Systems*, *44*(4), 342–356. doi:10.1108/00330331011083239

Chen, B., & Jiang, Z. M. J. (2016). Characterizing logging practices in Java-based open source software projects–a replication study in Apache Software Foundation. *Empirical Software Engineering*, 1–45.

Chesbrough, H. (2006). *Open business models: How to thrive in the new innovation landscape.* Cambridge, MA: Harvard Business School Press.

Chesbrough, H. W., & Appleyard, M. M. (2007). Open innovation and strategy. *California Management Review*, *50*(1), 57–76. doi:10.2307/41166416

Cibbarelli, P. R. (2008). Helping you buy ILSs. *Computers in Libraries*, *28*(9), 45–53.

Coase, R. H. (1937). The nature of the firm. *Economica, 4*(16), 386–405. doi:.tb00002.x10.1111/j.1468-0335.1937

Coase, R. H. (2007). The problem of social cost. In *Economic analysis of the law* (pp. 1–13). Blackwell Publishing Ltd.

Cohen, W. M., & Levinthal, D. A. (1990). Absorp-tive capacity: A new perspective on learning and innovation. *Administrative Science Quarterly, 35*(1), 128–152. doi:10.2307/2393553

Colchester, K., Hagras, H., Alghazzawi, D., & Aldabbagh, G. (2017). A survey of artificial intelligence techniques employed for adaptive educational systems within E-learning platforms. *Journal of Artificial Intelligence and Soft Computing Research, 7*(1), 47–64. doi:10.1515/jaiscr-2017-0004

College & Research Libraries News. (2009). Available at: http://crln.acrl.org/content/by/year/2009

Cook, J., Votta, L., & Wolf, A. (1998). Cost-effective analysis of in-place software processes. *IEEE Transactions on Software Engineering, 24*(8), 650–663. doi:10.1109/32.707700

Cornelissen, B., Zaidman, A., Deursen, A., Moonen, L., & Koschke, R. (2009). A systematic survey of program comprehension through dynamic analysis. *IEEE Transactions on Software Engineering, 35*(5), 684–702. doi:10.1109/TSE.2009.28

Corrado, E. M. (2007). *Libraries and the free and open source software movements.* Paper presented at the Fall Dinner Meeting of the New York Technical Services Librarians Association, New York, NY.

Crossley, A., & Shapira, Y. (n.d.). *Apache Tomcat 7.* Retrieved March 20, 2016, from https://tomcat.apache.org/tomcat-7.0-doc/logging.html

D'Ambros, M., & Lanza, M. (2010). Distributed and Collaborative Software Evolution Analysis with Churrasco. *Science of Computer Programming, 75.*

Dalle, J. M., Daudet, L., & den Besten, M. (2006). Mining CVS signals. *Proceedings of the Workshop on Public Data about Software Development,* 12-21.

Darcy, P., Daniel, L., & Stewart, K. (2010). Exploring Complexity in Open Source Software: Evolutionary Patterns, Antecedents, and Outcomes. In *Proceedings of the 2010 43rd Hawaii International Conference on System Sciences (HICSS).* IEEE Press. doi:10.1109/HICSS.2010.198

Dascalu, M. I., Bodea, C. N., Lytras, M., De Pablos, P. O., & Burlacu, A. (2014). Improving e-learning communities through optimal composition of multidisciplinary learning groups. *Computers in Human Behavior, 30,* 362–371. doi:10.1016/j.chb.2013.01.022

Dattero, R., & Galup, S. (2004). Programming languages and Gender. *Communications of the ACM, 47*(1), 99–102. doi:10.1145/962081.962087

Daugbjerg, C. (2001). *Governance Theory And The Question of Power: Lesson Drawing from The Governance Network Analysis Schools.* Paper to the 61st Political Studies Association Annual Conference, London, UK.

David, P. A., & Rullani, F. (2008). Dynamics of innovation in an 'open source' collaboration envi-ronment: Lurking, laboring, and launching FLOSS projects on SourceForge. *Industrial and Corporate Change, 17*(4), 647–710. doi:10.1093/icc/dtn026

de Jong, J. P. J., Kalvet, T., & Vanhaverbeke, W. (2010). Exploring a theoretical framework to structure the public policy implications of open innovation. *Technology Analysis and Strategic Management, 22*(8), 877–896. doi:325.2010.5227 7110.1080/09537

Delorey, D., Knutson, C., & Giraud-Carrier, C. (2007). Programming language trends in Open Source development: An evaluation using data from all production phase Sourceforge Projects. *Proceedings of the Second International Workshop on Public Data about Software Development (WoPDaSD'07).*

Deshpande, M., & Karypis, G. (2004). Item-based top-n recommendation algorithms. *ACM Transactions on Information Systems, 22*(1), 143–177. doi:10.1145/963770.963776

Ding, R., Zhou, H., Lou, J. G., Zhang, H., Lin, Q., Fu, Q., & Xie, T. et al. (2015, July). Log2: A Cost-Aware Logging Mechanism for Performance Diagnosis. *USENIX Annual Technical Conference*, 139-150.

Dorigo, M., Birattari, M., & Stutzle, T. (2006). Ant colony optimization. *IEEE Computational Intelligence Magazine, 1*(4), 28–39. doi:10.1109/MCI.2006.329691

Downes, S. (2005). E-learning 2.0. *E-learn Magazine, 2005*(10), 1.

Duesenberry, J. (1956). Innovation and growth. *The American Economic Review, 46*(2), 134–14.

Dyba, T., & Dingsyr, T. (2008). Empirical studies of agile software development: A systematic review. *Information and Software Technology, 50*(9-10), 833–859. doi:10.1016/j.infsof.2008.01.006

E.U. Connecta. (n.d.). Retrieved from http://eu.conecta.it/paper/Perceived_disadvan-tages_ope.html

Ebner, M. (2007). E-Learning 2.0= e-Learning 1.0+ Web 2.0? In *Availability, Reliability and Security, 2007. ARES 2007. The Second International Conference on* (pp. 1235-1239). IEEE.

Eby, R. (2007). Open source server applications. *Library Technology Reports*, 48–53.

Eclipse. (2013). Retrieved from Eclipse: http://www.eclipse.org/proposals/packaging/

Economides, N., & Katsamakas, E. (2006). *Linux vs. windows: A comparison of application and platform innovation incentives for open source and proprietary software platforms. The Economics of Open Source Software Development.* Elsevier Publishers. doi:10.1016/B978-044452769-1/50010-X

Egunjobi, R. A., & Awoyemi, R. A. (2012). Library automation with *Koha. Library Hi Tech News, 29*(3), 12–15. doi:10.1108/07419051211241868

EIFL-FOSS. (2013). *Koha (FOSS Integrated Library System).* Retrieved from http://www.eifl.net/ koha-fossintegrated-library-system

Ekanayake, J., Tappolet, J., Gall, H., & Bernstein, A. (2009). *Tracking Concept Drift of Software Projects Using Defect Prediction Quality.* MSR. doi:10.1109/MSR.2009.5069480

Elish, M., Al-Yafei, A., & Al-Mulhem, M. (2011). Empirical comparison of three metrics suites for fault prediction in packages of object-oriented systems: A case study of Eclipse. *Advances in Engineering Software, 42*(10), 852-859.

Elpern, J., & Dascalu, S. (2009). A Framework for Understanding the Open Source Revolution. *International Journal of Open Source Software and Processes, 1*(3), 1–16. doi:10.4018/jossp.2009070101

English, M., Exton, C., Rigon, I., & Cleary, B. (2009). *Fault detection and prediction in an open-source software project.* PROMISE. doi:10.1145/1540438.1540462

Enkel, E., Gassmann, O., & Chesbrough, H. (2009). Open R&D and open innovation: Exploring the phenomenon. *R & D Management, 39*(4), 311–316. doi:10.1111/j.1467-9310.2009.00570.x

ESCWA. (2007). *Economic and Social Commission for Western Asia: National Profil of the Information Society in Kuwait.* United Nations.

Espiau-Bechetoille, C., Bernon, J., Bruley, C., & Mousin, S. (2011). An example of inter-university cooperation for implementing *Koha* in libraries Collective approach and institutional needs. *OCLC Systems & Services: International Digital Library Perspectives, 27*(1), 40–44. doi:10.1108/10650751111106546

European Centre for the Development of Vocational Training (Cedefop). (2012). *International Qualifications*. Luxembourg: Publications Office of the European Union.

European Commission. (2004). *Commission concludes on Microsoft investigation, imposes conduct remedies and a fine*. Retrieved 25/06/2017 from http://europa.eu/rapid/press-release_IP-04-382_en.htm

European Commission. (2009). *European Interoperability Framework for pan-European eGovernment services, the European Interoperability Framework (EIF) Version 1.0*. Retrieved 25/06/2017 from http://ec.europa.eu/idabc/en/document/2319/5644.html

European Commission. (2013a). *Against lock-in: building open ICT systems by making better use of standards in public*. Retrieved 25/06/2017 from http://cordis.europa.eu/fp7/ict/ssai/docs/study-action23/d3-guidelines-finaldraft2012-03-22.pdf

European Commission. (2013b). *Open Standard*. Retrieved 25/06/2017 from http://ec.europa.eu/digital-agenda/en/open-standards

European Commission. (2017). *Strategy for internal use of OSS*. Retrieved 25/06/2017 from http://ec.europa.eu/dgs/informatics/oss_tech/index_en.htm

Evans, P. (2008). Is an Alternative Globalization Possible? *Politics & Society, 36*(2), 271–305. doi:10.1177/0032329208316570

Fenton, N. E., & Ohlsson, N. (2000). Quantitative analysis of faults and failures in a complex software system. *IEEE Transactions on Software Engineering, 26*(8), 797–814. doi:10.1109/32.879815

Fernandez-Ramil, J., Lozano, A., Wermilinger, M., & Capiluppi, A. (2008). Empirical Studies of Open Source Evolution. In T. Mens & S. Demeyer (Eds.), *Software Evolution* (pp. 263–288). Berlin: Springer. doi:10.1007/978-3-540-76440-3_11

Ferreira, K., Bigonha, A., Bigonha, S., & Gomes, M. (2011). Software Evolution Characterization-a Complex Network Approach. *Proceedings of the X Brazilian Symposium on Software Quality-SBQS*, 41-55.

Ferzund, J., Ahsan, S., & Wotawa, F. (2008). Analysing Bug Prediction Capabilities of Static Code Metrics in Open Source Software. *International Conferences IWSM*, 331-343.

Fitzgerald, B. (2006). The transformation of open source software. *Management Information Systems Quarterly, 30*(3), 587–598.

Fitzgerald, B. (2009). Open Source Software Adoption: Anatomy of Success and Failure. *International Journal of Open Source Software and Processes, 1*(1), 1–23. doi:10.4018/jossp.2009010101

Fluri, B., Würsch, M., Giger, E., & Gall, H. (2009). Analyzing the Co-Evolution of Comments and Source code. *Software Quality Journal, 17*(4), 367–394. doi:10.1007/s11219-009-9075-x

Fu, Q., Lou, J. G., Wang, Y., & Li, J. (2009, December). Execution anomaly detection in distributed systems through unstructured log analysis. In *2009 ninth IEEE international conference on data mining* (pp. 149-158). IEEE. doi:10.1109/ICDM.2009.60

Fu, Q., Zhu, J., Hu, W., Lou, J. G., Ding, R., Lin, Q., . . . Xie, T. (2014, May). Where do developers log? an empirical study on logging practices in industry. In *Companion Proceedings of the 36th International Conference on Software Engineering* (pp. 24-33). ACM.

Fuentetaja, E., & Bagert, D. (2002). Software Evolution from a Time-series Perspective. In *Proceedings International Conference on Software Maintenance* (pp. 226-229). IEEE. doi:10.1109/ICSM.2002.1167769

Fuggetta, A. (2003). Open source software—An evaluation. *Journal of Systems and Software, 66*, 77-90. DOI: 10.1016/S0164-1212(02)00065-1

Garnier, S., Gautrais, J., & Theraulaz, G. (2007). The biological principles of swarm intelligence. *Swarm Intelligence, 1*(1), 3–31. doi:10.1007/s11721-007-0004-y

Gassmann, O., Enkel, E., & Chesbrough, H. (2010). The future of open innovation. *R & D Management, 40*(3), 213–221. doi:10.1111/j.1467-9310.2010.00605.x

Gautam, K. S. (2016). OPAC Module in Open Source Library Management Software: A comparative Study. *DESIDOC Journal of Library and Information Technology, 36*(1), 56–61. doi:10.14429/djlit.36.1.9223

Gefen, D., & Schneberger, S. (1996). The Non-homogeneous Maintenance Periods: a Case Study of Software Modifications. In *Proceedings International Conference on Software Maintenance* (pp. 134-141). IEEE. doi:10.1109/ICSM.1996.564998

Genoese, L., & Keith, L. (2011). Jumping ship: One health science library's Voyage from a proprietary ILS to open source. *Journal of Electronic Resources in Medical Libraries, 8*(2), 126–133. doi:10.1080/15424065.2011.576605

Gensim: Topic modelling for humans. (n.d.). Retrieved March 19, 2016, from https://radimrehurek.com/gensim/models/ldamodel.html

Gerger, S. B., Basar, A., & Aglayan, B. (2011). Defect prediction using social network analysis on issue repositories. *ICSSP*, 63–71.

Ghafele, R., & Gibert, B. (2014). Open Growth: The Impact of Open Source Software on Employment in the USA. *International Journal of Open Source Software and Processes, 5*(1), 16–49. doi:10.4018/ijossp.2014010102

Ghosh, R. (2006). Economic impact of open source software on innovation and competitiveness of the information and communications technologies (ICT) sector in the EU. *Proceedings of the UNU-MERIT prepared for the European Commission*, 1-287.

Giger, E., Pinzger, M., & Gall, H. (2010). *Predicting the fix time of bugs*. RSSE.

Girba, T., Kuhn, A., Seeberger, M., & Ducasse, S. (2005a). How Developers Drive Software Evolution. In *Proceedings of the Eighth International Workshop on Principles of Software Evolution* (pp. 113-122). IEEE. doi:10.1109/IWPSE.2005.21

Girba, T., Lanza, M., & Ducasse, S. (2005b). Characterizing the Evolution of Class Hierarchies. In *Proceedings of the Ninth European Conference on Software Maintenance and Reengineering (CSMR)* (pp. 2-11). IEEE. doi:10.1109/CSMR.2005.15

Gkoumas, G., & Lazarinis, F. (2015). Evaluation and usage scenarios of open source digital library and collection management tools. *Electronic Library and Information Systems, 49*(3), 226–241. doi:10.1108/PROG-09-2014-0070

Glass, R. L. (2004). A look at the economics of open source. *Communications of the ACM, 47*(2), 25–27. doi:10.1145/966389.966409

Godfrey, M., & German, D. (2008). Frontiers of software maintenance track. In *International Conference on Software Engineering* (pp. 129-138). IEEE.

Godfrey, M., & Tu, Q. (2000). Evolution in Open Source Software: A case study. In *Proceedings of the International Conference on Software Maintenance* (pp. 131–142). IEEE. doi:10.1109/ICSM.2000.883030

Godfrey, M., & Tu, Q. (2001). Growth, Evolution, and Structural Change in Open Source Software. In *Proc. of the 2001 Intl. Workshop on Principles of Software Evolution (IWPSE-01)* (pp. 103-106). IEEE.

Goeminne, M., Decan, A., & Mens, T. (2014). Co-evolving Code-related and Database-related Changes in a Data-intensive Software System. *Proceedings of the IEEE Conference on Software Maintenance, Reengineering and Reverse Engineering (CSMR-WCRE)*, 353–357. doi:10.1109/CSMR-WCRE.2014.6747193

Goers, R., Gregory, G., & Deboy, S. (n.d.). *Log4j – Log4j 2 Guide - Apache Log4j 2*. Retrieved October 23, 2015, from http://logging.apache.org/log4j/2.x/

Goldberg, D., Nichols, D., Oki, B. M., & Terry, D. (1992). Using collaborative filtering to weave an information tapestry. *Communications of the ACM*, *35*(12), 61–70. doi:10.1145/138859.138867

Gonzalez-Barahona, J. M., Robles, G., Herraiz, I., & Ortega, F. (2014). Studying the laws of software evolution in a long-lived FLOSS project. *Journal of Software: Evolution and Process*, *26*(7), 589–612. PMID:25893093

Gorshenev, A., & Pismak, M. (2003). Punctuated Equilibrium in Software Evolution. *Physical Review E: Statistical, Nonlinear, and Soft Matter Physics*, *70*(6). PMID:15697556

Goulão, M., Fonte, N., Wermelinger, M., & Abreu, F. (2012). Software Evolution Prediction Using Seasonal Time Analysis: A Comparative Study. *Proceedings of 16th European Conference Software Maintenance and Reengineering (CSMR)*, 213-222. doi:10.1109/CSMR.2012.30

Gould, D. M., & Gruben, W. C. (1996). The role of intellectual property rights in economic growth. *Journal of Development Economics*, *48*(2), 323–350. doi:10.1016/0304-3878(95)00039-9

Gousios, G. (2013, May). The GHTorent dataset and tool suite. In *Proceedings of the 10th Working Conference on Mining Software Repositories* (pp. 233-236). IEEE Press.

Gousios, G., Vasilescu, B., Serebrenik, A., & Zaidman, A. (2014, May). Lean GHTorrent: GitHub data on demand. In *Proceedings of the 11th Working Conference on Mining Software Repositories* (pp. 384-387). ACM.

Government Launches Open Software Strategy Drafted by A2K4D. (n.d.). Retrieved from http://www.aucegypt.edu/business/newsroom/Pages/story.aspx?eid=107

Government of Jordan Selects Ingres to Drive Open Source Adoption Across the Country. (n.d.). Retrieved from http://www.businesswire.com/news/home/20100112005382/en/Government-Jordan-Selects-Ingres-Drive-Open-Source#.VZ1LGflViko

Grand, S. (2003). *Creation: Life and How to Make It*. Harvard University Press.

Grossman, G. M., & Helpman, E. (1990). Trade, innovation, and growth. *The American Economic Review*, *80*(2), 86–91.

Gulati, R. (1995). Does familiarity breed trust? The implications of repeated ties for contractual choice in alliances. *Academy of Management Journal*, *38*(1), 85–112. doi:10.2307/256729

Gupta, A., Cruzes, D., Shull, F., Conradi, R., Rønneberg, H., & Landre, E. (2008). An examination of Change Profiles in reusable and non-reusable Software Systems. *Journal of Software Maintenance and Evolution: Research and Practice*, *22*(5), 359–380.

Guzman, E., Azócar, D., & Li, Y. (2014, May). Sentiment analysis of commit comments in GitHub: an empirical study. In *Proceedings of the 11th Working Conference on Mining Software Repositories* (pp. 352-355). ACM. doi:10.1145/2597073.2597118

Hainich, R. R. (2009). *The End of hardware: augmented reality and beyond*. BookSurge.

Hall, T., Beecham, S., Bowes, D., Gray, D., & Counsell, S. (2012). A systematic literature review on fault prediction performance in software engineering. *IEEE Transactions on Software Engineering*, *38*(6), 1276–1304. doi:10.1109/TSE.2011.103

Hamburg, I., Engert, S., Anke, P., Marin, M., & im IKM Bereich, E. C. A. (2008). Improving e-learning 2.0-based training strategies of SMEs through communities of practice. *Learning, 2*, 610-012.

Hammouda, I., Laine, R., & Peltonen, J. (2010). *Transfer of Educational Methods through Open Sourcing of Learning Management Systems*. 2010 IEEE 10th International Conference Advanced Learning Technologies (ICALT), Sousse, France. doi:10.1109/ICALT.2010.185

Han, J., Pei, J., & Kamber, M. (2011). *Data mining: concepts and techniques*. Elsevier.

Harhoff, D., Henkel, J., & von Hippel, E. (2003). Profiting from voluntary information spillovers: How users benefit by freely revealing their innovations. *Research Policy*, *32*(10), 1753–1769. doi:10.1016/S0048-7333(03)00061-1

Hars, A., & Ou, S. (2001). *Working for free? Motivations of participating in open source projects*. Academic Press.

Hassan, A. (2009). *Predicting Faults Using the Complexity of Code Changes*. ICSE. doi:10.1109/ICSE.2009.5070510

Hassan, A., & Holt, R. (2005). *The Top Ten List: Dynamic Fault Prediction*. ICSM.

Hassan, A., Mockus, A., Holt, R., & Johnson, P. (2005b). Special issue on Mining Software Repositories. *IEEE Transactions on Software Engineering*, *31*(6), 426–428. doi:10.1109/TSE.2005.70

Hassan, A., Wu, J., & Holt, R. (2005a). Visualizing Historical Data Using Spectrographs. In *Proceedings of the 11th IEEE International Software Metrics Symposium (METRICS '05)*. IEEE Computer Society. doi:10.1109/METRICS.2005.54

Hattori, L., D'Ambros, M., Lanza, M., & Lungu, M. (2013). Answering Software Evolution Questions: An Empirical Evaluation. *Information and Software Technology*, *55*(4), 755–775. doi:10.1016/j.infsof.2012.09.001

Hattori, L., & Lanza, M. (2008). On the Nature of Commits. In *Proceedings of the 23rd IEEE/ACM International Conference on Automated Software Engineering-Workshops* (pp. 63-71). IEEE.

Hawkins, R. E. (2004). The economics of open source software for a competitive firm. *NETNOMICS, 6*(2), 103-117.

Heller, B., Marschner, E., Rosenfeld, E., & Heer, J. (2011, May). Visualizing collaboration and influence in the open-source software community. In *Proceedings of the 8th Working Conference on Mining Software Repositories* (pp. 223-226). ACM. doi:10.1145/1985441.1985476

Heller, M. A., & Eisenberg, R. S. (1998). Can patents deter innovation? The anticommons in biomedical research. *Science*, *280*(5364), 698–701. doi:10.1126/science.280.5364.698 PMID:9563938

Herder, E., Sosnovsky, S., & Dimitrova, V. (2017). Adaptive Intelligent Learning Environments. In Technology Enhanced Learning (pp. 109-114). Springer International Publishing. doi:10.1007/978-3-319-02600-8_10

Hermenegildo, M. V. (2012). *Conferences vs. journals in CS, what to do? Evolutionary ways forward and the ICLP/TPLP model*. Leibniz-ZentrumfürInformatik.

Herraiz, I., Gonzalez-Barahona, J., & Robles, G. (2007a). Forecasting the Number of Changes in Eclipse using Time Series Analysis. In *Proceedings of the 2007 Fourth International Workshop on Mining Software Repositories MSR'07* (pp. 32-32). IEEE. doi:10.1109/MSR.2007.10

Herraiz, I., Gonzalez-Barahona, J., & Robles, G. (2007b). Towards a Theoretical Model for Software Growth. In *Proceedings of the Fourth International Workshop on Mining Software Repositories* (p. 21). IEEE Computer Society. doi:10.1109/MSR.2007.31

Herraiz, I., Gonzalez-Barahona, J., Robles, G., & German, D. (2007c).On the prediction of the Evolution of libre Software Projects. In *Proceedings of the 2007 IEEE International Conference on Software Maintenance (ICSM '07)* (pp. 405-414). IEEE. doi:10.1109/ICSM.2007.4362653

Herraiz, I., Gonzlez-Barahona, J., & Robles, G. (2008). Determinism and Evolution. In A. Hassan, M. Lanza, & M. Godfrey (Eds.), *Mining Software Repositories*. ACM. doi:10.1145/1370750.1370752

Herraiz, I., Robles, G., González-Barahona, J., Capiluppi, A., & Ramil, J. (2006). Comparison between SLOCs and Number of files as Size Metrics for Software Evolution analysis. In *Proceedings of the 10th European Conference on Software Maintenance and Reengineering (CSMR '06)* (p. 8). IEEE. doi:10.1109/CSMR.2006.17

Hertel, G., Niedner, S., & Herrmann, S. (2003). Motivation of software developers in Open Source projects: An Internet-based survey of contributors to the Linux kernel. *Research Policy*, *32*(7), 1159–1177. doi:10.1016/S0048-7333(03)00047-7

Heylighen, F. (2006). *Why is open access development so successful? Stigmergic organization and the economics of information.* Arxiv preprint cs/0612071

Hillenius, G. (2017). Swedish policy makers want end to IT vendor lock-in. *Joinup*. Retrieved 25/06/2017 from https://joinup.ec.europa.eu/community/osor/news/swedish-policy-makers-want-end-it-vendor-lock

Hindle, A., German, D., Godfrey, M., & Holt, R. (2009a). Automatic Classification of Large Changes into Maintenance Categories. In *Proceedings of the 17th International Conference on Program Comprehension ICPC'09* (pp. 30-39). IEEE.

Hofmann, T. (2004). Latent semantic models for collaborative filtering. *ACM Transactions on Information Systems*, *22*(1), 89–115. doi:10.1145/963770.963774

Höllerer, T., & Feiner, S. (2004). *Mobile augmented reality. In Telegeoinformatics: Location-Based Computing and Services* (p. 21). London, UK: Taylor and Francis Books Ltd.

Hruska, J. (2016). Microsoft leaks Secure Boot credentials, shows why backdoor 'golden keys' can't work. *Extremetech*. Retrieved 25/06/2017 from https://www.extremetech.com/computing/233400-microsoft-leaks-secure-boot-credentials-demonstrates-why-backdoor-golden-keys-cant-work

Hu, J., Sun, X., Lo, D., & Bin, L. (2015). Modeling the Evolution of Development Topics using Dynamic Topic Models. *Proceedings of the 2015 IEEE 22nd International Conference on Software Analysis, Evolution and Reengineering*, 3-12. doi:10.1109/SANER.2015.7081810

Hyoju, D. (2012). *Pilot of Virtual Union Catalogue (VUC) Using KOHA ILS for Nepali Libraries*. Retrieved January 5, 2016, from www.eifl.net/resources/pilot-virtual-union-catalogue-vuc-using-Koha-ils-nepali-libraries.

Iannacci, F. (2002). The economics of open-source networks. *Communications & Stratégies*, *48*(4), 119–138.

Illes-Seifert, T., & Paech, B. (2010). Exploring the relationship of a files history and its fault-proneness: An empirical method and its application to open source programs. *Information and Software Technology*, *52*(5), 539–558. doi:10.1016/j.infsof.2009.11.010

International Conference on Open Source Software Computing (OSSCOM 2015). (n.d.). Retrieved from http://osscom2015.osscom.org/

International Development Association (IDA). (2003). *IDA issues Open Source Migration Guidelines.* Retrieved 25/06/2017 from http://ec.europa.eu/idabc/en/document/1921.html

Iroaganachi, M. A., Iwu, J. J., & Esse, U. C. (2015). Software Selection and Deployment for Library Cooperation and Resource Sharing Among Academic Libraries in South-West Nigeria. *DESIDOC Journal of Library and Information Technology, 35*(1), 3–8. doi:10.14429/djlit.35.1.6885

Israeli, A., & Feitelson, D. (2010). The Linux Kernel as a Case Study in Software Evolution. *Journal of Systems and Software, 83*(3), 485–501. doi:10.1016/j.jss.2009.09.042

ITA of Oman: The First Symposium on Free Source. (n.d.). Retrieved from http://www.ita.gov.om/ITAPortal/Media-Center/NewsDetail.aspx?NID=302

ITU Arab Regional Office. (2015). *Establishment of a network to support open-source software.* Retrieved from https://itunews.itu.int/en/2334-Establishment-of-a-network-to-support-open-source-software.note.aspx

Izurieta, C., & Bieman, J. (2006). The Evolution of FreeBSD and Linux. In *Proceedings of the 2006 ACM/IEEE international symposium on Empirical Software engineering* (pp. 204-211). ACM. doi:10.1145/1159733.1159765

Jaspersoft. (2010). T*he State of Enterprise Open Source Software After the Oracle Acquisition of Sun Microsystems.* Jaspersoft Report. Retrieved from http://www.jaspersoft.com/sites/default/files/Jaspersoft_Survey-Oracle_Java_White_Paper.pdf

Jenkins, S., & Kirk, S. (2007). Software Architecture Graphs as Complex Networks: A Novel Partitioning Scheme to Measure Stability and Evolution. *Information Sciences, 177*(12), 2587–2601. doi:10.1016/j.ins.2007.01.021

Jiang, Y., & Adams, B. (2015). Co-Evolution of Infrastructure and Source Code: An Empirical Study. In *Proceedings of the 12th Working Conference on Mining Software Repositories (MSR '15)* (pp. 45-55). Piscataway, NJ: IEEE Press. doi:10.1109/MSR.2015.12

Jiang, Y., Lin, J., Cukic, B., & Menzies, T. (2009). *Variance analysis in software fault prediction models.* Intl Symp. Software Reliability Eng. doi:10.1109/ISSRE.2009.13

Johari, K., & Kaur, A. (2012). Validation of object oriented metrics using open source software system: An empirical study. *Software Engineering Notes, 37*(1), 1–4. doi:10.1145/2088883.2088893

Johnson, J. P. (1999). *Economics of open source software.* Unpublished working paper. Massachusetts Institute of Technology.

Johnson, R. D., Hornik, S., & Salas, E. (2008). An empirical examination of factors contributing to the creation of successful e-learning environments. *International Journal of Human-Computer Studies, 66*(5), 356–369. doi:10.1016/j.ijhcs.2007.11.003

Jordan Open Source Association. (n.d.). Retrieved from http://www.jordanopensource.org/

Kabinna, S., Bezemer, C. P., Hassan, A. E., & Shang, W. (2016, March). Examining the Stability of Logging Statements. *Proceedings of the 23rd IEEE International Conference on Software Analysis, Evolution, and Reengineering (SANER).*

Kabinna, S., Bezemer, C. P., Shang, W., & Hassan, A. E. (2016b, May). Logging library migrations: a case study for the apache software foundation projects. In *Proceedings of the 13th International Conference on Mining Software Repositories* (pp. 154 164). ACM. doi:10.1145/2901739.2901769

KACST. (2013). *Enhancing Innovations through Free/Open Source Software in KSA.* King Abdulaziz City for Science and Technology.

Kalyuga, S., & Sweller, J. (2005). Rapid dynamic assessment of expertise to improve the efficiency of adaptive e-learning. *Educational Technology Research and Development*, *53*(3), 83–93. doi:10.1007/BF02504800

Kandar, S., Mondal, S., & Ray, P. (2011). A review of Open Source Software and Open Source movement in developing countries. *International Journal of Computer Science & Informatics*, *1*(1), 89–93.

Karaboga, D., & Akay, B. (2009). A comparative study of artificial bee colony algorithm. *Applied Mathematics and Computation*, *214*(1), 108–132. doi:10.1016/j.amc.2009.03.090

Karetzky, S. (1998). Choosing an Automated System. *Library Journal*, *123*(11), 42.

Kari, K. H., & Baro, E. E. (2014). The use of library software in Nigerian University Libraries and challenges. *Library Hi Tech News*. Retrieved from https://www.researchgate.net/publication/263287220

Karus, S., & Gall, H. (2011). A Study of Language Usage Evolution in Open Source Software. In *Proceedings of the 8th Working Conference on Mining Software Repositories* (pp. 13-22). ACM. doi:10.1145/1985441.1985447

Karypis, G. (2001, October). Evaluation of item-based top-n recommendation algorithms. In *Proceedings of the tenth international conference on Information and knowledge management* (pp. 247-254). ACM.

Katz, D., & Kahn, R. L. (1978). *The social psychology of organizations*. Academic Press.

Kaur, A., & Malhotra, R. (2008). Application of random forest in predicting fault-prone classes. *International Conference on Advanced Computer Theory and Engineering*, 37 – 43. doi:10.1109/ICACTE.2008.204

Kaur, K. (2013). Analyzing Growth Trends of Reusable Software Components. In H. Singh & K. Kaur (Eds.), *Designing, Engineering, and Analyzing Reliable and Efficient Software*. Hershey, PA: IGI Global; doi:10.4018/978-1-4666-2958-5.ch003

Keast, D. (2011). A survey of *Koha* in Australian special libraries: Open source brings new opportunities to the outback. *OCLC Systems & Services: International Digital Library Perspectives*, *27*(1), 23-39.

Kechaou, Z., Ammar, M. B., & Alimi, A. M. (2011). Improving e-learning with sentiment analysis of users' opinions. In *Global Engineering Education Conference* (pp. 1032-1038). IEEE. doi:10.1109/EDUCON.2011.5773275

Kemerer, C., & Slaughter, S. (1997). A Longitudinal Analysis of Software Maintenance Patterns. In *Proceedings of the eighteenth international conference on Information Systems* (pp. 476-477). Association for Information Systems.

Kemerer, C., & Slaughter, S. (1999). An Empirical Approach to Studying Software Evolution. *IEEE Transactions on Software Engineering*, *25*(4), 493–509. doi:10.1109/32.799945

Kenmei, B., Antoniol, G., & Penta, M. (2008). Trend Analysis and Issue Prediction in Large-scale Open Source Systems. In *Proceedings of the 12th European Conference on Software Maintenance and Reengineering (CSMR'08)* (pp. 73-82). IEEE. doi:10.1109/CSMR.2008.4493302

Khan, M. A., & Urrehman, F. (2013). *An Extendable OpenSource Architecture of E-Learning System*. Fourth International Conference on e-Learning "Best Practices in Management, Design and Development of e-Courses: Standards of Excellence and Creativity", Manama. doi:10.1109/ECONF.2013.51

Khan, M.T., Zahid, A. & Rafiq, M. (2016). Journey from Library management System (LMS) to *KOHA* by Government College University Libraries, Lahore. *Pakistan Journal of Information Management & Libraries, 17,* 184-190.

Khelifi, A., Abu Talib, M., Farouk, M., & Hamam, H. (2009, July-September). Developing an Initial Open Source Platform for the Higher Education Sector: A Case Study: ALHOSN University. *IEEE Transactions on Learning Technologies*, *2*(3), 239–248. doi:10.1109/TLT.2009.13

Kilamo, T., Hammouda, I., Mikkonen, T., & Aaltonen, T. (2012). From proprietary to open source—Growing an open source ecosystem. *Journal of Systems and Software, 85*, 1467-1478. DOI: 10.1016/j.jss.2011.06.071

Kim, L. (2015). *10 Most Popular Programming Languages Today.* Retrieved March 20, 2016, from http://www.inc.com/larry-kim/10-most-popular-programming-languages-today.htm

King, J. L., Gurbaxani, V., Kraemer, K. L., McFarlan, F. W., Raman, K. S., & Yap, C. S. (1994). Institu-tional factors in information technology innovation. *Information Systems Research, 5*(2), 139–169. doi:10.1287/isre.5.2.139

Kitchenham, B. (2004). *Procedures for Performing Systematic Reviews.* Joint Technical Report between Keele University and NICTA.

Kitchenham, B. (2004). *Procedures for performing systematic reviews.* Technical Report TR/SE-0401, Keele University, and Technical Report 0400011T.1, National ICT Australia.

Kitchenham, B. (2007). *Guidelines for Performing Systematic Literature Review in Software Engineering.* Technical report EBSE-2007-001.

Kitchenham, B., Pretorius, R., Budgen, D., Brereton, O. P., Turner, M., Niazi, M., & Linkman, S. (2010). Systematic literature reviews in software engineering- a tertiary study. *Information and Software Technology, 52*(8), 792–805. doi:10.1016/j.infsof.2010.03.006

Kläs, M., Elberzhager, F., Münch, J., Hartjes, K., & Von Graevemeyer, O. (2010). Transparent Combination of Expert and Measurement Data for Defect Prediction: an Industrial Case Study. In *Proceedings of the 32nd ACM/IEEE International Conference on Software Engineering* (Vol. 2, pp. 119-128). ACM. doi:10.1145/1810295.1810313

Klašnja-Milićević, A., Vesin, B., Ivanović, M., Budimac, Z., & Jain, L. C. (2017a). Introduction to E-Learning Systems. In E-Learning Systems (pp. 3-17). Springer International Publishing.

Klašnja-Milićević, A., Vesin, B., Ivanović, M., Budimac, Z., & Jain, L. C. (2017b). Recommender Systems in E-Learning Environments. In E-Learning Systems (pp. 51-75). Springer International Publishing.

Knab, P., Pinzger, M., & Bernstein, A. (2006). *Predicting defect densities in source code? les with decision tree learn-ers.* MSR.

Koch, S. (2005). Evolution of Open Source System Software Systems - a Large Scale Investigation. *Proceedings of the First International Conference on Open Source Systems.*

Koch, S. (2007). Software Evolution in Open Source Projects—a Large-scale Investigation. *Journal of Software Main-tenance and Evolution: Research and Practice, 19*(6), 361–382. doi:10.1002/smr.348

Kogut, B., & Metiu, A. (2001). Open-source software development and distributed innovation. *Oxford Review of Eco-nomic Policy, 17*(2), 248–264. doi:10.1093/oxrep/17.2.248

Korres, M. P. (2017). The Positive Effect of Evaluation on Improving E-Learning Courses Addressed to Adults: A Case Study on the Evolution of the GSLLLY Courses in Greece over a Decade. *Journal of Education and Training Studies, 5*(1), 1–11. doi:10.11114/jets.v5i1.1940

Koru, A. G., Zhang, D., & Liu, H. (2007). Modeling the effect of size on defect proneness for open-source software. *Third International Workshop on Predictor Models in Software Engineering.*

Korua, A., & Liu, H. (2007). Identifying and Characterizing change-prone classes in two large-scale open-source prod-ucts. *Journal of Systems and Software, 80*(1), 63–73. doi:10.1016/j.jss.2006.05.017

Kose, U. (2013). An Artificial Neural Networks Based Software System for Improved Learning Experience. In *Machine Learning and Applications (ICMLA), 2013 12th International Conference on* (Vol. 2, pp. 549-554). IEEE. doi:10.1109/ICMLA.2013.175

Kose, U. (2010). *Web 2.0 Technologies in E-learning. In Free and Open Source Software for E-learning: Issues, Successes and Challenges* (pp. 1–23). Hershey, PA: IGI Global.

Kose, U. (2014). On the State of Free and Open Source E-Learning 2.0 Software. *International Journal of Open Source Software and Processes*, 5(2), 55–75. doi:10.4018/ijossp.2014040103

Kose, U., & Arslan, A. (2016). Optimization with the idea of algorithmic reasoning. *Journal of Multidisciplinary Developments*, 1(1), 17–20.

Kose, U., & Arslan, A. (2017). Optimization of self-learning in Computer Engineering courses: An intelligent software system supported by Artificial Neural Network and Vortex Optimization Algorithm. *Computer Applications in Engineering Education*, 25(1), 142–156. doi:10.1002/cae.21787

Kose, U., & Koc, D. (2014). *Artificial Intelligence Applications in Distance Education*. IGI Global.

Kosinski, K. (2013, February). *Advanced CloudStack Troubleshooting using Log Analysis - a session at ApacheCon North America 2013*. Retrieved March 19, 2016, from http://lanyrd.com/2013/apachecon/scbrfk/

Kpodjedo, S., Ricca, F., Galinier, P., & Antoniol, G. (2013). Studying Software Evolution of Large Object Oriented Software Systems using an etgm Algorithm. *Journal of Software: Evolution and Process*, 25(2), 139–163.

Krill, P. (2015). *Java regains spot as most popular language in developer index*. Retrieved March 23, 2016, from http://www.infoworld.com/article/2909894/application-development/java-back-at-1-in-language-popularity-assessment.html

Kubat, M. (2015). Artificial neural networks. In *An Introduction to Machine Learning* (pp. 91–111). Springer International Publishing. doi:10.1007/978-3-319-20010-1_5

Kumar, V., & Jasimudeen, S. (2012). Selection and Management of Open Source Software in Libraries. *Annals of Library and Information Studies*, 59, 223–230. Retrieved from http://eprints.rclis.org/18198/1/ALIS%2059%284%29%20223-230.pdf

Kushwah, S. S. (2008). *Library Automation and Open Source Solutions Major Shifts and practices: A Comparative Case Study of Library Automating Systems in India*. International CALIBER.

Lal, S., Sardana, N., & Sureka, A. (2015). Two Level Empirical Study of Logging Statements in Open Source Java Projects. *International Journal of Open Source Software and Processes*, 6(1), 49–73. doi:10.4018/IJOSSP.2015010104

Lal, S., Sardana, N., & Sureka, A. (2016, June). LogOptPlus: Learning to Optimize Logging in Catch and If Programming Constructs. In *Proceedings of 40th Annual Computer Software and Applications Conference* (pp. 215-220). IEEE. doi:10.1109/COMPSAC.2016.149

Lal, S., Sardana, N., & Sureka, A. (2016b). Improving Logging Prediction on Imbalanced Datasets: A Case Study on Open Source Java Projects. *International Journal of Open Source Software and Processes*, 7(2), 43–71. doi:10.4018/IJOSSP.2016040103

Lal, S., Sardana, N., & Sureka, A. (2017a). ECLogger: Cross-Project Catch-Block Logging Prediction Using Ensemble of Classifiers. *e-Informatica. Software Engineering Journal*, 11(1), 9–40.

Lal, S., Sardana, N., & Sureka, A. (2017b). Three-level learning for improving cross-project logging prediction for if-blocks. *Journal of King Saud University-Computer and Information Sciences*. (in press)

Lal, S., & Sureka, A. (2016, February). LogOpt: Static Feature Extraction from Source Code for Automated Catch Block Logging Prediction. In *Proceedings of the 9th India Software Engineering Conference* (pp. 151-155). ACM. doi:10.1145/2856636.2856637

LaMantia, M., Cai, Y., MacCormack, A., & Rusnak, J. (2008). Analyzing the Evolution of large-scale Software Systems using Design Structure Matrices and Design Rule Theory: Two Exploratory Cases. In *Proceedings of theSeventh Working IEEE/IFIP Conference on Software Architecture (WICSA '08)* (pp. 83-92). IEEE. doi:10.1109/WICSA.2008.49

Latour, B. (1986). The Powers of Association. In J. Law (Ed.), *Power, Action and Belief: A New Sociology of Knowledge* (pp. 264–280). London: Routledge & Kegan Paul.

Latour, B. (1996). On actor-network theory. *Soziale Welt, 47*(4), 369–381.

Latour, B. (1996). On Actor-Network Theory: A Few Clarifications. *Soziale Welt*, 369–381.

Latour, B. (2005). *Reassembling the Social: An Introduction to Actor-Network Theory.* New York: Oxford University Press.

Lavji, N. Z., & Niraj, R. P. (2006). Application of WINISIS/GENESIS Software in Newspapers Clippings. *DESIDOC Bulletin of Information Technology, 26*(1), 17–26. doi:10.14429/dbit.26.1.3671

Law, J. (1999). After ANT: Complexity, Naming and Topology. In J. Hassard & J. Law (Eds.), *Actor-Network Theory and After.* Oxford, UK: Blackwell Publishers. doi:10.1111/j.1467-954X.1999.tb03479.x

Lazzarotti, V., & Manzini, R. (2009). Different modes of open innovation: A theoretical framework and an empirical study. *International Journal of Innovation Management, 13*(4), 615–636. doi:10.1142/S1363919609002443

Le, D., Behnamghader, P., Garcia, J., Link, D., Shahbazian, A., & Medvidovic, N. (2015). An Empirical Study of Architectural Change in Open-Source Software Systems. In *Proceedings of the 12th Working Conference on Mining Software Repositories (MSR '15)* (pp. 235-245). IEEE. doi:10.1109/MSR.2015.29

Lee, W., Lee, J., & Baik, J. (2011). *Software reliability prediction for open source software adoption systems based on early lifecycle measurements.* COMPSAC. doi:10.1109/COMPSAC.2011.55

Lehman, M. (1996). Laws of Software Evolution Revisited. In *Proceedings of the European Workshop on Software Process Technology* (pp. 108-124). Springer-Verlag. doi:10.1007/BFb0017737

Lehman, M., Ramil, J., & Sandler, U. (2001). An Approach to Modeling Long-term Growth Trends in Software Systems. In *Proceedings of the International Conference on Software Maintenance* (pp. 219–228). IEEE.

Leighton, L. J., & Crompton, H. (2017). Augmented Reality in K-12 Education. In Mobile Technologies and Augmented Reality in Open Education (pp. 281-290). IGI Global.

Lerner, J., & Tirole, J. (2002). Some simple economics of open source. *The Journal of Industrial Economics, 50*(2), 197–234. doi:10.1111/1467-6451.00174

Lerner, J., & Tirole, J. (2004). *The economics of technology sharing: Open source and beyond.* National Bureau of Economic Research. doi:10.3386/w10956

Lessmann, S., Baesens, B., Mues, C., & Pietsch, S. (2008). enchmarking classi?cation models for software defect prediction: A proposed framework and novel findings. *IEEE Transactions on Software Engineering, 34*(4), 485–496. doi:10.1109/TSE.2008.35

Levandowsky, M., & Winter, D. (1971). Distance between sets. *Nature, 234*(5323), 34–35. doi:10.1038/234034a0

Lewis, J. A. (2010). *Government Open Source Policies*. Retrieved from http://csis.org/publication/government-open-source-policies-0

Liaw, S. S. (2008). Investigating students' perceived satisfaction, behavioral intention, and effectiveness of e-learning: A case study of the Blackboard system. *Computers & Education*, *51*(2), 864–873. doi:10.1016/j.compedu.2007.09.005

Libraries, A. T. (2010a). Equinox announces *Koha* hosting, support services. *Advanced Technology Libraries*, *39*(3), 1–12.

Libraries, A. T. (2010b). Nelsonville public chooses ByWater Solutions. *Advanced Technology Libraries*, *39*(3), 2.

Library Journal (2010b). Open source ILS plan for Pennsylvania PLs. *Library Journal*, *135*(16), 16.

Library Journal. (2009a). LibLime and syndetic partner on enhanced content. *Library Journal*, *134*(10), 19.

Library Journal. (2010a). Equinox to support *Koha* open source ILS. *Library Journal*, *135*(5), 17.

Li, H., Shang, W., & Hassan, A. E. (2016). Which log level should developers choose for a new logging statement. *Empirical Software Engineering*, 1–33.

Li, H., Shang, W., Zou, Y., & Hassan, A. E. (2016b). Towards just-in-time suggestions for log changes. *Empirical Software Engineering*, 1–35.

Lin, S., Ma, Y., & Chen, J. (2013). Empirical Evidence on Developer's Commit Activity for Open-Source Software Projects. *Proceedings of the 25th International Conference on Software Engineering and Knowledge Engineering*, 455-460.

Li, P. L., Herbsleb, J., & Shaw, M. (2005). Finding predictors of? eld defects for open source software systems in commonly available data sources: a case study of openbsd. *International Software Metrics Symposium (METRICS)*. doi:10.1109/METRICS.2005.26

Lipkus, A. H. (1999). A proof of the triangle inequality for the Tanimoto distance. *Journal of Mathematical Chemistry*, *26*(1-3), 263–265. doi:10.1023/A:1019154432472

LocMetrics. (n.d.). Retrieved March 19, 2016, from http://www.locmetrics.com/

Lopata, C. (1995). Integrated Library Systems. *ERIC Digest*. Retrieved from http://www.Ericdigest.org/1996-1/library.htm

Lundvall, B., & Johnson, B. (2011). The learning economy. *Journal of Industry Studies*, *1*(2), 23–42. doi:10.1080/13662719400000002

Macan, B., Ferna'ndez, G. V., & Stojanovski, J. (2013). Open source solutions for libraries: ABCD vs *Koha*. *Electronic Library and Information Systems*, *47*(2), 136–154. doi:10.1108/00330331311313726

MacCormack, A. D., Rusnak, J., Baldwin, C. Y., & Harvard Business School. Division of Research. (2004). *Exploring the structure of complex software designs: An empirical study of open source and proprietary code*. Citeseer.

Mace, A. H. (2015). *Koha as a local circulation system?* Projekt Summary, January 2015 Stockholm University Library. Retrieved May 23, 2017, from http://www.sub.su.se/media/1114980/Koha-Project-Summary.pdf

Macleod, J., & Kefallonitis, E. (2017). Trends Affecting e-Learning Experience Management. In Strategic Innovative Marketing (pp. 753-758). Springer International Publishing. doi:10.1007/978-3-319-33865-1_93

Madhusudhan, M., & Shalini, A. (2014). Online public access catalogues of selected university libraries in Delhi: An evaluative study. *World Digital Libraries*, *7*(1), 15–42.

Madhusudhan, M., & Singh, V. (2016). Integrated library management systems Comparative analysis of *Koha*, Libsys, NewGenLib, and Virtua. *The Electronic Library*, *34*(2), 223–249. doi:10.1108/EL-08-2014-0127

Maher, M. (1999). Open source software: The suc-cess of an alternative intellectual property incentive paradigm. *Fordham Intell. Prop. Media & Ent. LJ, 10*, 619.

Mama, A. S. (2016). Perceived Impact on the Adoption of *Koha* on the State University Library's Management System. *International Conference on Research in Social Sciences, Humanities and Education.* Retrieved May 23, 2017, from http://uruae.org/siteadmin/upload/8346UH0516070.pdf

Mariani, L., & Pastore, F. (2008, November). Automated identification of failure causes in system logs. In *Software Reliability Engineering, 2008. ISSRE 2008. 19th International Symposium on* (pp. 117-126). IEEE. doi:10.1109/ISSRE.2008.48

Marsavina, C., Romano, D., & Zaidman, A. (2014). Studying Fine-Grained Co-Evolution Patterns of Production and Test Code. *Proceedings of the 2014 IEEE 14th International Working Conference on Source Code Analysis and Manipulation (SCAM)*, 195-204. doi:10.1109/SCAM.2014.28

Maskeri, G., Sarkar, S., & Heafield, K. (2008, February). Mining business topics in source code using latent dirichlet allocation. In *Proceedings of the 1st India software engineering conference* (pp. 113-120). ACM. doi:10.1145/1342211.1342234

McDermid, D. (2006). *Pragmatism.* Retrieved 25/06/2017 from http://www.iep.utm.edu/pragmati/

McGinnis, W. and Ransom, J. (2010). Kete and *Koha*: Integration built on open standards. *OCLC Systems & Services: International Digital Library Perspectives, 26*(2), 114-122.

McIntosh, S., Adams, B., & Hassan, A. (2012). The Evolution of Java build Systems. *Empirical Software Engineering, 17*(4), 578–608. doi:10.1007/s10664-011-9169-5

McIlroy, M. (1968). *Mass Produced Software Components.* Keynote address in NATO Software Engineering Conference.

Menell, P. S. (1999). *Intellectual Property: General Theories.* Berkeley Center for Law and Technology University of California at Berkeley.

Mens, T., Fernández-Ramil, J., & Degrandsart, S. (2008). The Evolution of Eclipse. In *Proceedings of the 2008 IEEE International Conference on Software Maintenance (ICSM)* (pp. 386-395). IEEE. doi:10.1109/ICSM.2008.4658087

Meqdadi, O., Alhindawi, N., Collard, M., & Maletic, J. (2013). Towards Understanding Large-scale Adaptive Changes from Version Histories. In *Proceedings of the 2013 IEEE International Conference on Software Maintenance* (pp. 416-419). IEEE. doi:10.1109/ICSM.2013.61

Merges, R. (1994). Intellectual property rights and bargaining breakdown: The case of blocking patents. *Tennessee Law Review, 62*(1), 74–106.

Milev, R., Muegge, S., & Weiss, M. (2009). Design Evolution of an Open Source Project using an Improved Modularity Metric. In *Proceedings of the 5th IFIP WG 2.13 International Conference on Open Source Systems OSS '09.* Skovde, Sweden: Springer. doi:10.1007/978-3-642-02032-2_4

Millien, R., & Laurie, R. (2008). Meet the middlemen. *Intellectual Asset Management (IAM) Magazine, 28.*

Minister of Development. (2017). *2015-2018 Bilgi Toplumu Stratejisi ve Eylem Planı.* retrieved 25/06/2017 from http://www.kalkinma.gov.tr/Pages/EylemVeDigerPlanlar.aspx

Minister, P. (2012). *E-Devlet: Kavram ve Genel Sorunlar* [E-State: Concept and General Issues Report]. Retrieved 25/06/2017 from https://www.tbmm.gov.tr/arastirma_komisyonlari/bilisim_internet/docs/sunumlar/Koordinasyon_Calismasi_Sunum-ea_06062012_1045.pdff

Ministry of National Education (MoNE). (2001, 2001, 2005, 2013). *Standart Türk Klavyesi.* Retrieved 25/06/2017 from http://www.resmigazete.gov.tr/eskiler/2013/12/20131210-9.htm

Ministry of National Education (MoNE). (2015). *MEB ile Microsoft Türkiye'den iş birliği projesi.* Retrieved 25/06/2017 from http://www.meb.gov.tr/meb-ile-microsoft-turkiyeden-is-birligi-projesi/haber/8695/tr

Ministry of Science, Industry and Technology (MoSIT). (2017). *T.C. Bilim, Sanayi ve Teknoloji Bakanlığı Sözleşmeli Bilişim Personeli Alım İlanı.* Retrieved 25/06/2017 from http://bid.sanayi.gov.tr/DokumanGetHandler.ashx?dokumanId=2071cce7-3a6d-48a9-a59d-fad83972c9eb

Mockus, A., Fielding, R., & Herbsleb, J. (2002). Two case studies of Open Source Software development: Apache and Mozilla. *ACM Transactions on Software Engineering and Methodology, 11*(3), 309–346. doi:10.1145/567793.567795

Monk, A. H. B. (2009). The emerging market for intellectual property: Drivers, restrainers, and implications. *Journal of Economic Geography, 9*(4), 469–491. doi:10.1093/jeg/lbp003

Moore, M. G. (Ed.). (2013). *Handbook of distance education.* Routledge.

Morpus, N. (2016). The Top 6 Free and Open Source School Administration Software. *Capterra – Blog.* Retrieved from http://blog.capterra.com/the-top-6-free-school-administration-software/

Müller, T. (2012). *How to Choose an Free and Open Source Integrated Library System.* Retrieved from http://eprints.rclis.org/bitstream/10760/15387/1/How%20to%20 choose%20an%20open%20source%20ILS.pdf

Murgia, A., Concas, G., Marchesi, M., Tonelli, R., & Turnu, I. (2009). Empirical study of Software Quality Evolution in Open Source Projects using Agile Practices. *Proceedings of the International symposium on Emerging Trends in Software Metrics (ETSM).*

Myrtveit, I., & Stensrud, E. (2008). *An Empirical Study of Software development Productivity in C and C++.* Presented at NIK-2008 conference. Retrieved from www.nik.no

Naama, K. (2006). *The State of Information Technology in the Arab World.* University of Veliko Turnovo.

Nagaraj, K., Killian, C., & Neville, J. (2012). Structured comparative analysis of systems logs to diagnose performance problems. *9th USENIX Symposium on Networked Systems Design and Implementation (NSDI 12),* 353-366.

Nakakoji, K., Yamamoto, Y., Nishinaka, Y., Kishida, K., & Ye, Y. (2002). Evolution Patterns of Open-Source Software Systems and Communities. In *Proceedings of the international workshop on Principles of Software Evolution* (pp. 76-85). ACM. doi:10.1145/512035.512055

Natural Language Toolkit. (n.d.). Retrieved March 19, 2016, from http://www.nltk.org/

Neamtiu, I., Xie, G., & Chen, J. (2013). Towards a Better Understanding of Software Evolution: An Empirical Study on Open-Source Software. *Journal of Software: Evolution and Process, 25*(3), 193–218.

Nesbitt, S. (2017). *4 open source tools for sharing files.* Retrieved from https://opensource.com/article/17/3/file-sharing-tools

Nile Center Technology Research. (n.d.). Retrieved from http://www.nctr.sd/en/index.php/nctr-opensource/foss.html

North, D. C. (1990). *Institutional Change, and Economic Performance.* Cambridge, UK: Cambridge University Press. doi:10.1017/CBO9780511808678

Nuvolari, A. (2004). Collective invention during the British industrial revolution: The case of the Cornish pumping engine. *Cambridge Journal of Economics, 28*(3), 347–363. doi:10.1093/cje/28.3.347

O'Reilly, T. (1999). Lessons from open-source soft-ware development: Introduction. *Communications of the ACM, 42*(4), 32–37. doi:10.1145/299157.299164

Obajemu, A. S., Osagie, J. N., Akinade, H. O. J., & Ekere, F. C. (2013). Library software products in Nigeria: A survey of uses and assessment. *International Journal of Library and Information Science*, *5*(5), 113–125.

Oduwole, A. A. (2005). Information Technology Applications to Cataloguing in Nigerian Universities. *The Electronic Library*, *23*(3), 1–2. doi:10.1108/02640470510603688

Ogbenege, J., & Adetimirin, A. (2013). Selection and use of *KOHA* software in two private Nigerian universities. *Library Hi Tech News*, *30*(6), 12–16. doi:10.1108/LHTN-04-2013-0020

Ojedokun, A. A., Olla, G. O., & Adigun, S. A. (2016). Integrated Library System (ILS) implementation: The Bowen University Library experience with *Koha*. *African Journal of Library Archives and Information Science*, *26*(1), 31–42.

Okoroma, F. (2010). Retrospective Conversion in Two Nigerian University Libraries: Comparative Study of Kenneth Dike Library and Obafemi Awolowo University Library. *Library Philosophy and Practice*, 1-26. Retrieved from http://www.Fags.org/periodicals/201005/ 2068075251.html

Okutan, A., & Yildiz, O. (2012). *Software defect prediction using Bayesian networks*. Journal Empirical Software Engineering.

Olssen, M., Codd, J., & O'Neill, A. (2004). *Education Policy: Globalization, Citizenship and Democracy*. Thousand Oaks, CA: Sage.

Olszak, A., Lazarova-Molnar, S., & Jørgensen, B. (2015). Evolution of Feature-Oriented Software: How to Stay on Course and Avoid the Cliffs of Modularity Drift. In *Proceedings of the 9th International Joint Conference Software Technologies, CCIS* (Vol. 555, pp. 183-201). Springer.

Oman Government. Free and Open Source Initiative. (n.d.). Retrieved from http://www.oman.om/

Omeluzor, S. U., Adara, O., Ezinwayi, M., Bamidele, M. I., & Umahi, F. O. (2012). Implementation of *Koha* Integrated Library Management Software (ILMS): The Babcock University Experience. *Canadian Social Science*, *8*(4).

Open software becomes a national strategy in Egypt. (n.d.). Retrieved from http://www.madamasr.com/news/open-software-becomes-national-strategy-egypt

Open Source Initiative. (n.d.). Retrieved from http://opensource.org/

OpenForum Europe. (2013). *OFE Procurement Monitoring Report 2013 – 1st Snapshot*. Retrieved 25/06/2017 http://www.openforumeurope.org/library/ofe-procurement-monitoring-report-2013-1st-snapshot/

Organisation for Economic Co-operation and Development (OECD). (1996). *The Knowledge Based Economy*. Paris: Author.

OSS prediction studies: Data collection Table. (2013). Retrieved from OSS prediction studies: Data collection Table: http://literature-review.weebly.com/

Ostrand, T., Weyuker, E., & Bell, R. (2003). Predicting the Location and Number of Faults in Large Software Systems. *IEEE Transactions on Software Engineering*.

Otunla, A. O., & Akanmu-Adeyemo, E. A. (2010). Library automation in Nigeria: The Bowen University experience. *African Journal of Library Archives and Information Science*, *20*(2), 93–102.

P.M., S., & Duraiswamy, K. (2011). An Empirical Validation of Software Quality Metric Suites on Open Source Software for Fault-Proneness Prediction in Object Oriented Systems. *European Journal of Scientific Research*, *52*(2).

Pagano, D., & Maalej, W. (2013). How do open source communities blog? *Empirical Software Engineering*, *18*(6), 1090–1124. doi:10.1007/s10664-012-9211-2

Page, B. W. (n.d.). *Welcome to Apache Hadoop!* Retrieved March 18, 2016, from http://hadoop.apache.org/#DownloadHadoop

Palfrey, T. R., & Rosenthal, H. (1984). Participa-tion and the provision of discrete public goods: A strategic analysis. *Journal of Public Economics*, *24*(2), 171–193. doi:10.1016/0047-2727(84)90023-9

Pan, W., Li, B., Ma, Y., & Liu, J. (2011). Multi-Granularity Evolution Analysis of Software. *Journal of Systems Science and Complexity*, *24*(6), 1068–1082. doi:10.1007/s11424-011-0319-z

Pappas, C. (2011). *Top 10 Free and Open Source eLearning Projects to Watch for 2012*. Retrieved from https://www.efrontlearning.com/blog/2011/12/top-10-free-and-open-source-elearning.html

Pappas, C. (2015). *The Top 8 Open Source Learning Management Systems*. Retrieved from https://elearningindustry.com/top-open-source-learning-management-systems

Pappas, C. (2016). *Top 6 Open Source Web Conferencing Software Tools for eLearning Professionals*. Retrieved from https://elearningindustry.com/top-6-open-source-web-conferencing-software-tools-elearning-professionals

Pasaréti, O., Hajdin, H., Matusaka, T., Jambori, A., Molnar, I., & Tucsányi-Szabó, M. (2011). Augmented Reality in education. *INFODIDACT 2011 Informatika Szakmódszertani Konferencia*.

Paul, O. (2010). *Koha developer wiki: Koha users around the world*. Retrieved March 12, 2013, from http://wiki.Koha.org/doku.php?id_Kohaausers

Paulson, J., Succi, G., & Eberlein, A. (2004). An Empirical Study of Open-Source and Closed-Source Software products. *IEEE Transactions on Software Engineering*, *30*(4), 246–256. doi:10.1109/TSE.2004.1274044

Pazzani, M. J., & Billsus, D. (2007). Content-based recommendation systems. In *The adaptive web* (pp. 325–341). Springer Berlin Heidelberg. doi:10.1007/978-3-540-72079-9_10

Perry, D., Porter, A., & Votta, L. (2000). Empirical studies of software engineering: A roadmap. *The Future of Software Engineering*.

Peters, M. A., & Besley, T. (2008). *Building Knowledge Cultures: Education and Development in the Age of Knowledge Capitalism*. Rowman & Littlefield Publishers.

Peterson, P. (2009). *An Introduction to Decision Theory*. Cambridge University Press. doi:10.1017/CBO9780511800917

Pfaffman, J. (2007). It's Time to Consider Open Source Software. *TechTrends*, *51*(3), 38–43. doi:10.1007/s11528-007-0040-x

Phadke, A., & Allen, E. (2005). *Predicting Risky Modules in Open-Source Software for High-Performance Computing*. SE-HPCS. doi:10.1145/1145319.1145337

Phipps, G. (1999). Comparing Observed Bug and Productivity Rates for Java and C++. *Software, Practice & Experience*, *29*(4), 345–358. doi:10.1002/(SICI)1097-024X(19990410)29:4<345::AID-SPE238>3.0.CO;2-C

Pressman, R. (2010). *Software Engineering – A Practitioner's Approach* (7th ed.). McGraw Hill Education.

Projektlink Konsult Limited. (2010). *Introducing Koha: An Integrated Library Management System*. Ibadan, Nigeria: Blue Print Concept.

Pruett, J., & Choi, N. (2013). A comparison between select open source and proprietary integrated library systems. *Library Hi Tech*, *31*(3), 435–454. doi:10.1108/LHT-01-2013-0003

Public Procurement Authority of Turkey. (2012). *Public Procurement Law*. Retrieved 25/06/2017 from, http://www2.ihale.gov.tr/english/4734_English.pdf

Punch, K. (2009). *Introduction to Research Methods in Education.* London: Sage.

Qiu, D., Li, B., & Su, Z. (2013). An Empirical Analysis of the Co-Evolution of Schema and Code in Database Applications. In Meeting on Foundations of Software Engineering, ser. ESEC/FSE 2013 (pp. 125–135). ACM. doi:10.1145/2491411.2491431

Rabkin, A., & Katz, R. H. (2010, November). Chukwa: A System for Reliable Large-Scale Log Collection. LISA, 10, 1-15.

Radtke, N. P., Janssen, M. A., & Collofello, J. S. (2009). What Makes Free/Libre Open Source Software (FLOSS) Projects Successful? An Agent-Based Model of FLOSS Projects. *International Journal of Open Source Software and Processes,* *1*(2), 1–13. doi:10.4018/jossp.2009040101

Rafiq, M., & Ameen, K. (2009). Issues and lessons learned in open source software adoption in Pakistani libraries. *The Electronic Library, 27*(4), 601–610. doi:10.1108/02640470910979561

Rafiq, M., & Ameen, K. (2010). Adoption of open source software in Pakistani libraries: A survey. *Information Age,* *4*(3), 35–38.

Rainer, A., Lane, P., Malcolm, J., & Scholz, S. (2008). Using N-grams to Rapidly Characterise the Evolution of Software code. In *Proceedings of the 23rd IEEE/ACM International Conference on Automated Software Engineering Workshops* (pp. 43-52). IEEE. doi:10.1109/ASEW.2008.4686320

Raja, U., Hale, D., & Hale, J. (2009). Modeling Software Evolution Defects: A Time Series Approach. *Journal of Software Maintenance and Evolution: Research and Practice, 21*(1), 49–71. doi:10.1002/smr.398

Ramzan, M. (2004). Levels of IT applications in muslim world libraries. *The Electronic Library, 22*(3), 274–280. doi:10.1108/02640470410541688

Randhawa, S. (2008). *Open source software and libraries.* Retrieved May 23, 2017, from http://eprints.rclis.org/16271/

Ranking, S. (2014). *Top 10 Programming Languages.* Retrieved from Top 10 Programming Languages: http://spectrum. ieee.org/computing/software/top-10-programming-languages

Ratzinger, J. T. S. (2008). On the Relation of Refactoring and Software Defects. MSR, 35-38.

Ratzinger, J., Gall, H., & Pinzger, M. (2007). Quality Assessment Based on Attribute Series of Software Evolution. In *Proceedings of the 14th Working Conference on Reverse Engineering WCRE '07* (pp. 80-89). IEEE. doi:10.1109/ WCRE.2007.39

Ratzinger, J., Sigmund, T., Vorburger, P., & Gall, H. (2007). Mining software evolution to predict refactoring. *International Symposium on Empirical Software Engineering and Measurement,* 354–363. doi:10.1109/ESEM.2007.9

Raymond, E. (1999). The cathedral and the bazaar. *Knowledge, Technology & Policy, 12*(3), 23–49. doi:10.1007/s12130-999-1026-0

Reeves, C. R. (2009). Genetic algorithms. Encyclopedia of Database Systems, 1224-1227.

Reilly, R. F., & Schweihs, R. P. (2004). *The hand-book of business valuation and intellectual property analysis.* McGraw-Hill.

Rentocchini, F., & Tartari, D. (2010). An Analysis of the Adoption of Open Source Software by Local Public Administrations: Evidence from the Emilia-Romagna Region of Italy. *International Journal of Open Source Software and Processes, 2*(3), 1–29. doi:10.4018/jossp.2010070101

Resnick, P., Iacovou, N., Suchak, M., Bergstrom, P., & Riedl, J. (1994, October). GroupLens: an open architecture for collaborative filtering of netnews. In *Proceedings of the 1994 ACM conference on Computer supported cooperative work* (pp. 175-186). ACM. doi:10.1145/192844.192905

Rizk, N., & El-Kassas, S. (2010). The software industry in Egypt: What role for open source? In Access to Knowledge in Egypt, New Research on 64 Intellectual Property, Innovation, and Development. Bloomsbury.

Rizk, N. (2012). Free and open source software (FOSS) as a vehicle for human development in Egypt: Some evidence and insights. *Int. J. Technological Learning. Innovation and Development*, *5*(3), 221.

Robles, G., Amor, J., Gonzalez-Barahona, J., & Herraiz, I. (2005). Evolution and Growth in Large Libre Software Projects. In *Proceedings of the International Workshop on Principles in Software Evolution* (pp. 165-174). IEEE. doi:10.1109/IWPSE.2005.17

Robles, G., Gonzalez-Barahona, J., & Merelo, J. (2006a). Beyond Source Code: The Importance of other Artifacts in Software Development. *Journal of Systems and Software*, *79*(9), 1233–1248. doi:10.1016/j.jss.2006.02.048

Robles, G., Gonzalez-Barahona, J., Michlmayr, M., & Amor, J. (2006b). Mining Large Software Compilations over Time: Another Perspective of Software Evolution. In *Proceedings of the 2006 international workshop on Mining Software repositories (MSR'06)* (pp. 3-9). ACM doi:10.1145/1137983.1137986

Robles-Martinez, G., Gonzlez-Barahona, J., Centeno-Gonzalez, J., Matellan-Olivera, V., & Rodero-Merino, L. (2003). Studying the Evolution of Libre Software Projects using Publicly Available Data. *Proceedings of the 3rd Workshop on Open Source Software Engineering.*

Rogers, M. (1998). *The definition and measurement of innovation.* Melbourne Institute of Applied Economic and Social Research. Retrieved from http://scholar.google.co.uk/scholar.bib?q=info:5oErPpbtQl8J:scholar.google.com/&output=citation&hl=en&as_ sdt=0,5&ct=citation&cd=24

Romero, C., & Ventura, S. (Eds.). (2006). *Data mining in e-learning* (Vol. 4). Wit Press. doi:10.2495/1-84564-152-3

Rossi, B., Russo, B., & Succi, G. (2009) Analysis of Open Source Software Development Iterations by Means of Burst Detection Techniques, In Open Source EcoSystems: Diverse Communities Interacting. In *Proceedings 5th IFIP WG 2.13 International Conference on Open Source Systems* (pp. 83-93). Springer.

Roy, C., & Cordy, J. (2006). *Evaluating the Evolution of Small Scale Open Source Software Systems.* Academic Press.

Russo, B., Mulazzani, F., Russo, B., & Steff, M. (2011). Building knowledge in open source software research in six years of conferences. *IFIP Advances in Information and Communication Technology*, *365*, 123–141. doi:10.1007/978-3-642-24418-6_9

Russo, B., & Succi, G. (2009). A Cost Model of Open Source Software Adoption. *International Journal of Open Source Software and Processes*, *1*(3), 60–82. doi:10.4018/jossp.2009070105

Sahraoui, S. M. (2009). ICT governance in higher education: Case study of the rise and fall of open source in a Gulf university. *International Conference on Information and Communication Technologies and Development (ICTD).* IEEE. doi:10.1109/ICTD.2009.5426692

Saini, M., & Kaur, K. (2014a). Analyzing the Change Profiles of Software Systems using their Change Logs. International Journal of Software Engineering, 7(2), 39-66.

Saini, M., & Kaur, K. (2014b). Software Evolution Prediction using Fuzzy Analysis. In *Proceedings of International Conference on Emerging Applications of Information Technology, organized by Computer Society of India at Indian Institute of Science.* Kolkata, India: IEEE Computer Society Press.

Saini, M., & Kaur, K. (2016). Fuzzy analysis and prediction of commit activity in open source software projects. *IET Software*, *10*(5), 136–146. doi:10.1049/iet-sen.2015.0087

Samoladas, I., Angelis, L., & Stamelos, I. (2010). Survival analysis on the duration of open source projects. *Information and Software Technology, 52*(9), 902–922. doi:10.1016/j.infsof.2010.05.001

Sánchez-Acevedo, M. A., Sabino-Moxo, B. A., & Márquez-Domínguez, J. A. (2017). Mobile Augmented Reality. *Mobile Platforms, Design, and Apps for Social Commerce, 153.*

Santos, E. A., & Hindle, A. (2016). Judging a commit by its cover; or can a commit message predict build failure?. *PeerJ PrePrints, 4*, e1771v1.

Sarwar, B., Karypis, G., Konstan, J., & Riedl, J. (2000, October). Analysis of recommendation algorithms for e-commerce. In *Proceedings of the 2nd ACM conference on Electronic commerce* (pp. 158-167). ACM. doi:10.1145/352871.352887

Sarwar, B., Karypis, G., Konstan, J., & Riedl, J. (2001, April). Item-based collaborative filtering recommendation algorithms. In *Proceedings of the 10th international conference on World Wide Web* (pp. 285-295). ACM.

Schach, S., Jin, B., Yu, L., Heller, G., & Offutt, J. (2003). Determining the Distribution of Maintenance Categories: Survey versus Measurement. *Empirical Software Engineering, 8*(4), 351–365. doi:10.1023/A:1025368318006

Schiaffino, S., Garcia, P., & Amandi, A. (2008). eTeacher: Providing personalized assistance to e-learning students. *Computers & Education, 51*(4), 1744–1754. doi:10.1016/j.compedu.2008.05.008

Schilling, A., Laumer, S., & Weitzel, T. (2012). Who Will Remain? An Evaluation of Actual Person-Job and Person-Team Fit to Predict Developer Retention in FLOSS Projects. *Hawaii International Conference on System Sciences*, 3446–3455.

Schumpeter, J. (1942). *Capitalism, socialism and democracy.* New York, NY: Harper.

Scientific and Technological Research Council of Turkey (TUBITAK). (2013). *25th Meeting of the High Council of Science and Technology Report.* Retrieved 25/06/2017 from http://www.tubitak.gov.tr/sites/default/files/btyk25_yeni_kararlar_toplu.pdf

SenthilKumaran, P., & Sreeja, K. P. (2017). A Study On Managing *Koha* Open Source Library Management System In the University Library, Central University Of Kerala. *International Journal of Research in Library Science, 3*(1), 91–101.

Shaffer, B. (2012). The Importance of Free Minds. *Lewrockwell.* retrieved 25/06/2017 from http://archive.lewrockwell.com/shaffer/shaffer250.html

Shafi-Ullah, F., & Qutab, S. (2012). From LAMP to *Koha*: Case study of the Pakistan legislative Assembly Libraries. *Electronic Library and Information Systems, 46*(1), 43–55. doi:10.1108/00330331211204557

Shah-Hosseini, H. (2009). The intelligent water drops algorithm: A nature-inspired swarm-based optimization algorithm. *International Journal of Bio-inspired Computation, 1*(1-2), 71–79. doi:10.1504/IJBIC.2009.022775

Shah, S. K. (2006). Motivation, governance, and the viability of hybrid forms in open source software development. *Management Science, 52*(7), 1000–1014. doi:10.1287/mnsc.1060.0553

Shang, W., Nagappan, M., & Hassan, A. E. (2015). Studying the relationship between logging characteristics and the code quality of platform software. *Empirical Software Engineering, 20*(1), 1–27. doi:10.1007/s10664-013-9274-8

Shani, G., Brafman, R. I., & Heckerman, D. (2002, August). An MDP-based recommender system. In *Proceedings of the Eighteenth conference on Uncertainty in artificial intelligence* (pp. 453-460). Morgan Kaufmann Publishers Inc.

Sharma, B., Chudnovsky, V., Hellerstein, J. L., Rifaat, R., & Das, C. R. (2011, October). Modeling and synthesizing task placement constraints in Google compute clusters. In *Proceedings of the 2nd ACM Symposium on Cloud Computing* (p. 3). ACM. doi:10.1145/2038916.2038919

Shatnawi, R., & Li, W. (2008). The effectiveness of software metrics in identifying error-prone classes in post-release software evolution process. *Journal of Systems and Software*, *81*(11), 1868–1882. doi:10.1016/j.jss.2007.12.794

Shen, L., Wang, M., & Shen, R. (2009). Affective e-learning: Using" emotional" data to improve learning in pervasive learning environment. *Journal of Educational Technology & Society*, *12*(2), 176.

Sigelman, B. H., Barroso, L. A., Burrows, M., Stephenson, P., Plakal, M., Beaver, D., . . . Shanbhag, C. (2010). Dapper, a large-scale distributed systems tracing infrastructure. Technical report, Google, Inc.

Singh, P. S. V. (2012). Empirical Investigation of Fault prediction capability of object oriented metrics of open source software. JCSSE, 323 – 327.

Singh, P. V., Tan, Y., & Mookerjee, V. (2008). Network effects: The influence of structural social capital on open source project success. *SSRN eLibrary*.

Singh, M., & Sanaman, G. (2012). Open source integrated library management systems: Comparative analysis of *Koha* and NewGenLib. *The Electronic Library*, *30*(6), 809–832. doi:10.1108/02640471211282127

Singh, P., & Verma, S. (2012). *Empirical Investigation of Fault prediction capability of object oriented metrics of open source software*. JCSSE.

Singh, S. (2008). A Computational Method of Forecasting Based on Fuzzy Time Series. *Journal of Mathematics and Computers in Simulation*, *79*(3), 539–554. doi:10.1016/j.matcom.2008.02.026

Singh, V. (2013). Experiences of Migrating to an Open-Source Integrated Library System. *Information Technology and Libraries*, *32*(1), 36. doi:10.6017/ital.v32i1.2268

Singh, V. (2014). Expectations versus experiences: Librarians using open source integrated library systems. *The Electronic Library*, *32*(5), 688–709. doi:10.1108/EL-10-2012-0129

Siy, H., Chundi, P., Rosenkrant, D., & Subramaniam, M. (2007). Discovering Dynamic Developer Relationships from Software Version Histories by Time Series Segmentation. In *Proceedings of the 2007 IEEE International Conference on Software Maintenance* (pp. 415-424). IEEE. doi:10.1109/ICSM.2007.4362654

Smith, N., Capiluppi, A., & Fernandez-Ramil, J. (2006). Agent-based Simulation of Open Source Software Evolution. *Software Process Improvement and Practice*, *11*(4), 423–434. doi:10.1002/spip.280

Smith, N., Capiluppi, A., & Ramil, J. (2005). A Study of Open Source Software Evolution Data using Qualitative Simulation. *Software Process Improvement and Practice*, *10*(3), 287–300. doi:10.1002/spip.230

Solow, R. M. (1957). Technical change and the aggre-gate production function. *The Review of Economics and Statistics*, *39*(3), 312–320. doi:10.2307/1926047

Solutions, K. (2011). *Koha Integrated Library Management System*. Retrieved May 23, 2017, from https://www.keep.pt/en/produtos/Koha

Sondakika News. (2013). *E Okul VBS girişi çöktü MEB sitesine girilmiyor*. Retrieved 25/06/2017 from, http://www.ihlassondakika.com/haber/E-Okul-VBS-girisi-coktu-MEB-sitesine-girilmiyor_568692.html#

Song, L., Singleton, E. S., Hill, J. R., & Koh, M. H. (2004). Improving online learning: Student perceptions of useful and challenging characteristics. *The Internet and Higher Education*, *7*(1), 59–70. doi:10.1016/j.iheduc.2003.11.003

Spencer, J. W. (2003). Firms' knowledge-sharing strategies in the global innovation system: Empiri-cal evidence from the flat panel display industry. *Strategic Management Journal*, *24*(3), 217–233. doi:10.1002/smj.290

Stallman, R. (2002). *Free Software, Free Society: Selected Essays of Richard M. Stallman.* Retrieved 25/06/2017 from http://www.gnu.org/philosophy/fsfs/rms-essays.pdf

Stallman, R. (2013). FLOSS and FOSS. *Free Software Foundation.* Retrieved 25/06/2017 from https://www.gnu.org/philosophy/floss-and-foss.en.html

Stamelos, I., Angelis, L., Oikonomou, A., & Bleris, G. L. (2002). Code quality analysis in open source software development. *Information Systems Journal, 12*(1), 43–60. doi:10.1046/j.1365-2575.2002.00117.x

Stephenson, N. (2004). *In the Beginning was the Command Line.* Retrieved 25/06/2017 from http://introcs.cs.princeton.edu/java/15inout/command.txt

Stewart, K., Darcy, D., & Daniel, S. (2006). Opportunities and Challenges Applying Functional Data Analysis to the Study of Open Source Software Evolution. *Statistical Science, 21*(2), 167–178. doi:10.1214/088342306000000141

Stol, K., & Babar, M. (2009). Reporting Empirical Research in Open Source Software: the State of Practice. In *Proceedings 5th IFIP WG 2.13 International Conference on Open Source Systems OSS '09.* Skovde, Sweden: Springer. doi:10.1007/978-3-642-02032-2_15

Stump, S. L. & Deegan, R. L. (2013). Open Source Opens Doors Repurposing Library Software to Facilitate Faculty Research and Collaboration. *Pennsylvania Libraries: Research & Practice, 1*(2).

Su, X., & Khoshgoftaar, T. M. (2006, November). Collaborative filtering for multi-class data using belief nets algorithms. In *Tools with Artificial Intelligence, 2006. ICTAI'06. 18th IEEE International Conference on* (pp. 497-504). IEEE. doi:10.1109/ICTAI.2006.41

Subramanyan, R., & Krishnan, M. (2003). Empirical analysis of ck metrics for object-oriented design complexity- Implications for software defects. *IEEE Transactions on Software Engineering, 29*(4), 297–310. doi:10.1109/TSE.2003.1191795

Sun, P. C., Tsai, R. J., Finger, G., Chen, Y. Y., & Yeh, D. (2008). What drives a successful e-Learning? An empirical investigation of the critical factors influencing learner satisfaction. *Computers & Education, 50*(4), 1183–1202. doi:10.1016/j.compedu.2006.11.007

Surman, M., & Diceman, J. (2004), *Choosing Open Source: A Decision making Guide for Civil Society Organizations.* The Commons Group. Retrieved from www.commonsgroup.com/docs/opensourceguide_fullversion_v1p0.pdf

Syeed, M., Hammouda, I., & Systa, T. (2013). Evolution of Open Source Software Projects: A Systematic Literature Review. *Journal of Software, 8*(11).

Syeed, M., Kilamo, T., Hammouda, I., & Systä, T. (2012). Open Source Prediction Methods: a systematic literature review. In *IFIP International Conference of Open Source Systems* (pp. 280-285). Springer. doi:10.1007/978-3-642-33442-9_22

Tahvildari, L., Gregory, R., & Kontogiannis, K. (1999). An Approach for Measuring Software Evolution using Source Code Features. In *Proceedings of the Sixth Asia Pacific Software Engineering Conference (APSEC '99)* (pp. 10-17). IEEE. doi:10.1109/APSEC.1999.809579

Tajoli, Z., Carassiti, A., Marchitelli, A. and Valenti, F. (2011). OSS diffusion in Italian libraries The case of *Koha* by the Consorzio Interuniversitario Lombardo per l'Elaborazione Automatica (CILEA). *OCLC Systems & Services: International Digital Library Perspectives, 27*(1), 45-50.

Tang, T. Y., & McCalla, G. (2003). Smart recommendation for an evolving e-learning system. *Workshop on Technologies for Electronic Documents for Supporting Learning, International Conference on Artificial Intelligence in Education,* 699-710.

Team, C. D. (n.d.). *Apache Commons Logging - Overview*. Retrieved March 18, 2016, from https://commons.apache.org/proper/commons-logging/

The Economist. (2006, March 16). Open source business. Open, but not as usual. *The Economist*, pp. 1-7.

The Free and Open Source Software Conference (FOSSC Oman). (n.d.). Retrieved from http://fossc.om/2015/

The Government of Jordan and open source database management company Ingres have signed an MOU to promote open source software adoption in the country. (n.d.). Retrieved from http://www.itp.net/578825-jordan-information-ministry-signs-deal-on-open-source

The Open Source Lebanese Movement. (n.d.). Retrieved from http://oslm.cofares.net/p/open-source-lebanese-movement.html

Thomas, S., Adams, B., Hassan, A., & Blostein, D. (2014). Studying Software Evolution using Topic Models. *Science of Computer Programming*, *80*, 457–479. doi:10.1016/j.scico.2012.08.003

Thung, F., Bissyandé, T. F., Lo, D., & Jiang, L. (2013, March). Network structure of social coding in github. In *Software Maintenance and Reengineering (CSMR), 2013 17th European Conference on* (pp. 323-326). IEEE. doi:10.1109/CSMR.2013.41

Thwin, M. M. T., & Quah, T. S. (2005). Application of neural networks for software quality prediction using object-oriented metrics. *Journal of Systems and Software*, *76*(2), 147–156. doi:10.1016/j.jss.2004.05.001

Thy, T., Ferenc, R., & Siket, I. (2005). Empirical validation of object-oriented metrics on open source software for fault prediction. *IEEE Transactions on Software Engineering*, *31*(10), 897–910. doi:10.1109/TSE.2005.112

Tian, K., Revelle, M., & Poshyvanyk, D. (2009, May). Using latent dirichlet allocation for automatic categorization of software. In *Mining Software Repositories, 2009. MSR'09. 6th IEEE International Working Conference on* (pp. 163-166). IEEE. doi:10.1109/MSR.2009.5069496

Tiemann, T. (2010). *Growing an Open Source Economy With Competence at the Centre*. Open Source Initiative Vice President, Open Source Affairs, Red Hat Inc.

Tiqqun. (2010). *The Cybernetic Hypothesis*. The Anarchist Library Anti-Copyright.

Tolu, H. (2013). Expendable 'Written' ICT Policies in a Digital Era, No Broken Promise. *International Free and Open Source Software Law Review*, *5*(2), 79–104. doi:10.5033/ifosslr.v5i2.86

Tolu, H. (2016). Techno-Social Policy of Free Open Source Software in Turkey, A Case Study on Pardus. *Journal of Software*, *11*(3), 287–311. doi:10.17706/jsw.11.3.287-311

Tunisian Open Source Software Unit. Ministry of Communication Technologies. (n.d.). Retrieved from http://www.opensource.tn/open-source/accueil/

Tu, Q., & Godfrey, M. (2002). An Integrated Approach for Studying Architectural Evolution. In *Proceedings of the 10th International Workshop on Program Comprehension* (pp. 127-136). IEEE.

Turhan, B., Menzies, T., Bener, A. B., & Stefano, J. D. (2009). On the relative value of cross-company and within-company data for defect prediction. *International Symposium on Empirical Software Engineering and Measurement2009*, *14*(5), 540–578. doi:10.1007/s10664-008-9103-7

Turski, W. (1996). Reference Model for Smooth Growth of Software Systems. *IEEE Transactions on Software Engineering*, *22*(8), 599–600.

Ukachi, N. B. (2012). Awareness, availability and utilisation of open source software in Nigerian libraries: the way forward. *International Research Journal of Library, Information and Archival Studies, 1*(1), 1-9.

Ukachi, N. B., Nwachukwu, V. N., & Onuoha, U. D. (2014). Library Automation and Use of Open Source Software to Maximize Library Effectiveness. *Information and Knowledge Management, 3*(4).

Ullah, N. (2015). A method for predicting open source software residual defects. *Software Quality Journal, 23*, 55-76. DOI: 10.1007/s11219-014-9229-3

UNESCO. (2008). *Intergovernmental Council for the Information for All Programme (IFAP) Fifth Session.* UNESCO.

United Nations. (2001). *Human Development Report.* Retrieved 25/06/2017 from http://hdr.undp.org/en/reports/global/hdr2001/chapters/

Uzomba, E. C., Oyebola, O. J., & Izuchukwu, A. C. (2015). The Use and Application of Open Source Integrated Library System in Academic Libraries in Nigeria: *Koha* Example. *Library Philosophy and Practice,* Paper 1250. Retrieved from http://digitalcommons.unl.edu/libphilprac/1250)

Van Eck, R. (2007). Building artificially intelligent learning games. In *Games and simulations in online learning: Research and development frameworks* (pp. 271–307). IGI Global. doi:10.4018/978-1-59904-304-3.ch014

Van Krevelen, D. W. F., & Poelman, R. (2010). A survey of augmented reality technologies, applications and limitations. *International Journal of Virtual Reality, 9*(2), 1.

Van Reijswoud, V., & Mulo, E. (2012). Evaluating the Potential of Free and Open Source Software in the Developing World. *International Journal of Open Source Software and Processes, 4*(3), 38–51. doi:10.4018/ijossp.2012070104

Vasa, R. (2010). *Growth and Change Dynamics in Open Source Software Systems* (Ph.D. thesis). Swinburne University of Technology, Melbourne, Australia.

Vaucher, S., & Sahraoui, H. (2007). Do Software Libraries Evolve Differently than Applications?: An Empirical Investigation. In *Proceedings of the 2007 Symposium on Library-Centric Software Design* (pp. 88-96). ACM. doi:10.1145/1512762.1512771

Villaverde, J. E., Godoy, D., & Amandi, A. (2006). Learning styles' recognition in e-learning environments with feed-forward neural networks. *Journal of Computer Assisted Learning, 22*(3), 197–206. doi:10.1111/j.1365-2729.2006.00169.x

Virtual Machinery - Sidebar 2 - The Halstead Metrics. (n.d.). Retrieved March 19, 2016, from http://www.virtualmachinery.com/sidebar2.htm

Von Hippel, E. (1988). *The Sources of Innovation* (Vol. 80). Oxford University Press.

Von Hippel, E. (2007). Horizontal innovation net-works—by and for users. *Industrial and Corporate Change, 16*(2), 293–315. doi:10.1093/icc/dtm005

Von Hippel, E., & Von Krogh, G. (2003). Open source software and the 'private-collective' innovation model: Issues for organization science. *Organization Science, 14*(2), 209–223. doi:10.1287/orsc.14.2.209.14992

Wahyudin, D., Schatten, A., Winkler, D., Tjoa, A. M., & Biffl, S. (2008). *Defect prediction using combined product and project metrics a case study from the open source apache, myfaces project family.* Euromicro Conference Software Engineering and Advanced Applications. doi:10.1109/SEAA.2008.36

Walid, K. (2010). Open Source Software in the Arab Region. *The Third International Symposium on Web Services.* Zayed University.

Walls, I. (2010). Migrating from Innovative Interfaces' Millennium to *Koha*: The NYU Health sciences Libraries' experiences. *OCLC Systems & Services: International Digital Library Perspectives, 27*(1), 51-56.

Walter, M., & Joann, R. (2010). Kete and Koha: Integration built on open standards *OCLC Systems & Services. International Digital Library Perspectives, 26*(2), 114–122.

Wang, L. (2001). Intelligent optimization algorithms with applications. Tsinghua University & Springer Press.

Wang, S. C. (2003). Artificial neural network. In Interdisciplinary computing in java programming (pp. 81-100). Springer US. doi:10.1007/978-1-4615-0377-4_5

Wang, L., Wang, Z., Yang, C., Zhang, L., & Ye, Q. (2009). Linux Kernels as Complex Networks: A Novel Method to Study Evolution. In *Proceedings of the 25th International Conference on Software Maintenance* (pp. 41-51). IEEE. doi:10.1109/ICSM.2009.5306348

Web Resources Depot. (2009). *7 Widely-Used and Open Source E-Learning Applications*. Retrieved from https://webresourcesdepot.com/7-widely-used-and-open-source-e-learning-applications/

Weber, S. (2000). *The political economy of open source software*. Retrieved from http://www. escholarship.org/uc/item/3hq916dc

Weber, S. (2004). *The Success of Open Source*. Cambridge, MA: Harvard University Press.

Webopedia. (n.d.). Retrieved from http://www.webopedia.com/TERM/O/open_source.html

Weicheng, Y., Beijun, S., & Ben, X. (2013). Mining GitHub: Why Commit Stops -- Exploring the Relationship between Developer's Commit Pattern and File Version Evolution. *Proceedings of the 20th Asia-Pacific Software Engineering Conference, 2*, 165–169. doi:10.1109/APSEC.2013.133

Welcome to Statistics How To! (n.d.). Retrieved March 19, 2016, from http://www.statisticshowto.com/

Welsh, E. T., Wanberg, C. R., Brown, K. G., & Simmering, M. J. (2003). E-learning: emerging uses, empirical results and future directions. *International Journal of Training and Development, 7*(4), 245-258.

Wenger, E. (2014). *Artificial intelligence and tutoring systems: computational and cognitive approaches to the communication of knowledge*. Morgan Kaufmann.

Wen-Shung Tai, D., Wu, H. J., & Li, P. H. (2008). Effective e-learning recommendation system based on self-organizing maps and association mining. *The Electronic Library, 26*(3), 329-344.

Wermilinger, M., & Ferreira, H. (2011). Quality Evolution track at QUATIC 2010. *Software Engineering Notes, 36*(1), 28–29. doi:10.1145/1921532.1960273

Wheeler, A. D. (2014). *Why Open Source Software / Free Software (OSS/FS)? Look at the Numbers!* Retrieved 25/06/2017 from http://www.dwheeler.com/oss_fs_why.html

Wheeler, D. A. (2007a). *How to evaluate open source/free software (OSS/FS) programs*. Retrieved July 15, 2016, from www.dwheeler.com/oss_fs_eval.html

Wheeler, D. A. (2007b). *Why open source software/free software (OSS/FS, FLOSS, or FOSS)? Look at the numbers!* Retrieved July 15,2016, from www.dwheeler.com/contactme.html

Whitley, D. (1994). A genetic algorithm tutorial. *Statistics and Computing, 4*(2), 65–85. doi:10.1007/BF00175354

Wiener, N. (1950). *The Human Use Of Human Beings: Cybernetics And Society*. Houghton Mifflin.

Wikipedia. (2011). *Integrated Library System*. Retrieved from http://en.Wikipedia.org/wiki/integrated Library System

Wikipedia. (2012). *Web 2.0*. Retrieved from http://en.wikipedia.org/wiki/ Web_2.0#History

Wikipedia. (2013). *Koha (software)*. Retrieved from https://en.wikipedia.org/wiki/Koha_% 28software%29

Williamson, O. (1979). Transaction-cost econom-ics: The governance of contractual relations. *The Journal of Law & Economics*, *22*(2), 233–261. doi:10.1086/466942

Willis, N. (2010). *Koha Community Squares off Against Commercial Fork*. Retrieved from https://lwn.net/articles/386284/

Wolf, T., Schroter, A., Damian, D., & Nguyen, T. (2009). Predicting build failures using social network analysis on developer communication. *International Conference on Software Engineering*, 1-11. doi:10.1109/ICSE.2009.5070503

Woolf, B. P. (2010). *Building intelligent interactive tutors: Student-centered strategies for revolutionizing e-learning*. Morgan Kaufmann.

World Bank. (1993). *Turkey: Informatics and Economic Modernization, A World Bank Country Study*. The World Bank. Retrieved 25/06/2017 from http://www-wds.worldbank.org/external/default/WDSContentServer/IW3P/IB/1993/03/01/000009265_3970128104047/Rendered/INDEX/multi0page.txt

World Economic Forum. (2014). *The Global Information Technology Report 2014*. Retrieved from http://www3.weforum.org/docs/WEF_GlobalInformationTechnology_Report_2014.pdf

Wrosch, J. (2007). Open source software options for any library. *MLA Forum*, *5*(3).

Wu, H. K., Lee, S. W. Y., Chang, H. Y., & Liang, J. C. (2013). Current status, opportunities and challenges of augmented reality in education. *Computers & Education*, *62*, 41–49. doi:10.1016/j.compedu.2012.10.024

Wu, J., & Holt, R. (2004). Linker Based Program Extraction and its use in Software Evolution. *Proceedings of the International Workshop on Unanticipated Software Evolution*, 1-15.

Wu, J., Holt, R., & Hassan, A. (2007). Empirical Evidence for SOC Dynamics in Software Evolution. In *Proceedings of the International Conference on Software Maintenance* (pp. 244-254). IEEE. doi:10.1109/ICSM.2007.4362637

Xie, G., Chen, J., & Neamtiu, I. (2009). Towards a Better Understanding of Software Evolution: An Empirical Study on Open Source Software. In *Proceedings of the International Conference on Software Maintenance* (pp. 51-60). IEEE. doi:10.1109/ICSM.2009.5306356

Xu, J., Gao, Y., Christley, S., & Madey, G. (2005). A Topological Analysis of the Open Source Software Development Community. In *Proceedings of the 38th Annual Hawaii International Conference on System Sciences (HICSS'05)*. IEEE.

Xu, W., Huang, L., Fox, A., Patterson, D., & Jordan, M. I. (2009, October). Detecting large-scale system problems by mining console logs. In *Proceedings of the ACM SIGOPS 22nd symposium on Operating systems principles* (pp. 117-132). ACM. doi:10.1145/1629575.1629587

Yang, S. Q., & Hofmann, M. A. (2010). The next generation library catalog: A comparative study of OPACs of *Koha*, Evergreen, and Voyager. *Information Technology and Libraries*, *29*(3), 141–150. doi:10.6017/ital.v29i3.3139

Yang, X. S., & Deb, S. (2010). Engineering optimisation by cuckoo search. *International Journal of Mathematical Modelling and Numerical Optimisation*, *1*(4), 330–343. doi:10.1504/IJMMNO.2010.035430

Yegnanarayana, B. (2009). *Artificial neural networks*. PHI Learning Pvt. Ltd.

Yener, D. (2017). *Handbook of Research on Geographic Information Systems Applications and Advancements*. IGI Global.

Yu, Y., Wang, H., Yin, G., & Ling, C. X. (2014, September). Reviewer recommender of pull-requests in GitHub. In *Software Maintenance and Evolution (ICSME), 2014 IEEE International Conference on* (pp. 609-612). IEEE. doi:10.1109/ICSME.2014.107

Yuan, D., Mai, H., Xiong, W., Tan, L., Zhou, Y., & Pasupathy, S. (2010, March). SherLog: error diagnosis by connecting clues from run-time logs. In ACM SIGARCH computer architecture news (Vol. 38, No. 1, pp. 143-154). ACM. doi:10.1145/1736020.1736038

Yuan, D., Park, S., Huang, P., Liu, Y., Lee, M. M., Tang, X., & Savage, S. et al. (2012). Be conservative: enhancing failure diagnosis with proactive logging. *10th USENIX Symposium on Operating Systems Design and Implementation*, 293-306.

Yuan, D., Park, S., & Zhou, Y. (2012b, June). Characterizing logging practices in open-source software. In *Proceedings of the 34th International Conference on Software Engineering* (pp. 102-112). IEEE Press.

Yuan, D., Zheng, J., Park, S., Zhou, Y., & Savage, S. (2012c). Improving software diagnosability via log enhancement. *ACM Transactions on Computer Systems*, *30*(1), 4. doi:10.1145/2110356.2110360

Yücel, N. (2017). *Pardus: Dünü Bugünü*. Retrieved 25/06/2017 from http://www.pardus.org.tr/forum/t/pardus-dunu-bugunu/1592

Yuen, C. (1985). An empirical approach to the study of errors in large software under maintenance. *Proc. IEEE Int. Conf. on Software Maintenance*, 96–105.

Yuen, C. (1987). A statistical rationale for evolution dynamics concepts. *Proc IEEE Int. Conf. on Software Maintenance*, 156–164.

Yuen, C. (1988). On analyzing maintenance process data at the global and detailed levels. *Proc. IEEE Int. Conf. on Software Maintenance*, 248–255.

Yu, L. (2006). Indirectly Predicting the Maintenance Effort of Open-Source Software. *Journal of Software Maintenance and Evolution: Research and Practice*, *18*(5), 311–332. doi:10.1002/smr.335

Yuming, Z., & Baowen, X. (2008). *Predicting the maintainability of open source software using design metrics*. Academic Press.

Zaidman, A., Rompaey, B., Deursen, A., & Demeyer, S. (2011). Studying the Co-Evolution of Production and Test Code in Open Source and Industrial Developer Test Processes through Repository Mining. *Empirical Software Engineering*, *16*(3), 325–364. doi:10.1007/s10664-010-9143-7

Zaid, Y. (2004). Automating Library Records Using GLAS Software: The University of Lagos Experience. *Nigerian Libraries*, *38*(1), 55–67.

Zaimi, A., Ampatzoglou, A., Triantafyllidou, N., Chatzigeorgiou, A., Mavridis, A., & Chaikalis, T. (2015). An Empirical Study on the Reuse of Third-Party Libraries in Open-Source Software Development. In *Proceedings of the 7th Balkan Conference on Informatics Conference* (pp. 4). ACM. doi:10.1145/2801081.2801087

Zazworka, N., & Ackermann, C. (2010). CodeVizard: a Tool to Aid the Analysis of Software Evolution. In *Proceedings of the 2010 ACM-IEEE International Symposium on Empirical Software Engineering and Measurement (ESEM '10)*. ACM doi:10.1145/1852786.1852865

Zhang, D., Zhou, L., Briggs, R. O., & Nunamaker, J. F. Jr. (2006). Instructional video in e-learning: Assessing the impact of interactive video on learning effectiveness. *Information & Management*, *43*(1), 15–27. doi:10.1016/j.im.2005.01.004

Zhongmin, C., & Yeqing, W. (2010,). The application of theory and method of time series in the modeling of software reliability. In *Proceedings of the 2010 Second International Conference on Information Technology and Computer Science (ITCS)* (pp. 340-343). IEEE. doi:10.1109/ITCS.2010.89

Zhoua, Y. (2010). On the ability of complexity metrics to predict fault-prone classes in object-oriented systems. *Journal of Systems and Software*, *83*(4), 660–674. doi:10.1016/j.jss.2009.11.704

Zhu, J., He, P., Fu, Q., Zhang, H., Lyu, M. R., & Zhang, D. (2015, May). Learning to log: Helping developers make informed logging decisions. In *Software Engineering (ICSE), 2015 IEEE/ACM 37th IEEE International Conference on* (Vol. 1, pp. 415-425). IEEE.

Zhu, A. (2017). *Artificial Neural Networks. The International Encyclopedia of Geography*. Wiley.

Zico, M. (2009). *Developing an Integrated Library System (ILS) using open source software KOHA: A Thesis*. Academic Press.

Ziedonis, R. H. (2004). Don't fence me in: Frag-mented markets for technology and the patent acquisi-tion strategies of firms. *Management Science*, *50*(6), 804–820. doi:10.1287/mnsc.1040.0208

Zimmermann, T., Herzig, K., Nagappan, N., Zeller, A., & Murphy, B. (2010). *Change bursts as defect predictors*. Intl Symp. Software Reliability Eng.

Zimmermann, T., Nagappan, N., Gal, H., Giger, E., & Murphy, B. (2009). *Cross-project Defect Prediction- A Large Scale Experiment on Data vs. Domain vs. Process*. ESEC/FSE.

Zimmermann, T., Nagappan, N., Gall, H., Giger, E., & Murphy, B. (2009, August). Cross-project defect prediction: a large scale experiment on data vs. domain vs. process. In *Proceedings of the the 7th joint meeting of the European software engineering conference and the ACM SIGSOFT symposium on The foundations of software engineering* (pp. 91-100). ACM. doi:10.1145/1595696.1595713

Zimmermann, T., Premraj, R., & Zeller, A. (2006). Predicting Defects for Eclipse. *Third International Workshop on Predictor Models in Software Engineering*.

Zimmermann, T., Premraj, R., & Zeller, A. (2007). Predicting Defects for Eclipse. *Proceedings of the Third International Workshop on Predictor Models in Software Engineering (Promise '07)*. doi:10.1109/PROMISE.2007.10

About the Contributors

Mehdi Khosrow-Pour, D.B.A., received his Doctorate in Business Administration from the Nova Southeastern University (Florida, USA). Dr. Khosrow-Pour taught undergraduate and graduate information system courses at the Pennsylvania State University – Harrisburg for almost 20 years. He is currently Executive Editor at IGI Global (www.igi-global.com). He also serves as Executive Director of the Information Resources Management Association (IRMA) (www.irma-international.org), and Executive Director of the World Forgotten Children's Foundation (www.world-forgotten-children.org). He is the author/editor of more than 100 books in information technology management. He is also the Editor-in-Chief of the *International Journal of Open Source Software and Processes*, *International Journal of Green Computing*, *International Journal of Digital Library Systems*, *International Journal of E-Entrepreneurship and Innovation*, *International Journal of Art, Culture, and Design Technologies*, *International Journal of Signs and Semiotic Systems*, and *International Journal of Disease Control and Containment for Sustainability*, and has authored more than 50 articles published in various conference proceedings and scholarly journals.

* * *

Manar Abu Talib is teaching at the University of Sharjah in the UAE. Dr. Abu Talib's research interest includes software engineering with substantial experience and knowledge in conducting research in software measurement, software quality, software testing, ISO 27001 for Information Security and Open Source Software. Manar is also working on ISO standards for measuring the functional size of software, and has been involved in developing the Arabic version of ISO 19761 (COSMIC-FFP measurement method). She published more than 40 refereed conferences, journals, manuals and technical reports, involved in more than 200 professional activities and sponsored research activities and supervised 30 capstone projects. She received the Best Teacher Award two times, the Exemplary Faculty Award in 2008 and 2010, Google CS4HS Award in 2014, QCRI ArabWIC and Anita Borg Institute Faculty scholarships in 2015, outstanding University & Community Service Award in 2016 and Exemplary Leader Award in WiSTEM 2016. She was the Counselor of IEEE Student Branch at Zayed University, 2012-2013 and founder and former CEO of Emirates Digital Association for Women (EDAW111). She is the ArabWIC VP of Chapters in Arab Women in Computing Association (ArabWIC), an executive member in UAE IEEE Section, the Sharjah Google Developer Group Manager, the UAE representative for the COSMIC-FPP Education Committee and the International Collaborator to Software Engineering Research Laboratory in Montreal, Canada.

Adekunle Adesola, a Chartered Librarian of Nigeria (CLN), presently heads Information Access Management Section which is the modern equivalent of what is known as Readers' Services and Circulation Control of the widely acclaimed Bowen University Library, Iwo, Osun state, Nigeria. He holds a Bachelor of Science degree B. Sc. (Hons) Political Science and Master of Library and Information Studies (M.L.S.) both from the University of Ibadan. He has attended a lot of training, conferences and workshops on Social Media and Web 2.0 applications for information gathering, processing and dissemination. In addition to his highly demanding professional and administrative duties, Adekunle teaches information literacy as an academic librarian in Bowen University. A savant of information science and au fait with ICTs and library software, Adekunle has published sizable number of articles in reputable and peer reviewed, mostly international journals. His research interests include social media applications, Web 2.0. technologies, library software, current and emerging ICTs, digitization and information literacy.

Abdelmalek Amine received an engineering degree in Computer Science from the Computer Science department of Djillali Liabes University of Sidi-Belabbes-Algeria, received the Magister diploma in Computational Science and PhD from Djillali Liabes University in collaboration with Joseph Fourier University of Grenoble. His research interests include data mining, text mining, ontology, classification, clustering, neural networks, and biomimetic optimization methods. He participates in the program committees of several international conferences and on the editorial boards of international journals. Prof. Amine is the head of GeCoDe-knowledge management and complex data-laboratory at UTM University of Saida, Algeria; he also collaborates with the "knowledge base and database" team of TIMC laboratory at Joseph Fourier University of Grenoble.

Kaniz Fatema is currently working as a Lecturer in the Department of Computer Science, AIUB, Dhaka. She completed her M.Sc in Software Engineering from Tampere University of Technology, Finland in 2015. Her research interest includes evaluating Project evolution, prediction and UML modeling.

Roya Ghafele is an Assistant Professor with the School of Law of Edinburgh University. At the same time, she holds three Fellowships with the University of Oxford, among them at the Said Business School and the Oxford Intellectual Property Research Centre. In addition to that she is a Founding Member of Oxfirst Limited, a boutique consulting firm specialized in the Economics of IP. Prior to that, she was an Assistant Professor with the University of Oxford and a Research Scholar with the Haas School of Business, University of California at Berkeley. From 2002 to 2007 she worked with the U.N.'s World Intellectual Property Organization (WIPO) and the Organization for Economic Cooperation and Development (OECD). In 2000 she started her career with the management consulting firm McKinsey & Company, where she moved from a five year long experience as a ballet dancer. Her Ph.D. was awarded the Theodor Koerner Research Prize by the President of the Republic of Austria. Dr. Ghafele was trained at Johns Hopkins University, School of Advanced International Studies, the Sorbonne and Vienna University. She is fluent in German, English, French, Italian and Persian.

Benjamin Gibert is a former research consultant with Oxfirst Limited. Within the University of Oxford, he held a research assistant role. He currently focuses on his artistic work as a composer.

Mohamed Guendouz received his Bachelor's degree in computer science from the Dr. Tahar Moulay University of Saïda, Algeria in 2012, he received his Master's degree from the same university. Now, Mohamed Guendouz is a PhD student at Dr. Tahar Moulay University of Saïda and a researcher at the GeCoDe Research Laboratory, he works on Big Data and Social Networks Analysis, he participated in several international conferences in Algeria as an Author.

Imed Hammouda is currently Professor and Dean of Mediterranean Institute of Technology (MedTech), South Mediterranean University, Tunisia. Before joining MedTech, he was Associate Professor of software engineering at Chalmers and University of Gothenburg, Sweden where he acted as programme manager for the Software Engineering and Management bachelor programme. His academic interests include software ecosystems, open source software, software architecture, software development methods and tools, and variability management. Before moving to Gothenburg, he was Associate Professor at Tampere University of Technology (TUT), Finland. At TUT, he was heading the international masters programme at the Department of Pervasive Computing. He was a founding member and leader of TU-TOpen - TUT research group on open source software. He has been the principal investigator of several research projects on various open initiatives. He has organizer and PC member of several international conferences and workshops such as OSS, SSE, MindTrek, and E-Learning.

Reda Mohamed Hamou received an engineering degree in computer Science from the Computer Science department of Djillali Liabes University of Sidi-Belabbes-Algeria and PhD (Artificial intelligence) from the same University. He has several publications in the field of BioInspired and Metaheuristic. His research interests include Data Mining, Text Mining, Classification, Clustering, computational intelligence, neural networks, evolutionary computation and Biomimetic optimization method. He is a head of research team in GecoDe laboratory. Dr. Hamou is an associate professor in technology faculty in UTMS University of Saida-Algeria.

Kuljit Kaur Chahal has 20 years of teaching and research experience. She is interested in Software Engineering, Distributed Systems, and Open Source Software Systems.

Utku Kose received the B.S. degree in 2008 from computer education of Gazi University, Turkey as a faculty valedictorian. He received M.S. degree in 2010 from Afyon Kocatepe University, Turkey and D.S. / Ph. D. degree in 2017 from Selcuk University, Turkey in the field of computer engineering. Between 2009 and 2011, he has worked as a Research Assistant in Afyon Kocatepe University. Following, he has also worked as a Lecturer and Vocational School - Vice Director in Afyon Kocatepe University between 2011 and 2012 and as a Lecturer and Research Center Director in Usak University between 2012 and 2017. Currently, he is an Assistant Professor in Suleyman Demirel University, Turkey. His research interest includes artificial intelligence, machine ethics, artificial intelligence safety, optimization, the chaos theory, distance education, e-learning, computer education, and computer science.

Sangeeta Lal is working as an assistant professor in Jaypee Institute of Information Technology, Noida, India. Her research interest is in Open Source Software and Mining Software Repositories. She has published papers in several national and international journals and conferences.

Grace Olla presently heads the Acquisitions unit of Bowen University library, Iwo, Osun state, Nigeria. She holds a Master degree, Information Science (M. Inf. Sc.) from the University of Ibadan and a Bachelor of Education in Library and Information Studies (B.L.S.) from Delta State University, Abraka. An erudite scholar, Mrs. Olla, teaches information literacy in Bowen University in addition to her very demanding schedule as the Acquisitions Librarian. A versatile information professional, Mrs Olla has attended lots of trainings, seminars, workshops bordering on building a balanced and systematic collection, library software, Web 2.0 and social media applications to library and information science, ICTs, etc. Her research interests include collection management, bibliographic control, information literacy and customer satisfaction.

Munish Saini is a Ph.D student in the Department of Computer Science, Guru Nanak Dev University, Amritsar, India. He received his B.Tech in Computer Science and Engineering from Sant Baba Bhag Singh Institute of Engineering and Technology, Jalandhar, India and M.Tech in Computer Science and Engineering from Dr. B. R. Ambedkar National Institute of Technology, Jalandhar, India. His research interest are in open source software, software engineering, and data mining.

Neetu Sardana is an Associate Professor in the Department of Computer Science in Jaypee Institute of Information Technology, Noida. She has more than 14 years of teaching experience. She has published papers in many national and international conferences and journal. Her research interest is in the area of Mining Software Repositories, Social Network Analysis and Web Mining. She had supervised several M.Tech Thesis and B.Tech Major Projects. Currently she is guiding four PhD's. She is also serving as a PC member of IC3 conference which is held every year in JIIT-Noida.

Ashish Sureka is an Associate Professor (Computer Science) at Ashoka University. He is also the founder and director of Robo Paathshaala (start-up) which is a robotics education service provider for school students. He was a Principal Researcher at ABB Corporate Research Center (India) for two years from 2015-2017. He was a Faculty Member (at IIIT-Delhi) from July 2009 to October 2014 and a visiting researcher at Siemens Corporate Research from August 2014 - July 2015. His current research interests are in the area of Mining Software Repositories, Software Analytics, and Social Media Analytics. He graduated with an MS and PhD degree in Computer Science from North Carolina State University (NCSU) in May 2002 and May 2005 respectively. He has worked at IBM Research Labs in USA, Siemens Research Lab (India) and was a Senior Research Associate at the R&D Unit of Infosys Technologies Limited before joining IIIT-D as a Faculty Member in July 2009. He has received research grants from Department of Information Technology (DIT, Government of India), Confederation of Indian Industry (CII) and Department of Science and Technology (DST, Government of India). He has published several research papers in international conferences and journals, graduated several PhD and MTech students, organized workshops co-located with conferences, and received best paper awards. He was selected for ACM India Eminent Speaker Program. He holds seven granted US patents.

Mahbubul Syeed is currently working as an Associate Professor in the Dept. of Computer Science, AIUB, Bangladesh. He got his PhD from Tampere University of Technology in 2015 and M.Sc from the same institute in 2010. Research interest of Syeed includes software engineering, software ecosystem, ecosystem enabling architectural design, patterns, and practices, evolution of software projects, socio-technical analysis of projects, big data mining and knowledge extraction. Additionally, Mr. Syeed has expertise in mobile application development in Android platform.

Hüseyin Tolu was born in Turkey and currently is working as a lecture of sociology of education and technology at the Recep Tayyip Erdogan University in Turkey. Tolu has finished his Master and PhD at the University of Bristol in the United Kingdom in 2014. Tolu has ten years of academic experience and interest in techno political management brokering (the trinity mechanisms of techno-politics in Cybernetic) to conceptualize current and future technology in social practices. In academia, Tolu has been interested in software related subjects, in particular cybernetic, sociology, futurism, globalization, privatization, educational policy, free open source software, public-private-partnerships, new public management, digital right management, digital divide and poverty, artificial and humanistic intelligences, technological and economical singularity, future education, philosophy and market (cynic, hedonist, dandy, materialist, activist, etc.), new social movement, etc.

Index

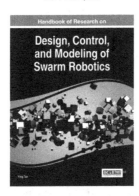

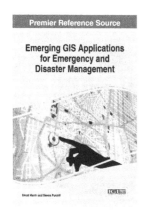
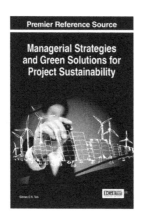

www.igi-global.com/infosci-ondemand

InfoSci®-OnDemand

Continuously updated with new material on a weekly basis, InfoSci®-OnDemand offers the ability to search through thousands of quality full-text research papers. Users can narrow each search by identifying key topic areas of interest, then display a complete listing of relevant papers, and purchase materials specific to their research needs.

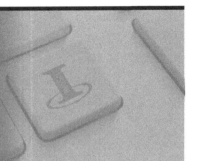

Comprehensive Service

- Over 81,600+ journal articles, book chapters, and case studies.
- All content is downloadable in PDF format and can be stored locally for future use.

No Subscription Fees

- One time fee of $37.50 per PDF download.

Instant Access

- Receive a download link immediately after order completion!

Database Platform Features:

- Comprehensive Pay-Per-View Service
- Written by Prominent International Experts/Scholars
- Precise Search and Retrieval
- Updated With New Material on a Weekly Basis
- Immediate Access to Full-Text PDFs
- No Subscription Needed
- Purchased Research Can Be Stored Locally for Future Use

"It really provides an excellent entry into the research literature of the field. It presents a manageable number of highly relevant sources on topics of interest to a wide range of researchers. The sources are scholarly, but also accessible to 'practitioners'."

– Lisa Stimatz, MLS, University of North Carolina at Chapel Hill, USA

"It is an excellent and well designed database which will facilitate research, publication and teaching. It is a very very useful tool to have."

– George Ditsa, PhD, University of Wollongong, Australia

"I have accessed the database and find it to be a valuable tool to the IT/IS community. I found valuable articles meeting my search criteria 95% of the time."

– Lynda Louis, Xavier University of Louisiana, USA

Recommended for use by researchers who wish to immediately download PDFs of individual chapters or articles.

www.igi-global.com/e-resources/infosci-ondemand

www.igi-global.com

Printed in the United States
By Bookmasters